FROM DREAM TO REALITY:

HISTORY OF THE APPALACHIAN TRAIL

FROM DREAM TO REALITY:

HISTORY OF THE APPALACHIAN TRAIL

By Thomas R. Johnson

APPALACHIAN TRAIL
CONSERVANCY®

Harpers Ferry

Cover photo courtesy of the Smoky Mountains Hiking Club (see page 194). The background map is Arthur Comey's 1925 suggested route through Maine to Katahdin, found in the Appalachian Trail Conservancy archives (see page 88).

First edition

Published by the Appalachian Trail Conservancy
          799 Washington Street (P.O. Box 807)
          Harpers Ferry, West Virginia 25425-0807
          <www.appalachiantrail.org>

Conclusions drawn about persons and events herein are those of the author and do not necessarily represent the opinions of the Appalachian Trail Conservancy or its staff members.

ISBN 978-1-944958-15-2

Library of Congress Control Number: 2020952148

Dedicated to the volunteers,

wherever they might be

TABLE OF CONTENTS

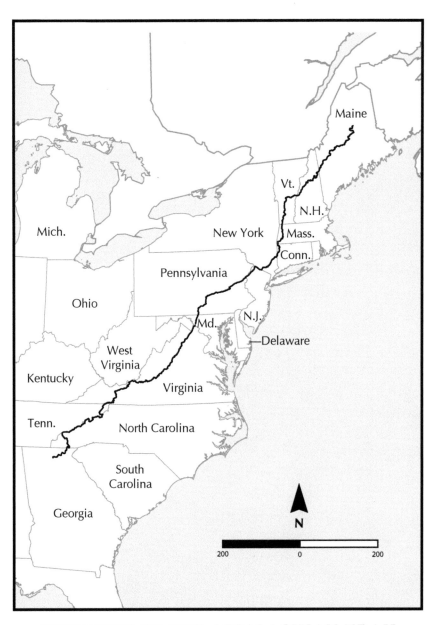

OVERVIEW OF THE APPALACHIAN TRAIL

INTRODUCTION:
LIKE MAGIC

When we bought our house in a mountain subdivision outside Front Royal, Virginia, our real estate agent told us that the Appalachian Trail was in the general vicinity. Looking at her, I judged that she was not herself a hiker, so how did she know? But, one day, soon after we moved in, I walked out the back door and walked down the gravel road where we lived. In a few minutes, I reached a small parking lot and saw two large rocks, with a sign on a tree — "U.S. Boundary." Squeezing between them, I found a primitive dirt path down a hillside. Five minutes or so later, I saw another set of rocks. I climbed over them and pushed through the forest beyond. And almost immediately, I stepped onto a trail, looked up, and saw a white blaze on a tree. I had stumbled into Nirvana.[1]

I have been a hiker since I was a kid growing up in southwest Washington state. My hiking had been around Mount Saint Helens, on trails that, since 1980, no longer exist. Now that I lived in the East, my hiking has been mostly on the Appalachian Trail. But, I am, in truth, just a day-hiker. Occasionally I throw on a pack and do an overnight, but my longest backpacking experience was only one week. True confessions: I have never thru-hiked and have no intention of doing so. It sounds way too hard. (I do not hesitate to

1. Apologies to Bill Bryson, whose experience in finding the Appalachian Trail was similar to mine.

congratulate those who have. As Ed Garvey once wrote, it is "the adventure of a lifetime.")

I am also a historian, as well as an intelligence professional. I have worked in the intelligence community in various capacities (even as a historian a few times) since 1964, and I have written a fair number of histories. My family is deeply frustrated that they can read so little of what I have written because of classification restrictions. They have been after me to write something that they can read.

I became fascinated with the history of the Appalachian Trail and have tried to learn more. The endless themes that have dominated its history — Benton MacKaye *versus* Myron Avery; the volunteer ethic; the struggle over the trail on private property; how the federal government came to protect the trail — all have unfolded in books and articles. This book discusses all those themes, but, in essence, it is about how the trail was built. That is the unifying theme.

I owe a huge debt of gratitude to a long list of people who helped me with the book. Leading off is one David Sherman, who guided my research and found much material. His knowledge is so all-encompassing that I've asked him several times why he didn't write it himself. He claims not to be a writer, but the e-mails that he has sent me show that he could have done it. If there is one significant person, both in a governmental capacity and in volunteer roles since the death of Myron Avery, it would be Dave.

There is a second Dave: Dave Field from Maine would be nigh on to Sherman as the preeminent influence on the trail since Avery. Like Sherman, Dave Field's role has involved both his organizational and volunteer capacities. Not only has he maintained a section of the Appalachian Trail since the 1950s (Saddleback, one of the hardest climbs on the entire trail) and personally designed a reroute of the trail in Maine, but he has also produced thousands of pages of copies and transcripts of Myron Avery's files in the Maine State Library.

INTRODUCTION

Three Appalachian Trail Conference/Conservancy executive directors have contributed to this history. Larry Van Meter, the fourth executive director of ATC, donated copies of his personal daily logs while he was in the job. Dave Startzell provided interviews, encouragement, and access to people. The seventh executive director, Ron Tipton, encouraged me to write this history, and his encouragement has kept me going. ATC's publisher, Brian King, certainly rivals Dave Sherman in his comprehensive knowledge of A.T. history, and his encouragement, likewise, has been important. The best archive on the history of the trail was under Brian's care at this writing.

JoAnn and Paul Dolan provided me sanctuary during the week that I spent going through various archives in New York. They themselves are historic figures in the history of the A.T. in their state. Laura Waterman, whose magisterial *Forest and Crag* is almost certainly the most important history of hiking ever written (at least in English), has offered interviews and encouragement. And, there is a long list of archivists who provided me access to files important in researching this history. Their names are in the bibliography, and each provided me with unstinting help in finding materials. I have been a historian full-time since 1985 but never had better cooperation than from those who tend those archives.

The volunteers, the members of Congress, and the government employees who worked to bring the Appalachian Trail to completion followed divergent paths, but they all worked toward the same goal and ended up in the same place. It is like a hike: Follow the blazes, and you won't get lost. It is like magic.

Tom Johnson
Front Royal, Virginia

Chapter 1

THE MOUNTAINS, THE FORESTS, THE HIKERS

Every Vermonter is a mountaineer....
— *James Taylor*

Creating a hiking trail the length of the country required overcoming natural obstacles and matching ideas to leadership.

This history begins in Vermont, with a schoolmaster named James Taylor, but Taylor's story comes at the end of the chapter. First, we consider the trail's environment — the mountains and the forests. Then, we move to New Hampshire, where recreational hiking in America began. Taylor's story then opens the book with the creation of America's first long-distance hiking trail.

The Mountains

Three great mountain chains divide the United States, north to south. In the west is the Sierra Nevada range, which is renamed the Cascades when it reaches north of Lassen Peak in northern California. In the center of the country are the Rocky Mountains, cleaving the continent in two. (The Rockies are the highest and most dramatic.) And, abutting the Piedmont of the U.S. eastern seaboard are the Appalachians. Looking from the west to the east, each chain is older.

At the Pacific Rim, the Cascades and Sierras were formed between four and seven million years ago, during the Tertiary period, merely a blink of an eye in geologic terms. They are the youngest and most active, producing the so-called Pacific Rim of Fire, a chain of active volcanoes and plate activity that produced the 1980 Mount Saint Helens eruption, and devastating quakes in California. The Rockies are much older, having been formed 80 to 100 million years ago, during the Cretaceous period. In the east, the barrier to westward expansion for the American colonists, their early frontier, were the Appalachians. In geologic terms, they are profoundly ancient. Their age becomes important to a hiker — there is a reason.

Each of the mountain chains is today traversed by a long-distance trail. Over the Sierras and Cascades is the Pacific Crest Trail, proposed originally only a scant three years after the Appalachian Trail itself by a school teacher from Bellingham, Washington. The Continental Divide Trail, which traverses the Rockies, was begun in the 1960s by a group of hiking enthusiasts and was authorized as a national scenic trail by Congress in 1978. And the Appalachian Trail (henceforth just the A.T.) travels the length of the Appalachians, although there is some dispute about where the chain really ends — Georgia or Alabama (or even Peru or Argentina, according to some research).

Mountain-building has its origins in what geologists term plate tectonics. This theory, which gained currency during the 1960s, holds that the geology of Earth is formed by the movement of vast plates some 60 miles below the surface, moving on a liquefied layer that causes them to shift one direction or another. The shift, called an orogeny, is generally measured in inches per year, and the clash of the underground plates occurs in slow motion, like molasses. Plates clashing together sometimes produce earthquakes. Although they are far more frequent on the Pacific Coast, they are not unknown on the East Coast.

Beginning in the Paleozoic era 251 to 542 million years ago, three great orogenic events occurred in the East. The plates shifted first west, creating high mountain ranges, followed by a shift eastward creating subsidence. During the Permian period, 285 to 230 million years ago, the Taconic orogeny resulted in the present-day Appalachian Mountains. That last great plate collision pushed the mountains and Piedmont farther west to their present positions. After that, the mountains began to erode, as rocks and soil were washed down into the lower lands.

During the Triassic and Jurassic periods (the age of the dinosaurs), the plates began to move apart again, and rift valleys formed. The Mid-Atlantic Ridge

Vertical sandstone upthrust

marks the great crack between the continents, and it widens at the rate of about an inch per year. So, too, the tops of the Appalachian Mountains erode at about an inch every 600 years. The constant subterranean upthrust, however, pushes them up at about the same rate, so that their height has remained essentially the same for millennia.

The movement of the rock plates caused them to clash, grinding against each other, and that resulted in a chaotic blend of rock upthrusts. The effect of orogenic events has been described as something like pushing against a rug to create folds, and one look at a map of eastern North America shows those folds as a vast, crenelated rug stretching the length of the East. As the hiker moves along the Appalachian Trail, he or she can see, or have to walk on, rocks that could have been formed as long as one billion years ago, during the Grenville period.

According to Collins Chew, the oldest rocks discovered on the A.T. are between Roan High Knob and Round Bald along the North Carolina–Tennessee border and are dated at 1.8 billion years old. The rocks that form the mountains of New England can be of similar vintage. Looking upward from a road cut in the Delaware Water Gap, one sees lines of rock from the Taconic orogeny all the way to the Alleghenian. The bluffs are a journey in time, and the hiker walks past rocks of many different time periods.

Dragons Tooth, a classic upthrust

Geology is messy. Often the hiker is on the rocks, which creates challenges all its own.[1]

The Appalachians, being the most aged of the three mountain chains, are also the most eroded. Many, if not most, hikers who have done all three major long-distance hikes (called the Triple Crown) call the A.T. the most difficult of the three, even though it is the shortest in terms of miles and relatively lower in overall elevation. Part of the difficulty is the rocky bed of the trail itself, and the fault lies not so much with overuse (which has become a problem over the years) but more in the weathering of the tops of the mountains and ridges of the Appalachians. A.T. hikers are walking on the oldest mountains in North America.

Three of the most distinct rock formations are in Virginia: Humpback Rocks, McAfee Knob, and Dragons Tooth. Those iconic formations are 500 million years old, dating back to the Paleozoic Era, and are comprised of Silurian sandstone. They are visited by legions of day-hikers and represent the very best of hiking in the Appalachian Mountains. In them, one can see a classic orogenal rock upthrust.

The Forests

"The Green Tunnel" — that is what the hiker sees today for much of the footpath's length. The forests in the Appalachian Mountains

---

1. Most of the material from this section came from Collins Chew, *Underfoot: A Geologic Guide to the Appalachian Trail*, 2nd edition (Harpers Ferry: Appalachian Trail Conference, 1993), and John McPhee, *In Suspect Terrain* (New York: Farrar, Straus, and Giroux, 1982)

are a vast, dense green and, in many places, almost impenetrable to light. The impression is of a forest that dominates the landscape and has existed forever. Rocky outcrops put a visual hole in the forest and are cherished because the hiker can see farther than just the few feet directly under his or her shoes. But, it was not always so. The Appalachian forest of today is something relatively new.

In the colonial period, naturalists explored and catalogued the Appalachian forests. John Bartram, a Pennsylvania farmer, was the first to make a detailed inventory of plant life in the southern Appalachians. He traveled through the South from North Carolina to Florida. His son, William, followed in his father's footsteps. His main journey was in 1773, and the William Bartram Trail in North Carolina is named after him.

The Bartrams were followed by Frenchman André Michaux, who gave his name to Michaux State Forest in Pennsylvania. (The Appalachian Trail bisects Michaux.) Although those naturalists ranged over the entire Appalachian chain, the Roan seemed to be the most fascinating for them. Michaux traveled into the southern Appalachians, arriving in the Roan area in 1796. He was followed only a few years later by Scotsman John Fraser, who visited the Roan in the 1780s and 1790s. Harvard biologist Asa Gray explored the Roan in 1840. Its plant life must have been one of the most thoroughly documented of any region in America.

Arnold Guyot, a Swiss naturalist, arrived in the United States in 1848, and his travels also ranged up and down the entire Appalachians. His list of mountaineering accomplishments would impress modern alpinists, and Myron H. Avery, a scholar of the mountains in addition to his other Appalachian Trail accomplishments, wrote that Guyot "was beyond question the most thorough explorer who ever penetrated the Appalachian mountain chain."[2] Guyot stayed in America and became a professor at Princeton University.

Before and after those explorers, waves of settlement surged over the mountain chain. New settlers pushed into the mountains in the

2. Guy and Laura Waterman, *Forest and Crag: A History of Hiking, Trail Blazing and Adventure in the Northeast Mountains*, 3rd ed. (Waterbury Center, Vt.: Green Mountain Club, Inc., 2011).

late Colonial period and brought their axes with them. They would down trees or would choose an even simpler method of girdling them so that they would die and lose their leaves. With additional light, a corn crop could be planted between the dead trees. And, in the higher elevations, where there might be meadows, they created pasture land. The march of settlement surged up from the coastal areas to the mountain chain, and the mountains began to lose their tree cover.

Unregulated timber cutting began denuding the eastern mountains. Vast areas from New England to the southern Appalachians were cut for timber, without any federal or state regulation. Iron smelting, which required charcoal, devastated large areas of the chestnut-oak overstory. Americans had assumed that the resource would last forever.

A clarion call for conservation was issued by George Perkins Marsh in 1864, in his seminal book, *Man and Nature*. Marsh, from a prominent New England family in Woodstock, Vermont, had a classical education, graduating from Dartmouth College in 1820. After college, he practiced law in Burlington, Vermont, and devoted himself to philological studies. Serving as a Whig representative to Congress from 1843 to 1849, he was subsequently as a Republican appointed envoy to Italy from 1861 to 1882, becoming the longest-serving ambassador in American history. His home has been preserved as part of the Marsh–Billings–Rockefeller National Historical Park just north of Woodstock (coincidentally, very near the A.T.).

Marsh's environmental message focused on what had happened in the Middle East. The forests of Mesopotamia, clinging to life in an area of sparse rainfall, had been cut down, with resulting environmental devastation that reduced the area to desert and permanent political and social turmoil. (The region remains unstable today.) He reasoned that, without some environmental regulations, the same thing could happen in the United States.

Marsh's warning was fast becoming true. With the introduction of narrow-gauge railways, vast areas fell to the saw, and slopes were robbed of the vegetation that would retain the soil. Between 1900 and 1933, sixty-three percent of the area that is now the Jefferson National Forest in Virginia was logged off. A series of devastating floods stripped the slopes of topsoil and buried communities downstream in huge slabs of mud and debris. In 1898, the Monongahela and Allegheny rivers flooded, and the debris cascaded down onto Pittsburgh, Pennsylvania, where the two rivers met. Similar devastation was visited on the southern Appalachians because of the rampant cutting of forests.

The same problem afflicted the White Mountains of New Hampshire. By the turn of the century, they were being logged catastrophically. Floods washed over towns like Manchester. Furthermore, the slash that was left behind fueled massive forest fires (not just in the Whites, but throughout the Appalachians). Tourism was one of the first sectors of the economy to suffer. One reaction to floods and fires was the creation of the Society for the Protection of New Hampshire

Denuded slopes in the White Mountains of New Hampshire.

Forests, and its forester in 1902 was Philip Ayres. Ayres began a campaign to turn public opinion against uncontrolled logging of the eastern forests.

Saving the forests started slowly. In 1876, twelve years after the publication of Marsh's book, Congress funded a study of American forest conditions and appointed Franklin Hough as a federal forest agent to make the study. Hough documented the destruction of the forests and recommended the withdrawal of public lands containing forests and the establishment of a permanent bureau to study and manage the forests. The Department of Agriculture responded by creating the Division of Forestry in 1881. For the time being, it was authorized only to continue studying the problem.

In the East, no federal land existed to be protected, and unregulated timbering continued unabated. By the 1880s, loggers had removed most of the marketable timber from New England and the Great Lakes region and were moving into the southern forests and the Pacific Northwest. Abandoned farms and cut-over land became endemic in the East and across the country.

In 1900, Congress launched another commission, requiring Secretary of Agriculture James Wilson to investigate forest conditions in the southern Appalachians of western North Carolina and adjoining lands. Wilson's report, issued the following year, was a 180-page litany of forest destruction, unregulated agricultural clearing, destruction of riparian areas, and downstream flooding. He stated that forests had to be preserved and that "federal action is obviously necessary." This report began a slow-motion effort to create forest reserves in the East, and it had a major impact on the movement.

The movement to preserve American forests was promoted most notably by the then-famous Boone and Crockett Club. Founded by Theodore Roosevelt in 1887, its purpose was to promote the hunting of game, but it took what some might see as a paradoxical turn toward forest conservation related to preserving the environment for game animals. Roosevelt, an enthusiastic hunter, advocated the preservation of game and never seemed to see a contradiction between the game trophies that adorned the walls of his mansion and the move to preserve the forest environment. Much of his hunting was in the West, and this is where he concentrated his conservation energies.

After hard lobbying by Roosevelt, President Benjamin Harrison signed the Forest Reserve Act in 1891. The act permitted the president to set aside any area of U.S.-managed forests and to prohibit timber cutting and hunting in those areas. Harrison promptly placed thirteen million acres under protection, creating eleven forest reserves (no tree cutting) and six timberland reserves (limited cutting). At the time, all the forest land owned by the federal government was in the West.

Management of the new forest reserves was originally allocated to the Interior Department (1897) in its organic act. Gifford Pinchot of Pennsylvania became the first head of the Bureau of Forestry in 1898. Roosevelt, as president, and Pinchot, as forester, were a team that brought modern forestry into the federal government.

The Interior organic act provided the underpinnings for an ecological approach to the management of public lands. It required the Forest Service to "improve and protect the forests," to "secure favorable conditions of water flow," and to "furnish a continuous supply of timber," which provided the basis for sustained-yield forestry. The act also provided for the allocation of funds to hire foresters and rangers.

In 1905, the Bureau of Forestry became the U.S. Forest Service, empowered to manage the forest reserves. In 1906, the forest reserves were transferred to the Department of Agriculture, and jurisdiction passed from the Land Office of the Department of the Interior to Gifford Pinchot's Division of Forestry in the Department of Agriculture. Forests thenceforth were to be treated as a sustainable and renewable crop. The activist President Theodore Roosevelt set aside more than 151 million acres and increased the forest reserves by more than 300 percent. The former president of a big-game club thus became the most conservation-minded president in history up to that point.

Forestry as a profession in America owed its origins to Pinchot, who George Vanderbilt hired as the first professional forester in the United States. This was in what would become later become Pisgah

Biltmore

National Forest, the first established in the East after the United States purchased much of the Vanderbilt lands near Asheville, North Carolina. Scientific forestry had originated in Germany in the nineteenth century, and Pinchot traveled to Europe to get instruction in forestry. Vanderbilt, who built a large mansion south of Asheville, owned more than 100,000 forested acres. In 1895, at Pinchot's recommendation, Vanderbilt established the first school of forestry in America. The Biltmore Forest School was founded on the Vanderbilt estate in 1895 and taught modern methods of forestry to the students.[3] The school became known as the Cradle of Forestry.[4]

Influenced by Pinchot, the Pennsylvania legislature created a Forestry Commission in 1893 and a Department of Forestry in 1901. And, another class of Pennsylvania lands became consequential to hikers. In 1895, Pennsylvania created a board of game commissioners. Game-commission lands ran along ridgetops, as would hiking trails. Since game lands were intended only for hunting, there was inherent conflict. That began a long-running battle to permit unrestricted hiking and camping on game lands in Pennsylvania, a conflict that is still going on to some degree.

Some states got out ahead of the federal government. Virginia, for instance, passed a legislative resolution in 1902 expressing support

---

3. The Biltmore school was opened just a few weeks before the opening of the New York State College of Forestry at Cornell University.
4. Chris Bolgiano, *The Appalachian Forest: A Search for Roots and Renewal.* (Mechanicsburg, Pa.: Stackpole Press, 1998).

for the establishment of an extensive national forest in the state and granting the federal government the right to acquire forest reserve land in Virginia.

At the same time, Virginia relinquished its right to tax those lands once they became national forests. Creation of eastern forests met fierce resistance from conservatives. Some felt that all vacant lands should be opened to development. Others believed that states' rights should rule and that the individual states themselves should take action, if any action were to be taken. There was an argument that the Constitution prevented the federal government from acquiring lands (although one would suppose that the Louisiana Purchase would have settled that argument).

More than forty bills were introduced in Congress over a ten-year period, but all were blocked. Even after Pittsburgh was devastated by a monumental flood in March 1907, caused by unrestricted logging in the headlands of the Monongahela and Allegheny rivers, Congress could not get legislation passed.

John Weeks seemed an unlikely candidate to reverse the trend. A Massachusetts Republican, he went to Congress in 1905 as a former naval officer and banker. Appointed to the Agriculture Committee by Speaker Joe Cannon, he had few farmers in his district and little connection with agriculture. But, he had grown up near the White Mountains, had a summer house there, and had become concerned about the rampant destruction of the forests in the Whites. Cannon — who had once proclaimed, "Not one cent for scenery" — now told Weeks that he was ready to support a forestry bill if Weeks could get it to the floor of the House. Weeks' first bill in 1908 dealt simply with purchasing lands near the headwaters of navigable streams, but, when that went nowhere, he added a provision in 1909 that the purchased lands would be maintained as federal forest reserves as a way to protect the water sources. After two years, the measure became law with the signature of President William Howard Taft on March 1, 1911.

The Weeks Act contained provisions for fire protection and authorized a National Forest Reservation Commission to approve land purchases. The Forest Service would recommend land purchases after the U.S. Geological Survey evaluated them for suitability under the provision for the protection of navigable streams. It was now possible to have federal forests in the East. The Appalachian Trail would come to depend heavily on this legislation and the subsequent creation of national forests.

Following the passage of the act, the federal government began creating eastern forests. First was the Pisgah in North Carolina, and that was followed by the White Mountain National Forest in New Hampshire in 1918. All told, twenty-one national forests would be created in the East.

The process of creating national forests in the East was jurisdictionally messy. For instance, the Jefferson eventually emerged from the original Whitetop Purchase Unit, in what is now Mount Rogers National Recreation Area. This purchase unit was eventually (1920) combined with other newly acquired lands in Tennessee and North Carolina to create the Unaka National Forest. All the while, the Forest Service began the appraisal and purchase of various tracts scattered through southern Virginia.

Those purchase units eventually were collected within a "proclamation boundary" to create the Natural Bridge National Forest (NBNF), immediately south of what would become Shenandoah National Park in 1926. When NBNF was officially created in 1925, it consisted of a gross acreage of 279,000 acres, of which the government owned 153,000 acres. The entire area had suffered greatly from timber harvesting and denuded slopes. Finally, in 1936, President Franklin D. Roosevelt declared the Jefferson National Forest out of the lands that originally comprised the Unaka and Natural Bridge forests.

That problem of defining public lands surfaces another issue that would affect the Appalachian Trail, but many hikers are simply unaware of the problem. When a forest was first created, the units that had been purchased would be collected within a congressionally authorized "proclamation boundary." For instance, the proclamation boundary for Natural Bridge National Forest was the aforementioned 279,000 acres. The boundary was simply a line on a map, within which the Forest Service was authorized to acquire the lands. Since it was all private property, the government had to purchase the acreage. Over the years prior to creation of that particular forest, the government owned 153,000 acres. The remainder was called "inholdings," widely scattered within the proclamation boundary.

Thus, when the A.T. was first scouted, much of it ran through private land, and the hiker was often unaware whose land he or she was hiking through. The Forest Service had to go through the laborious process of buying up the tracts that the trail was on or moving the trail onto existing public property. Acquisition of the tracts needed was often a contentious and drawn-out process that sometimes created local opposition to any federal presence whatsoever. Unsuspecting hikers were sometimes caught in the middle.

The Forest Service, unlike the Park Service, did not normally condemn lands (although there were exceptions). The Forest Service would acquire lands from willing sellers, using the eminent domain condemnation process only to clear land title or in the case of an egregious attack (bulldozing across the corridor). Under the Weeks Act, the Forest Service also had to obtain permission from the states. Thus, for each state, a consent agreement had to be approved by the legislature. Most of the inholdings acquired to create a corridor for the A.T. remained in private hands when the National Trails System Act was passed in 1968.

In 1921, when the idea of an Appalachian Trail was first proposed, the forests did not look much like they do today. Rather than the oak and poplar forests that predominate today, the American chestnut was the most prominent species.

In 1904, forester H.W. Merkel of the New York Zoological Society noticed small orange spots on the bark of American chestnut trees in the Bronx. The spots were thought to have originated from Chinese chestnuts imported from Asia. The Chinese variety was resistant, but the American chestnut was not. This was the beginning of the disastrous chestnut blight that quickly swept through the forests of New York, Connecticut, and Pennsylvania. The blight continued to march on down the Appalachian chain, killing nearly every chestnut in its path. A few of the trees were mysteriously resistant, but only a few.

When hikers began scouting the trail, especially in the mid-Atlantic states, they were confronted with "ghost forests" where chestnuts once grew (see page 147). It was a tragedy almost beyond calculation, not just for hikers, but also for wildlife. Chestnuts were one of the staples for countless animals. And, chestnuts were a staple for Appalachian mountain residents, and its timber defined many livelihoods.

The hikers

If Asheville, North Carolina, was the "cradle of forestry," New England was the cradle of hiking in America.[5] That hiking began in New England probably owed much to the history and culture of the place — not to mention the existence of some very fine mountains. For humans, from the time they have been able to communicate feelings, something has been endlessly fascinating, even primordially sacred, about mountains. The enthusiasm for hiking and climbing as leisure probably was spurred by the transcendental movement, that uniquely New England intellectual phenomenon that was the first philosophy to be generally credited to Americans.

Many of the early hikers and climbers also were identified with Transcendentalism. Ralph Waldo Emerson, whose publication *Nature* in 1836 marked the beginning of Transcendentalism, was indeed a lover of nature. Henry David Thoreau was the most famous outdoorsman of the movement and of New England in general. If there was a "back to nature" movement in America, it originated with the Transcendentalists, and they influenced all subsequent nature movements in New England. Transcendentalism was strongly Romantic, with a large admixture of East Indian Hindu and Buddhist asceticism. The urge to climb mountains, however, predated the transcendentalists. (One thinks of Moses, for example.)

---

5. Much of the information in this section is taken from *Forest and Crag*.

Recorded mountain ascents in New England began with the legendary Darby Field, who climbed Mount Washington in 1642.[6] (He was the first transplanted European known to have set foot on what would become centuries later the Appalachian Trail.[7]) Subsequent accounts of Field's climb originally favored the Boot Spur route, but more recently that has come under question, and the Crawford Path route (Crawford Path itself had not yet been built) is now thought by many to have been his route.

Mount Washington became a popular mountain for early climbers. John Josellyn climbed it in 1663 and 1671. In 1784, the Reverend Jeremy Belknap led a large expedition up the mountain. (Belknap himself did not make it to the top, but the Reverend Manasseh Cutler, described by David Mazell as perhaps the first serious botanist in New England,[8] did.) The result of the Belknap expedition was the naming of the mountain after George Washington, who had commanded the armies of the Continental Congress.

The history of New England trails and hiking is documented in Laura and Guy Waterman's seminal book, *Forest and Crag*, first published in 1989. They report that very few would venture into serious mountain climbing until the period of the Transcendentalists. But, beginning in 1830, the Watermans wrote, climbers began venturing into the mountains of New England, inspired partly by a hiking and climbing movement in Europe. Emerson was a dedicated walker. At the age of 22, Thoreau climbed Mount Washington and followed this with ascents of Greylock, Monadnock, Lafayette, Wachusett, and Katahdin. He was unsuccessful at the latter, and his description of the attempt is a classic in Transcendental literature. Thoreau wrote that

Perhaps I most fully realized that this was primeval, untamed, and forever untamable Nature, or whatever else men call it, while com-

---

6. Dave Field, his direct descendant and one of the great volunteers in the history of American trail-building, makes his first appearance in Chapter 5 of this book.

7. Native Americans, often ignored in literature, were surely the first people to set foot on the route of the A.T., and Field is reported to have led two of them on his trek to counter their spiritual beliefs about the summit.

8. David Mazell (ed.), *Pioneering Ascents: The Origins of Climbing in America, 1642-1873* (Vienna, Va.: Potomac Appalachian Trail Club, 1991).

ing down this part of the mountain…. Nature was here something savage and awful, though beautiful. I looked with awe at the ground I trod on, to see what the powers had made there…. This was what Earth of which we have heard, made out of Chaos and Old Night…. It was not lawn, nor pasture, nor mead, nor woodland, nor lea, nor arable nor waste-land. It was the fresh and natural surface of the planet Earth.[9]

Other mountains, perhaps somewhat less difficult, became very popular in the second half of the nineteenth century. Monadnock became the second most popular climb in the world after Mount Fuji in Japan. (To the Japanese, climbing Fuji is part of the national religion. To the New Englander, it was Monadnock.) In Vermont, oft-climbed Mount Ascutney was a relatively easy hike. The first known organized recreational hike in America took place on May 2, 1863, a six-mile hike from Williamstown, Massachusetts, to Birch and Prospect glens.

A few definitions are in order. "Organized" means that an organization sponsored it. The organization was the Williamstown Alpine Club, which had been organized only a month before as the first known hiking club in America. The other key word is "recreational." It was not a government survey (think about the Mason–Dixon Line or the survey in Maine to establish the border between the United States and Canada) nor an exploration (Lewis and Clark, Zebulon Montgomery Pike, John Wesley Powell.) The purpose was just to hike — this was for fun and was sponsored by a hiking club. If you assumed that the Williamstown Alpine Club was spawned entirely by Williams College, one of the most famous of New England liberal arts colleges, you would be wrong. Williams College was all male, and nine of the twelve organizers of the Alpine Club were women. Women were some of the most enthusiastic hikers of the day.

In New England, women represented a large component of hikers, climbers, and trail-builders. The first women known to climb Mount Washington were the Austin sisters in 1821 — they chose the

---

9. *Ibid*, pp. 148-49, quoting Thoreau.

Crawford Path. In 1840, Mrs. Daniel Patch climbed Moosilauke, and two women, Mary Cook and Fannie Newton, made the first known ascent by women of Mount Marcy in New York in the 1850s.

Some notable climbs in America were not undertaken in New England. Elisha Mitchell in 1835 climbed the peak now named Mount Mitchell, which eventually became documented and accepted as the highest point in the United States east of the Mississippi. (The unfortunate Mitchell climbed it again in 1857 but drowned in a creek during a storm on the way back.) André Michaux made the first European ascent of Roan Mountain in 1796. Many famous nonnative climbs were recorded out west in the nineteenth century, including climbs of Pike's Peak, Long's Peak, Mount Shasta, Lassen Peak, and Mount Saint Helens.

The Watermans document the era of pure walking in the mid-1850s, led by such famous long-distance walkers as Alden Partridge and Edward Payson Weston. Weston, for instance, walked twelve to fifteen miles every day and once walked 100 miles in less than twenty-four hours. New England was the home of those remarkable people. Much of the interest came from outing clubs at colleges, such as Mount Holyoke and Dartmouth. Harvard, Brown, Yale, and Williams were all well-known for their clubs. Williams seems to have been in the forefront, and its proximity to Mount Greylock, the highest point in Massachusetts and immediately south of the campus, apparently inspired the students.

The Watermans recount an early instance of trail-building by the outing club. "On May 12, 1863 [only ten days after their first organized hike], a noisy horde of Williams College students cut a path from the end of this road to the top on a one-day blitz, armed with axes, bush hooks, crow bars, hoes and tin horns." The trail thus constructed was called the Hopper Trail after the road where it began. It goes up the west side of Greylock but did not become part of the Appalachian Trail, which had to be routed in such a way as to connect with the Long Trail in Vermont, just to the north.

The Watermans wrote about the infrastructure that provided the underpinning for the walking, hiking, and climbing endeavors. Vacation lodges began in the early nineteenth century, many of them in the iconic White Mountains. They tell the story of the inn that the Crawford family began at what came to be known as Crawford Notch. Beginning with the purchase of a cabin in the notch in 1791, the family built a lodge, which in 1828 became a major resort, the Crawford House. Not satisfied with just providing an overnight, the Crawfords also provided recreation. Earlier, in 1819, they had built an 8.4-mile trail toward the north and Mount Washington, which became known as the Crawford Path. That is the oldest, continuously used hiking trail in the United States. Ethan Crawford later built a second trail toward Mount Washington up Ammonoosuc Ravine, another trail that is still used today. It intersects the Crawford Path just south of Lakes of the Clouds Hut.

Later in the century, other vacation lodges sprang up, and, in the latter half of the century, railroads connected the vacation areas with metropolitan areas, especially Boston. This infrastructure greatly expanded the opportunities to hike in the mountains, in an era before the motor car. New England was ripe for the formation of hiking and trail clubs.[10]

The first organized hiking club is credited to the aforementioned Williams College, at the foot of Greylock. Professor Albert Hopkins organized the club in April 1863. (One of the founding members of the club, Samuel Hubbard Scudder, would play a prominent role in organizing the Appalachian Mountain Club of Boston.) Called the Alpine Club of Williamstown, it kept up a vibrant hiking schedule for several years, traveling to Vermont and New Hampshire. In 1864, it organized eighteen expeditions, but enthusiasm waned, and the club appears to have faded out two years later.

The second known trail club in the Northeast was the White Mountain Club of Portland, Maine. Established in 1873 by George Vose, John Anderson (designer for the family of the trail route through Crawford Notch), and several others, it eventually faded as the Appalachian Mountain Club increasingly dominated New England hik-

---

10. Generally speaking, "trail clubs" had a dual mission of recreation and trail-building. "Hiking clubs" usually confined their activities to recreational hiking.

ing and trail-building. Before it folded in 1894, the club explored the Mahoosucs and Old Speck.

The Appalachian Mountain Club broke the mold and became the granddaddy of trail clubs in the United States. The idea for a new club based in Boston came from a Massachusetts Institute of Technology (MIT) physics professor, Edward Pickering, who in 1875 began talking about a club to explore the mountains and build trails. All the early recruits to his idea were academics. (And, to this day, academics and office workers play an outsized role in trail-building.) Edward F. Morse from Harvard and Samuel Scudder, who had recently left Williamstown to join the Harvard College faculty, met with Pickering on January 8, 1876, to found the Appalachian Mountain Club (AMC). The historic meeting was in a MIT building, and Pickering became the first president. Scudder succeeded him the next year.

The club founders were interested in exploring the mountains, mapping and documenting their elevations, preserving the wilderness environment, and, not least, building trails. With a headquarters just a few short blocks off the Commons at 5 Joy Street in downtown Boston until late 2017, AMC became the largest and most influential trail club in the country. It was to become much more than just a hiking and trail-building organization, but a true outdoors club, sponsoring skiing, rock climbing, whitewater canoeing, social events, and much else, including significant land-conservation programs in this century. But, a large component was early trail construction, especially in the White Mountains. Many of New England's trails owe their existence to AMC.

A regional organization, the club envisioned a connected network of trails to create a regional trail system. When the idea of an Appalachian Trail took hold, it was only a matter in New England of selecting the route — the trails were already there.

Other clubs would pop up in New England after 1876. A few were locally influential, such as the Agassiz Association of Lennox, Massachusetts, which would reach 10,000 members at its peak. But, few had trail-building as a principal objective, and most were short-lived. There was no true challenge in New England to the pervasive influence of AMC. The Sierra Club, the first national group, organized in 1892, took AMC as its model. In later years, a few organizations came and endured. The most significant and enduring were the New England Trail Conference, the Randolph Mountain Club, and several college outing clubs (Dartmouth Outing Club and the Wonalancet Out Door Club).

The small town of Randolph, New Hampshire, was a summer vacation destination for many urbanites in the mid-1850s. In the days before the Civil War, it began attracting mountain explorers, who led enterprising vacationers into the Whites. Mount Adams and Mount Madison, both now on or along the Appalachian Trail, were favorite destinations. James Gordon was the most sought-after guide in the early days, and he was followed by Eugene Cook, Charles Lowe, and the Englishman William Peek. A young MIT student, Louis Cutter, went to Randolph in 1885 to test barometric readings and began making maps that became the standard for the Randolph Mountain Club and AMC. Judith Maddock Hudson, the club historian, writes that, in the early days, no trails in the modern sense existed — just primitive tracks that went straight up the mountainside. Men and women climbed up those tracks, the women often dressed in floor-length gowns that must have caught under their boot heels constantly.[11] Guy and Laura Waterman write a moving description of this early burst of enthusiasm for mountain climbing:

> Randolph in the eighties was one of those rare and precious moments in any region's history when the bloom was fresh, and new worlds of enterprise and adventure were there to be grasped, amid lots of hard work, camaraderie, and joy.[12]

The Randolph group began building huts in 1876, the year that AMC was founded, twelve years before AMC built its first hut, the Madison Spring Hut in 1888. The "huts" were really locked cabins, solidly constructed with glass windows, overhead kerosene lighting,

---

11. Judith Maddock Hudson, *Peaks and Paths: A Century of the Randolph Mountain Club* (Gorham, N.H.: Randolph Mountain Club, 2010).
12. Watermans, *op. cit.,* p. 223.

and such amenities as table cloths.[13] Until 1910, no formal club organization existed, just a group of inspired hikers taking their summer vacations in the Randolph area. What caused that to change was a devastating result of rampant timber-cutting. Timber companies moved into the Whites in the late nineteenth century, leaving cleared slopes and mountains of slash. The result of all this was damaged trails and forest fires all over the Whites.

The attempt to manage timber production and create sustainable forestry began in 1881 with the creation of the New Hampshire Forestry Commission, and such other private groups as the Society for the Protection of New Hampshire Forests, formed in 1901. Those measures did not come in time to save the trails in the northern Whites, but they did lead to the creation of the Randolph Mountain Club. In the spring of 1910, John Boothman, recognizing that tourists were attracted to Randolph because of hiking trails, proposed that a formal organization be established to clear the damaged trails.[14] The Randolph club became a subsidiary of AMC in the sense that it built and maintained the trails in the Northern Presidentials as part of AMC's trail-work program.

The matter was highly significant in that it was one of the earliest examples of a local trail club doing the actual work. While AMC's territory was all of New England, Randolph had a defined territory and a relationship with AMC that was replicated in other areas. The organizational pattern moved down the Appalachian chain as hiking trails expanded. A later umbrella organization, the Appalachian Trail Conference, defined the trail movement in the East and eventually across America.

A second trail club that would endure was the Wonalancet Out Door Club, some distance to the south of Randolph, near Waterville Valley. There, Katherine Sleeper, a local inn owner possessed of incredible energy, founded the club in 1898. Sleeper led the effort to create a trail network south of Waterville. Her singular accomplishments remind one of a latter-day fireball, Elizabeth Levers of the New

---

13. Hudson, *op. cit.*, p. 5 ff.
14. *Ibid*, pp. 30-41 and 50-52.

York–New Jersey Trail Conference (see chapter 8). Physically close to Wonalancet was the Chocorua Mountain Club. An offshoot of the Wonalancet club and once independent, it built yet another network of trails near Waterville.

Like the activity in Randolph, trail-building in the immediate Waterville area originated with summer residents: Paul Jenks, Charles Blood, and Nathaniel Goodrich. They did not confine their energies to Waterville but ranged far afield, north in New Hampshire (Wildcat Ridge, Kinsman Ridge) and all the way to the Mahoosucs in Maine. They did a great deal to create the underpinnings of a unified trail system.

The Dartmouth Outing Club (DOC), established in 1909, became yet a third club that has continued over the long term. The founder, Dartmouth student Fred Harris, was an avid skier. Seeing no organized skiing activity at the college, he advocated that an outdoor club be formed to take advantage of the winter in New Hampshire and Vermont. One of the activities that the club got involved with (although by no means the principal enterprise) was trail-building, and DOC created yet another network of trails in New Hampshire, southwest of Waterville. It also eventually assumed responsibility for about seventy-five miles of the A.T. from Hanover to a connection with the Long Trail in Vermont, as well as more than fifty miles in New Hampshire. (Today, DOC's section, which had pulled back from the Long Trail about twenty-three miles to Vt. 12 near Woodstock, is wholly in New Hampshire, from the Connecticut River to Mount Moosilauke.)

The idea of a unified trail system was promoted by Louis Cutter, a mapmaker and member of the Randolph group. When Cutter became councillor of improvements for AMC in 1901, he called for connecting the trail system in the Waterville area with various trails farther north, so that it would become a single trail system, rather than a disparate group of local trails. In 1903, he enlisted Sturgis Pray to cut a trail up the Swift River Valley, following roughly the present Kancamagus Highway, and then past Greeley Ponds to Waterville.

By 1921, when Benton MacKaye published his vision of a long trail extending the length of the Appalachian chain, a network of trails and trail clubs already existed in New England, poised to pounce on the idea.

Pray, MacKaye's collegiate hiking partner, became known as an AMC master trail-builder. He laid out a trail in the Whites along the Swift River, which linked for the first time trails of the Sandwich Range with those of the East Branch of the Pemigewasset River and the Franconia Range. According to MacKaye biographer Larry Anderson, "The trail was a harbinger of a new era of hiking activity, which emphasized connecting local trail networks — previously radiating from resort hotels and railroad stops — into one grand network."[15] Pray urged AMC to adopt the concept of "trunk trails," with side trails providing an enhanced hiking experience. It was an idea that MacKaye adopted with the Appalachian Trail.

Many of the smaller organizations have not survived to the present day but were active in building trails in the early years. An example was the Ascutney Mountain Club, formed in 1906 by residents of Windsor, Vermont. Prior to its organization, local volunteers had already built a trail to the summit of Ascutney, one of the most popular mountains in the state, and had built a stone house, sleeping up to twenty.[16] The short-lived Stratton Mountain Club, organized in 1912, made an enduring mark on Vermont history by building a trail to the top of Stratton Mountain and a sixty-five-foot observation tower on top. A burst of energy in New York led to the founding of the Adirondack Mountain Club in the 1920s. The Catskills also sported trail clubs. And, New York City became a hotbed of hiking activity with the very fast and athletic Fresh Air Club (1877), Tramp and Trail Club (organized in 1914 by Frank Place), Inkowah (all women, 1918), and many others.[17]

---

15. Larry Anderson, *Peculiar Work: Writing about Benton MacKaye, Conservation, Community* (Little Compton, R.I.: Quicksand Chronicles, 2013), p. 43.
16. Vermont State Archives, Barre, Vt., Box 241/1.
17. The most complete account of the activity in New York is Glenn Scherer's *Vistas and Visions: A History of the New York New Jersey Trail Conference* (New York: New York–New Jersey Trail Conference, 1995).

South of New York, things moved much more slowly. Pennsylvania was an interesting exception. The state is possessed of low, rocky ridges, seldom exceeding 2,500 feet, but they provided Pennsylvanians with many choices for their ridgeline trails. Major population centers in Philadelphia, Harrisburg, and Pittsburgh and centers of college life produced an environment similar to New England. Thus, trail clubs popped up there earlier than in most areas south of New England. Before the idea of a long trail became popular, the Blue Mountain Eagle Climbing Club, founded in 1916, whose unique history will be discussed later, had pride of place. Coming along almost at the same time was the Pennsylvania Alpine Club of Harrisburg in 1917, the Allentown Hiking Club in 1931, and the Susquehanna Trailers of the Wilkes-Barre area.[18]

The early trail clubs were typically exclusionary. One had to be sponsored, and not everyone was considered appropriate for membership. Most of the clubs required someone to attest to the person's character before they could become a member. This tradition carried on into the southern regions, and some of the original clubs, having been founded by college professors, continued to carefully restrict membership well beyond World War II. Hiking was not regarded as a plebian activity — one had to be elected.

A few groups existed south of Pennsylvania, but the region, blessed with outstanding mountains, could not replicate the culture of trail-building in the Northeast. Trail clubs centered around large urban centers and were founded typically by college professors. New England had plenty of both. But, the Southern Appalachians needed a push. That push was provided by Myron Avery and did not begin until the late 1920s.

---

18. Silas Chamberlain, master's thesis, "'To Ensure Permanency': Expanding and Protecting Hiking Opportunities in Twentieth-Century Pennsylvania" (*Pennsylvania History*, Vol. 77, No. 2, 2010). Chamberlain's graduate work has since been published as *On the Trail: A History of American Hiking* (New Haven, Conn.: Yale University Press, 2016).

The builders

Trail-building began in the earliest days. The first trail up Mount Washington, for instance, was done by George Biggs, a mineralogist. He probably selected what is now the Tuckerman's Ravine route. Boott Spur (named after Francis Boott, a British botanist) was another path that gained early popularity as a possible route that Biggs might have taken.

Early trails were for work, not recreation. Surveyors cut trails, as did botanists, mineralogists, and scientists of various stripes. Builders were often intent on discovery, not hiking. In Pennsylvania, for instance, trails into the mountains were often cut by workers in slate quarries, coal mines, and iron foundries. Trails to charcoal pits were common. The Horse-Shoe Trail, one of the earliest recreational trails in the state, followed segments of a path used to link forges and furnaces. The famed Thousand Steps on the Standing Stone Trail were built by workers in a limestone mine up a steep mountain that bypassed the switchbacks that followed the railroad grade. In the Northern Presidentials, Charles Lowe's system of paths from Randolph to Mount Adams was begun in 1875. Lowe had been recruited for the task by William Nowell, a great trail-builder of AMC.

Those early trails were quite primitive, and builders generally tried to reach the top of the mountain by the shortest possible route. One innovative trail builder, Rayner Edmands, had no patience for such rudimentary trails. He wanted trails that people would like to hike. His wife, to whom he was intensely devoted, had hiked with him on some of the primitive mountain trails in the Northern Presidentials. She wore the long skirts universally worn by women in those days, and, to Edmands, the trails that she hiked were completely inappropriate for those skirts.

Edmands decided to build trails to a different standard, one that we now call "graded trails." Rather than just cutting overhanging bows and painting blazes, he built true paths, hewed from the ground with metal tools. He laid out the trails with string, and limited elevation gains to a more moderate degree, which required sidehill and switchbacks. To divert water, he built water bars. That was hard work, but it created a trail standard that encouraged the less hardy to hike in the Presidentials. In a way, Edmands was the great leveler and brought to hiking a much more diverse group. Men such as Cook and Peek strongly opposed the Edmands paths and refused to hike on them. (Edmands, in return, refused to hike on those created by Cook and Peek.)[19] In the long, long run, Edmands' style won out in most places. The graded trail is more common today than are other types.

Before AMC, many of the mountain paths were maintained by lodge employees, and trail maintenance was very haphazard in the early days. Hikers loved to create new trails but were generally loathe to go back and keep them clear. The theory was that continuous use would be sufficient. In New England, where a cold climate stunted growth, this often worked. It did not work farther south, as the early pioneers of the Appalachian Trail discovered.

AMC also forged ahead with early paid trail crews. Local woodsmen were sometimes hired to maintain trails, and, in 1911, AMC hired its first paid trail crew, only a few years after the Green Mountain Club began paying crews to maintain the Long Trail in Vermont.

AMC pioneered in overnight accommodations, originally called huts. The impulse for this in the White Mountains is self-evident. The weather is one of the most unpredictable, if not most outright dangerous, in the continental United States. Storms can blow across the Whites with frightening speed, and it is instructive to note that the highest wind speed ever recorded on the surface of Earth (231 miles per hour) was recorded on Mount Washington on April 12, 1934. AMC early on recognized the Whites as a unique ecosystem and began taking precautions.

AMC huts in those early days were very primitive and often did not last from one year to the next. Early locations were on Lowe's Path and in Carter Notch, both in the Randolph domain. The first hut to last was Madison Spring, on the ridgeline between Adams and Madison, built in 1888.

---

19. Hudson, *op. cit.,* pp. 21-23.

Lakes of the Clouds Hut had its own dark history. In June 1900, AMC held a meeting on top of Mount Washington. Most of the group went up by cog railway, but two intrepid mountaineers, William Curtis (regarded by many as the most athletic man in the country) and Allan Ormsbee (not far behind Curtis in physical condition), decided to go by way of the Crawford Path. A fierce storm blew in, and both men were frozen to death on the trail. AMC erected a primitive hut where their bodies were found, and, in 1915, they built Lakes of the Clouds Hut not far away.

Maps and guidebooks were also pioneered by AMC, which seemed to hold every record for innovation in the hiking community. The Watermans mention hiking guidebooks published as early as 1852, but the first modern guidebook, produced by Moses F. Sweetser, dates from 1876. It contained route descriptions of ascents of virtually all the New England peaks and concentrated on what the climber would see on the climb, rather than a turn-by-turn description of the route. This format was not replaced until AMC guidebooks began to appear in 1907.

Taylor

The Green Mountains were created from an upthrust along a fault line that can be seen near Burlington, Vermont, a line that extends all the way to Canada. Compared with the Whites, the Green Mountains tend to be of somewhat more modest height, between 3,000 and 4,000 feet above sea level. Stratton Mountain, a peak of unique historical importance to the A.T., is 3,936 feet. South of Killington Peak, the elevations are lower; it is the last 4,000-foot summit on the southbound Appalachian Trail before reaching Virginia. Compare this with the elevations in the White Mountains: Mount Washington, the highest peak in the Whites (and all of New England), is 6,288 feet. But, the Green Mountains define the state, and the state is full of history.

During the Revolutionary War, the Green Mountain Boys, led by Ethan Allen, marched across the mountains to capture Fort Ticonderoga on Lake Champlain. Brother Ira Allen and four others probably made the trek along what is now the Long Trail, bushwhacking some forty miles along the ridgeline. Vermont later won its independence from New York, and residents have always maintained a fierce independent spirit.

Vermonters have a sense of their own uniqueness. Vermont culture is replicated nowhere else, some believe. They regard themselves as an entity separate from the other forty-nine states and don't propose to join the Union culturally. The Appalachian Trail, which runs through the southern part of the state, earns little respect from true

James P. Taylor

Vermonters. It is the Long Trail that gets their loyalty.

The Long Trail, at 272 miles, is advertised as America's first long-distance hiking trail. The concept of a long-distance trail was revolutionary in some ways. When it was created, trails in the Northeast were a disparate collection of short trails clustered around vacation spots that could be reached by railroads. Linearity was just an emerging concept farther east.

One James P. Taylor emerged into the trails community of Vermont as the headmaster of the Vermont Academy for Boys at Saxton River and sometime head of the local chamber of commerce. But, first and foremost, he was a promoter. It was he who first began promoting the idea of a long-distance trail along the Appalachian chain.

Born in New York City in 1872, educated at Colgate, Harvard, and Columbia, he moved to Vermont to take on the job of school head-

Stratton Pond

master. But, Taylor was also a hiker and became frustrated by the lack of trails in the Green Mountains. His academy was near Mount Ascutney, and he would hike around the mountain but could not find trails anywhere else. For two days, according to the Taylor legend, he tried in vain to find the Lake of the Clouds on Mount Mansfield in central Vermont. He reached his nadir when he fell into a concealed potato cellar in an abandoned lumber camp. He failed to find his way from Pico Peak to Killington. He was thoroughly frustrated.[20]

Taylor wrote about his frustration and about his own personal revelation. He sat in a tent at the base of Stratton Mountain (now on the Appalachian Trail) waiting for the rain to clear. He spent the days in "meditation and dreaming" and came up with the idea of a long trail the length of the Green Mountains.[21] There is now a plaque on

20. Vermont State Archive, Box 241/5: Article by Cornelia Wilber, *Long Trail News*, Feb. 1941.
21. Taylor article, undated, found in Box T2/24 in the Vermont State Archives; Tom Slayton (ed.), *A Century in the Mountains: Celebrating Vermont's Long Trail* (Waterbury, Vt.: Green Mountain Club, Inc., 2009): Chapter 2, "A Century of Change–and Growth, A Short History of the GMC" by Reidun Dahle Nuquist, p. 32.

top of Stratton reading, "Cradle of the Appalachian and Long Trails," crediting Taylor with the vision.[22]

Reidun Nuquist, the historian of the Green Mountain Club (GMC), points to the Champlain Tercentenial on July 8, 1909, when 50,000 people gathered in Burlington to see William Howard Taft and other notables at City Hall Park. James Bryce, the British ambassador to the United States (and also a famous historian), advocated for keeping the Green Mountains open to recreation. His words resonated with the audience, and Louis Paris, second only to Taylor in the creation of the Long Trail, credited Bryce with inspiring the founding of the club. It was Paris who first publicized the Long Trail in the May 1911 issue of *The Vermonter*.[23]

After Bryce's speech, Taylor founded the GMC at a community meeting in Burlington on March 11, 1910. He invited twenty-three men (but no women) to that first meeting. The twenty-three founders were all community leaders — doctors, lawyers, editors, journalists, a school principal, a college professor, a former governor, and United States senators.[24]

Taylor was the catalyst but not the main trail-builder. That honor belonged to one of the early members — lawyer Clarence P. Cowles (who eventually became a judge and was thereafter always addressed by his formal title, Judge Cowles). The very first five-mile stretch was scouted by Cowles and Craig Burt on October 1, 1910, a little more than six months after the club was founded.

The first section of the trail was a thirty-mile stretch between Mount Mansfield and Camel's Hump east of Burlington. Taylor's marking technique was, like Rayner Edmands', to unravel a ball of string along the proposed path. This technique was still being used by Myron Avery in the 1930s to mark the Appalachian Trail route through Virginia and Maryland.

Taylor continued to expand and flesh out the idea of this long trail and discussed it publicly in an address in 1914 to the Western New

22. Anderson, *op. cit.*, p. 367.
23. Jane and Will Curtis, "*Green Mountain Adventure, Vermont's Long Trail* (Montpelier, Vt.: Green Mountain Club, Inc., 1985), p. 15.
24. Nuquist, *op. cit.*, p. 32.

England Chamber of Commerce in Greenfield, Massachusetts. By then, his idea for a long trail included the mountains to the southwest of Vermont — the Taconics and Housatonics — and even extended into New York State, south across the Hudson River and along the top of the Palisades.[25] North, it would even reach Canada. He made a map of this long trail and showed it to audiences. According to Louis Paris, the Long Trail was modeled after *Der Hoheweg* (the High Way), a German long-distance trail that began in Pforzheim in Baden and ended in Basel, on Lake Constance in Switzerland.

Enthusiasm began to wane, and, by 1912, little was being done to lay out other trail sections. Paris, the GMC treasurer, was the most active member, but his treasury was about out of money. At that point, Austin F. Hawes, the Vermont state forester, went to the GMC trustees. Hawes needed trails for fire suppression and proposed that his fire roads be combined with the route of the Long Trail — killing, in a way, two birds with one stone. He would supply the labor if GMC provided the money. With Hawes' proposal as inspiration, the club went on a campaign for donations and rounded up $475 almost immediately. That was a way to get trail rapidly on the ground, and Hawes delegated the job to Robert Ross, one of his young foresters.

By the fall of 1913, 150 miles already were on the ground, from Killington to a point north of Smuggler's Notch. Almost all the construction was north of the present Appalachian Trail. The Forestry Service continued to push ahead with the project, funded by the Green Mountain Club. The club eventually raised more than $1,000 toward the effort.

Trails and fire roads did not turn out to be the best of partners. Within GMC was considerable dissension about the routing of the trail, which was laid out according to fire-road precepts, without any evident consideration given to a scenic hiking trail. It went through some heavily logged sections — the Vermont Forestry Service wanted a fire road and nothing else.[26]

It was at this point that Will Monroe entered the GMC scene with the idea of a new trail route that came to be known as the Monroe Sky-

25. Vermont State Archives, Box T2/25.
26. Curtises, *op. cit.*

line. Monroe had established a New York Section of GMC, a venture that was so controversial that it was challenged as illegal under the
GMC bylaws. (An article by Louis Paris in *The
Vermonter* settled the controversy and "proved"
that an out-of-state chapter was legal.) Monroe,
the interloper from Montclair, New Jersey, was
a game-changer. Vividly described by the Watermans, his photographs usually showed him
as surrounded by a bevy of large, shaggy dogs
(collies, Saint Bernards, Newfoundlands, Great
Pyrenees). Judge Cowles called him "the most
scholarly man I ever knew."

Will Monroe

Monroe was strong-willed and probably
difficult to get along with when arguing for his skyline trail. The
Watermans describe the history of the New York Section under Monroe as a "stormy, independent fiefdom within the parent GMC, frequently at odds with the club as a whole, always vigorous, often the
largest section in membership, never the quietest."[27] Monroe began
his skyline trail in 1916, a trail section that also was entirely north of
what would become the Appalachian Trail.

Meanwhile, GMC pushed trail scouting south of Killington, and,
by 1917, the Long Trail was complete south of Sherburne Pass all the
way to Massachusetts. It linked up with trails constructed by Williams College. The trail in the north, to the Canadian border, was not
completed until later, so the section that was later adopted as part of
the Appalachian Trail was in place earlier.

The Long Trail garnered a number of firsts. It was, indeed, America's first "long trail," although that designation depends to some
extent on definitions. (How long did a trail have to be to merit the
definition "long"?) It was the first to use the idea of a "linear trail,"
as opposed to shorter loop trails typical of New Hampshire. And, according to Myron Avery, it was the first one to use paint as a way of

---

27. Watermans, *op. cit.*, p. 364.

marking trails.[28] Avery adopted the white blaze from its first use by GMC on the Long Trail.

In later years, Taylor began moving away from direct involvement in the trail that he inspired.[29] He was, at heart, a promoter who fastened onto many causes and was very diverse in his interests. He left trail-building to others. The Watermans characterized Taylor as

> ...this shabby, slightly disreputable chamber of commerce huckster, this amiable schemer, this compulsive promoter, this mercurial and most un-Vermonterish grand champion of Vermont [who] was on the field first, waving his baton and ready to lead the field.[30]

Philip Ayres

His 1914 address to the Western New England Chamber of Commerce in Greenfield, Massachusetts, set out his broader vision of the Long Trail, extending it north to Canada and all the way to New York state. It would be necessary to form a region-wide trail organization, he proclaimed. Attending the talk was Philip Ayres, forester for the Society for the Protection of New Hampshire Forests. Ayres seized on Taylor's idea of a region-wide organization of trail groups and began pushing for a formative meeting.

Ayres enlisted Allen Chamberlain, a newspaper columnist for the *Boston Evening Transcript* and an avid hiker. On December 16, 1916, the great formative meeting finally happened, hosted in Boston by AMC. Chamberlain credited Taylor with the vision to bring the leaders in the New England trail movement together in one room. Taylor was elected president of the New England Trail Conference. The organizing committee consisted of Taylor, Ayres, Chamberlain, H.A. Perkins of Wakefield and the AMC, and Nathanial Goodrich of the Dartmouth Outing Club.

---

28. PATC archives, Avery papers, 1934, draft of an article by Avery.
29. Slayton, *op. cit.*, p. 40.
30. Watermans, *op. cit.*, p. 479.

At the meeting, Sumner Hooper from Maine pushed the idea of the Long Trail's connecting to the trails in New Hampshire, but the most revolutionary idea came from one Bill Hall, a federal forester, who speculated that the New England trails might eventually connect with new trails in the southern Appalachians, most of which were being built in the newly created southern forests: Pisgah, Cherokee, and Chattahoochee.[31]

Ashton Allis provided a more well-defined map in 1921. His vision brought the Long Trail into eastern New York State, across the Hudson to Storm King, down the Hudson Highlands, through the Palisades Interstate Park to Greenwood Lake, down into northern New Jersey, and thus all the way to Delaware Water Gap.[32] In this, he was following Taylor's vision of extending the Long Trail south and added his own segment to the Delaware River at the Pennsylvania border.

In New York, hiking groups had begun emerging as early as the mid-nineteenth century. At the time, no formal trails existed, and groups of those rugged and very enthusiastic clubs would use woods roads. The emerging railway systems played a major contribution in getting people out of New York City and into the woods, as they had in New England.

Fortunately for hikers, a great deal of public land was available for them to hike on. The Palisades Interstate Park was established in 1900, and, in 1910, Mary Williams Harriman, the widow of Edward H. Harriman, a railroad magnate, made a land gift to the state of New York for the Bear Mountain and Harriman State Park system.

In 1920, an outdoors writer named Raymond Torrey began a column on hiking called the Outing Page in the *New York Tribune*. In 1923, he changed the name to the "Long Brown Path," taken from Walt Whitman's "Song of the Open Road" — "The long brown path before me, leading wherever I choose." It was Torrey who inspired the trail system in New York that eventually became a major section

---

31. Vermont State Archives, Box T2/25, article by Chamberlain in the *Boston Evening Transcript*; Watermans' article in the *Appalachian Trailway News (ATN)*, September/October 1985, pp. 7-9; *Forest and Crag*, pp. 475-83.
32. *ATN, ibid.*

of the Appalachian Trail. The first "official" section (in 1922) was the Ramapo–Dunderberg Trail west of the Hudson. (See chapter 2.)

When Benton MacKaye published his 1921 article proposing an Appalachian Trail, the scene was set.

What happened to Taylor? He continued to promote Vermont, and, when a skyline-drive controversy raged in the 1930s, he advocated for those roads as a way to increase tourism in the state. In September 1949, his body was found floating in Lake Champlain, the evident victim of a boating accident. At his funeral, all the ushers were GMC members, and, in 1951, the club dedicated a lodge in his memory.[33]

The Taylor tale fades into legend, and, through the haze of time, one is no longer sure how to separate Taylor the promoter from Taylor the hiker. His vision of trails along the height of the land similarly faded into legend as it worked south. Benton MacKaye gets the credit, but James Taylor deserves a slice, too.

33. Vermont State Archives, Box 225/29.

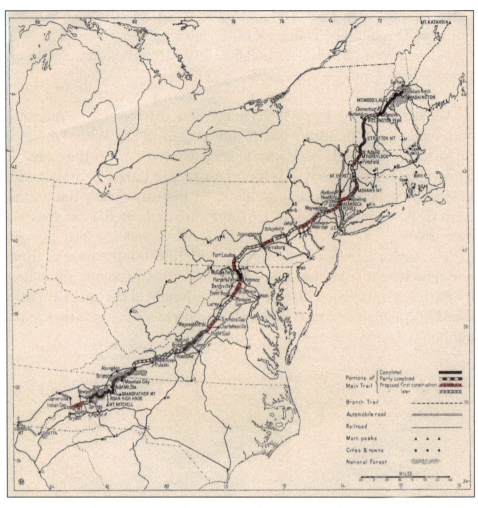

A very early Benton MacKaye map of the proposed Appalachian Trail

Chapter 2

BENTON MACKAYE HAS A GRAND IDEA

*Another feature about the Appalachian Trail is that it is entirely
the result of volunteer labor, the work of men and women who have
received no compensation for their service other than the satisfaction of having a hand in putting across so magnificent a project.
The budget of the Conference, including the cost of postage, is only
about $500.00 per year. No officer of the Conference draws a cent of
salary or even expense money. The tasks of scouting, routing, clearing, and marking the trail have been done by volunteers, the working parties being mostly composed of professional men and woman,
office workers, college students, and others — the white collar class
— who have welcomed this opportunity to get into the out-of-doors.*
— Paul Fink, 1938

The idea of extending the New England trail system south along
the Appalachian chain was being discussed by such people as James
Taylor, Ashton Allis, Allen Chamberlain, and Bill Hall, particularly
at the first meeting of the New England Trail Conference (NETC) in
1916 in Boston. Hearing about their discussions later, Benton Mac-
Kaye probably connected their ideas with his own, arrived at independently. The trail that people at the NETC were talking about did
not yet have a publicist. Benton MacKaye became its publicist.

MacKaye soon after Harvard

It would be hard to imagine two more dissimilar personalities. Taylor was the consummate promoter, a P.T. Barnum in hiking boots. MacKaye was a consummate intellectual — a hiker and avid outdoorsman since childhood who spent his adult life researching, writing, advocating, and working in midlevel professional positions until the 1940s. Yet, they had the same vision — which says something about the attraction. At forty-two, MacKaye, schooled and initially employed as a forester from Stamford, Connecticut, published the vision that others were discussing.

Born in 1879, MacKaye became one of New England's itinerant philosophers. His father, Steele MacKaye, was a playwright and actor from a wealthy family who, through a series of bizarre events, did not inherit any of the family's wealth and was constantly in need of money. He died suddenly in 1894 after a series of spectacular financial failures. Fortunately for the next generation, Steele's son Will purchased a house in the small town of Shirley Center, Massachusetts. That became the center of the family's holdings and was used, off and on, by Will's brother Benton. It gave him a place that he could return to, often between jobs.[1]

Benton received a classical education at Cambridge Latin School and then enrolled at Harvard College. In 1901, after graduating from undergraduate school, he rambled from one job to another with a fair bit of hiking when he could. Beginning as a tutor of schoolboys in New York City, he became a camp counselor in New Hampshire in 1902.

---

1. Most of the biographical information for this chapter was drawn from Larry Anderson, *Benton MacKaye: Conservationist, Planner, and Creator of the Appalachian Trail* (Baltimore: The Johns Hopkins University Press, 2002).

*The "Sky Parlor" at the rear of the family "cottage" in Shirley Center —
the second-floor den where Benton often did his writing and research.*

In 1903, he became the first student to pursue a graduate degree
in the newly created Harvard forestry program, the fourth such curriculum in the country (after schools at the Biltmore estate, Cornell,
and Yale). Next-door New Hampshire was, by one account, regarded
as the most heavily logged state in the nation, and MacKaye, already
an avid hiker, warmed to the new profession. Just before he started
his graduate studies, he had survived a near brush with death in an
attack of appendicitis. Emerging from his sick bed, he decided that
his mission in life was to save the forests.

After Harvard, in 1905, he was hired by Gifford Pinchot as one
of a group of new foresters authorized under new federal legislation
that gave Pinchot control of the new forest reserves, then entirely in
the West (see page 9).

As a forester, MacKaye spent his early years in New England, advising private landowners, but he moved around. In 1908, he was
posted first to Kentucky, then was moved to Massachusetts later that

year, doing various forest surveys under Pinchot. He studied timber overcutting in the Great Lakes region, and he was in Washington state, investigating conditions in the mills, lumber camps, and mill towns. He witnessed the violent strikes in the Northwest lumbering industry, particularly in Everett, a mill town north of Seattle. Mac-Kaye was deeply influenced by the labor-management conflicts there.

Between 1906 and 1910, he was simultaneously teaching forestry at Harvard and working, usually in the summer, for the USFS.

Leaving the Forest Service, he worked for the Labor Department studying various issues related to labor-management relations and was let go in mid-1919 after a dispute with a congressman and budget crunches. He then had a temporary job with the Postal Service, studying the postal delivery system as the basis for a cooperative agricultural marketing program. In 1920, he moved to Milwaukee to become an editorial writer for the *Milwaukee Leader,* a socialist newspaper from which he resigned, partly on principle and partly in reaction to criticism of his activist wife's views.

His socialist leanings had a long history. While teaching at Harvard between other jobs, he joined the Harvard Socialist Club, which numbered among its members such prominent early twentieth-century liberals as John Reed, Walter Lippmann, and Lincoln Steffens. Theirs was a "soft" socialism, similar to the British Fabian socialism of Beatrice and Sidney Webb at the turn of the century. Still, it was out of the American political mainstream, where the Progressives had captured the hearts of the political left.

In 1919, he had moved to a row house on DuPont Circle in Washington, D.C., which was a center for political liberals in the capital, including a young Dean Acheson, Frederic Howe, and other more controversial figures further to the left. At the end of World War I in 1918, MacKaye had harbored thoughts of following John Reed to Russia to help the new Bolshevik government, but his application to go was never acted on. That was about as close as MacKaye ever got to international political activism in a lifetime of domestic political activism.

MacKaye married late in life, at thirty-six, in 1915. Jesse Belle Hardy "Betty" Stubbs, a widow, was a political radical in the wom-

Jesse Belle ("Betty") Hardy Stubbs MacKaye

en's suffrage and antiwar movements with views similar to those of MacKaye. She became increasingly depressed and committed suicide in 1921, after only six years of marriage.

41

Betty's suicide was in key ways the impetus for MacKaye to put on paper his vision of a great long-distance trail, a vision that had its roots at least twenty-four years earlier. She ran from him in Grand Central Station, to avoid a trip to the upstate camp of a friend, where she had stayed during previous episodes, and jumped into the East River off Manhattan, as recorded on the front page of *The New York Times.*

It was a tragedy that followed Benton the rest of his life, making him a solitary individual, even more itinerant in his ways, requiring little in the way of creature comforts and little sense of place, except for Shirley Center. He would show up at friends' homes and stay for periods of time, then move on. His intellectual attainments were such that he must have been a very pleasant companion. In any case, he remained a perpetual house guest all his life, entertaining his friends with his ideas and his wit.

MacKaye's ideas about trails came early in life. At 18, in August 1897, he disappeared into the New Hampshire forest with Sturgis Pray, the future Appalachian Mountain Club (AMC) master trail-builder, and several companions. Pray, who became head of the land-scape architecture curriculum at Harvard, was scouting connecting trails in a broad sweep of the White Mountains. MacKaye spent several weeks tramping through the Whites on that journey of exploration. Describing the experience for the Appalachian Trail Conference (ATC) meeting in 1972, MacKaye wrote:

> *It was the summer of 1897 that I waded with two companions, across Swift River, scrambled through a blowdown, and ascended Tremont Mountain overlooking the southern White Mountain ranges. The blowdown ushered me into the true genuine sure-enough 'forest Primeval,' for such it yet was in the 1890s. And it was hell. A scrambled mess of fallen broken trunks and boughs, a choking chaos impossible to describe....* [2]

---

2. Rauner Library, Dartmouth College, MacKaye collection, Box 159, folder 19.

On August 17, MacKaye awoke early near the top of Mount Tremont. At about 4:30 a.m., he clambered up the remaining quarter-mile to the top of Tremont and was visited with what he described as a mystical experience. "The grandest sight I ever saw was now before me, nothing but a sea of mountains and clouds."[3] Larry Anderson, MacKaye's biographer, speculates that this might have been the original vision that motivated him on conservation and trail matters. The days with Pray probably influenced MacKaye's course in life and his love of trails.

Three years later, MacKaye took a backpacking trip with Horace Hildreth, a fellow Harvard student. Following MacKaye's graduation, they threw on rucksacks and headed for Vermont, a state that had as yet very few trails. Beginning in the southern Green Mountains, they worked their way north. They reached Killington Peak, Sherburne Pass, Camel's Hump, and Mount Mansfield, bushwhacking most of the way. This adventure made a lasting impression on MacKaye, and, he said several times later, it was on Stratton Mountain in the southern Green Mountains that he had his grand vision of a trail the length of the Appalachian chain. He described the experience in 1964:

We walked up through the trailless woods to the top of Stratton Mountain and climbed trees in order to see the view.... It was a clear day with a brisk breeze blowing. North and south sharp peaks etched the horizon. I felt as if atop the world, with a sort of 'planetary feeling.' I seemed to perceive peaks far southward, hidden by old Earth's curvature. Would a footpath someday reach them from where I was then perched?"[4]

MacKaye credited this experience as the inspiration for his vision of an Appalachian Trail (although he sometimes cited other moments, depending on his audience). Stratton Mountain has gone down in history as the place where both he and James Taylor experi-

---

3. Larry Anderson, *Peculiar Work*, p. 22.
4. Appalachian Trail Conservancy archives, Stanley Murray Box. Murray, in a letter to Gasteiger on May 26, 1966, quotes from a letter from MacKaye to Nancy Durham, reproduced in the July 1964 edition of *American Forests*.

enced their respective transcending moments. Is it possible that both he and Taylor experienced their revelations at the same mountain? In any case, it was a stunning coincidence that Taylor had his vision at the bottom of Stratton and MacKaye at its top.

The vision was something that nagged at MacKaye for many years before he wrote about it. In 1902, for instance, Anderson writes, when MacKaye was a camp counselor, he told the headmaster, Virgil Prettyman, that there should be a trail from Mount Washington in New Hampshire to Mount Mitchell in North Carolina. By 1916, an article discussing the recreational possibilities of national forests cited the thinking of Allen Chamberlain, who had recommended that forests be physically linked. MacKaye went on to discuss the potential to link the forests of New Hampshire, Vermont, Massachusetts, and Connecticut. He was aware of proposals by the Green Mountain Club to extend its Long Trail to the Canadian line and then south to the Berkshires, the Hudson Highlands, and then downriver all the way to New York City itself. He then speculated that it might be possible to some day extend the northern trails down through New Jersey and Pennsylvania, the Blue Ridge of Virginia, and thence to the Southern Appalachians. He also proposed linking the east and west *via* river transport. "Once in the Rockies, the many systems of roads and trails, from the Canadian to the Mexican border, would take the traveler by any number of routes to the Cascades, the Sierras, the Coast ranges, and to the Coast itself." Here was the master planner at work.[5]

He wrote of the role of rail lines to connect the urban population with the mountains and even discussed the idea of forest camps for them to stay in. Here, indeed, was his first design for a long-distance trail, printed the same year that forester Bill Hall proposed such an idea at the founding meeting of the New England Trail Conference.

MacKaye's ideas, published in the *Journal of the American Institute of Architects* six years later, did not resonate in 1916. They did resonate in 1921. All good ideas eventually have their moment, and one must wait for the moment.

---

5. Benton MacKaye, "Recreational Possibilities of Public Forests," *Journal of the New York State Forestry Association*, October 1916.

"An Appalachian Trail: A Project in Regional Planning"

MacKaye's ideas for a long-distance trail were part of his planning mentality and led to his association with Clarence S. Stein, a relationship that was to last the rest of his life. The two were almost exactly contemporary — Stein was born in Rochester, New York, in 1882, just three years after MacKaye, and died in 1975, the same year as MacKaye. Stein grew up in New York City in a well-to-do Jewish family that made caskets. His early life and education were highly eclectic as he absorbed ideas from various schools of humanistic thought. He took courses at Columbia University and the *Ecole des Beaux Arts* in Paris. He became interested in the settlement-house movement in New York, and that led him to consider the problems of urban living and the need to plan for a more attractive environment.

Stein designed, consulted on, and was a leading advocate for a number of urban-development projects. Stein planned several so-called "garden cities" that would provide a green environment that separated living and walking space from the ever-present automobile.

Stein became an architect, but one whose architectural planning was of broad sweep, rather than building designs. He cofounded the Regional Planning Association of America (RPAA) in 1923, and he and MacKaye, who had given thought to the problems of urban and regional planning, established a close, lifetime friendship.

On Sunday, July 10, 1921, MacKaye was introduced to Stein by Charles Harris Whitaker, who edited the *Journal of the American Institute of Architects* (AIA). The historic meeting took place at Hudson Guild Farm, in the highlands of New Jersey, a recreational retreat maintained by New York's Hudson Guild Settlement House (and now a 3,800-acre private hunting club for the wealthy).

MacKaye had retreated to Whitaker's home in New Jersey after the suicide of his wife, and there, at his friends' urgings, his thoughts turned to the idea of committing his trail-project ideas to paper. Whitaker recognized MacKaye's ideas as applicable to regional planning and invited his friend Stein to visit and to discuss MacKaye's ideas.

The article that brought MacKaye to prominence, written at Whitaker's home after that Hudson Guild Farm meeting, reads today to many as a convoluted piece, suffused with utopian ideas pasted together into a not especially well-organized treatise. Philosophically, it smacked more of Utopians such as Edward Bellamy than pragmatists such as John Dewey. (It later must have mystified more practical people such as Myron Avery.)

The Appalachian Trail was not even the central idea, although it appears in the title of the article as *"an* Appalachian Trail." Preliminary drafts and other meeting notes show that, under the rubric of recreation, he intended a flanking attack on the contemporary industrial system—with an eye to the sensitivities of the audience. He, Stein, and Harris excised most explicitly political terms.

MacKaye began with a philosophical consideration of the problems of economics, labor, and leisure time in the early 1920s. Linking them together, he concluded that the answer to the problems that he posed was to create forest camps in the Appalachians. That would solve problems, as he saw them, of a need to disperse the eastern population, create a project for leisure time, and establish an economic base in the mountains. He dealt with the most basic problems of modern industrial economy and proposed solutions.

Several different types of forest camps would be established — those based on forestry and timbering, those producing crops to feed the residents, and those concentrating on recreation as a restorative exercise for urban populations. Much was left unanswered about who would populate the camps, how long they might stay, whether or not there would be a constant shift from urban to rural and then back again. By implication, the camps would require permanent residents as managers — but that, too, was left unaddressed in the article.

He wrote, "No scheme is proposed in this particular article for organizing or financing this project. Organizing is a matter of detail to be carefully worked out. Financing depends upon local public interest in the various localities affected." (MacKaye later expanded on those ideas, and his later writings answered many of the questions left hanging in 1921.)

Connecting all would be a "sky-line trail," a walking path that would provide recreation, as well as a physical connection between forest camps. The trail was almost incidental to the concept of forest camps.

He envisioned the Long Trail in Vermont as the launching point for that new trail. That Appalachian Trail would be an extension of the Long Trail, but Vermont

MacKaye's 1921 map of the proposed A.T.

would not be the northern terminus. That would be Mount Washington in New Hampshire. The southern terminus would be Mount Mitchell in North Carolina, the highest point east of the Mississippi. The new trail would be divided into sections, generally within state boundaries, managed by local residents. MacKaye envisioned the use of eminent domain to acquire needed rights of way. He did understand trails and noted that not all of it could be built right away. Construction would require years — and it would all be done by volunteers.

A second type of camp, the "shelter camp," should be spaced along the trail one day's walk apart. "They should be equipped always for sleeping and certain of them for serving meals — after the fashion of Swiss chalets," according to MacKaye. They would be similar presumably to the larger shelters on the Long Trail or AMC huts, rather than the shelters that eventually evolved on the A.T. "Community camps" would naturally grow out of the shelter camps. These would be located near the trail, perhaps on neighboring lakes, with permanent residents. They should be part of the project, purchased and owned by sponsoring entities along the trail. "Food and farm camps" would also be necessary, although not, perhaps, at the inception of the project. His model for those was Hudson Guild Farm in New Jersey.

Accompanying all that was a map of the East Coast with the new trail depicted from New Hampshire to North Carolina. He drew in side trails — for instance, from somewhere in northern Virginia (perhaps from what was to become the northern district of Shenandoah National Park?) north across Maryland to Pennsylvania and on into western New York. Its southern stretch vaguely resembled what was to become the Tuscarora Trail, which was eventually built as an A.T. side trail. In its general contours, MacKaye's depiction closely resembled what actually became the Appalachian Trail, with extensions — in the south on to northern Georgia and in the north into central Maine. An intriguing line went north to a location that could have been Katahdin in Maine.

In southern Virginia, the proposed trail diverged at the New River, with an eastern prong and a western prong. The eastern prong took the trail to Mount Mitchell but did not stop there. It continued down through North Carolina into northern Georgia, quite close to Springer Mountain, then on to a point that appears to be Chattanooga. The western prong carried the trail into Tennessee, with a dotted line on to southern Alabama. MacKaye drew a short, dotted line into southern Maine, in the direction of Katahdin.

The map showed rail lines from various cities. Some, such as Cleveland, Cincinnati, Philadelphia, Buffalo, and Boston, were specifically identified, while others were unidentified but could be interpreted as Nashville, perhaps Atlanta, Birmingham, possibly Richmond, and other spots. In the absence of widespread automobile ownership, railroads were regarded as the key to accessing vacation spots.

It is a wonder that the idea of a trail caught on. The *Journal of the American Institute of Architects* was normally read by a small constituency of architects and devotees of urban planning. The way he laid out his ideas might be regarded as fuzzy and incomplete in today's world, and the idea that took off (the trail) was not even the core thesis of the article. It was, to use today's parlance, simply a vector. Yet it was the part of the plan that MacKaye and Stein pushed immediately following publication.

The trail was a means to an end, an end that was suffused with MacKaye's urban planning and socialist thinking. Socialists and urban planners had a great deal of material to think about — to connect modern American urban living with the natural world. But, it was not the socialist or the urban planner who was to be captured by the idea. It was the hiker. The concept of long-distance trails certainly had caught on within the outdoor leadership community in New England and was soon to infuse downstate New York with its infectious enthusiasm.

Following publication of the article, MacKaye continued to expand his ideas for the project and to fit the trail into the larger context of the forest realm. Larry Anderson notes, "For Benton MacKaye, the Appalachian Trail was never merely a footpath.... The Appalachian Trail, that is, was the axis of what he envisioned as a vast expanse of protected public land, stretching along the mountains between Maine and Georgia." MacKaye stated at a 1931 ATC meeting in Gatlinburg, Tennessee, "A realm and not a trail marks the full aim of our effort."[6] Creating a wilderness domain was more important than the trail itself.

That intellectual ferment stayed with him all his life and drove the spilling out of a veritable cornucopia of ideas. Much of what he proposed, he never formally published. But, the ideas drove him forward and pushed him to organize the effort.

His unpublished writings further defined his ideas to make the new trail usable. He defined his idea for the placement of forest camps and wrote about the need for side trails to connect to the main line

---

6. Anderson, *Peculiar Work*, p. 80.

trail. He thought about "trail towns," and how a hiker could reach them by rail and then stay overnight prior to taking a side trail to the skyline route. Campsites on the trail, MacKaye wrote, should be purchased by local organizations, and they should charge for their use. Railroads loomed so large in his thinking that he stated at once point, "Without stations, the trail is not a trail." He used a trail section from Stratton in Vermont to Greylock in Massachusetts as an example of how recreational use of the mountains might unfold.[7]

Organizing the Appalachian Trail Project

Having published the article, the next step in MacKaye's mind was to create the trail and the camps. He wrote, hesitantly, in the journal *Appalachia* in December 1922, "Some day a permanent central organization will have to be born, but it has not yet been determined just what sort of thing this will be." While he hoped that most of the new trail would be on Forest Service or Park Service land, he acknowledged that some parts of the trail would be on private land and that permissions would be needed. He wrote that the new organization would have to "get permissions where we can, make detours where we must...." The Committee on Community Planning of the American Institute of Architects became the initial sponsor of the idea.

Thinking about the geography of the Appalachians, he divided the trail into eight long sections:

In the far north, he acknowledged that the trail system in New England provided the basis for a skyline trail through New Hampshire and Vermont. Contacts had already been made with the New England Trail Conference. New Hampshire and Vermont had the best-organized trail system. Sections in Massachusetts and Connecticut were in a less organized state. He expected the work in Connecticut would be done by the state Forest and Park Commission.

The next section south was New York and New Jersey, where a trail club (New York–New Jersey Trail Conference) had already been

---

7. Rauner Library, MacKaye Collection, Box 177, folder 8; undated mimeographed article, possibly not published.

organized and was at work on a trail system in the Palisades Interstate Park and Harriman State Park.

He named the next section "Schuylkill," Delaware Water Gap to Harrisburg, Pennsylvania. Pennsylvania had an active hiking community but so far no organized trail-builders.

Section 4 was called North Potomac (Harrisburg to the Potomac River).

Then there was South Potomac, the Potomac River to Luray, Virginia. Shenandoah National Park had not yet been created, so that was at the time private land. Here again was a vibrant hiking culture without organized trail-building.

The Natural Bridge section was from Luray to Roanoke, Virginia.

The New River section was from Roanoke to Unaka National Forest.

Finally, there was Tennessee and North Carolina, from the New River (near its origins in North Carolina) to Mount Mitchell.

He found contacts with seven of the eight districts, with only the New River district remaining to be contacted. He was in touch with several national forests and so far was meeting with a positive response.[8]

The farther south the section, the sketchier was the detail in his plan. Still, that New Englander displayed an unusually precise knowledge of each area. (His organization by regions by 1925 had nothing to do with geography and everything to do with the presence of, or prospect for, a volunteer organization.) It provided a good basis for moving forward. He knew that organizing the volunteer organizations would be a big job, especially in the far South, where the hiking culture was very different from that in New England.

"Beginning" that new trail at Mount Washington presented certain risks. The Presidentials were the weather barrier between coastal New England and the arctic mass sweeping down from Canada. The entire trail was above timberline and had cost hikers' lives. The wind gusts on Mount Washington were phenomenal. Yet, the fame of the mountain made it a logical choice for a northern terminus.

---

8. MacKaye, article in *Appalachia*, December 1922, pp. 244-52.

He also proposed to begin expanding local trails from Boston, New York, Washington, and Charlottesville, Virginia, to serve as connecting trails to the Appalachians.

The trail would begin in pieces, and, as the individual pieces were expanded and eventually connected together, hikers could walk individual sections, traveling by train from one section to another. It was a grand vision.

As he moved forward, MacKaye spun out organizational proposals. In unpublished writings, he proposed an initial conference with local group leaders in each provisional section. That would be followed by a field examination to determine the local route of the trail and the camps. The result of that would be a "field report" on the prospects. Then, a follow-up conference with the same local leaders would discuss implementation of the plan. Volunteer groups would raise funds to purchase places for camp sites. "Work on trails should be started promptly and snappily all along the line — preferably in the spring."[9] (He presumably meant the very next spring!)

In the spring of 1922, MacKaye began meeting with local trail leaders to promote and organize his new trail. Beginning in New England, he lunched with Albert Turner and Austin Hawes of AMC. Turner was the field secretary for the Connecticut State Park and Forest Commission and was working out a route for the trail through his state and in Massachusetts. He advised MacKaye that William Welch of the Palisades Interstate Park Commission was working on the idea of a bridge at Bear Mountain and that appeared to be the best place for the Appalachian Trail to cross the Hudson River.[10]

On April 6, he had dinner at the City Club in New York, with Clarence Stein, J. Ashton Allis of AMC, and Raymond Torrey, the influential columnist for the *New York Evening Post.*

The very next day, Torrey published a column describing MacKaye's idea. He outlined the trail movement in New England — AMC's work in the White Mountains and the Green Mountain Club's creation of the Long Trail in Vermont. He then turned to the New

---

9. Rauner Library, MacKaye Collection, typescript of an unpublished article.
10. ATC archives, MacKaye Box, Turner letter to MacKaye, March 24, 1922.

Raymond Torrey's first column on MacKaye's idea

York situation, where a number of hiking groups had built a trail from Tuxedo to Jones Point on the Hudson and had more recently extended it north to Bear Mountain. The New Jersey Forestry Department, he noted, had made eight miles of new trail on the summit of Kittatinny Mountain. Allis proposed extending that trail system, also called the Ramapo–Dunderberg Trail, both north and south — to Kittatinny Mountain in New Jersey and across the Hudson to the Berkshires in Connecticut.

MacKaye then travelled to Washington to meet with Francois Matthes, a geologist with the U.S. Geological Survey, and with L.F. Schmeckebier, an economist with the Brookings Institution. Matthes had been made aware of the proposal for a trail by the secretary of the American Civic Association. The next day, he met with a larger group: Matthes, Schmeckebier, journalist Frederick M. Kerby, Harry Slattery (counsel to the National Conservation Association), and Louis F. Post (former assistant secretary of labor under President Wilson and Mac-

Kaye's boss in his last government position before TVA). They formed a committee with Matthes as chairman. That early organizing committee had a short life, and only Schmeckebier continued on in any significant capacity. (He became Myron Avery's deputy and later succeeded Avery as president of the Potomac Appalachian Trail Club.) The rest of them rapidly disappeared from the project, and, by 1925, when the Appalachian Trail Conference was formed, only Matthes' name was still mentioned in correspondence, and he attended that meeting.

While in Washington, MacKaye talked with Arno Cammerer, then deputy director of the National Park Service, and was in touch with Vernon Rhoades of the forest service, who took a keen interest in routing the trail through the southern forests. MacKaye also made contact with Paul Fink of Jonesboro, Tennessee, a banker and avid backpacker who became an early supporter and scout of the trail route in the south.

But, his most consequential contact was with a physician from Charlottesville. Halstead Hedges devoted considerable time to the mountain folk of the Blue Ridge and probably knew the area better than anyone who lived in town. Even before the end of May 1922, Hedges had scouted south as far as the Tye River (today, thirty trail miles south of Rockfish Gap). He also began scouting a trail route north of Rockfish Gap in what was to become the southern section of Shenandoah National Park.[11] At the time Hedges began laying out a trail route, Congress had not even authorized a national park in Virginia. MacKaye was more than impressed with Hedges' scouting trips. In 1967, he gave Hedges credit for being "the first of the on-ground pioneers."

Before leaving Washington, MacKaye rode to Harpers Ferry, Berryville, and Snickers Gap with Kerby, Slattery, and Matthes. The Appalachian Trail, when it was finally put on the ground, actually went through Snickers Gap, and Berryville was only 10 miles to the west.[12]

In Washington, MacKaye also met with Harlan Kelsey, a member of a committee selecting potential national park locations in the East.

---

11. MacKaye, "Some Early A.T. History," PATC *Bulletin*, October–December 1957, pp. 91-96.
12. He was undoubtedly driven, as he didn't own a car. The meetings in Washington are discussed in MacKaye's diaries and in the PATC *Bulletin* for January 1953.

Doctor Halstead S. Hedges.

The first person to scout the route of the A.T. south of the Potomac in Virginia was Halstead Hedges. Hedges, an ophthalmologist living in Charlottesville, was born in 1867 in West Orange, New Jersey, but at 15 his family moved to Charlottesville. He graduated from the University of Virginia in 1882, and by 1899 was in private practice. A groundbreaking surgeon, he was the first person in the United States to perform a corneal transplant and received many honors for his medical work. But, he also became famous for his hiking. As a young man, he hiked with his brother from Georgia to Virginia, over ridges with no trails, bushwhacking most of the way in a six-week hike. When Benton MacKaye published his idea for a trail through Virginia, it was Hedges who knew the area north of Rockfish Gap better than anyone. Hedges was a consummate outdoorsman — a hunter (he only used a bow and arrow), canoeist, and camper. His favorite spot was Loft Mountain, then called Big Flat. At age 87, he went camping in a wilderness area of Ontario, Canada. The doctor died in September 1968, just eleven days short of his 101st birthday.

Kelsey said, "Hell, don't take your Trail to Mount Mitchell — take it through the Smokies — that's where the scenery is."[13]

Come October, MacKaye was back up north, and, on the 27th, he was attending a conference at Bear Mountain Inn. There he gave the *spiel* on his trail proposal, followed by discussions of possible trail linkages. Allen Chamberlain of AMC again told of the possibility of extending the trail through the Berkshires. That meeting included many who would become prominent in the early trail movement, including urban historian Lewis Mumford, Harlean James, Albert Turner, Harlan Kelsey, and Raymond Torrey. This conference adopted Major William Welch's logo for the Appalachian Trail; he was the conference's host as the general manager of the state park there and the Palisades

13. Rauner Library, MacKaye Collection, Box 182, folder 4, Cosmos Club Bulletin, June 1959.

Interstate Park. It has survived as the A.T. logo to this day — first as a square and then as a diamond, officially adopted at another meeting in 1924 and trademarked by the conservancy in the mid-1970s.

In January 1923, MacKaye attended a meeting of the New England Trail Conference in Boston. His Appalachian Trail idea was discussed at length, and Sturgis Pray and Allen Chamberlain took prominent roles. The leaders discussed the idea of extending the New Hampshire trail system into Massachusetts (where it would link up with the Long Trail coming down from Vermont) and on into Connecticut.[14]

Allen Chamberlain

So, within a year of the article's appearance, MacKaye's idea for a trail had caught the attention of a very influential group, people who could make it happen. But forest camps? Few people seemed interested in that part of the proposal. It was only the trail that had captured their imagination, and that group did not become a sustainable center. There was still no organization.

Building Support for the Idea

MacKaye continued to publish articles explaining his ideas and advocating for the trail and for forest camps. In 1922, he authored an article in the influential AMC journal, *Appalachia*. He emphasized that the Appalachian Trail was just the spine of a whole system of trails and camps. Commenting on the vexing issue of rights-of-way, he stated that there was no plan yet to secure the right to walk but wrote, "Ultimately the hiker is as much entitled to his appropriate highway as the automobilist is to his."[15] That expansive view of public right was more in the British than in the American tradition. In

14. MacKaye, "Some Early A.T. History," PATC *Bulletin*, October-December 1957, pp. 91-96.
15. *Appalachia*, Volume XV, No. 3, December 1922.

The evolution of the trail marker from Major Welch's original at top left.

England, historic walking paths were ultimately protected by English common law. American jurisprudence relied more on written statutes than common law.

The idea of the Appalachian Trail was just one aspect of MacKaye's ideas about recreation and the use of public forests. As early as 1916, he had published "Recreational Possibilities of Public Forests" in the *Journal of New York Forestry Association*.[16] In that article, one sees an early proposal for a recreational trail the length of the Appalachians. His fixation on forest camps remained, and he once wrote to the secretary of labor advocating a "new homestead principle," proposing that the government retain permanent title. In 1919, he promoted the idea of colonization of forest-service lands in a substantial report published by the Department of Labor, "Employment and Natural Resources." His ideas were visionary but "politically unachievable" and quickly achieved oblivion.[17]

16. Volume 3, October 1916.
17. Anderson, *Benton MacKaye*, pp. 90-92.

His characterization of the Appalachian Trail remained fixed. In a letter to Fred Davis, president of Natural Bridge Appalachian Trail Club, he stressed, "It is a real *trail-path* and not a road; it is a wild way and not a tame way. The foot replaces the wheel, the cabin replaces the hotel, the song replaces the radio, and the camp fire replaces the movie."[18] But, the clarity and directness of that statement was not always duplicated elsewhere. A 1927 "Statement by Benton MacKaye on the purpose of the Appalachian Trail" was a mishmash of disparate thoughts. A similar statement to the Green Mountain Club two years later was fuzzy and poorly focused and dealt mostly with environmental protection, barely mentioning the Appalachian Trail at all.[19]

In 1922, he had tried to answer, "Why the A.T.?" His answer began by asking how the trail could conserve resources and human labor. The trail would not be an end in itself, but a means to an end. "It would be an open air laboratory in applied economics.... The base for these educational operations is the trail. The first job is to build it."[20]

He continued to scratch down ideas. In his mind, he tried to link the sections of the trail to the economics of each area. He related the Green Mountains and the southwestern New Hampshire hills to beef cattle and sheep; the Boston area to the dairy industry; the Hudson Valley to dairy and apples; the Kanawah area to water power, coal, and hardwoods; the Tennessee River Valley to coal, sheep, and dairy; and so on. He tried to link the crest trail to those economic zones, with a rather hazy timeline for development. MacKaye surfaced the idea of scout troops getting involved with the trail and wrote about the need to visit the economic zones and recruit leaders to begin laying out the trail and the camps.

MacKaye continued to pursue the more utopian aspects of his 1921 article. He worked on his early idea of "townless highways," using a highway around Boston as an example of what could be achieved. (The proposal resembled in some respects the later ring road or beltway around the city, and some see that paper as a fore-

---

18. Rauner Library, MacKaye Collection, Box 178, folder 28.
19. *Ibid*, folder 14.
20. Rauner Library, MacKaye Collection, handwritten draft, February 1922.

runner of the interstate highway model.) He began to build a circle of friends prominent in the area of regional planning.

He met Lewis Mumford during the formation of the RPAA and both attended the October 1923 conference at the Bear Mountain Inn. In 1931, they co-authored an article in *Harpers Monthly* promoting the "town-less highway" idea. He met Bob Marshall in 1933 when he (Mac-Kaye) was active in the job market. When a job with the Roosevelt administration in the Indian Service led to a transfer to the Southwest, he first met Aldo Leopold, a pioneer in the en-

MacKaye and H.C. "Andy" Anderson, circa 1931.

vironmental movement and author of *Sand County Almanac*. Fired from that job, too, he was hired in April 1934 by the Tennessee Valley Authority in Knoxville, Tennessee, where he reunited with Harvey Broome and the circle of friends who, with people such as Andy Anderson of PATC, would form The Wilderness Society in 1934 (see page 158). In Knoxville, he came the closest to people who would go out and build a section of his Appalachian Trail other than Torrey's crew in New York.

MacKaye envisioned the Appalachians as a "wilderness belt" that would block East Coast urban expansion. He proposed to have small communities along the wilderness belt, the residents of which would keep traditional Appalachian crafts alive. His planning goal was to keep wilderness intact, in contrast to the "urban core." The Appalachian Trail was to be a chain of those wilderness links.

Enlisting the national forests' leaders was one of the most important avenues of support. In 1922, MacKaye had sent a letter to Franklin W. Reed, district forester for District 7, which included Washington.[21] MacKaye asked for the addresses of national foresters and said that he hoped to route much of the trail through the national forests. He specifically mentioned both Unaka and Natural Bridge national forests. Reed enthusiastically endorsed MacKaye's proposal and promised to provide the requested maps and contacts. He wrote to MacKaye, "I am glad to tell you that the idea of the Appalachian Trail seems popular with the Forest Supervisors...." He also promised to send a copy of MacKaye's map to the forest districts and ask the district foresters to begin considering routes, including what trails already existed. Reed noted some difficulties he anticipated: "It will be particularly difficult in the Southern States to popularize the idea as the recreationists are not given to hiking as a means of recreation...."[22] Reed's admonition was a harbinger of what Myron Avery encountered when he began laying out a route of the A.T. through the South.

Reed named many Forest Service trails that could become part of MacKaye's new trail. Included in his list were forty miles in Natural Bridge National Forest, seventy-eight miles in Unaka, ninety-eight in Pisgah, and seventeen in Nantahala. The foresters in the East thus became enthusiastic sponsors of MacKaye's idea, even though it is impossible today to know how many of those new trail miles, built by foresters, eventually became part of the A.T.

Responses were also arriving from state forests. A letter from the North Carolina state forester stated that he would like to see such a trail because of the potential to develop the mountains for visitors. MacKaye also received letters from F.W. Besley of the Maryland State Board of Forestry and Chapin Jones, the state forester of Virginia. Besley later became an important contact for Myron Avery and helped pioneer the A.T. in his state.[23]

---

21. ATC archives, MacKaye Box, undated letter.
22. *Ibid*, Reed to MacKaye, June 23, 1922.
23. *Ibid*, North Carolina: Letter to MacKaye, March 12, 1923; Maryland, May 10, 1922; and Virginia., May 11, 1919.

Late in 1922, MacKaye got the support of Gifford Pinchot of Pennsylvania, under whom he had served in the new Forest Service just out of graduate school. "I have just been over your admirable statement about an Appalachian Trail for recreation and health and recuperation, and for employment on the land.... I am greatly interested and wish you the very best of success."[24]

MacKaye's spadework from 1921 to 1925 was, according to Larry Anderson, his most significant work in promoting and organizing for the trail—"the very years...when MacKaye made his greatest contributions to the small details, as well as the overarching concept of the trail project, and at the greatest personal sacrifice."[25]

His contacts included many of the people who became influential in regional trail planning, such as Austin F. Hawes (the state forester for Connecticut), Albert Turner (president of the New England Trail Conference), Robert Sterling Yard (executive secretary of the National Parks Association and a key associate of Park Service Director Stephen Mather), as well as Torrey, Allis, and Chamberlain. It also included Paul Fink. Fink proposed that the new trail be extended all the way to Lookout Mountain outside Chattanooga, Tennessee.

The National Park Service also became a player when Stephen Mather began working to create national parks in the East. All the existing national-park land was then in the west, so eastern parks would begin with a handicap — there was no land, and no money to buy land. Undaunted, Mather in February 1924 appointed a committee to study the matter. A year later, the committee was renamed the Southern Appalachians National Park Commission. The committee got recommendations from the various states. That resulted in many recommendations, so Mather split the committee up into subgroups so they could visit all the proposed parks. The committee established the principle that, to become a federal entity, the park must have at least 500 square miles. That requirement eliminated from consideration some obvious candidates, such as Roan Mountain.

---

24. Hunter Library, Sherman Collection, Western Carolina University, Cullowhee, N.C., Pinchot to MacKaye, December 22, 1922.
25. Anderson, *ibid*, pp. 165-166.

The idea of making outdoor recreation part of the national agenda and using public land for the purpose was slowly emerging. Nineteen twenty-four marked the first National Conference on Outdoor Recreation in Washington. MacKaye attended as a representative of the Regional Planning Association of America (RPAA), and the group discussed forest camps, the Appalachian Trail, and the use of national-forest land. Still lacking any organizational framework for his ideas, MacKaye described the trail as "a movement, not an organization."[26]

On January 27, 1925, Congress passed a bill providing for two national parks in the Appalachians, plus Mammoth Cave in Kentucky. The bill to establish Great Smoky Mountains National Park on the Tennessee–North Carolina state line and Shenandoah National Park in Virginia was signed by the president just two months later. No money was appropriated, however.

Half the money for the Smokies was raised in the two states, while John D. Rockefeller donated most of the rest. The local contribution fell $1.5 million short, and, after he was sworn in as president in 1933, Franklin D. Roosevelt donated the remainder from the federal treasury. In the case of Virginia, the state was expected to raise the money, and that made the park in that state hang in the balance for several years.

The result of that was to place two prospective national parks directly in the path of MacKaye's proposed trail. The national parks and national forests in the East gave a huge shove to the prospects for completing the Appalachian Trail, and, without that, the idea of a long-distance trail over fourteen states might never have come to pass.

In the spring of 1925, MacKaye had gone to see Franklin Roosevelt, then chairman of the Taconic State Park Commission. At least one personal interview occurred, for MacKaye wrote, "I thoroughly enjoyed my talk with you the other day in your office and shall be glad to hear further from you upon the subject." MacKaye pressed his case with Roosevelt in 1926. His letter to Roosevelt set out a description of the trail and the camps and how MacKaye thought they might relate.

---

26. Quoted from Anderson, *MacKaye*, pp. 178-179.

His very detailed prescription assumed that a working-class family in New York City could leave the city after a half-day's work and get to a mountain environment by nightfall. The family thus could be able to hike the Appalachian Trail the next day and get back to the city by nightfall. (In the 1920s, most office workers worked five-and-a-half-day weeks, ending at noon on Saturday.) The family would travel by train from the central city and would get off at a railway station in the forest — MacKaye was not specific as to what forest or what railway station. The family would be met by a car and driver that would take them to a forest camp, where a caretaker would provide them with water, firewood, and blankets, referred to as the "basic necessities." There would also be food — "No valuable time should be lost in hunting up provisions."

He used a proposed trail route from Bear Mountain to Mount Everett, Massachusetts, as the area of interest and proposed that the state purchase land for fourteen camps between the two locations. A "field survey" would be necessary to find the best locations for the camps. All that would take money, for the construction of buildings at the camps would be professionally done. But, the trail itself, true to MacKaye's original prescription, would be scouted and built by volunteers, perhaps some of the early campers. He wrote, "Indeed, an important value — if not the main value — of having a trail at all consists of its blazing, its marking, its cutting, and its maintaining by parties of volunteer workers. The folks themselves should do the work. This gives them a definite, exhilarating pursuit in common (the doing of a big job together) which lies at the bottom of the keen interest and zest which is always shown at the prospect of 'trail making.'"[27]

That is one of the most explicit statements of how MacKaye's program would work in practice. The role of the trail was integrated into the "forest camps." The central idea was recreation and how to get an urban family into the forest for a healthy recreational experience. The trail was a means to the end.

That meeting was followed, only two weeks later, by a letter from Raymond Torrey to Roosevelt. He had learned from MacKaye that

---

27. ATC archives, MacKaye Box, MacKaye to Roosevelt, January 13, 1926.

he (Roosevelt) was interested in building the Taconic section of the Appalachian Trail in New York. Torrey wrote that he had personally hiked the proposed route and the various alternates. MacKaye favored a route through the Housatonic Valley of Connecticut, but Torrey favored a route inside New York, ending at Mount Riga in the tristate border region before drifting off to Mount Everett, Massachusetts, in the east. His objective in lobbying Roosevelt was clearly to advocate for the state to buy land in eastern New York that would protect the trail. The early contact with Roosevelt undoubtedly played a role in the future president's support for the Appalachian Trail and in his decision to task the first Civilian Conservation Corps (CCC) camp in the nation with building it, although those two connections were not the only connections Roosevelt would have with the trail project.

Torrey's letter was important, but not for the impact it might have had on Roosevelt. Taconic State Park was indeed created, but by then the trail was already in Connecticut, and the park played no role in protecting it.

Rather, Torrey discussed a recent meeting of the New England Trail Conference in Boston, where plans were discussed to make connections in the New England trail sections to establish an Appalachian Trail that would be fully connected. Torrey wrote to Roosevelt of the plans by the Green Mountain Club to continue its trail to the Massachusetts line, where it would connect with a trail route down to Mount Greylock in Blackinton State Forest. GMC had also formulated plans to connect the Long Trail in central Vermont with a trail section being built by the Dartmouth Outing Club in New Hampshire. He also wrote that the A.T. to the west of the Hudson River was complete within Palisades Interstate Park. The trail from Arden in New York to Greenwood Lake through the Harriman estate was complete as far as Lake Mombasha, by permission of the Harriman family. Plans were afoot to extend the trail into northern New Jersey on the Wawayanda Plateau. Torrey's enthusiasm fairly bubbled over.[28]

Roosevelt was favorable to the proposals of MacKaye and Torrey, but his commission had opposition within it, and nothing immediate was done. Roosevelt was evidently taken by the idea, though, and

28. ATC archives, MacKaye Box, Torrey to Roosevelt, February 14, 1926.

became a key supporter of MacKaye's trail. He continued to advocate for it at the governors' conference in Salt Lake City in 1930. As president, he linked the A.T. with the CCC and, in 1935, wrote to Robert Underwood Johnson of AMC: "The studies are being pushed, and the first step seems to be the continuation of the skyline Trail along the Blue Ridge. Later on we plan for the development along the crest of the watershed and also a trail along the more westerly slopes. At least the nation is becoming conservation minded!"[29]

Back in January 1922, Harlan Kelsey had contacted Paul Fink. "Will you not read the enclosed article on 'A Project for an Appalachian Trail' and let me know what you think of it? At a recent conference with Mr. MacKaye and Mr. Stein I suggested Lookout Mountain as a Southern terminus and it met their approval. You are a real tramper and know the Smoky Mountain section. I hope you will give me your full ideas on this matter."[30] Fink was, at the time, the acknowledged expert on hiking the Smokies (and later his exploits were published in *Backpacking Was the Only Way*).

In the South, development lagged far behind New England, but clubs were beginning to spring up. The first was the Carolina Mountain Club, established in 1920 as the southern chapter of AMC. Dr. Chase Ambler, a successful leader of the long campaign to secure the Weeks National Forest Land Purchase Act, was the first president. The club withdrew from AMC when it discovered seventy percent of its chapter membership dues was being sent to New England and nothing was being returned to the club. In 1930, the Carolina Appalachian Trail Club was formed with George Stephens as president, and, in 1931, it was merged with Carolina Mountain Club, taking CMC as its name. The Carolina Mountain Club was one of two earliest clubs in the South to take on a section of the A.T., the section in the Unakas from the Virginia state line to the Smokies — an impossibly long section that surely strained the club's resources.[31]

---

29. ATC archives, MacKaye Box, series of letters.
30. Knoxville, Tennessee, McClung Collection, Paul Fink papers, Kelsey to Fink, January 16, 1922.
31. *ATN*, January 1964.

New York: Home to the First Section

The Hudson River was blessed with spectacular natural scenery. The Palisades, a long cliff on the west side of the river, provided iconic viewing from the east bank of the river and breathtaking views from atop sheer rock walls on the west. But, the cliffs also made good gravel when crushed, and rock crushers moved onto the narrow beach at the foot of the wall. A huge gravel industry was established, and the cliffs began to disappear.

What New York also was blessed with were wealthy citizens with a strong environmental bent. Many had homes on the east side of the river, looking out across to the Palisades and the rock crushers that were going night and day, as if it were some sort of race to bring down the cliffs in the shortest amount of time. The owners of the rock crushers did not fear anyone, but they soon found their match, because the Roosevelts, the Harrimans, the Rockefellers, and the Hewitts, rich and politically influential, became determined to save the Palisades.

In 1895, the governor of New Jersey appointed a study commission, and Governor Levi P. Morton of New York appointed a commission to confer with their New Jersey counterparts concerning the future of the Palisades. Morton hoped to engage the United States government by connecting the cliffs with national defense, wording it "for the purpose of fortification and reservation in order that the brink of the precipice may be securely held and defended against attack and hostile occupation."[32]

That ploy did not engage the federal government, but the rock-crushing business provoked a huge cry by the New Jersey Federation of Women's Clubs, who became the organized advocates for conservation of the Palisades. In 1900, largely as a result of the women's clubs' advocacy, Palisades Park was established at the foot of the Palisades on land acquired by the Palisades Interstate Park Commission (PIPC). PIPC was under the leadership of George Perkins, one of the wealthy citizens from across the river.

---

32. Robert O. Binnewies, *Palisades: 100,000 Acres in 100 Years* (New York: Fordham University Press and Palisades Interstate Park Commission, 2001), p. 9.

The New York legislature continued to provide support for the environmental movement. People feared that timber companies would cut down virtually every tree along the Hudson, and, in 1909, New York passed the Hudson Forest Preservation Act.

As it happened, the extremely wealthy Harriman family, whose wealth began by the acquisition of railroads in the West, had acquired a large estate west of the Hudson, where their land was managed by the Yale School of Forestry. Prior to his death in 1909, E.H. Harriman proposed to donate thousands of acres of his estate to PIPC if Governor Charles Evans Hughes would direct the board of state prisons to change the planned construction of a new Sing Sing prison in the deep gorge on the west side of the Hudson at Bear Mountain, easily visible from West Point Military Academy. Mary Harriman repeated the offer as the widow of E. H. Harriman — 10,000 acres of her private Hudson Highlands estate if the state would move the prison elsewhere. The state got the message, Sing Sing was moved, and Bear Mountain–Harriman State Park emerged. Those acquisitions added protection to areas that had already become favorites for hikers.[33]

New York achieved one of the largest state park systems in the United States. Established originally in 1900, it came to encompass some 75,000 acres. As the public area expanded, trail prospects improved, and the area enjoyed a huge trail-building boom.

New sections of the Appalachian Trail were part of an emerging trail system. By the 1920s, New York City was a cauldron of hiking activity. The so-called Fresh Air Club, recruited by founder Bill Curtis in 1917, was perhaps the most energetic. It was said that ordinary trampers could not keep up with that group, which Curtis recruited from the athletic clubs downtown. AMC founded a New York City chapter in 1912, and Raymond Torrey became an active member. The New York Tramp and Trail Club was founded in 1914 by Frank Place, a New York librarian. In 1916, college professor Will Monroe had established a chapter of the Green Mountain Club (see page 32). He and his assistant, J. Ashton Allis, began blazing trails in New Jersey's

---

33. *Ibid*, p. 43.

Wyanokie Mountains. By 1920, seventy-five hiking clubs existed in the New York City area.[34]

New York hikers already were experienced with the trails on the west side of the Hudson River. One of their favorite hikes began at Tompkins Cove. They would take the ferry from the west end of 42nd Street in Manhattan up to Weehawken and then go by train to Tompkins Cove. Tompkins Cove was established as an adjunct to a limestone quarry, a common sight below the Hudson Massif. At that point, they would detrain and follow old woods roads until they arrived at the Timp, an almost vertical climb up a steep rocky crag. At the top of the Timp were signs pointing the hiker to the beginning of the Timp–Torn Trail, which continued north toward Bear Mountain from a place in the trail called Five Points, the junction of two trails and two roads. One continued north along the trail of the Six Chins to the Bald Spot of the Timp. According to the very first hiking guide (by Torrey), "The view from this point is superb. Bear Mountain and Anthony's Nose frame the river to the north; to the west is a tumultuous sea of mountain tops and slopes, over which the R-D [Ramapo–Dunderberg] Trail runs...."[35] One can imagine the exhausting rock climb involved in this trail along the Hudson Highlands. The trail then descended to Jones Point, where hikers caught a ferry back to New York.[36] That seminal trail, part of the first section of the A.T. ever so designated, was originally called the Tuxedo–Tom Jones Trail.

Hikers there never had a friendlier and more useful ally than Major William A. Welch, general manager of the Palisades Interstate Park Commission. Welch, always referred to as "Major Welch" from his time in the Army Corps of Engineers, had been invited in 1912 by George Perkins to become the first superintendent of the Palisades Interstate Park. Welch had achieved a measure of renown as an engineer building railroads in South America. In the summer of 1920, he began working with hiking clubs to build a system of trails in Bear Mountain–Harriman State Park.

34. Scherer, *op. cit.*
35. Raymond Torrey, Frank Place, Jr., and Robert L. Dickinson, *New York Walk Book* (New York: American Geographical Society, 1923), pp. 79-82.
36. *Ibid.*

Major Welch (right) with Franklin D. Roosevelt

He wanted to create recreational opportunities in his domain, and, in September 1920, he met with a group of prominent organizers at the Waldorf Hotel in New York to discuss the formation of a so-called League of Walkers. Welch convened a second meeting at Abercrombie & Fitch a month later. It was attended by representatives from the prominent hiking groups in New York: Fresh Air Club, Tramp and Trail Club, and others. Welch included Torrey of the *New York Evening Post* and Albert Britt of *Outing Magazine* to ensure that he got publicity. At the meeting, a new group was formed, the Palisades Interstate Park Trail Conference, with Britt as the first president. Welch outlined a proposed cross-park trail but at first discouraged volunteers, "because we did not want any amateurs marking out these trails nor attempting to clear them."[37] (That edict did not survive for very long.) Welch's group renamed itself the New York–New Jersey Trail Conference in 1922.

Torrey, who would became the most significant promoter of the Appalachian Trail in New York, was born in Massachusetts in 1880, the son of a sea captain. His life was journalism, and, after living and writing for newspapers in the Berkshires, he moved to New York City, where he worked for several different newspapers before finding his life's work at the *New York Evening Post*. There, he began publishing a weekly column, titled "The Long Brown Path," after a line in Walt Whitman's *Song of the Open Road*. (See page 52.) The column became the bible for New York's hiking community, and its publication was eagerly anticipated every week. It included a listing of hikes that were running every weekend, as many as twenty or thirty. Torrey also used the column for advocacy, promoting the environment and environmental causes, organizing letter-writing campaigns for forest preservation, and the like. If New York had a trail leader, it was Raymond Torrey.

When Welch sought to create hiking trails in Bear Mountain–Harriman State Park, he turned to the influential Torrey to lead the effort. Welch actively helped the volunteers, providing transportation and shelter when needed and also the metal markers that Welch himself designed.

When MacKaye connected with the New York hiking scene in 1922, he met with Welch, Allis, and Torrey. MacKaye had the right people for the state. Torrey would go on to build that very first section of trail ever designated as an official part of the A.T. His chief

---

37. Binnewies, *op. cit.*, pp. 132-33.

collaborator was Allis, and Welch was the "landowner" who gave permission for the new trail.

Torrey began building the new Appalachian Trail with legions of trail builders. He described the process that he used in one of his columns. The work crew was divided into three groups. The scouts, who knew how to lay out a trail, led the enterprise, identifying the route with string looped over branches. The clearing group Torrey called the Elephant Squad — they brought hatchets and loppers and followed the string. They cleared to a width of four feet, the U.S. Forest Service trail standard and still the standard for the A.T. At eight feet in height, the trail would be high enough that a person with a pack would not get hung up. The third group painted blazes, built rock cairns in bare spots, and nailed up the markers that Welch supplied.

In October 1923, the first six miles of the A.T. were finished in Bear Mountain–Harriman State Park. From the Timp–Torn Trail, the new section of trail went from Dunderberg, a point of land jutting into the Hudson River on the old Timp–Torn Trail. It proceeded over West Mountain, eventually joining the present-day A.T. route; over Black Mountain; over Letterrock Mountain; across Seven Lakes Drive at Lake Tiorati; and along Fingerboard Mountain. It then dipped south, crossing N.Y. 106 at Tom Jones Mountain and ending at Parker Cabin Hollow, close to the Ramapo River. The only portion of that original route that approximated the present-day A.T. is from West Mountain to Fingerboard Mountain and along Fingerboard some distance before diverging south. The new trail, from Tuxedo on the Ramapo River, over Dunderberg Mountain, and ending at Jones Point, was named the Ramapo–Dunderberg Trail.

The eastern end of that trail system arrived abruptly at the Hudson, after a steep downhill section from the top of Bear Mountain. But, in 1924, the Harriman family finished building the Bear Mountain Bridge, and at that point the trail could cross the Hudson. They built it with their own money, and for years it was privately run and charged tolls. At 2,258 feet long, the Bear Mountain Bridge was at the time the longest suspension bridge in the world, and it opened a connection for the Appalachian Trail from Bear Mountain to Anthony's

Bear Mountain Bridge with Anthony's Nose in the background.

Nose on the east side of the river.[38] It was then, and sometimes still is, recognized as the lowest point on the trail although the field below the bridge, between it and the park's zoo, on the west bank of the Hudson, is the actual low point.

By the mid-1920s, Torrey, working with Welch, had established a vibrant trail-building program in the Palisades and Harriman parks. The core trail, the Ramapo–Dunderberg, was by then twenty-four miles long, and the Appalachian Trail used parts of it. Torrey's map appeared in a newspaper article and showed the very extensive trail system.

In New Jersey, scouting had already begun, following an Ashton Allis plan. Randall Hains and H. Harriman Grimm of the Quest Club scouted a route over Pochuck Mountain and Wawayanda. A route was opened over the north end of Kittatinny Ridge by AMC and GMC volunteers. So far, it was only a trail fragment, unconnected with other sections of the long-distance A.T.[39]

---

38. *ATN*, March/April 1983, article by Larry Luxenberg, pp. 8-9.
39. Scherer, *op. cit.*, p. 5.

The Appalachian Trail Conference

Benton MacKaye's original vision for a new trail organization at first contained few details. His correspondence in the archives at Dartmouth contains an undated draft of a plan for an organization he called the Appalachian Trail, Incorporated. It would be a nonprofit corporation governed by an executive committee of sixteen members. There would be a membership structure comprised of charter, active, and associate members. It was evidently a very early formulation, because his ideas about forest camps and wilderness preservation were still unfolding.[40]

Moving from concept to reality was on the minds of the active participants, particularly the trail-builders in New York. The idea for an organizational structure came up at the 1923 conference at Bear Mountain Inn. In late 1924, the General Council of the National Conference on Outdoor Recreation moved the idea along. It was at that meeting, attended by both Welch and Torrey, that Welch's logo with the official "Maine to Georgia" motto was adopted. Welch agreed to preside.

The formative meeting for that new organization was sponsored by two organizations. One was the Federated Societies on Planning and Parks, a new organization established in January 1925. (The Federated Societies was comprised of five national organizations, including the American Civic Association.) Also directly involved was the Regional Planning Association of America (RPAA), which had been established in 1923. That organization became the principal sponsor of MacKaye's idea for the Appalachian Trail, and organizing for the trail became its early preoccupation.

To launch the effort, Welch contacted Harlean James, executive secretary of the American Civic Association. The organization that emerged was due in no small degree to the organizing talents of that remarkable woman.

The Appalachian Trail Conference was established on March 2 and 3, 1925, at a meeting at the Raleigh Hotel in downtown Washington, D.C., sponsored by the Federated Societies. After an opening speech by Frederick Delano, president of the Federated Societies,

---

40. Rauner Library, Dartmouth College, MacKaye Collection, Box 177, folder 11.

Harlean James, born in Mattoon, Illinois, in 1877, blazed an amazing path through corporate America. At 29, she was already the general manager of the huge California and Hawaii Sugar Refining Company — an almost unheard-of position for a woman in those days. In 1911, she went into nonprofit and government work and, by 1918, was executive secretary of the U.S. Housing Corporation within the Department of Labor. In 1921, she became executive secretary of the American Civic Association and served as executive secretary for a long list of national organizations, most of them associated in some way with regional planning. Her awards were numerous and, among many others, included the Pugsley Gold Medal Award. In 1990, she was designated a "National Planning Pioneer" by the American Planning Association. Major Welch truly knew his woman when he picked Harlean James to organize the conference that led to the formation of ATC. She was its secretary for fourteen years.

Welch took the chair and introduced Benton MacKaye to describe his trail concept. At that date, MacKaye was still focused on his purpose "to conserve, use and enjoy the mountain hinterlands which penetrates the populous portion of America from north to south." Comparing the Appalachian Trail to the western railways that opened up that region, he said, "Instead of a railway we want a 'trailway' [a term he later disparaged]." The trail was to be the connecting link to the forest camps where people would find food and shelter. In that way, the entire Appalachian region would be opened up, and urban populations would enjoy the natural beauty and healthful climes of the mountain region.

He talked about five regions of the trail, including New England, New York and New Jersey, Pennsylvania, the central region (Delaware, Virginia, West Virginia, Washington, and Maryland), and the southland, including North Carolina, Tennessee, South Carolina, Kentucky, Alabama, and Georgia. Paul Fink and Vernon Rhoades of the USFS were the only representatives from south of Virginia. It was MacKaye's speech that was supposed to set the tone for the group.

As other members rose to speak, it was clear that MacKaye's vision did not transfix everyone. Each member seemed to look at the objective through a slightly different lens. Raymond Adolph, forester of the Palisades Park, viewed the project mainly as a guard for fire suppression. Francois Matthes of the U.S. Geological Survey in Washington viewed the trail as a "nature guide service" so that people could experience nature. Fred Schuetz from the Scout Leader's Association talked only about side trails from adjacent cities. Clarence Stein came the closest to MacKaye's vision, placing the A.T. in the context of regional planning. And, Arthur Comey of NETC, already a famed hiker, drew the discussion the closest to trail values, talking about "going light" as a hiker and backpacker.

Despite the divergent formulations from the people in the room, the "vision" that emerged was the trail and only the trail. The central connector to the forest camps had become the objective in itself. The conference then proceeded to organize itself into the Appalachian Trail Conference, with a constitution. It was to be run by an executive committee comprised of twenty-five members: four from each of the five regions that MacKaye had outlined, plus five at-large members.

Welch was to preside, and many prominent members came from New York and New England, including Comey, Torrey, Stein, Charles Cooper, and Frank Place. The conference struggled for geographic diversity. Only A.E. Rupp represented Pennsylvania, while George Freeman Pollock and Halstead Hedges were from Virginia,

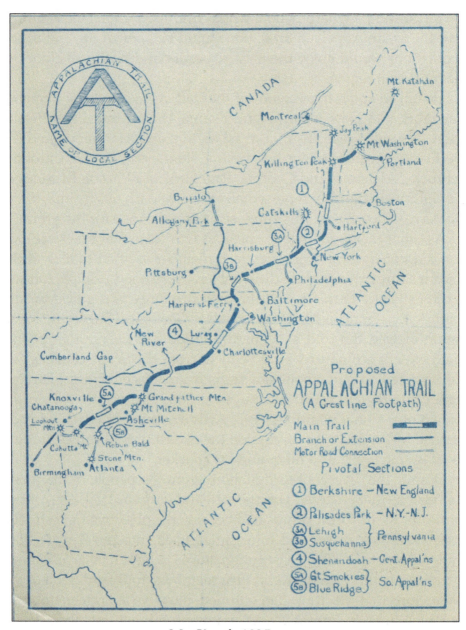

MacKaye's 1925 map

and Rhoades and Fink came from North Carolina and Tennessee, respectively. No one attended from Georgia or Alabama, reflecting, perhaps, an uncertainty as to the southern terminus of the trail and a lack of contacts in the region. Harlean James was named secretary.

At the conference, MacKaye presented a newer map than the one in his 1921 paper, modified by the suggestions that he had received since the original publication four years earlier. The main line still terminated at Mount Washington in the north, but the southern terminus was now designated as Cohutta Mountain in North Georgia, not a singular summit but a range that is now a designated federal wilderness area. That strange choice might have been selected from a lack of knowledge of southern geology.

For the first time, Katahdin was shown as a northerly extension from Mount Washington. In the south, the trail diverged. At Grandfather Mountain, it split in two, the main trail moving over to the Unakas while retaining a branch trail over Mount Mitchell, Rabun Bald, and on to Stone Mountain outside Atlanta. To the west, it appeared to go over the recently named Great Smoky Mountains National Park and from Cohutta extended to Lookout Mountain in Chattanooga, with a side trail all the way to Birmingham, Alabama. The map depicted other side trails to Buffalo, New York; the Catskills; Cumberland Gap, Tennessee; and from the Long Trail to Jay Peak in Vermont. The new map was emblazoned with Major Welch's A.T. logo. MacKaye's five zones were depicted and discussed.

A certain amount of fanfare accompanied that first meeting. Stephen Mather, director of the National Park Service, was the noon speaker the second day. Holding the meeting in Washington the week of Calvin Coolidge's inauguration lent an air of importance to the proceedings. ATC had gotten off to an auspicious beginning, with high-level government support.

But, surprisingly, MacKaye was not appointed to the executive committee. Rather, he was designated as "field organizer," a position that had no definition and a large amount of ambiguity. We do not know today what ran through the minds of the attendees who came to that peculiar decision — we don't even know who picked the members of the executive committee, although Welch was undoubtedly a member of the inner circle and presented the organizing resolution on page 92. MacKaye might have been viewed as simply the "inspirer in chief," but hardly a practical man who would be involved with day-to-day decisions about organization — although it was he who had spent three-and-a-half years personally contacting the key individuals in forests and other agencies, generating relentless publicity, and organizing events. Perhaps it was thought that he was be the chief scout who would locate the trail on the ground. Perhaps he would go out to distant towns and organize clubs to build the trail. But, we simply don't have any documentation for what was on the minds of the 1925 organizers.

"Field organizer" did not even approximate MacKaye's talents or capabilities. He was the idea man, not the organizer. The Conference clearly needed someone to scout a route and organize trail clubs, but that someone would not be MacKaye. The Conference awaited a person to fill that role, but so far it hadn't found one.

MacKaye did not exercise his role as "field organizer," whatever that was intended to mean. Although a longtime, dedicated hiker, he did not go out and scout the route — that role fell to others, chiefly Myron Avery beginning late in 1927.

MacKaye had made preliminary contacts up and down the Appalachians prior to 1925, contacts that could have been turned into trail clubs to scout and build the trail, but neither MacKaye nor anyone else did it. He did not create forest camps, and, other than his brief contact with Franklin Roosevelt, the record does not show that he advocated for public land acquisition to protect the trail until the next decade. But, he was hardly done with the project. Instead, he devoted himself to writing and publicity.

In 1932, he published an article in *Scientific Monthly* under the title, "The Appalachian Trail: A Guide to the Study of Nature." He contended that the study of nature was the original purpose of the trail, and he wrote sections on geology, flora, and fauna.[41] That same year, he took a crack at writing a trail guide. Never published, it was more of a philosophical disquisition on the physical environment of the Appalachians than a hiking guide.[42] Still later, in 1936, he pro-

---

41. Rauner Library, Dartmouth College, MacKaye Collection, Box 159, folder 15.
42. *Ibid*, Box 178, folders 66-67.

posed a scenic resources board at the federal level. It would include both the secretary of the interior and the secretary of agriculture (so as to get the two main owners of the land on which the A.T. was being built). MacKaye proposed that federal property be divided into zones, ranging from more to less intensive use.

Larry Anderson suggests that MacKaye's most significant piece, aside from the 1921 article, might be an unpublished 1923 manuscript discussing a proposed regional plan for the Columbia Valley in northwestern New Jersey—a side trail from Hudson Guild Farm (a "community camp") to the likely route of the A.T. He viewed that as a possible template for the Appalachian region. It was a careful analysis of the available resources and how they could be employed to benefit the economic structure of the region.[43]

Perkins

The founding conference adjourned on March 3, everyone went home, and then nothing happened beyond the normal activity level in New England. The trail through the Mahoosucs, for instance, was completed in 1926. But, one searches in vain for evidence of central direction from ATC. The executive committee consisted of the right people, but no one was taking the lead.

In January 1927, at the annual New England Trail Conference meeting in Boston, a new figure stepped forward. Arthur Perkins, a lawyer and retired local judge from Hartford, Connecticut, listened to MacKaye speak about "Outdoor Culture: The Philosophy of Through Trails" and became very interested in the project. Later in the meeting, he spoke informally with Welch and MacKaye. Welch seems to have never viewed himself as anything but a figurehead — others would do the actual work — and was anxious to get out of the titular presidency. (Welch's view of his role was probably why nothing was moving forward at the ATC level.) Perkins was so taken by the idea of

---

43. Anderson e-mail to author, May 2015.

Born in 1864 and educated at Yale, **Arthur Perkins** worked with his father at the law firm of Perkins and Perkins. He assumed control in 1889, and the firm later became Howard, Kohn, Sprague and Fitzgerald, the oldest continuously operating law firm in the United States. As a youth he had climbed the Matterhorn, but, as an adult, he devoted himself to the law and became a municipal-court judge. But, in 1923, at the age of 59, he got back into hiking in New England. By 1927, he had become chairman of AMC's Connecticut chapter and become enamored of Katahdin — where he can be seen here tacking up the first signs for the new A.T. before he became involved with ATC. That same year, he began working on a second ATC conference, to be held again in Washington, D.C.

the trail that he volunteered to assume leadership from Welch, who accepted, probably with great relief.[44]

On October 17, 1927, a young government lawyer from Washington wrote to Perkins. His name was Myron H. Avery, and he said that he had heard about that new trail and had been told that MacKaye had been in Washington in 1922 to talk to some people, but none of them was connected to any of the local hiking organizations (most prominently the Red Triangle Club), so word had not spread further. Avery wanted to know more.

Perkins was delighted that he had found someone from the Washington area who was interested in the Appalachian Trail and opened

---

44. See Brian King's article in the July/August 2000 *ATN*, p. 2ff.

a lengthy and vigorous correspondence with Avery. Avery, at 27, was less than half Perkins' age and was bubbling over with enthusiasm. Perkins had opened correspondence with others south of New York, but Avery appeared to be his man. After MacKaye's dalliance with Hedges, Matthes, and Schmeckebier in 1922, no movement was noted in the Washington area except for Hedges' scouting trips, and now someone in the nation's capital wanted to work.

Perkins wrote that scouting was going on all the way to Delaware Water Gap, and some people from Pennsylvania had scouted a route across Pennsylvania to Hagerstown, Maryland, but that proposed route was very tentative and would probably cross the Potomac River at Harpers Ferry. What Perkins needed was some progress from Harpers Ferry to Georgia.[45]

The Pennsylvania route troubled Perkins. The clubs in the state (the Blue Mountain Club was taking the lead) were conflicted about the route south of the Susquehanna River. Two routes had been proposed, and Perkins was relying on Avery to advise him, since Avery was already scouting the trail in that area. The matter was not resolved before an ATC meeting in 1928, and it would not be decided then either.[46]

(As for the particular route south of the Susquehanna, the clubs disagreed over the routing southwest of Harrisburg. An early proposal by several Pennsylvania clubs proceeded along Tuscarora Mountain and arrived on the Potomac at Hancock, Maryland. Hikers would then walk the sixty-four miles east along the Chesapeake and Ohio Canal towpath to Harpers Ferry. The second route, advocated by Avery and the Potomac Appalachian Trail Club (PATC), branched south across Cumberland Valley and then along South Mountain in Pennsylvania and Maryland, emerging on the towpath just three miles east of Harpers Ferry.)

Perkins was careful to note that he was not the authority for ATC, having had only informal go-ahead from Welch. Nonetheless, he was willing to become a conduit for reports from Avery. He suggested

---

45. ATC archives, Perkins Box, a series of letters: The earliest was from Perkins to Avery on October 17, 1927, but it refers to an Avery letter of two days earlier that evidently opened the dialogue.
46. *Ibid*, various dates.

that Avery organize as a chapter of AMC. However, only eleven days before, Avery and five others had established PATC as an independent organization. Avery was already moving too fast to be caught.[47]

One letter in the chain of correspondence established a precedent that still holds. Rather than referring to sections of the A.T. on the diamond markers, for instance the Harriman Section, Perkins proposed that habit be replaced by the words "Maine to Georgia," the adopted official motto. And so it was done.[48] (The phrase was not without controversy, however. For many years, the southern clubs introduced a resolution at each conference to change the phrase to read "Georgia to Maine." Each time, it was voted down.)

The ATC Meetings of 1928 and 1929

Avery began an intense lobbying effort to convince Perkins to hold the second ATC conference in Washington. Knowing that PATC was only a fledgling group, Perkins favored Bear Mountain and dealing with the more mature organization headed by Raymond Torrey. (Torrey himself was on Perkins' side.) But, when PATC agreed to undertake all the tasks of organizing, Perkins finally agreed to let Avery and the PATC be the host.

The second ATC conference thus convened at the National Museum on May 19 for general sessions. Avery opened the session. Major Welch did not attend, so Perkins was in the chair. That odd arrangement must have felt awkward to Perkins, for he exercised no authority except informally from Welch, yet it underlined Welch's determination to retreat from the broader organization and concentrate on the Palisades Interstate Park. Perkins was elected temporary chairman and asked attendees for trail reports.

It became evident that some scouting had been done, but, outside of New Hampshire and Vermont, very little trail was actually on the ground, enthusiasm notwithstanding. Descriptions of routes that had been temporarily adopted were almost all on roads, Torrey's

---

47. *Ibid*, Perkins to Avery, November 11, 1927.
48. *Ibid*, Perkins to Avery, February 27, 1928.

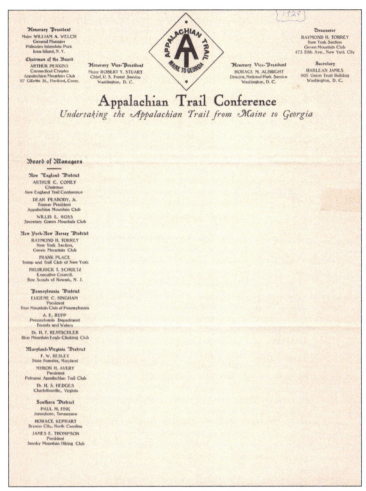

ATC letterhead in 1928.

built sections west of the Hudson being the longest exception. Most speakers were concerned about the trail on private property, since most of the Appalachians were then in private hands. Avery stated that, in laying out the trail south of Harpers Ferry, "private property had been ignored." Speakers from the Forest Service optimistically summarized all the trails that had already been built, expecting that these would eventually be adopted as part of the new trail.[49]

49. ATC archives, Box 6-1-1.

The next day, conferees adjourned to Black Pond near Potomac Gorge and were entertained by George Freeman Pollock, advocate for Shenandoah National Park. Pollock gave an illustrated talk about the area that would become the future park.

Perkins stated that Katahdin was now the official northern terminus, but that no official route had been adopted in Maine south of the mountain. The conference officially adopted Welch's diamond logo — the third time an organization had done so. The group decided that a third ATC conference would be held in 1929, and Perkins, Torrey, and a Mr. Morton were appointed a committee of three to decide where and when it would be. With that, the conference adjourned, although some of them stayed to hike PATC's new route south of Harpers Ferry.

The committee decided that the third meeting would be held at Lafayette College in Easton, Pennsylvania, in May 1929. Although having it in Washington again had been discussed earlier, Perkins found out that the Blue Mountain Club expected to be the host and was already making arrangements. (Perkins noted to Paul Fink that perhaps having it in Washington every year was a bad idea and surfaced a proposal to alternate between north and south locations.[50]) The host club was headed by Hiram Bingham of the Blue Mountain Club. Perkins, now securely in the chair following Welch's withdrawal to honorary status, opened the conference to more than 50 attendees.

At Lafayette College, MacKaye once again gave a "keynote" address and estimated that around fifty percent of the route was now on the ground — a highly fanciful contention. That was followed by extensive reports from the participants. The trail through southwest Virginia was the longest unresolved route, and little was known about the terrain. The route through southwest Pennsylvania was still unresolved, and a committee was formed to decide the issue.

The new organization adopted a constitution that gave ATC a structure that it would retain for decades. It was headed by a president, honorary president (Welch), two honorary vice presidents, a secretary, and a treasurer. Harlean James and Raymond Torrey were elected to the last two offices. The honorary vice presidents were

50. McClung Collection, Fink papers, Perkins to Fink, April 15, 1959, and May 3, 1929.

MEMBERS PRESENT AT 1929 CONFERENCE
SATURDAY A.M.
MAY 11, 1929.

Arthur Perkins.
Marian E. Lappo
Eugene C. Bingham
murray H. Stevens
Myron H Avery - P A. T. C.
Wm J. Cooper, Blair Co Chapter, P.A.G.
K F Rentschler
J Bruce Byall
Benton MacKaye
Frank Place. T+TCNY
P.J. Renner Catskill Hiking club n.y. City
Mortimer Bishop - Mead Air Club Wfc
C. P. Wilber - N.J. Dept. Conservation + Development.
A M. Turner Field Secretary, Conn. State Park & Forest Commission
Anna Rigo Wilson
Katherine C. Erwin
Harold G Anderson
Kathryn G. Fulkerson
Wm F. Shanaman,
a N. Parker.
Raymond H. Torrey. Green Mountain Club, New York and Vermont
A Dream Piper Paterson Rambling Club
(Penna Alpine Club) Torrey Botanical Club. N.Y. Chapter. Adirondack Mt. Club

Horace Albright, director of the National Park Service, and Robert
Stuart, chief of the Forest Service.

Naming honorary vice presidents had a clear political purpose,
but the decision not to establish a "real" vice president had conse-

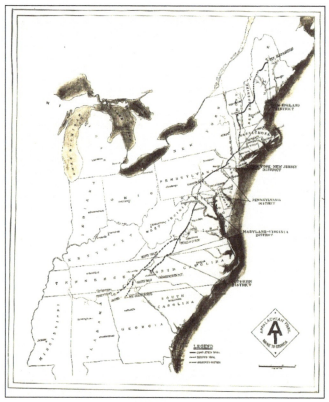

1929 map

quences in 1930, because, if Perkins became unable to preside, no clear line of succession was established. Leadership would be exercised by a board of managers and, from that group, an executive committee. Avery was on the board of managers and the executive committee, and the largest contingent from any club was from PATC.

The constitution adopted an overly long statement of purpose, which would be "to promote, construct and maintain a connected trail, running as far as practicable, over the summits of the mountains and through the wild lands of the Atlantic Seaboard and adjoining states from Maine to Georgia, to be supplemented by a system of primitive camps at regular intervals, so as to render accessible for tramping, camping and other forms of primitive travel and living in the said mountains and wild lands, and as a means for conserving and developing, within this region, the primeval environment as a natural re-source." The statement of purpose — which did not change for decades — was almost identical to one that had been submitted by MacKaye in December 1928.[51] His idea of forest camps still was part of the official plan.

The ATC map of the trail in 1929 eliminated the side trails and con-necting rail lines that had cluttered up earlier depictions. It only showed the trail, although there were three places where routing decisions needed to be made. In Pennsylvania, both the Avery route and the one promoted by the Pennsylvania Alpine Club were shown. The map de-picted both a southwestern Virginia and a North Carolina route. And, in Georgia, both termini were shown — the original route to Cohu-tta Mountain, and a more easterly route ending at Mount Oglethorpe. (That was the first time that Oglethorpe made its appearance.)

Soon after the conference concluded, Perkins headed south by train to connect with southern hiking clubs. His avowed purpose was to discuss the trail with Forest Service and National Park Service authorities. He stopped in Lynchburg, Virginia (headquarters of the Natural Bridge National Forest); Bristol, Virginia; Jonesboro, Tennes-see (home of Paul Fink); Bryson City, North Carolina (home of Hor-ace Kephart); Erwin, Tennessee; Asheville, North Carolina (where the Carolina Mountain Club was based); Knoxville, Tennessee; and Atlanta, Georgia. In Knoxville, he was hosted by Harvey Broome and the Smoky Mountains Hiking Club (SMHC),[52] so the Forest Service and National Park Service were not his only objectives. Connecting with Kephart, Fink, and Broome put him in good position to expand the Appalachian Trail south of Virginia. According to Broome, the trip by Perkins inspired SMHC to become a trail-building club as well as a hiking group.[53] There *was* a difference.

Scouting reports were coming into Perkins. Enthusiastic hikers, very taken with the idea of that long, long trail, wanted to get their trails scouted and on the ground. In New Hampshire, Dartmouth Out-

---

51. Rauner Library, MacKaye Collection, Box 177, folder 78.
52. McClung Collection, Harvey Broome papers; Perkins to Broome, October 18, 1929.
53. *Ibid*, Broome to Ed Garvey, January 17, 1967.

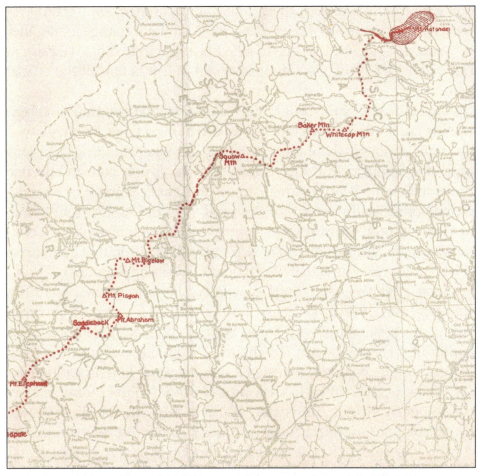

Arthur Comey's 1925 map of a proposed route in Maine.

ing Club workers had scouted at least part of a new trail route from Hanover toward a connection with the Long Trail at Sherburne Pass in Vermont. The Connecticut Chapter of AMC was out scouting a route from Blackiston State Park (now a historic district in nearby North Adams) to the north side of Mount Greylock south of Williamstown.

In Maine, Arthur Comey's early trail scouting was being supplemented by reports from Maine game wardens from Katahdin south to Squaw Mountain. Claims by game wardens that the trail "is in fairly good shape" were probably overly optimistic — Walter Greene's trail scouting, beginning in 1932, was to become the actual initial route of the trail (see page 247). In 1929, Comey and G. Arnold Wiley scouted north from Grafton to Old Blue and Indian Pond on the Kennebec River. But, Comey was not optimistic about the prospects north of the Grafton–Bigelow area. There was a distinct lack of local interest, and he anticipated that the timber companies would oppose an official trail.[54] Comey did produce a map showing a possible route as far east as Saddleback, however.

Perkins began an early discussion about trail standards, and that led to a long-running discussion about trail markers. Welch's early logos were made of copper and were first produced at his park workshop on Bear Mountain for a cost of six cents each. They became prey to souvenir hunters; many disappeared. Because copper was relatively expensive, Perkins began experimenting with galvanized iron markers. Those were less expensive but still tended to disappear, and so many of them were required that clubs could not afford the expense.

Myron Avery began experimenting with unpainted axe blazes. A downward slice, followed by a quick horizontal chop, produced a divot in the tree. Avery found these to be satisfactory in the north woods of his home (he was from Maine), but tree and bark growth in the mid-Atlantic was so rapid that the blazes became obscure in a fairly short time. So, Avery began dabbing white paint in the axe chop, and the white blaze eventually (although not without a long struggle) became the standard marker for the A.T.

Lacking a vice-president, Perkins used Avery, and they continued a long and detailed correspondence on every aspect of trail construction. Noting that PATC had already written a trail-construction manual, Perkins suggested that, with slight modifications, it could be adopted by ATC.

Then, in May 1930, Perkins reported to Avery that he had been taken by a dizzy spell with impairment of vision and intense nausea. He reported that he was improving from what was diagnosed as a stroke but was terribly disappointed that he could not join ATC at its upcoming conference at Skyland in what was to become Shenandoah

---

54. David B. Field manuscript, "Compiled History of the Appalachian Trail in Maine: The Early Years."

National Park. Avery would be in the chair, and Perkins asked that Avery take over the running of ATC, at least as a temporary measure.[55]

In preparation for the conference, Perkins made a full report to Avery on trail conditions and progress up and down the Appalachians. He had fragmentary information on many areas of New England and was very discouraged about Connecticut because of forest fires but had made contact with a new trail enthusiast there named Ned Anderson. South of Pennsylvania, he dealt almost exclusively with national forest supervisors, with varying degrees of success. He was willing to personally fund the expense of scouting some areas of the South in order to get things moving in the national forests in areas where he was getting a tepid response.[56] With that, and with no actual vice president, he handed control to Myron Avery.

Perkins never recovered. He began telling people that Avery was to be considered as leading ATC and never attended another ATC meeting. From May 1930, Avery continued to run ATC for more than two decades, until 1952.

Arthur Perkins died on May 16, 1932, almost two years to the day after his first stroke. Avery personally gave Perkins credit for keeping MacKaye's dream alive.[57]

In 1934, MacKaye got a job with the Tennessee Valley Authority (TVA), and he worked in an office in downtown Knoxville until 1936, when he was let go. He was hired to be a regional planner, and he proceeded to spin out broad, long-range plans that many in the TVA viewed as impractical. David Lilienthal, one of the three TVA directors, commented, "Planning is a subject that attracts those who are in a hurry but are rather hazy as to where they want to go."[58] The more realistic Lilienthal was convinced that such economic and social engineering as that which MacKaye proposed had little chance of success, even in the very liberal environment of the New Deal.

55. ATC archives, Perkins Box, Perkins to Avery, May 27, 1930.
56. *Ibid.*
57. PATC *Bulletin,* July 1932, p. 53.
58. Anderson, *ibid,* p. 253; quoted from Arthur Schlesinger's *The Coming of the New Deal* (American Heritage Library Edition, Boston: Houghton Mifflin, 1988), p. 331.

The experience in Knoxville, however, had other benefits unrelated to the job. It was there that he first formed associations with Harvey Broome, Bernard Frank, Bob Marshall, and others who, with MacKaye, formed The Wilderness Society in October 1934. Many were members of the Smoky Mountains Hiking Club. They often hiked in the new Great Smoky Mountains National Park — stronger hikers moving rapidly up steep hillsides, with the more relaxed and philosophical Benton trailing along. MacKaye was the intellectual leader of the group, which was dubbed the Philosopher's Club, with Benton as the chief philosopher. His experiences in Knoxville had an enormous influence on his subsequent life.

In Knoxville, his ethereal ideas of social and economic planning ran headlong into the reality of a chaotic and unplanned American economy.

Benton MacKaye's role was seminal. His articulation of a long-distance trail through the mountain vastness of the East Coast began what was to become a successful movement for recreational trails throughout the nation. Sometimes, dreamers carry the day.

Americans tend to be intensely practical, rather than philosophical. American philosophers there have been, of course, but they tend toward the John Dewey type rather than the model of such German philosophers as Immanuel Kant. Daniel Boorstin, the preeminent historian of the colonial period of American history, makes this point in his writings. The American character works against the armchair philosopher and in favor of the person who is "up and doing" (to use Longfellow's words). The eventual conflict between the philosophical Benton MacKaye and the get-it-done Myron Avery (see page 154) is thus embedded in the nation's culture as well as the trail's.

RESOLVED, by the Appalachian Trail Conference assembled in Washington, D.C., March 3, 1925,

(1) That this Conference be made permanent;

(2) That the following provisional constitution be adopted:

ART. I. The name of this Conference shall be the "Appalachian Trail Conference".

ART. II. The purpose of this Conference shall be to promote and establish the Appalachian Trail as a working, functioning service, as a system of camps and walking trails for rendering accessable to campers and walkers the mountainous and wild lands and areas of the eastern United States, such service to be developed as a means for stimulating public interest in the protection, conservation, and best use of the natural resources within such areas.

ART. III. The members of this Conference shall consist of the persons and groups who adopt hereby this constitution and of additional persons and groups who are interested in carrying out the purpose of this Conference and who may be hereafter admitted under rules formulated by the Executive Committee herein created.

ART. IV. The control of the affairs of this Conference shall be vested, provisionally, in an Executive Committee of fifteen persons, as follows:

Five persons representing respectively the following nation-wide organizations:

The Federated Societies
The Regional Planning Association of America
The National Conference on Outdoor Recreation
The U.S. Forest Service
The National Parks Service

Two persons from each of the five following regional organizations:

The New England Trail Conference
The New York - New Jersey Trail Conference
The Appalachian Trail Committee of Pennsylvania
The Appalachian Trail Committee of the Blue Ridge Region (Maryland, Delaware, District of Columbia, Virginia, West Virginia).

The beginning of the 1925 resolution establishing ATC.

Chapter 3

THE LEADER: MYRON AVERY

It seemed simply not possible for Myron Avery to be associated with an enterprise without running it. He was possessed of singular intelligence, energy, discipline, organizing skill, aggressive drive, and personal egotism…. Although he appointed numerous committees, he generally knew more about their activities than the chairmen he appointed and often dictated letters for their signatures, not always discussing the contents with them in advance.

— Laura and Guy Waterman

With the untimely death of Arthur Perkins, Myron Avery, his appointed successor, grabbed the tiller. For the next twenty-two years, he was the unchallenged leader of the Appalachian Trail effort. No one else ever emerged quite like Avery; it was as if the trail movement lived in the middle of a cyclone.

Larry Anderson, Benton MacKaye's biographer, credited Avery with a central role that MacKaye never took: "Despite Myron Avery's relatively short life, the energies and efforts he had packed into the quarter century he devoted to the Appalachian Trail had…enabled him to witness the completion of the A.T. as a continuous footpath from his beloved Katahdin to Georgia, the establishment of the ATC as a durable, functioning steward of the trail, and the forging of constructive, official agreements with federal and state agencies, which laid the groundwork for the passage and implementation of the 1968 trails bill."[1]

Carlos Campbell, one of the leaders of the Smoky Mountains Hiking Club, wrote to Avery (while Arthur Perkins was still alive), "We in Knoxville have long since learned to look upon you as the power behind the throne — or, in other words, as the Col. House of the Appalachian Trail Movement."[2]

Avery radiated an unique, manic energy. The descriptions of him are vivid. Arch Nichols, himself the unchallenged leader of the North Carolina section of the A.T. for many years, recalled a time that Avery was coming through Asheville on his way to Florida and wanted to stop to talk to the forest rangers in that district:

> *He asked me to arrange a meeting with the forest supervisor. He had his mail forwarded to me, and, two days before he arrived, two big, fat brown envelopes came with his letters. That Saturday…he sat there in the supervisor's office with a letter opener, wastebasket and briefcase, quickly sorted through the letters and arranged them in his briefcase to study and answer on the train. The remainder of the weekend he met with the Carolina Mountain Club, went down and hiked Wayah Bald, interviewed the forest supervisor and got back to Asheville barely in time to catch the train."[3]*

Frank Schairer, Avery's chief lieutenant at PATC, wrote about a scouting trip with Michaux (Pennsylvania) state foresters: "[T]he State Forester met us at dawn, and it was pretty clear he thought we might last till 10 a.m. Myron said, 'Let him set the pace until 10, then we'll step out.' Long after dark we arrived at Pine Grove Furnace with the Forester's tongue dragging, but with a firm and enduring respect in his heart thus established for Myron and his 'Trail Gang.'"[4]

1. Larry Anderson, *Peculiar Work*, p. 98..
2. ATC archives, Avery correspondence, 1930-1932, Campbell to Avery, April 7, 1931. The allusion is to President Woodrow Wilson's chief assistant, Edward M. House.
3. ATC archives, Raymond Hunt correspondence, Box 11-3-3.
4. David Bates, *Breaking Trail in the Central Appalachians — a Narrative* (Washington: Potomac Appalachian Trail Club, 1987), p. 102.

Avery possessed a meticulously detailed mind. In a PATC eulogy after Avery's death, Ken Boardman, the PATC photographer, wrote, "Of Myron's meticulous care for detail: As exemplified by the Smokies hike in 1937, when he left detailed instructions to the 'pack train,' until Doc Sossman finally convinced him that

Avery's childhood home

the drivers could not read...." Fred Blackburn, who followed Avery as PATC president several years later, wrote in a eulogy that "the enduring picture of Myron pushing the measuring wheel over miles and miles of trail is one which even a comparative newcomer can never forget."[5]

Avery was born in 1899 in Lubec, Maine, on Canada's southeastern Atlantic border, where the morning sun first strikes the continental United States, into a family that emigrated to "Massachusetts" in 1650. (The Province of Maine was gradually absorbed into the Massachusetts Bay Colony in the 17th century and did not become a state until 1820.) The town, a center for sardine packing, is almost surrounded by water, and Avery's father ran a sardine packing business.

But, the sea never attracted Avery as a young man (although it became the focus of his lifelong legal career). Instead, he spent his summers in the mountains, working with agencies that managed the timber industry. In college, he was a member of the outdoor club, and, by all accounts, he was interested in hiking from the beginning. Katahdin and the nearby lakes were among his favorite places.[6]

After graduation from high school, Myron went to Bowdoin for his bachelor's degree and then to Harvard Law School. His academic record was excellent, and, on graduation, he began the practice of law.

5. *Ibid*, p. 103.
6. Avery correspondence in the Maine State Library. Letter to Frank C. Hinkley, May 8, 1932, stated that he worked for the Forestry Department while at Bowdoin.

Within ATC and related circles, mystery surrounded his first job for decades. It was long believed in PATC circles that he began his law practice in Hartford, Connecticut, with the law firm headed by Arthur Perkins, but there is no record of Avery in the firm. Robert Rubin of ATC speculated that Myron might have clerked for Perkins in the summer.[7] PATC members, including no less than Frank Schairer, believed that Avery worked for Perkins, was enlisted by Perkins to pursue the Appalachian Trail project, and moved to Washington for that purpose. PATC historian Dave Bates accepted this as probable, but it remained unverified.[8]

Avery in 1925

There is evidence to refute all those claims of Hartford before 1926. A copy-proof of his official biography in a family photograph album, copied by Dave Field, says that, after Harvard in 1923, he *immediately* "became an admiralty attorney for the U.S. Shipping Board (later U.S. Maritime Commission)."

Avery's correspondence also indicates that he never knew Perkins until he (Myron) was living in Washington. The first contact with Perkins was by mail in October 1927. It is clear from the wording of that letter that Avery and Perkins had never met (see page 80).

Presumably, he moved to Washington after law school, although the only record of the date is that posthumous proof in the family album. It was there that he met the woman he married, Jeannette Leckie. They leased a home in the American University area, on Columbia Road. By 1926, he was already hiking in the Skyland area. George Freeman Pollock, creator of Skyland and self-described father of Shenandoah National Park, went hiking with Avery that summer and commented about how hard it was to keep up with him.

7. Robert Rubin, *ATN,* July/August 2000, "The Short Brilliant Life of ^Myron Avery."
8. Bates, *op. cit.,* p. 23.

Avery developed a passionate following in the new club he helped found, PATC. He did not suffer fools gladly but could be kind and understanding, especially to new hikers without his experience. With a few notable exceptions, the club would "go to war" for their leader, and there were simply no defections in the

Camped out in 1927, the year Avery got involved with the A.T.

ranks for the first years. To them, he was a hero. And, he did develop a dedicated following up and down the trail.

Joseph Bartha, former chairman of the New York–New Jersey Trail Conference, wrote on the tenth anniversary of Avery's death, "To know him was to love him. Anyone who was ever privileged to come in close contact with him never forgot the twinkle of his eye, his genial smile, his characteristic friendly salutation, and his quick response to cooperate in every movement for the advancement of having well-cleared and well-marked trails."[9] Carlos Campbell from the Smoky Mountains Hiking Club, a key trail builder in the park, was another dedicated Avery fan.

But, his temper was legendary, too, and his pen — or, often, typewriter (*via* dictation) — could be acerbic. Avery got into many spats, particularly with the Appalachian Mountain Club (AMC) and other northern clubs. To cite one example of many possible, Avery took strong exception to a review of one of his trail guides by Robert Underwood of AMC. Although Underwood insisted that the review was quite moderate in tone and generally favorable, Avery sent him an irate letter. In reply, Underwood returned a barbed missive that pretty well encapsulated the problem that Avery had with criticism.

I had not intended to reply to your letter, even to explain my final disposition of this whole matter, as my disgust at your complete

9. *ATN*, September 1962, p. 41.

inability to understand in the slightest a viewpoint other than your own, at the pettiness of most of the points you manage to bring up, and at your absurd and utterly inappropriate threat to attempt legal action against us, would necessarily have given to my letter a tone which I should consider most regrettable between representatives of clubs which themselves are on thoroughly good terms.[10]

To that, Avery replied with another acerbic letter.

Avery had an acrimonious exchange with Edgar Heermance of the New England Trail Conference (NETC) in 1938. He took exception to Heermance's using some of his material in a draft guidebook and incorporating it into one of his. He threatened a lawsuit for plagiarism and actually contacted a law firm in New Haven, Connecticut, Heermance's home state. Heermance attempted to smooth over the disagreement, writing, "I am a peace loving person, and hate to get into a fight with you, as we both have the best interest of the A.T. at heart. Though I frequently differ with you in opinions and methods, I honor you as the man who has made the Appalachian Trail a reality. No one else could have done it." Unmoved, Avery called Conrad Wirth, assistant director of the National Park Service, into the fray. One can imagine that Wirth was smart enough to stay disengaged. Nothing more of the dispute was recorded by Avery, but, since peace-making seemed unproductive, Heermance proposed that NETC withdraw its membership in ATC, which the organization fortunately voted down.[11]

Avery also kept up a long-running dispute with Ashton Allis, one of the original fathers of the A.T. The source of the dispute is obscure but might have related to Allis' support of Benton MacKaye's position that the trail environment be kept truly wilderness in character. At one point, Avery wrote to Allis, "I have appreciated that, by reason of our environment and circumstances, our points of view on many matters are as far apart as the poles. On matters of effective organizational policies, fundamental principles of conservation, our experience and our approaches are totally different. However,

10. ATC archives, Avery correspondence, Underwood to Avery, June 22, 1932.
11. *Ibid*, Avery correspondence, 1936-1937; correspondence between Avery and Heermance, 1938

Arthur Comey skiing above Katahdin's Great Basin in 1928.

despite these difference of opinion and viewpoint…, I should like to say that I have always held you in the highest personal regard."[12] But, Avery continued to hold a grudge, and, in 1948, contending that Allis was not sufficiently supportive of ATC, he unsuccessfully opposed the election of Allis as Conference treasurer.[13]

Avery's correspondence with Arthur Comey of the New England Trail Conference was unfailingly combative. Comey — a Massachusetts Institute of Technology landscape architect and legendary hiker, skier, and mountain climber — was credited with laying out the A.T. route north of Grafton Notch, almost all the way to Saddleback in Maine. He enjoyed a wide reputation in the regional-planning circles of MacKaye and other founders. His relationship with Avery seesawed between bumpy and argumentative and sometimes productive.

Those disputes became a theme in Avery's life, a character flaw that he seemed unable to erase. One supposes that they originated from his legalistic frame of mind, in which every letter became a le-

---

12. *Ibid*, Avery letter to Allis, June 18, 1942.
13. *Ibid*, 1948-1949.

gal brief. It was as if he were still in college, participating in debate, in which he was compelled to take a view opposite from that of the other team and never back down. (He rarely did.)

His relationship with the other A.T. clubs varied according to geography. To clubs in the South, Avery was an icon. That resulted from the fact that he worked with them to lay out the trail south of Damascus, Virginia. He hiked with them and engaged cooperatively with their leaders, and they regarded him as almost a member of their club. There seemed to be no daylight between Avery and the South (with the possible

Myron Avery in 1934

exception of the Georgia Appalachian Trail Club).

With the New England clubs, Avery had rocky relationships. The northern clubs, which had already created the initial sections of this new trail, regarded Avery as a Washington upstart, determined to take control of *their* trail away from them. That was to be a continuing theme reflected often in private correspondence among leaders in AMC, NETC, and the component clubs. To their suspicions, Avery responded in kind, reinforcing the impression that this Washington lawyer had co-opted their trail for his own aggrandizement and personal promotion. Avery could not see their view and did not understand their reluctance to simply give control of their A.T. section to the crowd in Washington and this insolent lawyer.

The New Englanders must have been struck by the paradox that Avery was from Maine, their home turf.

Avery could be very engaging and acquired friends in high places that could benefit the trail. He had a long-running friendly relation-

Arno Cammerer (July 31, 1883 – April 30, 1941) was the third director of the National Park Service. The National Park Service's first director, Stephen Mather, recognized Cammerer's competence as executive secretary of the Fine Arts Commission and appointed him as assistant director in 1919, replacing previous assistant director Horace M. Albright, who then became director. Cammerer served as Mather's right-hand man in Washington and acted for him in his frequent absences over the next decade. He succeeded Albright as director on August 10, 1933. He fell out of favor with Harold Ickes, the secretary of the interior, later in his career, and finished as the superintendent of the newly created Eastern Region. His untimely death in 1941 at the age of 57 removed Avery's principal advocate in the federal government.

ship with both Arno Cammerer and Conrad Wirth when they were successively assistant directors and then directors of the National Park Service. His relationship with Cammerer, beginning in the spring of 1928,[14] shortly after Avery helped found the Potomac Appalachian Trail Club, was especially close. Cammerer admired Avery's energy and wrote him in 1931, "As I had not been in contact with the actual deliberations of the preceding days [referring to the ATC conference in Gatlinburg] I did not know how far the recognition of your splendid and enthusiastic and unselfish work on behalf of this trail had gone. I want you to know that I am just as happy as any one of your friends could be over this well-deserved honor [his election as Conference chairman] your associates have bestowed upon you."[15]

Avery had strong opinions about how the trail was to be built, and one of his most settled policies was that it remain a volunteer enterprise. He strongly opposed the tendency of New England clubs

14. Bates, *op. cit.,* p. 4.
15. ATC archives, Avery correspondence, 1930-1932.

to hire trail crews, and, in 1932, he wrote, paraphrasing Lincoln, "It was said in days before the Civil War that the Union could not exist half slave and half free; I am very doubtful whether an organization of our kind can exist half paid and half free."[16] In this, he tracked well with Benton MacKaye.

Avery's energy spilled over into academic pursuits. He researched the history of the entire Appalachian chain, and some of his discoveries were ground-breaking. For example, he discovered Arnold Guyot's "Notes on the Geography of the Mountain Region of Western North Carolina" in the archives of the Coast and Geodetic Survey. He extensively annotated the manuscript for publication in *The North Carolina Historical Review* for July 1938 and then by ATC itself.

PATC

Like other major cities in the East, the Washington area had hikers and trail clubs. At least two clubs were organized by 1918: the Red Triangle Club and the Wildflower Preservation Society. No records have come down about the Wildflower Preservation Society, but Red Triangle kept archives that have survived, so we know something about hiking in and around Washington at the time.

Because few families owned cars, hikes tended to be close in, and transportation was by bus or street car. The Chesapeake and Ohio Canal towpath was the most popular location — not only was it close in, but a street car took hikers to trailheads. They also hiked in Rock Creek Park, along Sligo Creek, and parks on the south bank of the Potomac River. Farther afield, they often walked on dirt roads, of which there were many in those early days.

They sometimes hiked even farther afield, on the trails in the future Shenandoah National Park, hiking to Old Rag, Mount Marshall, and others. Stoney Man and Skyland were favorite destinations. They once hiked the twenty-two miles from Linden (near Front Royal, Virginia) all the way to Harpers Ferry. They did joint hikes with the Wildflower Preservation Society and with the Wanderlusters, a Bal-

---

16. *Ibid,* July 25, 1932.

timore hiking club. One Red Triangle hike drew ninety-five participants. The Washington area was becoming a vibrant hiking capital.[17]

The Wildflower Preservation Society (WPF) was headed by noted
naturalist, photographer, and traveler P.L. Ricker. Its focus was, of
course, natural history, but many of its members were hikers first and
naturalists second.[18] Andy Anderson, who later became a founding
member of The Wilderness Society, was a regular WPF participant.
Anderson obviously was aware of ATC as an umbrella organization
established in 1925. It was Anderson who recorded the incident that
led to the founding of PATC:

> It was a rainy Saturday in November 1927. A trip had been scheduled
> by the Wildflower Preservation Society, but the downpour was so
> steady and persistent that I concluded it was no day for botanizing.
> Around noontime the rain stopped and the sun came out. I was debat-
> ing what to do with myself when I remembered that the Red Triangle
> Club had a hike scheduled for that afternoon. I joined the party and
> there I met Myron Avery for the first time…. We discussed equip-
> ment for a while, and then I mentioned that P.L. Ricker, President of
> the Wildflower Preservation Society, had been talking to me about or-
> ganizing a club to work on the Appalachian Trail. Myron reacted with
> such enthusiasm that it appeared that he had been thinking along the
> same line. He wanted to call a meeting right away.[19]

The three of them (Anderson, Avery, and Ricker) met several
days later in Anderson's offices in the Metropolitan Bank Building
in downtown Washington. Anderson was asked to write to AMC to
see what members there were in the Washington area. (No record of
a response from AMC was found.)

---

17. PATC archives, records of the Red Triangle Club.
18. WPS archives did not survive, and our knowledge of the club has come down to us
chiefly from an article by Kathryn Fulkerson in the PATC *Bulletin* for July 1953, p. 92, and
from Grant Conway's article in the *Bulletin* for January-March 1971, p. 6-7.
19. PATC *Bulletin*, October 1952, p. 89. Anderson was wrong about the month. Avery was
already in touch with Perkins in late October, stating that a group in Washington would
meet to form a new club, according to Avery's papers in the Maine State Archives (Avery
to Perkins, October 24, 1927).

A few days later, Ricker called Anderson to say that one Frank Schairer, a recent Yale graduate, had been on a wildflower trip and was anxious to get out into the mountains. Anderson called Schairer, and they decided to take the bus to Ashby Gap, some sixty miles west of Washington. On the bus, they met Avery, who was accompanied by Joseph Cox and Cox's son, on the way to hike. When they arrived at Ashby Gap, they decided to split up and scout a possible route for the Appalachian Trail. Avery and the two Coxes, junior and senior, hiked north, while Anderson and Schairer hiked south. It was the first known mid-Atlantic Appalachian Trail scouting trip, even before PATC was founded.

Anderson described Schairer: "I had never before met such an enthusiastic hiking companion, and I had done considerable hiking in the hills in southern New York and northern New Jersey and in the Adirondacks. Whenever we emerged on an expansive view, loud shouts of 'Hot Dog!' 'Oh Boy!' *etc.* could be heard." He and Schairer made their way to Manassas Gap, about ten miles north of the future Shenandoah National Park, and took the train back to Washington.[20]

PATC was founded on November 22, 1927, at a meeting also held in Anderson's office. Avery, Anderson, Ricker, Schairer, Homer Corson, and L.F. Schmeckebier became the "immortal six," and the dynamic Avery was elected president.

Looking back on those days years later, Avery described the scene:

This was in the fall of 1927. Up in New England a retired lawyer in Hartford, Connecticut, by the name of Arthur Perkins, was trying to revive Benton MacKaye's project of a continuous trail from somewhere in New England to somewhere in the far Southern Appalachians. The plan was nebulous indeed. Mount Washington was suggested as the northern terminus, Mount Mitchell as the southern; the divergence of the final route from the proposed route only emphasizes the utter lack of knowledge of the Appalachian mountain area. In this year, of 1927, many of us were newcomers to this region. We wished to see, at close hand, the blue haze-covered ridges

---

20. *Ibid.*

*which loomed up a as barrier to westward travel. We thought, then,
that we might be able to open some small link in this proposed master Trail. So we began work.*[21]

Uncertainty was not part of Avery's personality, and he was determined to explore those blue haze-covered ridges. Trail scouting
and marking trips began immediately that winter of 1927–1928. The
very first PATC work trip was in February 1928, barely two months
after the club's formation. Avery, undeterred by winter weather, was
unwilling to wait for spring.

Their first objective was to scout, mark, and clear a trail from
Harpers Ferry to Linden, about forty-five miles. But, none of them
had ever built a trail, and they experimented with techniques. According to Schairer,

*We learned our trail technique the hard way. We used…mainly Boy
Scout axes…. When it came to trail markers, we had a few copper ones
that Major Welch had made at Bear Mountain and had given to us as
his contribution to getting started. Ricker's idea was that we needed
something to mark turns, so we bought those little wooden garden
labels — little slats an inch wide and a foot and a half long or so. Ricker
printed on them 'Appalachian Trail' or 'Spring' or 'viewpoint.'*

When they could, these pioneers used woods roads or primitive
paths made by local residents. But, in some areas, they had to cut
through the forest. Axes and pruning hooks took off the branches,
but they avoided treadwork. There was simply no time, and they
hoped that hikers' boots would keep the lower vegetation cleared.[22]

It is not possible to actually know precisely where the new sections of the Appalachian Trail were. Maps, once PATC began making
them, were very sketchy, with a few place names and no details at
all. Documentation consisted mainly of periodic reports in the new
PATC publication, the *Bulletin*, printed quarterly.

---

21. *Potomac Appalachian, 50th Anniversary Issue*, November 1977, p. 4, quoting an earlier Avery document.
22. Interview with Frank Schairer in the PATC *Bulletin*, October 1942, pp. 101-106.

PATC began publishing guidebooks as early as 1930, and the turn-by-turn descriptions were quite detailed. Avery himself always hiked with a measuring wheel, which became his trademark. In films the club made in those early days, he could be seen stopping to make detailed notes as he moved along the trail. But, where these little notebooks disappeared to is unknown. None has survived in the PATC archives or in the Maine State Library. The ATC archives contain one small notebook that Avery kept on a scouting trip through the Smokies in 1930, and that apparently is the only Avery notebook that has survived. It is puzzling that such a record-keeper as Avery did not keep his trail notes collected in one place.

The work consumed almost everyone. (Schairer once remarked that, in the first two years, he spent a single weekend at home.) Trail work trips went through the winter, into the spring, and on through the summer of 1928, and, by the end of that year, PATC had blazed the trail from Harpers Ferry all the way to Chester Gap, just north of the future Shenandoah National Park.

The territory for the trail was on ridge lines some sixty miles west of the Washington metropolitan area. The mountains in that area were not exceptionally high, with few above 1,000 feet in elevation, but were very rocky. All of it was private property, hardscrabble farms inhabited by hardscrabble farmers. The land was poor, and many farmers had left for more fertile land west of the Appalachians. The area was difficult to access, because roads were bad. In some places, no roads existed at all in the eastern approaches to the mountains, and the trail had to be accessed by driving or taking public

Avery and Schairer at work on blowdowns, whacking weeds.

transportation to places west of the ridge and looping back toward the east. U.S. 50 from Washington to Winchester had no bridges, parts of it were still dirt, and all the streams had to be forded. The road up to the top of Snickers Gap (Va. 7) was so steep that the passengers sometimes had to get out and push.

Once the trail was completed, it was necessary to keep it from becoming overgrown with vegetation. That came as a surprise to Avery, whose experiences in Maine did not prepare him for the prolific plant growth in the mid-Atlantic. In Maine, a trail cleared was a trail completed, with only occasional checking and minor clearing. But, when in Virginia the first summer came, plant growth obscured the trail, and it had to be done again. Avery wrote to Schairer, "The growth in the Blue Ridge is prolific beyond belief. A trail, cut in April, will appear wide and open as a boulevard; in August, one would never believe that there was a trail in the locality." Avery and Schairer hit upon an overseer system. One Walter Jex was assigned the stretch of trail from Harpers Ferry to Bluemont, about eighteen miles south of Harpers Ferry. Jex was the first officially appointed PATC trail overseer.[23]

PATC (and ATC) needed a place to meet, and Harlean James, who had organized the seminal Appalachian Trail conference in March 1925, provided a venue at her offices, allowing the new club to use space at the American Planning and Civil Association in the Union Trust building in downtown Washington. That began a succession of temporary, sometimes leased quarters until the club purchased a townhouse at 1916 Sunderland Place in northwest Washington after World War II.[24]

Avery insisted that everything be documented, and the first club bulletin was issued in February 1928, less than three months after the club was founded.[25] Harold Allen, another close Avery associate, began working on a trail guidebook, and, in February 1930, the club published its first guidebook, covering the A.T. from the Maryland–Pennsylvania line north to the Susquehanna River.[26] A more

23. *Ibid,* July-September 1969, p. 72; *Bulletin,* April 1947, p. 24.
24. PATC *Bulletin,* October 1947, p. 70.
25. Bates, *op. cit.,* p. 4.
26. *Ibid,* p. 8-9.

ambitious project was the 1932 *Guide to Paths in the Blue Ridge*, which covered the territory from Duncannon, Pennsylvania, on the Susquehanna all the way to the New River in southwestern Virginia. The guidebook resulted from Avery's early scouting trips in that territory and was highly praised by none other than Raymond Torrey of New York, himself a master at writing hiking guides.

Others looked with awe at the explosive growth and manic activity of PATC. An article in *Nature Magazine* in 1931 remarked over the "live wire Potomac Appalachian Trail Club." Major Welch marveled at the speed at which the trail was being put on the ground and at Avery's organizational ability. In 1930, he congratulated Avery for "what I consider to have been the most successful conference on the Appalachian Trail. Your arrangements were perfect, the attendance was all that anyone could wish and the spirit even beyond my fondest dreams."

Welch highlighted, in the same letter, a cultural shift that he considered significant. In New England (and in certain areas of the South as well), trail clubs were considered the preserve of the well-to-do and socially prominent. Referring to AMC, he wrote, "Of course, you know that the older Clubs, who control and have built the northern end of the trail are, what shall I say, Harvard and Boston — I think probably that will cover it. They do not properly realize that in order to carry this work on we must have recruits and that these recruits are coming from all kinds and all classes of people...and that we have no right to confine our trails to just a few of the old timers...."[27] PATC was inviting anyone to become a member who would participate in a work trip, and the element of exclusivity was gradually disappearing (at least in Washington). In recognizing this, Welch showed a broad vision of what trails and trail clubs in the East would become. He knew that the dynamic Avery would lead the way.

---

27. ATC archives, Perkins Box, Welch to Avery, June 7, 1930.

ATC

Avery started out as the president of PATC, but, four years later, he got a second hat — chairman of ATC. All of a sudden, the president of a local trail club was running the entire effort. Avery settled into his new role immediately, and the two organizations tended to merge. ATC was PATC, and PATC was ATC. The two combined in Myron Avery. His correspondence had two signature blocks, depending on who he was writing to, and what the subject was.

The relationship between the two was not necessarily ATC the senior, PATC the junior. In fact, it was often the other way around. ATC rented spaces from PATC in downtown Washington, emblematic of the power relationship. This juxtaposition of relationships caused unending trouble between ATC on one side and the New England Trail Conference and AMC on the other.

The ATC constitution established a board of managers (*i.e.*, directors) consisting of the active officers (chairman, secretary, and treasurer, but, again, no vice president), and eighteen representatives, three from each of the now-six regions: New England, New York and New Jersey, Pennsylvania, Maryland–Northern Virginia, a Unaka District from the Peaks of Otter to the Big Pigeon River, and a Southern District, everything south of the Big Pigeon. This established a geographic focus that was to continue until after the turn of the century. It seemed to be assumed that the three representatives from each section would lead trail selection and construction, but no such language appeared in the constitution. The division into sections mirrored MacKaye's approach to organization.

Likewise, the purpose statement could have been written by MacKaye, and several indicators suggest it was. After describing the trail itself, the constitution talked about "a system of primitive camps at proper intervals, so as to render accessible, for tramping, camping and other forms of primitive travel and living, the said mountains and wild lands, and as a means for conserving and developing, within this region, the primeval environment as a natural resource." Taken literally, it sounded like MacKaye's forest camps, but no such structure evolved. Three-sided shelters for overnighting backpackers came the closest to forest camps.

The officers were Welch as honorary president, Avery as chairman, Raymond Torrey as treasurer, and Harlean James as secretary. The eighteen board members comprised many of the most significant trail leaders for the ensuing decades: Arthur Comey from Massachusetts, Ned Anderson from Connecticut, Murray Stevens from New York, Harry Rentschler and Eugene Bingham from Pennsylvania, Fred Besley from Maryland, Fred Davis and S.L. Cole from Virginia, George Masa and John Byrne from North Carolina, Paul Fink and James Thompson from Tennessee, and Eddie Stone from Georgia.

ATC very early took on the personality of Myron Avery. He insisted on detailed and meticulous documentation of everything. He was strong on organization, and ATC followed his lead in that as in everything else. He believed in periodic meetings so that ATC members (almost entirely organizations) and officers could meet in person. (There was nothing like a face-to- face meeting, he believed.) He wanted periodic reports to the membership about progress in getting the trail on the ground, on trail standards (so that everyone did everything the same way), on communicating with the membership in writing at frequent intervals, and in central publishing of hiking guides so that there would be some form of higher level control. He did not want every club doing its own thing, and his propensity for centralization reflected how Avery himself viewed the trail, as an integral unit rather than as separate sections.

Avery put himself on the road. His travels were legendary, and he liked to drop in on people, his way of getting to know his organization. (It was also probably one of his ways of achieving control of this far-flung enterprise.) In the days before commercial air travel became common, he took the train. His first long trip for the A.T. was in 1929, before he had an official position with ATC. He journeyed south to Knoxville, where he met the leaders of the Smoky Mountains Hiking Club and formed life-long associations. From then until the mid-1930s, he maintained a very heavy travel schedule. He enthralled the southern clubs on those trips, although the northern

Undecided route south of Smokies   Undecided route south of Roanoke

clubs viewed his proclivity for popping up in their territory with a certain amount of suspicion.

He seemed to be on the train all the time. In 1930, for instance, the whirlwind Avery hiked from Bear Mountain to Greenwood Lake. The day following that excursion, he left for Pennsylvania to hike with the foresters from Mont Alto and Michaux state forests. He appealed to Perkins for 500 more markers — he needed them all up and down the trail. Three days later, he sent another frantic appeal for markers. "Things are moving fast down here, BUT our crying need is markers." It must have been difficult for Perkins to keep up with the demand for markers that followed Avery's trips. One can only gasp at Avery, striking out in every direction.

ATC enlisted *Mountain Magazine*, published in Boston, and the journal *Appalachia*, the AMC mouthpiece, to publicize the new trail. Beginning in 1930, he sent long and detailed trail updates, first to *Mountain Magazine* and later to *Appalachia*. A piece in *Appalachia* discussed his trip through the Smokies in considerable detail, and he stated, "[T]he rapid development of the Appalachian Trail has created such a startling reversal of conditions that it is probably true today that the extent of marked Appalachian Trail south of the Mason and Dixon line is greater than in the north." (This might have been literally true, but the trail through New England and New York was in much more stable condition. The route in the South might have been marked in places, but it was hardly "built.")

An article in *Mountain Magazine* in February 1930 claimed that some 500 miles were finished, of a projected 1,300 miles (underestimating the length total by some 700 miles). He admitted that much of it was on private land "with the permission of the owners," an exaggeration because, in most cases, trail enthusiasts chose not to inform the owners. Avery was aware of this and felt it prudent to avoid the issue at that time.

Acknowledging that no specific route had been declared in most of Maine, Avery wrote that Arthur Comey of NETC had done considerable scouting from Grafton Notch toward Katahdin, but that a precise route needed to be established. South of Maine, Avery could be more specific, because much of the proposed route had been preliminarily scouted, and some of it had been marked.

He highlighted the three places where alternate routes were under discussion. They were the same three that had existed since the 1928 conference. The first was where the trail would go in southern Pennsylvania, whether to dip south through Cumberland Valley and then follow the crest of South Mountain to Harpers Ferry, or to continue on Blue Mountain, and eventually to Tuscarora Mountain, ending at the Chesapeake and Ohio Canal towpath some sixty-four miles west of Harpers Ferry.

The second undecided section was south of the Peaks of Otter northeast of Roanoke. Should the trail continue due south on the Blue Ridge watershed, down to Grandfather Mountain, and then head west into Unaka National Forest? Or should it break off of the eastern edge of the Appalachians and head southwest of Roanoke and then down through the Unaka? At the time, there was no public land for either route.

The third controversy began in the Smokies. The most direct route into North Carolina was south from Silers Bald, across the Little Tennessee River into the Nantahala National Forest, and on into Georgia, terminating at Mount Oglethorpe. The alternate route continued on down to the western tip of the Smoky Mountains National Park and then terminated at Cohutta Mountain. It was surprising that Cohutta was still in play, but at least the proposal by MacKaye to continue to Chattanooga was no longer under consideration.

Perkins strongly advocated Oglethorpe and the Georgia route[28] but was incapacitated. He wrote Avery, "I do not think there will be any objection to the change in the Constitution as to the southern end of the Trail from Cohutta Mountain to Mount Oglethorpe except, perhaps from Ben MacKaye, who selected the former location from a map and has always had it in his mind." Avery wrote back, mystified by Cohutta. "I have long wondered who designated Cohutta as the end of the trail, and nobody seemed to know. Fink wrote that, long

Continued on page 118

---

28. ATC archives, Perkins Box, Perkins to Avery, May 27, 1930.

Roy Ozmer

The history of the Appalachian Trail has no stranger story than that of Roy Ozmer. In 1929, having heard about the trail, Ozmer contacted MacKaye, Welch, Avery, Harold Allen, and others to learn more. Learning more about the project, he decided to scout the route, beginning at its southern terminus. This got him into communication with Eddie Stone and Charles Elliott of the Georgia Appalachian Trail Club, and they convinced him that he should start at Oglethorpe. At the time, Cohutta was still in play, so even this preliminary decision was fraught with controversy.

Ozmer was a character, with a wit and a will. His own description of the decision to do the trip was earthy. "At the time I first became interested in the movement it was impossible to find anyone south of Washington who knew whether the Appalachian Trail was a liquid or solid. Even in the North, where the idea had been brewing for some time, few and far between were those who knew much of the movement, much less anything at all of the factors influencing the actual location of the proposed 'highroad for hikers.'"[1] His discussions with Stone, Elliott, and Horace Kephart, a well-known Southern writer, hiker, and early explorer of the Smokies, convinced him that he could begin at Oglethorpe and walk north through Georgia and North Carolina, blazing the route as he went.

Ozmer began at Jasper, the nearest town to Mount Oglethorpe, and, on May 2, 1929, he began walking. His trail report detailed the difficulties he had trying to find, and blaze, a virtually nonexistent trail. Ozmer wrote at one point, "Next day I made poor progress, having considerable difficulty in locating the desired route through such a confusion of abandoned roads and faint cattle trails between Southern's and the Falls [Amicalola]." His route took him past Amicalola to a succession of locations: Bucktown Mountain, Black Mountain, Winding Stair Gap, Hightower Mountain, Sassafras Mountain, Crane Gap, Grass Gap, Woody Gap, Baker Mountain, Henry Gap, Blood Mountain, Frogtown Gap [Neel Gap], Cowrock Mountain, and Strawberry Mountain, following mostly Forest Service trails to the Little Tennessee. Eleven of the fifteen place names on this list are on today's A.T. maps, and it is remarkable that today's trail generally follows the

1. GATC, *op. cit.*, p. 5.

very earliest A.T. trail scouting, done by Roy Ozmer. But, it is hard to know how much influence Ozmer had on route selection.

Ozmer entered what is now Great Smoky Mountains National Park at the Little Tennessee River and hiked up Forney Ridge to Silers Bald.[2] This was the most direct route, a straight line north into the park. (At the time, the river was much narrower than it is today, because Fontana Dam had not been built.) It intersected the Smoky Mountains Hiking Club (SMHC) trail not far west of Clingmans Dome, near the center of the park.

This route through the Smokies got Ozmer into a scrap with the SMHC. It advocated for the trail running the length of the park, exiting on the Little Tennessee west of Gregory Bald, crossing the river on the bridge at Tapoco, North Carolina, and continuing on to Cohutta. Using the Silers Bald route made sense only if the trail were to end at Oglethorpe instead of Cohutta, missing the western end of the park completely. At a meeting with Jim Thompson (SMHC president) and other members of the club, Ozmer advocated for the Oglethorpe route and was supported by Horace Kephart. According to Ozmer, Kephart broached a compromise, in which both termini would be retained, but only if SMHC would finance and build its section from Gregory Bald over to Cohutta.

Ozmer wrote to Avery on November 1, 1929, "I feel badly about the Knoxville crowd, looking at my endeavors as they do, but I have no regrets to express to them. I did not tramp the Smokies to provide any sort of reproach to them, of course, but I felt that such a course would react favorably to the Trail here in the South…." In another letter, he proclaimed, "It would be mighty nice if the Trail could be so routed to cover the Smokies, but it cannot be wrapped all over the world to reach every place of beauty and interest…."[3]

North of the Smokies, Ozmer got sick and dropped off the trail for the rest of the year. He convalesced at home in Tennessee. As 1930 dawned, Avery suggested he scout farther north to lay out a route through southwest Virginia. Ozmer agreed and decided to begin at the Peaks of Otter in Natural Bridge National Forest northeast of Roanoke.[4] Instead of hiking north, he would go south toward Damascus.

---

2. *Ibid*, p. 6.
3. *Ibid*, p. 7.
4. ATC archives, Avery correspondence, Ozmer to Avery, July 11, 1930; Avery to Perkins, July 22, 1930.

Ozmer's report on the Virginia section from the Peaks of Otter to Galax, Virginia, laid out a proposed route that Avery later followed in locating the Appalachian Trail along the Blue Ridge. From the Peaks of Otter, Ozmer turned south, following roads, dirt tracks, and faint trails from homestead to homestead in the high mountain ridges east of Roanoke. He meandered through the mountain ridges until he came to the Blue Ridge escarpment, marking the end of the Piedmont and the beginning of the Appalachian range. This escarpment is well-defined and in places very steep in the east, but westward it is a gentle slope toward the river valleys south and west of Roanoke. Ozmer was frustrated that the area appeared more like tableland than ridgeline. It was mostly farmland, crisscrossed with roads, farms, and occasional stores. It was completely unlike the Unakas further south, and, the farther south Ozmer ventured, the less enchanted he became.

At a point about 30 miles north of Galax on the New River, he gave up, got a car (he did not explain how he acquired a car), and drove to see S.L. Cole, reputed to know the area better than anyone. He and Cole formed a bond, and Cole drove Ozmer eastward, where they found the escarpment, the Pinnacles of Dan, and the cliff known as Lover's Leap. Ozmer described the Pinnacles as the most spectacular and scenic spot that he had seen, and it completely turned around his view of the Blue Ridge route. At that point, he gave over the selection of the route on to Galax to Cole, who, he wrote, had already recruited several groups living in the area to lay out a trail.[5]

Ozmer carried USGS topographical maps and took distances at 0.001 of a mile. Lacking GPS technology, it is hard to know how he came to such precise measurements. The record does not indicate that he pushed a measuring wheel, and he did not mention blazing. The entire report is a bit of a mystery.

Avery proposed to Perkins that Ozmer's entire route should be adopted.[6] Perkins, still inclined to compromise at that point, followed Kephart's suggestion that both routes, the Oglethorpe and the Cohutta routes, should be adopted, thus creating a bifurcated trail southwest of Clingmans Dome. The route advocated by the Smoky Mountains Hiking Club would continue west of Silers Bald,

5. PATC archives, PATC *Bulletin* #23.
6. PATC archives, Avery papers, Avery to Perkins, July 24, 1929.

Ozmer (right) with Arthur Woody (of Woody Gap), a legendary Georgia forest ranger, who for 30 years was chief ranger for the Blue Ridge District of Chattahoochee National Forest. "He ruled his domain like a benevolent patriarch," wrote Ronald M. Fisher in a National Geographic Books volume on the trail.

past Gregory Bald, and then south to Twentymile on the Little Tennessee, where there was a bridge over the river to Tapoco. Eddie Stone replied hotly, and the matter remained unresolved at the time. The SMHC route at least had the advantage of being able to cross the Little Tennessee on an auto bridge. There was no bridge at Forney Ridge.

Aside from the scouting trips, little is known today about Ozmer. Born in 1899, the same year as Avery, he came originally from Georgia and lived in Tennessee at the time of the scouting trips, and his correspondence referred to fighting fires with the Forest Service. After the Virginia trip, he disappeared from the scene and was not heard from for decades. But, in 1959, a reporter for the *Miami Herald* "rediscovered" the former trail scout living as a hermit on an island in the Everglades. "Bearded and wearing a beachcomber outfit of beret, slacks, sport shirt and sandals, Ozmer (a university-educated former merchant seaman) surprises tourists with his excellent English and scholarly dissertations."[7] He died in 1969.

---

7. GATC, *op. cit.*, p. 197.

ago, Kelsey and another asked him about it."[29] Avery in 1930 was still not in a position to dictate the solution — in a very short time, he would be.

Avery scheduled frequent meetings. At first, they were to be yearly, and the 1930 meeting was, like the 1928 conference, hosted by PATC at Skyland in the future national park. Making PATC the host placed Avery in charge, a role that Perkins had given him in any case. And, it eased the transition from Perkins to Avery, a move that no one in 1930, least of all Perkins, realized would be necessary. Arthur Perkins expected to return as soon as he was able.

Although PATC was the host and Avery was the master of ceremonies, the 1930 conference was the last that he did not himself dominate. He allotted ten minutes for each speaker, and he himself had only five minutes on the program. His position was still tenuous, given that people expected that Perkins would recover. Perkins was, after all, only 66 years old and had seemed to be very vigorous.

The conference featured Eddie Stone from Georgia as the Saturday-evening after-dinner speaker. Perkins and Avery could have sent no clearer message that Cohutta was not to be the end of the trail.[30] Perkins sent Avery an amendment to the constitution making Oglethorpe the southern terminus, and it was passed unanimously.[31]

By the time of the 1931 conference, Avery was piloting the ship. An ATC conference had never been held in the South beyond Virginia, and Avery proposed to Perkins that the next one be in Knoxville. Almost two months later, Jim Thompson, president of the Smoky Mountains Hiking Club, offered to host the event in Gatlinburg, on the Tennessee side of the new national park.[32] Avery decided in favor of Gatlinburg, and SMHC became the host.

Just prior to the conference, Avery got on the train, traveled to Georgia, and hiked the entire proposed route from Oglethorpe up to

29. Georgia Appalachian Trail Club (GATC) History Committee, *Friendships of the Trail: The History of the Georgia Appalachian Trail Club, 1930-1980* (Atlanta: Georgia Appalachian Trail Club, 1981), p. 6.
30. ATC archives, Conference meetings, box 6-1-1, Program for the Fourth ATC Conference, Skyland.
31. PATC, Avery papers, Harold Allen to Perkins, June 4 1930.
32. PATC, Avery papers, Avery to Perkins, May 2, 1930; Thompson to Avery, June 26, 1930.

Gatlinburg. He was joined in Georgia by Stone and later by Warner Hall. In a single day, Avery covered 34 miles with a full pack over the poorest of trails through the Nantahalas. In Gatlinburg, he got off the trail and chaired the meeting.

The event was heavily promoted in the PATC *Bulletin,* which advertised that the club was chartering a bus for the club members from Washington to Gatlinburg. It was a ten-day vacation, only one day of which was spent at the conference — the rest was hiking or traveling. Avery led hikes to the highest peaks in the Smokies, and the first one, a climb up Mount LeConte, advertised as "moderate," began with a 5,000-foot ascent!

In 1931, Avery traveled almost constantly. His trip from Georgia to Gatlinburg was only one of several hiking trips covering much of the East Coast. He hiked east of the Hudson on a route scouted by Murray Stevens, covering 55 miles in two days. On another trip, he hiked from Swatara Gap to the Susquehanna River in Pennsylvania, a distance today of 34 trail miles (somewhat less then because of subsequent reroutes).

In a letter to Perkins in April 1931, he discussed his plans for standardization. He wanted each club to write guidebooks and used Raymond Torrey's classic *New York Walk Book* as a model. Avery wanted a manual setting out standards for trail construction. PATC had already published a manual, but he complained that "it had no Authority." He was writing a manual for general use and would send it to Torrey and Comey before publication.[33]

Avery continued to issue periodic reports on trail news through the 1930s. He kept reissuing the map, drawing the final route down from an indefinite track to one that had been approved by ATC (that is, approved by Avery) and recognized up and down the East Coast. Finally, in 1939, he accepted a solution to the irregular reports. It was a newsletter, called the *Appalachian Trailway News,* or *ATN.*

The editor, whose idea it was originally and who paid for the early editions herself, was Avery's partner in publication and one of his

---

33. PATC archives, Avery to Perkins, April 23, 1931.

A Texan by birth, **Jean Stephenson** went to Washington to work in the Navy Department. She had a doctorate in judicial science (and five others), in those days an unusual accomplishment for a woman. She joined PATC in 1933 and quickly became a fixture in the leadership. She became the guidebook editor and chair of the history committee and the publicity committee. A maintainer, too,

Avery and Stephenson on Sentinel Mountain in Maine in 1939

she went to Maine with Avery to help clear the trail, and she headed a group of women who sewed blue-denim covers on mattresses destined for PATC cabins. Outside of PATC, she was nationally known in the field of genealogy. Jean was a longtime member of the board of managers at ATC. Anything that needed editing and publishing, Jean did. In the early days, she funded the publication of the *ATN* out of her own pocket. With the possible exception of Frank Schairer, she was the closest person in PATC/ATC to Myron Avery.

closest associates, Jean Stephenson.[34] (The publication was succeeded in 2005 by *A.T. Journeys*.)

In 1931, Avery had announced that the three gaps in the planned route had been resolved. The most northerly, in Pennsylvania, had

---

34. Bates was probably the most through source on Jean Stephenson to date, but she is one of three ATC leaders profiled in depth in a 2020 book from ATC, *We Were There, Too*, by Gwen Loose.

been resolved in favor of the Cumberland Valley–South Mountain route, which had been laid out by Avery and Schairer. For the route south of Roanoke, the eastern route over the Blue Ridge had been selected, mostly because no one had scouted a western route. And, south of the Smokies, Oglethorpe had been selected instead of Cohutta. Although it would have been more democratic to have done this by committee, Avery resolved all three himself.

By 1931, Avery was discussing the A.T. route all the way from Grafton Notch to Oglethorpe. It only excluded the trail north from Grafton Notch to Katahdin, which Comey had scouted, because considerable work needed to be done to specify and mark the route. New England had plenty of trails; the trick was to select those that would comprise the A.T.

Massachusetts was one of those states where the specific trail sections had not yet been chosen. Williams College Outing Club and the Berkshire School Outing Club were working on the problem, while the newly formed Trails Committee of the Connecticut Forest and Park Association under Chairman Edgar Heermance was working on the Connecticut section. Closer to Washington, the Pennsylvania clubs had laid out the trail all the way from Delaware Water Gap to Harrisburg. The PATC section ran from the trail on Blue Mountain, south of the Susquehanna, to Rockfish Gap in Virginia.

Avery was pleased with a new section from the Peaks of Otter to Unaka National Forest on the Virginia–North Carolina line. "Its development into a completed 300-mile link of the Appalachian Trail has been the outstanding event of the past year." He praised S.L. Cole of Floyd, Virginia, and Cole's Southern Virginia Appalachian Trail Association, with branch clubs in Galax, Floyd, and The Pinnacles. Those clubs were to be short-lived, and the trail was entirely on private property or roads. Those factors finally pushed Avery to sponsor a new route west of Roanoke. (The Blue Ridge trail was eventually abandoned, although one can occasionally spot a white blaze on the old route, which follows the Blue Ridge Parkway through Virginia.)

By 1931, a dog-leg from Grandfather Mountain west to Unaka National Forest was abandoned. Instead, from the New River near the North Carolina border, the trail was routed over Iron Mountain and into Virginia at Damascus. MacKaye's original proposal to route the trail from Grandfather to Mount Mitchell was changed. The new Unaka route had been decided at a May 1931 meeting in Jonesboro, Tennessee, the home town of Paul Fink. Curiously, Avery did not attend but later certified the decision.

In the Smokies, the trail was fully laid out south of the Big Pigeon River, except for a very wild section east of Newfound Gap. Avery described this section from personal experience: "The intervening section is a trailless, inaccessible ridge-crest where trail construction is a matter of such extreme difficulty that it must await development by the National Park Service."[35] Discussing the route south of the Smokies and into Nantahala National Forest, Avery acknowledged that a great deal more work needed to be done before a final route selection south of the Little Tennessee River could be made. South of Tellico Gap in North Carolina, however, existing Forest Service trails could be used all the way to the Georgia border, where Eddie Stone had completed selection of a route from Oglethorpe to the North Carolina border.[36]

Trail Standards (or, Building to Avery's Specifications)

Just what should the Appalachian Trail be? A trail, indeed, could be almost anything. Since the A.T. began in New England, it initially looked like AMC leaders thought it should look. The leadership came from the intellectual elite and envisioned a challenging experience. No climb was too steep, no trail was too rocky, no section too exhausting for their taste. To this day, trails in New England are more challenging.

The contrary view was promoted by Rayner Edmands, who began building graded trails, with gentler climbs accommodated with switchbacks (see page 25). Edmands modeled his trails after graded trails in the Rockies and stuck fiercely to his standards but failed to convert the AMC leadership.

---

35. Avery had personally scouted the route east of Newfound Gap and had written a journal describing the hike. It is the only Avery trail journal to survive today and was found in the ATC archives in one of the boxes of maps that Avery had accumulated.

36. This detailed route description comes in a document in a publication titled *Associated Outdoor Clubs of America* in the Maine State Library. The article by Avery is entitled, "Progress of the Appalachian Trail."

Eugene Cook led the "primitive" group, and later Sturgis Pray (with MacKaye's approval) and Warren W. Hart (AMC's councillor of improvements) continued the tradition of "hard" trails. They believed that hikes should be more of an adventure, while Edmands felt that the public would avoid such trails and that a large hiking population would never be built up if the trails were too hard.[37] The AMC leadership did not seem to care if they built a constituency or not — it was part of the elitist tradition of the hiking community at the time.

National Park Service and Forest Service officials defended graded trails, saying that not everyone could handle the rough trails and that the public that visited national parks and forests would not hike on them. And so, the controversy continued.

The tradition of hard trails migrated down to New York. Raymond Torrey once referred to graded trails as "sissy trails." His early trail construction tended to be well-blazed but not cut down to mineral soil.[38]

Torrey fully understood, however, the need to establish firm standards for trail construction. Several different hiking clubs were building trails in the Palisades Interstate Park, and trail standards became chaotic. Because of that, Torrey established a committee on trail standards, headed by William Burton, the Green Mountain Club's New York Chapter president, and Frank Place of the New York–New Jersey Trail Conference. They published a manual, *Program for the Coordination of Volunteer Trail Work Recommended by the New York–New Jersey Trail Conference*. Torrey was a trail-standards pioneer.[39]

At this point, Myron Avery entered the scene. His early trails were very primitive, consisting solely of marking the route, lopping branches, and cutting large blowdowns. That was necessary under the circumstances, because he was intent on getting a route on the ground, and time for trail-work was limited. Within the first six years of PATC's existence, it had laid out a route from near Harrisburg and Duncannon, Pennsylvania, to Rockfish Gap, Virginia, a distance

---

37. Watermans, *op. cit.*, pp. 287-91.
38. N.Y.–N.J. Trail Conference archives, Torrey, "Long Brown Path" (originally published in the *New York Post*, March 13, 1936).
39. Rima Nickell, *ATN*, May/June 1990, pp. 11-18.

today of some 260 miles. Because there was no construction, there were no switchbacks, and the original PATC section of the A.T. went straight up and straight down mountains. This section resembled to some extent the trails in New England, less the steep, rocky summits. It was a phenomenal achievement as it was. With just more than 150 members, the club could not possibly have done more than that.

First, Avery set standards for scouting. A scouting party laid out a temporary route and should not paint blazes. Better to tie rags on branches so that a blazing or construction party could find the route later. The scouts should make a written record of their trip, a sort of strip map identifying features such as water sources, road intersections, side trails, and approximate distances.[40]

In the mid-1930s, the Civilian Conservation Corps (CCC) had to relocate the Appalachian Trail in many places to accommodate Skyline Drive construction in Shenandoah National Park. The CCC built trails to National Park Service standards, that is, graded trails, down to mineral soil. After having laid out the early, primitive trail, Avery heartily approved of the new CCC trail. In a 1934 letter to Oliver Taylor, chief of the engineering branch for NPS, Avery wrote: "The new trail is superbly located…. The ease of grade will permit the use of the new trail by many people for whom the old route was far too difficult." Defending the CCC-built trail against criticisms from New England, he wrote: "I am at a loss to see why the hiker should complain if presented with something better than the irreducible minimum." Seeing the need to work with the Park Service, Avery had become a convert to graded trails.

Later, discussing the new, wide trails, he complained about the prolific growth in the mid-Atlantic. This required a wider trail so that it would not be obscured by summer growth. Building graded trails eliminated some of the work of cutting back the vegetation and gave the hiker a marked trail to follow, rather than one that had been simply stomped down.[41]

40. Avery correspondence in the Maine State Library, Avery to "Fogg," May 23, 1934.
41. ATC archives, Avery correspondence, 1934, Avery to Taylor, October 16, 1934.

Dr. L.F. Schmeckebier at work.

In 1952, Avery reminisced about the gradual conversion of the trail to a graded standard:

Incidentally, the type of graded trail in the Shenandoah and East-
ern Smokies was decidedly novel to Eastern walkers, who were
not familiar with this type of construction. When the Park Service
undertook the construction of a crest line trail, its standards and en-
gineering practices were, of course, those used in its Western Parks.
As you may know, the Park Service was violently attacked by the
'wilderness school,' who considered this highly engineered trail to be
an intrusion upon the naturalness of the forest.[42]

That same year, an ill and retiring Avery sent a letter to the ATC conference in Skyland. "There is set forth, in detail in The Appalachian Trail Conference publication, 'The Appalachian Trail,' the story of its development, the techniques evolved and the essentials to maintain this Trail to creditable standards so that its traverse is a matter of pleasure rather than an endurance contest against uncut growth with a bewildering uncertainty as to the route."[43]

The fight over graded trails continued for years. Back in 1936, PATC's vice president, L.F. Schmeckebier, took issue with those who didn't like graded trails. "Perhaps we are getting old, but we do not

42. ATC archives, Stanley Murray papers, Avery to Edwards, May 12, 1952.
43. *ATN*, September 1952, p. 42.

consider it essential to a true trail to have to step from rock to rock over every fallen log, or to scramble down a talus slope, watching the ground all the while to avoid falls, or a sprained ankle or broken leg."[44]

To impose construction standards, Avery proposed a general trail construction and maintenance manual. As early as 1928, he wrote to Judge Perkins that PATC had already written and published its own manual, and he suggested that it be adopted by ATC for the use of all the clubs. Perkins replied with approval (he and Avery seemed to think alike on all matters) but noted that he himself was working on such a manual and proposed that Avery's standards be inserted into the Perkins draft. Since Perkins never published a manual, his illness and the press of business in his last few years probably overcame his project.[45]

Avery's project, however, continued forward, and, in 1931, he was still writing to Perkins proposing a standard trail manual be issued by ATC. He told Perkins that he was working with Comey and Torrey on a draft that he, Harold Allen, and Andy Anderson were editing and would soon bring the draft forward to the board for approval.[46] *Publication No. 5* became an ATC bible until the 1980s.

Marking

Marking the route of the Appalachian Trail became an industry unto itself. The first program centered around Major Welch's diamond logos. The original square logos were four-inch copper markers, manufactured in the workshop on Bear Mountain for a cost of six cents each. When PATC was established, the club's main expense was ordering markers for its trail section, and, when Avery began expanding his field of view into southern Virginia, North Carolina, and Tennessee, he ordered the markers in large quantities.

The expense of copper soon led Perkins to begin experimenting with galvanized iron and enamel markers. His first markers were produced in 1927, and those were the ones that Avery ordered for

---

44. PATC archives, L.F. Schmeckebier memo, December 17, 1935.
45. ATC archives, Perkins papers, Avery to Perkins, October 18, 1928, and Perkins to Avery, October 23, 1928.
46. *Ibid,* Avery to Perkins, April 23, 1931.

ATC and PATC.[47] But, as the trail mileage increased, even that became a burdensome expense, and, as with PATC, much of the ATC budget was consumed by the purchase of markers.

Avery double-blazing and placing a marker.

Adding to the financial burden was the desirability of the markers. As soon as they were nailed up, souvenir hunters began pulling them down. Letters began pouring into ATC from frustrated hikers, complaining about the difficulty of following the trail because so many markers were gone. Avery himself complained in 1932, "I am amazed at the way the enamel A.T. markers have been removed. They are fastened only with 1" screws; a jackknife will take them out…. Some scheme is needed to outwit the souvenir hunters."[48]

Grasping for a solution, Avery began leaning toward blazes. According to Avery, "As near as I can determine, the use of paint for marking trails originated with Prof. Will S. Monroe, founder and president emeritus of the New York Section of the Green Mountain Club, who adopted white paint to mark the scenic Monroe Skyline Section of the 260-mile Long Trail in Vermont."[49]

At first, Avery's blaze was preceded by an axe chop. A swift downward chop of the axe, followed by a horizontal swing, would cause a chip to fly off the tree. He acknowledged that his early ax-chop program for PATC did not work because the chop quickly became obscured by

---

47. PATC archives, Avery papers, 1934, draft article by Avery for the PATC *Bulletin*.
48. ATC archives, Avery correspondence, 1930-1932, Avery to Ralph C. Larrabee, September 20, 1932.
49. PATC archives, Avery papers, 1934, draft article by Avery for the PATC *Bulletin*.

tree growth and faded over time, thus making it hard to see from any distance. So, the blaze was then daubed into the divot. Renowned botanist Egbert Walker, who reputedly painted the first white blaze in Virginia, opposed the axe chop, arguing that it damaged the tree. He convinced the attendees at the ATC conference in 1935 to stop the axe chop. Instead, he had found a one-and-a-half-inch Red Devil paint scraper at a hardware store that permitted the trail worker to scrape the outer bark without going through the cambium.[50]

PATC adopted the white blaze, at first slapped into an axe chop. (Avery also advocated white paint as being a much cheaper alternative to metal markers.) In 1929, Arthur Comey of the NETC wrote to Avery, concurring with white paint, especially in reference to the long distances needed to mark the trail in Maine. "I would suggest instead of AT markers set more frequently that the intermediate marks be simple daubs of paint...."[51]

Paint blazes, now used universally on the trail, became the most controversial program in ATC. Among dedicated trail workers, nothing seemed to excite them more than a good long argument about blazes.

Avery advocated for the use of white aluminum-oxide paint. He had standards about how often to blaze (more often in the South, less so in New England), and the use of the double blaze to mark turns. The double blaze came up in correspondence as early as 1931, and Avery urged all the clubs to use it whenever the trail changed direction or character (for instance, from a trail to a road).

As to the blaze *color*, chaos reigned. In Connecticut, clubs were using blue. In North Carolina, blazing in Nantahala National Forest was orange. Many sections were not blazed, while hiker Ed Garvey was still seeing axe chops in 1970. In Massachusetts, clubs were nailing up diamond logos rather than painting blazes. AMC sections stolidly resisted ATC authority to govern their A.T. sections and did whatever they chose for many years. The Park Service did not accept blazes and used wooden signs at trail intersections.

---

50. Raymond Torrey, "The Long Brown Path," N.Y.-N.J. TC archives, undated [1935].
51. PATC archives, Avery papers, Comey to Avery, August 1, 1929.

Clubs in Pennsylvania refused to blaze their sections, although this was not unanimous. Dr. Harry Rentschler, the most influential member of the Blue Mountain Eagle Climbing Club, at first opposed blazing, contending that it spoiled the natural environment. (The club used the axe chop instead.) According to an article by Maurice Forrester, Rentschler's opposition to blazing was changed by Mary Dorsey, one of Avery's close associates. She took her problem to Avery, and together, they came up with a strategy. She went to Rentschler with a problem — she was a single woman alone in the forest, and, to avoid getting lost, she needed an occasional paint blaze. Rentschler relented and told her she could paint the occasional blaze. Having her foot in the door, she proceeded to blaze the entire 100 miles of the BMECC section.[52]

The situation in New York was especially difficult. There, the Conservation Department had already established blazing standards: blue for north-south, red for east-west, yellow for diagonal, and white for side trails. The A.T., being a diagonal trail, was marked yellow. William Burton, president of the New York section of GMC, called a meeting in 1931 to try to work out a solution, but this did not resolve the problem, and controversy (and multicolored blazes) continued. In 1939, the New York–New Jersey Trail Conference finally voted to change the blaze color to white.[53] Still, it took the war years to effect a complete change, and Jean Stephenson congratulated Joe Bartha, who had headed the reblazing project there, for finally completing the task in 1947.[54]

Blaze frequency could also touch off an argument. Avery insisted that hikers be able to stay on the trail. That did not mean that one should be able to see the next blaze when standing at a tree with a blaze, but they should not be restricted to major trail intersections, as some in the Forest Service advocated. Instead, Avery opted for what he called a "reassurance" blaze, meaning that a hiker needed to see an occasional blaze to be reassured that he or she was still on the A.T.[55]

---

52. *ATN*, August 1974, p. 42. Mary Dorsey became one of the most renowned women hikers on the East Coast.
53. ATC archives, Avery correspondence, 1939, Frank Place to Avery, April 28, 1939.
54. N.Y.–N.J. TC archives, Bartha file, Stephenson to Bartha, February 21, 1947.
55. See, for instance, ATC archives, Avery correspondence, 1930-1932, Avery to Joseph Kircher, Regional Forester Eastern Division, June 20, 1931.

From top: Mosby Shelter in northern Virginia,
Tumbling Run double shelters in Pennsylvania, and
Black Rock Hut in Shenandoah National Park.

Blazing became an artistic endeavor. Avery insisted on a precise two-inch by six-inch blaze. There could be no sloppiness or stray drips. There was to be no slapdash blazing.

Discussions about blazing did not end for many years, and controversies over blaze color, blaze frequency, double blazing, and offset blazing continued to roil ATC and the constituent clubs. Avery was convinced that the trail would not be integrated until standards such as blazing were imposed the length of the trail.

Ultimately, the A.T. ought to result in a pleasing experience for the public. Avery wrote that "trails should be marked and maintained in a manner to eliminate the necessity of labor and uncertainty in finding one's route. They should be an open course, a joy for travel."[56]

Shelters

The trail would not be complete, Avery felt, until all the "amenities" were in. That was, for him, especially important in regard to shelters, then called "lean-tos." But it also included other things: maps, guidebooks, signs, access trails, and side trails to viewpoints.[57] To him, the A.T. was not a single linear path — it was a whole system. His standards set the tone for the A.T., and all long-distance trails that came after.

At the landmark 1937 ATC meeting, Ed Ballard of NPS (see page 140) teamed with Avery to successfully propose a chain of shelters along the entire trail, and NPS published guidelines for them the following year. The classic AMC Adirondack shelter became the model for early A.T. lodgings. It was a simple three-sided structure with an overhang. The standard width was fifteen feet, eight inches. Bunks should be of wire, unless the shelter was in New England, where conifers were available. ATC recommended adding a stone fireplace in front of the shelter for cooking. PATC evolved its own modification of the Adirondack, partially enclosing the front, presumably to give hikers more cover from winds. PATC documented its recommended shelter model in Publication No. 12, *Plans for an Appalachian Trail Lean-to*.

---

56. Avery's final message to ATC, 1952, in *ATN*, July/August 2000.
57. ATC archives, scrapbook 8, Avery article in *The Regional Review*, January 1940.

Most shelters were built of logs with chinking, as was Mosby Shelter, depicted at top left on page 130. Torrey preferred stone shelters, and that was the model for many shelters built in Shenandoah National Park and elsewhere. In Pennsylvania, state Forest Service employees in Mont Alto Forest preferred a double-shelter system, a tradition that has survived to the present (but was not replicated elsewhere).

Arguments arose about spacing. Many hikers regarded the Ballard/Avery standard of eight to ten miles between shelters to be too close, but Avery defended his standard. "This might, to the hardened tramper, seem unduly low. However, the purpose of trail travel is to find pleasure by the route and not emulate the marathon or endurance contest."[58]
Avery understood that not all hikers wanted to backpack more than thirty miles in a day. In 1941, a chart of lean-tos on the A.T. listed 103 built specifically for the A.T. and an additional forty-six that were already in existence. This came out to an average of just more than thirteen miles between shelters. Obviously, the eight- to ten-mile standard had not yet been achieved along the entire trail.

It may seem paradoxical that Avery, the fittest and most accomplished hiker of his day, advocated relentlessly for easier trail construction standards and frequent amenities, but he wanted a broad spectrum of Americans to use the trail. One tends to look on Avery as fanatical and single-minded, but, in real life, he had a very complex personality, and one gets many different views of Myron Avery.

Avery's preferred term "lean-to" survived into the 1950s, until it was changed to "shelter" (except for Maine). He hung tenaciously to the name, despite widespread criticism. A.E. Demaray, acting director of the National Park Service at one time, tried to convince Avery that most people associated the term "lean-to" with a shed on the side of a barn.[59] Orville Crowder, founder of Mountain Club of Maryland and one of the earliest hikers to cover the entire trail (Avery was the first), complained to Jean Stephenson about the term. "All up and down the trail on this recent trip I have run into dislike for the term

---

58. Avery papers, PATC *Bulletin*, April 1942, pp. 39-45.
59. ATC archives, Avery correspondence, 1939-1940: Demaray to Avery, December 26, 1939, and Avery's reply, January 10, 1940.

In 1934, a group of Baltimore hikers got tired of driving to Washington to join PATC hikes and work trips, and an enthusiastic young hiker, **Orville W. Crowder**, took the lead in establishing a Baltimore-based club, Mountain Club of Maryland. A gifted naturalist and world traveler, he organized the World Nature Association and led the nation's first overseas nature tours, which eventually totaled 128 trips. He was a skilled mountaineer and climbed to  the highest point in each of the original 48 states and was the fifth person to complete hikes of the whole A.T. (He also was first cousin to Orville and Wilbur Wright, from whom he got his middle name.) Crowder died in 1974 at age 70, and PATC dedicated a grove of trees on its land in Harpers Ferry to his memory.

'lean-to,' and in many cases plain bewilderment at its use, and since I have always been a rabid anti-lean-to dictionist I have been in no position to defend the according-to-standard-or-bust Avery usage."[60]

Nothing frustrated Avery more than clubs and government organizations that refused to build shelters. Superintendent J.R. Eakin in the Smokies declined to build them "until the need arose." To Avery, simply having a long-distance trail in place defined the need, and he wrote to Eakin, "A trail system — particularly an extended trail system — without shelters is on the same basis as full dress without collar or shirt." He appealed to his friend, NPS Director Arno Cammerer, for relief, and promptly got it. Cammerer wrote back to Eakin requesting that a shelter system be built immediately. By 1941, the Smokies had eight shelters in

---

60. ATC archives, Avery correspondence, 1940, Crowder to Stephenson, October 23, 1940. Crowder was a close associate of Avery for many years, nearly equaling the roles of Frank Schairer and Jean Stephenson.

place.[61] The trail clubs in the densely populated northern states were able to maintain higher trail standards than those in the more sparsely populated South. When Orville Crowder hiked through the southern A.T. in 1940, he assessed trail conditions there. Crowder was highly critical of trail quality as compared with his normal mid-Atlantic A.T. standard. His detailed report reached Avery and resulted in a decision at the ATC level to send a "hit squad" to the area most in need. A combined Baltimore–Washington group headed to Tennessee and worked on eighteen miles of the A.T. from Spivey Gap to Devils Fork Gap.[62]

Whose Land?

Avery emphasized the need for a *connected* trail, as opposed to one that was fragmented. Since there were long stretches without a footpath, he designated road shoulders as part of the trail, an anathema to MacKaye. Avery argued that the road walks would eventually be eliminated as a true hiking trail was put into place. In 1931, he wrote to Harvey Broome in Tennessee, "Of course, this automobile road [between the Smokies and Tellico Gap in North Carolina] is simply a temporary connection for anyone who wants to travel from one place to the other at the present time."[63]

The matter of private land remained a serious obstacle to completing the trail. Should a local club attempt to get formal landowner agreement, or should they avoid pressing the point? The concern was that, if a legal right to walk were requested, the landowner, fearing it might cloud the deed, might then refuse permission to allow workers to put in the trail or even evict the trail from the property, if it were already there. The consensus was to avoid asking the question.

Avery wrote in 1933, "As to the crossing of land and the marking on private property, I think it is futile to try to get anything more than the acquiescence of the owner or an oral permission…. Every owner is

61. PATC archives, Avery papers, 1937, Avery to Cammerer, December 4, 1937, and Cammerer to J.R. Eakin, December 4.
62. *Ibid*, Avery correspondence, 1940, Avery letter to Board of Managers, December 10, 1940.
63. ATC archives, Avery correspondence, 1932-34, Avery to Broome, July 7, 1931.

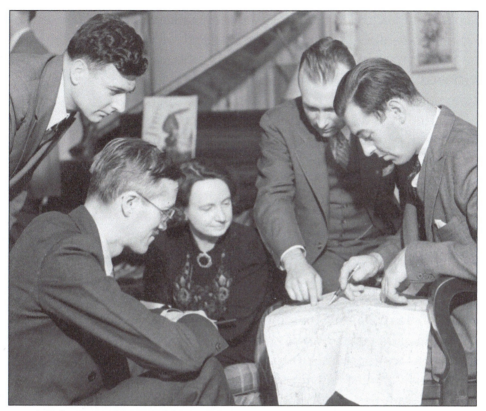

A February 1939 PATC excursions-committee meeting, planning for the September ATC meeting. Marion Park is at center, next to Avery.

naturally afraid to give a written permission of his land lest it constitute an easement or cloud on the title of his land."[64] Thus, for decades, most of the trail crossings on private land were by a "handshake agreement" rather than a formal easement recorded in court with the deed.

In 1938, Edgar Heermance of Connecticut wrote Avery questioning the legal liability of a landowner if a hiker were injured on his land. In those days, many states did not have laws limiting liability of the landowner to "gross negligence," and the matter was cloudy in many jurisdictions.[65] Thus, liability also deterred property owners from freely giving permission. Again, trail clubs found it convenient to avoid opening the

64. *Ibid*, Avery to Gates, February 15, 1933.
65. ATC archives, Avery correspondence, 1938-39, Heermance to Avery, December 9, 1938.

subject and just asked for a handshake agreement. That became a principal prod behind the drive to get federal legislation protecting the trail.

And what about competing uses on the trail? MacKaye had envisioned a hiking trail unencumbered by other forms of transportation, but how to enforce that?

Curiously, it was easier on private property, because the handshake agreement between hikers and the landowner implied that other uses, principally horses, would not be permitted. Horseback riding was sometimes allowed on public property. The superintendents of both Great Smoky Mountains National Park and Shenandoah National Park (SNP) permitted horses on certain sections of their respective A.T. routes, and the local clubs were powerless to stop the practice.

The main issue seemed to be destruction of the trail tread rather than hikers being run down by horses. PATC President Dorothy Walker wrote to the SNP superintendent in 1947, "Obviously a large number of horses frequently passing over the Trail will destroy the present desirable plant cover, break up the surface, thus exposing it to erosion and in wet spots creating deep mud or a rough pitted treadway."[66] Jean Stephenson chimed in with one of her usual acerbic letters, this one to National Park Service Region One in Richmond, Virginia. Her letters, especially to federal authority figures, gave no quarter.[67]

Having what amounted to a public trail, but not necessarily on public land, the A.T. was essentially defenseless against misuse. In 1942, Avery published "A Message to Those Who Walk in the Woods," pleading for cooperation by hikers. He was chiefly concerned about backpackers starting fires that got out of control, which could cause forest fires, but he was also concerned about boisterous singing and trash. Avery was also concerned about personal appearance, recommending proper garb (including having enough of it to cover strategic parts), grooming, and presenting a pleasing appearance to the public and to landowners.[68]

He knew that handshake agreements could be withdrawn.

---

66. *Ibid*, Avery correspondence, 1947, Walker to Eduard D. Freeland, March 18, 1947.
67. PATC archives, Avery correspondence, Stephenson to Thomas J. Allen, July 21, 1947.
68. ATC archives, Scrapbook 8.

The Appalachian Trailway Agreement

At the 1937 ATC conference, Edward Ballard, a National Park Service "field coordinator" and a member of ATC and AMC and rather constant silent partner of Myron Avery, called for increased public protection for the trail. This, he said, should be done by increased purchase of lands along the A.T. to protect it from the threat of being evicted from private land. The federal government and the states should work together to acquire the trail corridor and should move to protect the corridor from encroachments and incompatible uses.

Acknowledging that the trail did not run entirely through wilderness, public agencies should protect what was left of wilderness. Now that the trail was "finished," it should be relocated in places to improve the hiking experience, the proposal went. Land should be acquired by direct purchase or protected through scenic easements. Further, shelters and campsites were an essential component of a protected and relocated trail.[1] The conference adopted a resolution of support.

Ballard's proposal was revolutionary. At a single step, it would bring governments all up and down the East into the task of protecting a hiking trail. Avery worked closely with Ballard and was probably the inspiration for the proposal.

The idea for a trailway was not original with Ballard. It had been proposed in 1924 by Albert Turner of Connecticut. That same year, the Massachusetts legislature authorized the purchase of lands or easements for state trails.[2] Nothing much happened after that, until Ballard's 1937 proposal.

Ballard's most original idea was for an "interstate compact." Such agreements had been authorized by Congress in the 1936 Park, Parkway and Recreational-Area Act. The matter was taken up by the Park Service and Forest Service in 1938, and a new "Trailway Agreement" was signed on October 15, 1938. The two federal agencies agreed to protect the trail one mile on each side of the path.

1. Proceedings of the Eighth Appalachian Trail Conference, "The Appalachian Trailway," by Edward Ballard.
2. Ibid.

Within that zone, no parallel roads would be allowed, with no unnecessary cutting of timber or roads within 200 yards of the trail.

The historic agreement provided an *intent* to protect the environment around the trail but contained enough qualifying provisions that the two agencies could wiggle out without violating the specific terms (although they might still violate the intent).

A second step was to get the fourteen states to sign on to protect their portions of the trail. A draft agreement for states to sign was crafted. Like the federal agreement, it was an *intent* — which Major Welch termed, at a subsequent meeting in Amherst, Massachusetts, to discuss the agreement, a "moral endorsement," not a legal one.[3]

What, specifically, could be protected? Of the estimated two thousand miles of the trail, about seven hundred miles was in federal government ownership. Were all fourteen states to sign on, another 150 miles would be protected, for a total of around 850 trail miles, just more than forty-one percent.

ATC conducted two follow-on meetings to discuss the agreements and plan a strategy to get the states to sign on. ATC drafted a model state agreement, and the first regional meeting was held at Hungry Mother State Park in Virginia. Those southern states, having less private property to contend with, were more enthusiastic. Charles Elliott, the representative from Georgia, signed his state agreement on the spot.

The second regional conference, held in Amherst, Massachusetts, the following month, met with less enthusiasm at first because New Englanders had more private land to contend with. Ernest J. Dean, one of the attendees, pointed out to Arno Cammerer of the National Park Service before the conference that a two-mile zone of protection would be impractical for the states because their parks and forests tended to be much smaller than, say, Great Smoky Mountains National Park, where a two-mile zone was more or less trivial. This consideration caused the Na-

---

3. ATC archives, Minutes of the Amherst meeting; Fairfax, Sally K., "Federal-State Cooperation in Outdoor Recreation Policy Formation: The Case of the Appalachian Trail," doctoral dissertation, Duke University, 1973, pp. 29-30.

tional Park Service to change the zone of protection for the states to a quarter-mile on either side of the trail. When delegates met in Amherst, Dean was pleased and willing to sign on.[4]

A campaign resulted to get the states (besides Georgia) to sign their agreements. All but Maine signed almost immediately. According to a Myron Avery letter on April 15, 1940, that was because one Sterling Edwards, writing on PATC letterhead, urged Maine officials to revise their fire laws. At that point, Maine officials decided to have nothing to do with the agreement.[5] It has also been suggested that Avery's feud with Percival Baxter led Baxter behind the scenes to scuttle the state's participation.

The Appalachian Trailway Agreement, while lacking judicial weight, was a significant milestone in the history of the Appalachian Trail. The principle had been established that protecting this unique recreational resource was a governmental concern.

John Seiker, chief of recreational land planning for the Forest Service, stated at the 1941 ATC conference at Bear Mountain, New York, that the agreement made the A.T. the dominant recreational resource along the corridor.[6] The precedent weighed heavily on Stanley Murray when, in the 1960s, he began working on federal legislation to protect the trail by purchasing it.

More than a half-century later, it became the earliest example of what works for the A.T., cited by all sides in a Supreme Court case that threatened to upend decades of A.T. management principles.

4. ATC archives, Avery correspondence, 1938-39, contains numerous letters to and to and from Avery, Cammerer, Dean, and John Vondell (who Avery asked to host the Amherst conference); also *ATN*, July 1939, p. 6.
5. ATC archives, Avery correspondence, 1940. The Sterling Edwards issue was an interesting subplot to A.T. history. Edwards was an independent gadfly who often wrote letters claiming to represent ATC. This drove Avery absolutely crazy, but he was unable to stop Edwards.
6. *ATN*, September 1941, p. 41.

Ed Ballard

Edward B. Ballard (1906-2000) is perhaps the most uncelebrated of all early Appalachian Trail leaders whose proposals and actions instigated fundamental changes in the course of the project and the resulting experience, for both users and managers. At the 1937 ATC meeting, it was he — with Avery's full backing — who proposed what became the Appalachian Trailway Agreement among ATC, the agencies, and 13 states and he who proposed a chain of overnight shelters or lean-tos roughly a day's apart along the length of the footpath. Avery like to introduce him as a member of AMC (which he was, along with membership in PATC), but he was, in fact, associate field coordinator for trails and winter sports for NPS — the person to whom Avery was joined in the hip when it came to issues he didn't have to take directly to his director colleagues. He had many other connections to the A.T. and ATC: In a 1988 reminiscence he sent to ATC, he studied under Sturgis Pray (see page 22) at Harvard's landscape-architecture graduate school, worked with Harlan Kelsey (page 55) in selecting Shenandoah and Great Smokies lands, filled in for Arthur Comey (page 74) at a New England Trail Conference meeting in 1934, met Harlean James (page 55) at the 1934 ATC meeting, and had a chance "discussion" with Percival Baxter on a train to Boston about his opposition to a national park (page 259). Ballard left the NPS to serve in the Army in the Pacific during World War II, then worked for state park agencies in Maryland, Kentucky and Pennsylvania, and then spent 23 years in the office of the chief of the Army Corps of Engineers, before a much-lauded career in private landscape-architecture practice in the Washington area.

Chapter 4

HORACE KEPHART, PAUL FINK, AND THE TRAIL THROUGH THE SOUTHERN APPALACHIANS

Myron Avery left two trails. One was of hurt feelings and bruised egos. The second was the Appalachian Trail. The first will disappear – the second will last.

— Quote attributed to Bill Mersch,
PATC bus driver and member of the council

There was never a time when the trail was not to go through Harpers Ferry, West Virginia — as *planned* anyway. The town was the most historic place on MacKaye's planned trail. First settled in 1733, it took its name from one Robert Harper, who, in 1748, purchased the land at the confluence of the Potomac and Shenandoah rivers and operated a ferry over the Potomac (hence the name). The Wager family, heirs to Harper, operated the ferry until 1824, when they erected the first bridge over the Potomac. The story of the town and trail was henceforth a story of bridges and floods.

At the edge of town, overlooking the confluence of the rivers, was a pile of shale slabs, originally so precarious that one could sway the pile back and forth. This is the famous Jefferson Rock, deriving its

Jefferson Rock

name from Thomas Jefferson's *Notes on the State of Virginia*, in which he wrote, "The passage of the Patomac [sic] through the Blue Ridge is perhaps one of the most stupendous scenes in Nature," and concluded that "this scene is worth a voyage across the Atlantic."

In 1796, the new nation purchased 118 acres at the confluence of the rivers for an armory, only the second federal one after Springfield, Massachusetts. Armories were especially important in the colonial period, when the colonies had no standing armies and the militias had to be self-armed. John Hall, a Maine inventor who had patented a breech-loading rifle, received a contract from the federal government to manufacture rifles, most of which were stored at the armory.

In 1832, the town became the center of a transportation competition. The mid-Atlantic states were competing with New York to become the manufacturing center, and that required a transportation corridor to the rapidly expanding Midwest. To provide cheap transportation, the Chesapeake and Ohio Canal, beginning in Washington, was being dug alongside the Potomac by Irish laborers, with the intention of eventually reaching the Midwest. At the same time, the Baltimore and Ohio Railroad was being built, also intending to reach the Midwest. The competition was intense and led to armed clashes between Irish laborers. In 1832, both had reached the narrow defile on the north bank of the river across from the town.

Although they both squeezed through, only the railroad reached Pittsburgh and farther — the canal stopped at Cumberland and never became the economic engine for Washington, which in turn never became a manufacturing center. The railroad benefitted Baltimore, which did indeed become a commercial and manufacturing hub. The canal continued to be an economic drag, until barge service was finally ended in 1924 after one of the river's regular, disastrous floods. But, an artifact remained — the C&O towpath, originally for mules pulling barges and later for generations of hikers. It provided a stable and permanent footpath.

The most famous incident in the town's history was John Brown's raid in 1859. Hoping to spur a slave revolt, he needed rifles from the armory to arm the enslaved. The failure of the raid only highlighted the strategic importance of the town and made it a target, if the geography were not already sufficient, for Confederate and Union forces during the Civil War. Possession of Harpers Ferry swayed back and forth during the war, not finally coming into possession of the Union until General Philip Sheridan evicted Jubal Early and the Confederates in 1864.[1]

After the war, the nation's first college dedicated to the education of "freemen" (freed enslaved men) was established by the Reverend Dr. Nathan C. Brackett of the Free Will Baptist Church. Brackett was an abolitionist dedicated to educating the freed slaves and had the backing of the Freedmen's Bureau established by General O.O. Howard and John Storer of Maine, who financed the venture. In 1867, after receiving financing from Storer, Brackett opened Storer Normal School[2] (later Storer College) on the hill above the town. The college first was in the Brackett House, erected in 1858, named after the first president of the college.

---

1. The history of Harpers Ferry can be found in any one of several short histories of the town. See, for instance, Dave Gilbert, *A Walker's Guide to Harpers Ferry, West Virginia* (Harpers Ferry: Harpers Ferry Historical Association, 1991).
2. Teachers' colleges were earlier called "normal schools."

After Storer College closed in 1954, the National Park Service (NPS) acquired the thirty-acre property and renamed the main college building at that time the Mather Center, after its first director, Stephen Mather (who coincidentally had spoken at the founding meeting of the Appalachian Trail Conference in 1925). The Brackett House was later to figure in the history of the Appalachian Trail, serving as the first headquarters of the Appalachian Trail Conference in Harpers Ferry in 1972 after it left its Washington space shared with the Potomac Appalachian Trail Club (PATC).

The canal and towpath were acquired by the federal government in 1938 to preserve it as a historical/recreational parkway. (Fortunately, it never became a parkway.) By that time, the towpath had become part of the Appalachian Trail. Much of the entire town of Harpers Ferry became a national monument in 1944.

The Appalachian Trail passed through the town in 1928 and for the first eight years thereafter. The first access was over a bridge erected across the Potomac after a flood destroyed spans of an old Bollman iron truss bridge built in 1852. But, floods were endemic to the spot, and no bridge was permanent, it seemed. After a 1936 flood destroyed the bridge, hikers bypassed the town, walking across an existing automobile bridge from Maryland into Virginia and then climbing the bluff to the ridgeline along the Virginia–West Virginia border.

In 1985, the Goodloe E. Byron Memorial Pedestrian Bridge was cantilevered on an existing railroad bridge from the Maryland bank into the town (see page 463) and thus the trail returned to Harpers Ferry.[3] Continuing through town, it passed Jefferson Rock and returned to the Virginia side of the river over an automobile bridge. Once across, it climbed Loudoun Heights to intersect with the earlier trail. (Days before Christmas 2019, a freight-train derailment obliterated the top of one third of the pedestrian bridge, breaking the continuity of the A.T. until it was repaired in July 2020.)

---

3. The history of the A.T. through Harpers Ferry is well-covered in Paula Strain, *The Blue Hills of Maryland: History Along the Appalachian Trail on South Mountain and the Catoctins* (Vienna: Potomac Appalachian Trail Club, 1993).

When a bridge was not available in the earlier decades, hikers used commercial boat services. At one time, a rope-drawn ferry operated from the Loudoun Heights shore in Virginia across the Shenandoah River to West Virginia and Harpers Ferry. But, the boatmen were alcoholics, and sometimes hikers had to wait for someone to go wake up an operator.

Myron Avery, Frank Schairer, and Andy Anderson first scouted the trail south of town, two weeks before PATC was established.[4] The route proceeded down the ridgeline separating

Opening of the pedestrian bridge in 1985 with U.S. Senator Robert Byrd (right).

West Virginia from Virginia until it reached a point just north of Va. 7, where it left the state line and was entirely in Virginia. Six trail miles south of Route 7 was Mount Weather, first established as a weather research center in 1901. It slowly sank into decline, the victim of parsimonious congressional funding, personnel defections, and a fire that burned down the main building in 1907. The A.T. passed along the western border of the federal land. South of Paris at U.S. 50, it used a road that had been built by the CCC for fire prevention.

---

4. PATC archives, Avery papers, letter from Avery to F. C. Pederson, Virginia state forester, August 20, 1935.

Crossing the Shenandoah in the early days.

From Harpers Ferry to the boundary of what would soon become Shenandoah National Park, the trail initially was entirely on private property. (In the 1960s, a state wildlife-management area was created just north of Linden, and that provided a small slice of public land.) Although hiking across private property worked for years, it would eventually become a huge stumbling block to a through trail and was one spark that lit the flame that, in 1968, resulted in the federal government's declaring the Appalachian Trail a government responsibility.

Shenandoah National Park

South of Chester Gap, near Front Royal, was a vast territory that Avery knew was to become a new national park. The land looked nothing like it does today and certainly did not resemble a national park. It was occupied by Appalachian farmers, most of them squatters, and it has been estimated that approximately one-third of the acreage was high pasture.[5] Much of what was left of the forest was dead, owing to the catastrophic chestnut blight. This blight, which began in

5. Bolgiano, *op. cit.*

"Ghost forests" of dead chestnuts along proposed Skyline Drive route

New York Zoological Park in 1904, was already well established by 1928 in the Blue Ridge Mountains of northern Virginia.

When Avery and his pioneer trail-blazers first entered what would become the new national park, they encountered what they called "ghost forests" of dead chestnuts. The tree was not just ornamental — it provided sustenance for man and animal alike, and its loss helped to impoverish the people living in the mountains. Darwin Lambert, the chronicler of the early Shenandoah Park, wrote, "Advocates of a national park in the Blue Ridge between Front Royal and Waynesboro would claim in 1924 that the mountain forests were 'virgin' or 'primeval.'... A professional report of 1914, detailing the true situation, somehow hadn't reached these advocates."[6]

Bears, iconic residents of the present-day park, had been exterminated. Not a single bear was known to exist in the future park in 1930, even though today the park has more resident bears per acre than any other park in the nation.[7]

---

6. Darwin Lambert, *The Undying Past of Shenandoah National Park* (Lanham, Md.: Roberts Rinehart, Inc., 1989), p. 169. Lambert's book is the source of what I believe to be the most reliable information about the history of the park, and the information in this section was drawn mostly from his book.
7. Lambert discusses the bear population when the park was established.

The lands of Virginia had been granted by King Charles to various court favorites, and the land between the Potomac and Rappahannock rivers was granted to various owners and eventually to Thomas, the sixth Lord Fairfax. The headwaters of the Rappahannock had not been specifically located, and the Rapidan, it was thought, might be a tributary of the Rappahannock, so the southern boundary of the Fairfax lands had not been established. By the time Peter Jefferson (Thomas Jefferson's father) had done a survey and concluded that Lord Fairfax owned some five million acres, Lord Fairfax had sold most of it to various wealthy landowners and court favorites. Some three-fifths of the present-day park was in possession of those landowners, many of whom had never actually traveled to America to see their holdings.[8]

What happened in a case like this was that locals occupied the land, either as leaseholders or squatters. Squatting became much more common than legal claims, and it has been estimated that only about seven percent of the land was occupied by legal owners.

A few large landowners actually occupied the land and produced crops, using enslaved labor. By far the largest landowner was Thomas Shirley, who owned 48,000 acres near Syria, on the east side. Shirley died a few years before the Civil War, and, after that, the plantation system began breaking down.

German farmers tended to locate in valleys where arable land was in good supply, while Scotch Irish tended to occupy the uplands. Neither group had slaves. Tobacco dominated early planting, but rapidly depleted the soil, and farmers usually switched to corn. This, too, eventually depleted the land, which was, in any case, fairly rocky and difficult to farm. Much of the high hillsides wound up as grazing land. The chestnut blight hurried that along.

At the turn of the century, a few commercial ventures were in place: a hotel at Panorama, part of a real estate venture, and a hotel at Black Rock, on the west side of the ridge, which burned to the ground in 1909 and was never rebuilt. The footings can still be seen off the Ap-

---

8. Lambert, *op. cit.*, pp. 34-45. Governor Spottswood disputed the Fairfax claims, and the state of Virginia began selling land in the disputed area. That wound up in the Supreme Court, which decided, in the famous case of *Martin v. Hunter's Lessee*, that state claims were always subordinate to claims by the federal government.

palachian Trail.[9] But, the most significant commercial operation was Skyland.

In the middle nineteenth century, the region south of Thornton Gap, where present-day U.S. 211 cuts through from Warrenton to Luray, was thought to have commercial-grade deposits of copper. That turned out not to be the case, but it brought new investment to the region, and one of the investors was one George H. Pollock of Massachusetts, who was part owner of what was called the Stony Man tract, named after a mountain with a well-known overlook off to the west. Once the copper bug had been nipped, the senior Pollock suggested that his son, George Freeman, visit the tract, as it might furnish hunting opportunities.

That the young Pollock did in 1886. Pollock was intrigued with the area and proceeded to build a new road, under considerable difficulties, from Luray to a spot just south of Stony Man. He erected a tent city and hired local residents to build permanent structures. They became Skyland, a resort for the well-heeled. Some of the cabins originally constructed by Pollock's laborers still exist at Skyland, now part of the park.

One of the principal industries in the mountains was corn liquor, and Pollock had difficulties with some of the residents who were suspicious of his presence because many of them had stills. No good, they felt, could come of bringing a bunch of tourists up into their territory. The most prominent resident, who formed a tenuous bond with Pollock, was Aaron Nicholson, who ran a moonshine business on the east side of the ridge in a narrow valley known as Nicholson Hollow. The community that sprang up around the hollow was known as the Nicholson Free State, as if to advertise its independence from federal control (particularly federal *revenuer* control.)[10]

Congress passed the legislation creating two new parks in the east in February 1925. One was on the border of Tennessee and North Carolina, and the other was in Virginia.

---

9. *Ibid*, p. 190.
10. The best source for information about Skyland and Pollock is a book by Pollock himself, *Skyland: The Heart of the Shenandoah National Park* (Chesapeake Book Company, 1960).

The location for the Virginia park was not yet established and became the subject of intense competition. The first major ridgeline in the east was the Blue Ridge, running between 2,000 and 4,000 feet. West of that was a series of ridges called the Massanutten. The Massanutten option was being promoted by a group calling itself Shenandoah Valley Incorporated. The group was headed by Hugh Naylor of Front Royal. Pollock and a Ferdinand Zerkel of Luray met with Naylor and drove out to Fort Valley, between the two Massanutten ridges. A single visit converted Zerkel to Pollock's promotion of the Blue Ridge option, and he thus became one of the principal promoters of Skyland as the center for the proposed park. They formed their own association, printed brochures, and began an intense lobbying campaign to convert the committee that had been established to survey the options being proposed for the two parks.

The investigating committee that Congress created in 1924 had its sights fixed on the Smokies. Major William Welch was a key member of the committee. Regarding the park in Virginia, some converting was necessary, and Pollock concentrated on one member of the investigating committee, Harlan P. Kelsey, a native North Carolinian then living in Boston. He enticed Kelsey to visit Skyland and took him on a long horseback ride lasting several days, through what is now the central district of the park. This convinced Kelsey of the merits of the Blue Ridge option. The Blue Ridge was dramatically superior to the Massanutten option, and it is fortunate indeed that Pollock won the argument. (In 1969, Benton MacKaye credited Kelsey as the originator of the phrase, "Maine to Georgia" as the A.T.'s official motto.)

The new park was to include 385,000 acres. The two states in question were to raise the money to finance the purchase of the lands, and Will Carson was named by the state to head a Virginia State Commission on Conservation and Development. Carson immediately saw two problems. First, 385,000 acres exceeded the amount of suitable land for a national park. And second, raising that amount of money was probably beyond the capacity of the committee. Carson convinced the secretary of the interior to authorize a "resurvey," and Arno Cammerer was appointed to head the effort. This resulted in what became known as the Cammerer Line, and Congress agreed to cut the size of the park to the area inside the line, 327,000 acres.

The Virginia legislature appropriated $1 million for the purchase, and Carson and his committee raised almost another $1 million. They were in discussions with the people promoting the Smokies to combine their forces, when the Rockefellers stepped in to pledge $5 million for the park in the Smokies. The people in Tennessee and North Carolina became uninterested in their partnership with the Virginians. At this point, Carson was still about $2 million short. He planned to raise that amount, but the stock market crash of 1929 made that unrealistic.

Noting that the Virginia group was strapped for cash, Congress agreed to lower the amount of territory still further, to 160,000 acres. This made the project feasible, depending on the price of the land. The Virginians found a friendly judge, who agreed to land appraisals that were substantially below the actual value. In this way, the land area of Shenandoah National Park finally was purchased, and the families on the land were infuriated.

That was the "easy part." The hard part was moving the 465 families who lived on the land into towns outside the new park boundary. Some had been there for generations, and some owed much of their income to the illegal production of whiskey, which could not be moved elsewhere. In addition, they were resentful of the undervaluation of the land. Some agreed to the buy-out but left with a bitter taste. Others resisted, leading to instances where whole families had to be physically dragged onto trucks and taken to new lodgings outside the park boundary. A few residents secretly were granted a life estate and were allowed to stay. Only 197 families actually owned the land, and the rest were paid nothing for the privilege of being evicted. The bitterness and hard feelings lasted for decades and can still be detected when talking to members of the evicted families.[11]

The evictions were going on when PATC became involved in blazing a trail through the new park, and the club sent out pleas for

---

11. Lambert describes all this in his book, pp. 207-240. A former PATC president, Jack Reeder, has written several books detailing the trauma attending the resettlement, as have others.

donations of clothing. Kathryn Fulkerson, one of the early founders of the club, stated, "The Club has responded most liberally." It was important for PATC to be friends with residents, who could make life miserable for "flatlanders" making trails through their territory.[12] An early PATC cabin was almost burned down by unknown assailants, presumed to be local residents.

As those events were taking place, the irrepressible Myron Avery was poking around the territory for the new park. Avery was hiking there as early as November 1926 and was already in touch with Cammerer. It was Avery's understanding (probably from Cammerer) that the Park Service intended to have a trail the length of the park. On November 9, the *Page County News and Courier* discussed Avery's recent visit there and his talks with Pollock. The newspaper marveled that "on Tuesday Mr. Avery took a hiking trip which, in Mr. Pollock's estimation, excels any on record for this vicinity."[13] Avery was already making his mark and his plans. This was a full year before he, Anderson, and Schairer decided to establish a trail club and was Avery's earliest known involvement with hiking in the mid-Atlantic.

PATC's first work trip in what would become the new park did not begin at Front Royal, the northern entrance. It began, instead, at Thornton Gap. This area, to become the central district of the park, already had trails built by Pollock's people, and the developers of the hotel at Panorama had built an earlier trail to Mary's Rock, a spectacular viewpoint south of the gap named by Thornton after his wife in 1733. Thus, the initial PATC section was from Thornton Gap to Mary's Rock. (We do not know if PATC just improved that trail or built an entirely new trail.) That trip, in April 1928, was the first foray into the park to build the Appalachian Trail.

Those early work trips marked PATC's real initiation into the type of trail work already common in New England. Frank Schairer described it as a true learning experience. The club did no tread work — they mainly removed vegetation, painted blazes, and moved on.[14]

---

12. Shenandoah National Park (SNP) archives, Zerkel collection, SHEN 21205, Box 7.
13. ATC archives, Avery correspondence, general, 1938.
14. Lambert, "Administrative History of Shenandoah National Park, 1924-1976," unpublished manuscript, 1979.

President Roosevelt at Skyline Drive site in 1933 with CCC Director Robert Fechner (back seat, center), en route to lunch with CCC enrollees.

Club members removed brush and scrub oak, leaving the heavier work of cutting blowdowns to Avery and Schairer.

Skyline Drive construction began in 1933 by the newly created Civilian Conservation Corps (CCC). Knowing that PATC was already building the Appalachian Trail, park rangers were concerned that their activities mesh with those of the volunteers. Demaray, assistant superintendent of Shenandoah National Park, wrote to James R. Lassiter, the engineer in charge, "It is important that you make contact with Mr. [L.F.] Schmeckebier so that you may fully explain our trail building activities and learn from him as much as possible of the Club's recommendations. The Club has been very active.... We want to give full consideration to their ideas."[15]

Park officials were very concerned that Avery would get out ahead of them on trail building in territory that was still private but

Continued on page 164

15. SNP archives, Demaray to Lassiter, August 4, 1933.

The Skyline Drive Controversy of 1935

Completing the Appalachian Trail was a monumentally difficult enterprise. It had so many problems arrayed against it that a betting person would have bet against its ever coming to completion. But, it was also torn apart internally by a catastrophic dispute between the two leaders. Benton MacKaye, the creator, feuded with the organizer, Myron Avery. It all came to a head over the matter of skyline drives.

In 1930, President Herbert Hoover, while on a horseback ride with National Park Service Director Stanley Albright near Big Meadows, directed him to begin construction of a ridgetop road through the new Shenandoah National Park. Hoover justified this executive action partly as a drought-relief measure, partly as a Depression jobs program for local residents, and partly as a scenic drive through the new and soon-to-be national park.[1] The new road would begin at Panorama, where a federal highway cut through Thornton Gap, and proceed to George Freeman Pollock's Skyland resort. That would not be the end of it, however — it would bisect the park at least from Swift Run Gap in the south to Front Royal in the north.

The president had spoken, and no one — not Myron Avery, not Benton MacKaye, not even Congress — could reverse the decision. It was an executive order that was within the authority of the president. It confronted volunteers working to build the Appalachian Trail in the same place, but it was not original to Herbert Hoover.

The idea of a skyline road had come up in an early meeting of the Southern Appalachian Park Committee, a group formed by Congress to create new national parks in the East, including Major Welch and other A.T. pioneers. The discussions revolved around a great parkway that would connect the two parks, Great Smoky and Shenandoah.[2] In 1924, William C. Gregg, a member of the committee, spoke in Harrisonburg, Virginia, predicting that, if a park were established in the area, a drive would be built all the way along the top of the park.[3]

In the 1930s, automobile-based tourism was all the rage, as private-vehicle ownership exploded, and all the East Coast was talking about skyline drives. At the same time that Vermont was beating back a proposal to run a drive along the top of the Green Mountains, New Hampshire

1. Lambert, *op. cit.*, *The Undying Past of Shenandoah National Park*, p. xi.
2. Anderson, *op. cit.*, *Benton MacKaye*, p. 230.
3. SNP archives, Series I, Park Central Files, box 117, folder 5, article in the *Harrisonburg Daily News-Record*, October 25, 1924.

residents were dealing with a similar proposal in their state. The chairman of the Crawford Notch Recreational Development Committee was advocating a drive over the Presidentials, and the highway department already was surveying for a possible route.[4] Talk of extending the planned Skyline Drive in Shenandoah National Park into national forests to the south, calling it the Blue Ridge Parkway, picked up. How far would it go? Some were advocating an extension all the way to north Georgia, where one would run out of mountains.

The Park Service began acquiring the right-of-way in Shenandoah National Park, the U.S. Bureau of Public Roads flagged the route, and ground-breaking was on July 18, 1931, not quite a year before Franklin D. Roosevelt would be nominated to oppose Hoover for a second term. Initially, 161 workers were hired, and they were dealing with the drought, the chestnut blight, and unemployment.[5] When Roosevelt as president formed the Civilian Conservation Corps (CCC) in 1933, CCC workers took over much of the construction.

At the time, PATC was engaged in building the Appalachian Trail through the future park. The decision to build the parkway came as much a surprise to them as to everyone else. The impact on the club was that the new drive would undoubtedly destroy the trail, because both were on the ridgetop. Avery immediately contacted the Park Service to see what could be done.

The push for ridgetop roads evoked strong opposition all up and down the Atlantic Coast, and Benton MacKaye was one of the early leaders. At the ATC meeting in Skyland in 1930, he emphasized, "The Appalachian Trail is a footway and not a motorway because it is a primeval way and not a metropolitan way."[6] Everywhere he went, he talked the same theme. In a letter to Fred Davis, secretary of the Natural Bridge A.T. Club, he wrote, "It is a wilderness way through civilization — not a civilized way through the wilderness. Be sure to get this point."[7]

MacKaye felt, biographer Anderson writes, that "the Appalachian Trail was never merely a footpath.... The Appalachian Trail, that is, was the axis of what he envisioned as a vast expanse of protected public land, stretching along the mountains between Maine and Georgia."[8]

4. Appalachian Mountain Club archives, speech by Col. William Barron, December 21, 1933.
5. *Potomac Appalachian*, November 1977, p. 51.
6. PATC archives, Avery papers, MacKaye speech, May 30, 1930.
7. *Ibid.*
8. Anderson, *op. cit., Peculiar Work*, p. 80.

Benton MacKaye – M. H. Avery

A small snapshot from a Bake Oven Knob meeting in 1931, found in Avery's personal photograph album (Avery's handwriting).

Avery never argued with MacKaye about this. He was not opposed to the concept of a trail through wilderness. Rather, his focus was elsewhere. He wanted a completed trail and regarded that as the first objective. A *wilderness trail* could come later — first, you had to have a *trail*. In a letter to the Smoky Mountains Hiking Club, he wrote, "As a subject of fireside contemplation, the Trail project is a delightful philosophy. It requires, however, a less ephemeral existence. Its very existence must depend upon a demonstration of the actual Trail, adequately marked for present use."[9]

That was as clear an articulation of Avery's thinking as exists. His focus was work, building the trail. He could not disagree with MacKaye's objective but thought that it was a bit premature. The trail had to come first, in his view. The tragedy was that the two could not compromise, could not harmonize their objectives.

The first face-to-face meeting of MacKaye and Avery that we know of was at the May 1929 ATC meeting at Lafayette College (see page 84). Two years later, at Bake Oven Knob in Pennsylvania, the Blue Mountain Eagle Climbing Club (BMECC) hosted a grand celebration marking the completion of its trail section and commemorating the tenth anniversary of MacKaye's article. The *Allentown Morning Call* claimed 1,000 celebrants, although Raymond Torrey wrote that about half that number actually showed up. Among those with speaking parts were Torrey, Hiram

9. ATC archives, Avery correspondence, Avery to SMHC, May 17, 1932.

Bingham, William Shanaman, Daniel Hoch (of whom more will be said later), Dr. Harry Rentschler, MacKaye, and Avery. The only known photo of MacKaye and Avery together was at that event; ironically, the original resides in Avery's personal photo album.[10]

MacKaye consulted with a diverse group of trail advocates — William Welch, Ashton Allis, Raymond Torrey, Halstead Hedges — but the record does not show whether he sat down with Avery during the various meetings both attended to share views. There was neither physical nor intellectual closeness between the two.

As early as 1932, Andy Anderson, Avery's close associate in PATC, recognized the divergence. Intellectually, Anderson stood with MacKaye but was close enough to Avery to understand his thinking. The two (Avery and MacKaye) were headed for a clash if one of them did not retreat, and Anderson recognized it very early. He wrote to MacKaye in 1932, "Myron has not yet grasped the idea of the incompatibility of the road [Skyline Drive] and the trail...."[11]

When the CCC jumped into the trail-construction business to replace the tread overtaken by the drive, Avery was enthusiastic. He began calling it a "super trail" and compared it favorably with the "primitive" job that volunteers had done with the original route through the central district." To the board of managers, he reported, "This has superseded the original route, rough, difficult to maintain and a considerable exertion for many hikers."[12] Avery's enthusiasm, probably driven by the reality of the situation, seemed genuine.

MacKaye, Anderson, and others were not so happy. In their view, a graded trail smacked too much of what existed of suburbia in those days, desecrated the wilderness, and provided too easy a footpath. The arguments back and forth echoed similar arguments in New England over the Rayner Edmands approach to trail construction (see page 25).

Arguments went back and forth about trail construction. Was the CCC version of the Appalachian Trail too easy? The trail in the photograph on page 165 was exactly what the New Englanders jeered. The trail sections along steep cliffs with crib walls would have been difficult for the small PATC club to have built in those days.

The open break came in 1934.

10. ATC archives, Avery personal album and scrapbook #4, 1931-33; Anderson, *Peculiar Work*, p. 79.
11. McClung Collection: Harvey Broome papers, Anderson to MacKaye, August 12, 1934.
12. ATC archives, "Report of the Chairman of the Board of Managers of the A.T.C.," October 1, 1934.

The Wilderness Society

Back in Knoxville, the place was in ferment about the idea of creating wilderness areas in the United States. MacKaye, a strong advocate of wilderness, was there working for the Tennessee Valley Authority, and he joined socially with SMHC on a regular basis. The club was led by Harvey Broome, another wilderness advocate, and SMHC had many others of a similar mind.

In 1934, the Park Service was building Skyline Drive in Shenandoah National Park and continued to push ever more ridgeline automobile roads in the East to provide scenic driving opportunities for the public. Andy Anderson, who had started out as one of Avery's closest confederates, diverged from Myron on Skyline Drive in the park and proposed to his allies in ATC that they should form a committee to try to derail Skyline Drive (whose construction had already begun).

According to Larry Anderson, MacKaye's biographer, this was the spark that lit a fire under Bob Marshall, an independently wealthy chief of forestry for the Bureau of Indian Affairs. Marshall was convinced that it was time to advocate for a national organization to promote wilderness. Later in the year, Anderson and Marshall met in Washington to flesh out the idea for a new organization. Anderson drafted a statement of principles and sent it to MacKaye in Knoxville.

The whole thing came together on October 19, 1934, in Knoxville, when the leaders of the wilderness movement met to attend the American Forestry Association convention. On a journey to inspect a Civilian Conservation Corps (CCC) camp near LaFollette, MacKaye, Marshall, and Broome all piled into a car driven by Bernard Frank and joined the motorcade to LaFollette. Near Coal Creek, Frank pulled the car onto the road shoulder, and the four of them sat beside the road, working on the draft statement of principles, and thus "the basic outline of the Wilderness Society was born."[13]

This legendary first step had consequences for the Appalachian Trail. MacKaye now had an organization to push his idea of conservation, and it fit in well with his idea that, above all else, the trail must be in wilderness. Were it not, it would not be the Appalachian Trail that he advocated.

Avery didn't dislike wilderness and wanted, above all else, to have a *connected* trail. In this, he fell out with Harvey Broome and other members of SMHC. A frustrated Broome wrote Avery in 1932, "As I have written

13. Anderson, *op. cit., Benton MacKaye*, p. 274; article by Michael Nadel in PATC *Bulletin*, April 1962, p. 30.

you many times before, I cannot see why the Trail needs to be completed by any particular date, and I am confident, after extensive correspondence with Benton MacKaye, that he himself is not one who would strive feverishly after the fashion of this machine mad world to complete a task."[14]

Avery's personality sometimes worked against him in the Smokies. After years of submitting to Avery's interference, the mild-mannered Carlos Campbell, Avery's chief ally, wrote hesitantly to him: "It is a little bit difficult to tell you things that I feel I must tell you without, possibly, leaving the impression that I am angry at you personally…. You surely know, however, that at many times you have been criticized by your fellow-workers up and down the line because of what they have termed a dictatorial attitude."[15] The specific dispute was about shelters, and Avery gave the decision over to the local club. Perhaps Campbell's letter convinced him.

At an ATC meeting in Rutland, Vermont, in the spring of 1934, MacKaye rounded up the forces opposed to skyline drives and graded trails. MacKaye himself could not attend, but he sent an "expression of sentiment" to be read at the conference. Broome, who would team with MacKaye, Bob Marshall, and others to form the Wilderness Society later that year, advocated MacKaye's position and demanded that any roads that might be built be in the valleys, not the ridgetops.[16] Given that the president had made the decision about Skyline Drive in Shenandoah, the matter concerning that park seemed moot — the very best that could be accomplished was to advocate against extending the drive in other places.

That same year, MacKaye published an article in *Appalachia* entitled, "Flankline *versus* Skyline," in which he attempted to resolve the conflict with a compromise. Rather than building skyline roads, a road lower down on the mountain would be a better alternative, in his view, to skyline roads. They would provide better scenic views and a cheaper alternative to difficult ridgetop roads. He might have hoped to bring Avery's viewpoint around to his, but, if so, it was a faint hope.

MacKaye might have been right, but his position was unrealistic. President Hoover had made the decision, and President Roosevelt was following Hoover's example. Avery, the realist, understood this. If a compromise were not reached with the federal government, there would be no Appalachian Trail.

14. McClung Collection, Broome papers, Broome to Avery, September 22, 1932.
15. ATC archives, Avery correspondence, Campbell to Avery, March 29, 1939.
16. Hunter Library, Sherman Collection.

Avery anticipated trouble at the 1935 meeting, and, like MacKaye, began to round up allies. In the months before the conference, Avery was in touch with Arno Cammerer, discussing the NPS position on skyline drives, and stating that he was looking for allies on the issue. He clearly did not want to damage his relationship with Cammerer and, in fact, had already come out in favor of skyline drives in such places as Vermont.[17] His relationship with authorities such as Cammerer, who were acquiescing in skyline drives, was regarded by many as far too cozy.

The seventh Appalachian Trail Conference was held at Skyland, on Avery's home turf, June 22 and 23, 1935. Saturday, the 22nd, was the only business day. Most of the program was a set-piece report by Avery, his officers, and the various clubs, along with speeches on special topics from allies and supporters of the trail. Only two sessions tipped attendees off to what was in store. In the morning, they were to vote on changes to the constitution. And, at nine p.m. came the report of the resolutions committee.

The membership section of the constitution, normally of little interest, was where disagreements began. It was proposed, and passed, that Class A members (that is, trail-maintaining clubs) would have one vote for the president, one for the secretary, and one for each ten miles of trail maintained. Since PATC had the longest section in those days, 240 miles, it would thus get 26 votes and would have the largest voting bloc. Although this provision was hotly contested, it passed and became the method of voting. (And it is, more or less, the same vote allocation used today.) Those opposed to the new provision claimed that it was the way that Avery packed the voting and thus gave him reasonable assurance that he could run ATC the way he wanted to.

Raymond Torrey, Avery's former ally, headed the pro-MacKaye forces at the conference. He offered a resolution supporting MacKaye's position: "Resolved, that this Conference favors as a general proposition, the routing of scenic highways through valleys or along the slopes of mountain ridges rather than along their crests." The resolution did not pass — Avery had the votes.

MacKaye sent a letter to the meeting opposing skyline drives, stating that the proposed parkways would "not only obliterate the trails, but what was far more vital, would stifle and strangle the atmosphere of the wilds. The Appalachian Trail Conference, existing for the preservation of the

17. ATC archives, Avery correspondence, Avery to Cammerer, March 30, 1935; Report of the Chairman to the Board of Managers, October 1, 1934.

wilderness, tolerates the construction of no motorways where they would gut the wilderness of its primeval atmosphere…and demands that any roads built in the vicinity of this mountain fastness be located in the valleys and along the lower slopes instead of on the skyline."

Anderson was quick to see the situation as it really was. Commenting on MacKaye's position paper, he wrote only a few days after the conference, "I fear, however, that the point you make will be pretty well lost on Myron…. You are a dreamer, inclined to be fanatical, while he is a practical man, getting things done."[18] Anderson, who with Avery had planned the creation of PATC, knew his hiking partner well and understood, too, about MacKaye. He could see the possibilities for compromise disappearing.

The conference ended with Avery in the saddle and the disaffected MacKaye forces in retreat. But, Avery had made enemies. In the months that followed, he and Torrey, his former friend and ally, hurled invectives at each other. Torrey had the pulpit of the New York Evening Post and his "Long Brown Path" column, and he used it to attack Avery and ATC. The two, Avery and Torrey, eventually reconciled, but it did not happen until the Skyline Drive controversy was well back in the rear-view mirror.

Andy Anderson wrote an article in the November issue of Appalachia, entitled, "What Price Skyline Drives?" "This great voluntary recreational project…was intended to be something more than a through footpath connecting Maine to Georgia. It was to be a thread connecting wild and primitive areas…."[19] He was clearly in the MacKaye camp.

Jean Stephenson had already fired back at Torrey. In December, L.F. Schmeckebier and Harold Allen wrote a counterweight to publications by Torrey and Anderson. In an article entitled, "The Shenandoah National Park, the Skyline Drive and the Appalachian Trail," they tried to counter every argument that the other side had thrown out. As for the new trail built by the CCC, they defended the graded trail.

In the end, even Avery proposed a compromise. He wrote a letter to Cammerer late in 1935, proposing that the drive in the southern district of the park be a flankline road, rather than continue Skyline Drive south of Swift Run Gap.[20] But, it was too late. Contracts had already been let for the construction project in the south district of the park. Moreover, the political push to retain the drive throughout the park was strong from Harry Byrd

18. ATC archives, MacKaye papers, Anderson to MacKaye, June 27, 1935.
19. PATC archives, Anderson file.
20. PATC archives, Avery papers, 1935, Avery to Cammerer, December 3, 1935.

(former governor of Virginia and now a U.S. senator whose home in Berryville, Virginia, was just a few miles west of the trail).[21]

That led, in late 1935, to an increasingly bitter exchange of letters between Avery and MacKaye. Accusing MacKaye of dilatory elitism and of a lack of work ethic, Avery stated, "[P]assing resolutions and everlastingly talking is of little use. We must be ready to take action."[22]

The matter had gone far beyond a policy dispute — it had devolved into personal animus and *ad hominem* attacks, especially from Avery. MacKaye realized that continuing the dialogue was useless. "I have noticed in you a growing, self-righteous, overbearing attitude and a bullying manner of expression.... In your present frame of mind, therefore, I feel that further words are futile."[23] Although Avery is often portrayed as the sharper, personal tongue, a 1934 going-away scrapbook from MacKaye's TVA friends contains a number of scathing, even juvenile limericks directed at Avery (and even Harlean James, despite his public praise for her in the 1920s). Those were friends, not reticent MacKaye himself.

As far as is known, it is the last words they ever shared, and Avery died in 1952 without ever having reconciled with MacKaye, although he did allow a later ATC meeting to commend him.

One of the claims that Avery made in his letters to MacKaye, and in publications by PATC and ATC, was that the Appalachian Trail project had effectively died in 1925 and was only resurrected in 1927 because of Arthur Perkins. This became settled ATC historical fact until the 1980s, and it followed Avery's line that MacKaye, for all his grand vision, remained a dreamer. Avery craved action and believed that only concerted and organized activity would create a trail. For all his faults (and he had many), Avery was essentially right in this claim. Did he consciously write MacKaye out of the history? Little evidence supports this claim, and much refutes it, although, in fact, Avery himself wrote much of the early history.[24]

The two came from the same New England (and Harvard) world but seem to have come to different conclusions about life. One area of difference was in the very composition of trail clubs, which both interreacted with extensively (in different regions). In those days, joining a trail club, any trail club, on the East Coast, required more than just

---

21. Lambert, *op. cit.,* and unpublished manuscript, 1979.
22. ATC archives, Avery correspondence, Avery to MacKaye, December 19, 1935 (although a handwritten note in the corner suggests it was not sent until Christmas Eve).
23. *Ibid,* MacKaye to Avery, February 4, 1936.
24. One place where one can read the theory is in Larry Anderson's *Peculiar Work,* pp. 86-87, but it is not the only source, and Anderson is not the only writer to make the claim.

sending in dues. This policy may have come from fraternal organizations, which also restricted membership. Most trail clubs had very restricted memberships, as attempts were made to keep only the "better" types on the membership rolls. That was the view of many clubs. When MacKaye participated in the creation of The Wilderness Society, an advocacy group that never was a trail club, it was his view that the political position of members should be like a political party. The founding statement included the sentence, "Above all, we do not want in our ranks people whose first instinct is to compromise." In a letter to Bob Marshall, MacKaye wrote, "If the purpose is Cannibalism...then nobody but a Cannibal should be admitted."[25]

Avery, on the other hand, played a huge role in democratizing the trails movement. Part of the vibrancy of PATC was its democratic character. If one came out on a couple of work trips, one could apply for membership, and the number of members was unrestricted, as opposed to many of the other clubs. As a result, PATC's membership steadily increased. It was a large factor in the club's dominance.

Skyline drives were to bedevil the trails movement for years. They were irresistible to a large segment of the population in the East and thus had considerable political backing. Avery, ever the politician, opposed them when he could and acceded to them when resistance was futile. He believed that it would be possible to fend off a skyline drive in the Smokies,[26] but, in Shenandoah National Park, he recognized the political realities. (And, anyway, the president had already decided — it wasn't an arguable case.)

In 1933, Avery had opposed the Blue Ridge Parkway, another *fait accompli*. But, dissatisfaction got him nowhere, so he used his influence with Cammerer to get the federal government to rebuild the Appalachian Trail through Natural Bridge National Forest, as it would the trail through the park. Cammerer answered back, "You and I talk the same language" and told Avery that the matter already was set in motion. It is interesting to note that MacKaye also wrote to Cammerer, protesting the new road and demanding that a flankline road be built. Avery's letter achieved more, because he asked for federal assistance.[27]

---

25. Quoted from Anderson, *Peculiar Work*, p. 92.
26. ATC archives, scrapbook #8, Avery article in *The Regional* review, January 1940.
27. ATC archives, Avery correspondence: Avery to Cammerer, November 27, 1933; Cammerer to Avery, December 3; MacKaye to Cammerer, December 30.

would eventually be part of the park, while the park was still legally restricted from building trails there.[16] The park needed to build trails to government standards, while PATC volunteers were roaring through the terrain using their own standards.

Part of the nervousness on the part of park officials was Avery's relationship with their boss, the assistant director of the National Park Service, Arno Cammerer (see chapter 3). The two carried on a direct correspondence, bypassing the park rangers. Cammerer became the director in his own right in 1933, and Avery used his relationship with the new director to overcome obstacles and work around opposition from officials of Shenandoah National Park. Park officials had be careful with Avery.

The CCC, created as a jobs program by the new Roosevelt administration, had, as an additional objective, environmental conservation. FDR, wanting to demonstrate the impact of the new program, established the first CCC camp in the nation outside of Edinburg, Virginia — it was, of course, called Camp Roosevelt (see page 153). The first two work camps in national parks were both in Shenandoah, at Skyland and Big Meadows. The earliest CCC projects in the nation involved building roads and trails.

Rerouting the Appalachian Trail because of Skyline Drive construction was one of the first big projects. Trail building was, in a way, similar to road building, and the CCC boys built a new trail that everyone (everyone in PATC, that is) praised. It was a graded trail, built to National Park Service standards, a very different type of trail than the one it replaced.

The CCC was run by U.S. Army sergeants, who employed military discipline. Reveille roused the young men in the morning, and taps sent them to bed. On the trail, they worked with military precision. The state of Virginia alone produced more than 100,000 veterans of the CCC program.

Cabin and shelter building was sometimes a PATC project and sometimes a park project. For instance, Meadow Spring, a cabin (then called a shelter), was built by PATC very close to Mary's Rock. Sex-

---

16. *Ibid*, Demaray to Lassiter, May 9, 1933.

A CCC crew builds Shenandoah National Park trail.

ton Cabin also was built by PATC. On the other hand, Rock Spring and Pocosin cabins were originally built by the CCC in the 1930s, as were Rip Rap and Big Run (which no longer exist). The organizations would negotiate over interior construction, and who did the work seemed to depend on who had the resources at the time.

As the new Appalachian Trail took shape in the park, Avery and park officials continued to negotiate the final route through the central district. In December 1935, Frank Schairer announced to his overseers that the Appalachian Trail was finished from Thornton Gap to Swift Run Gap, which marked the southern boundary of the central district. The other two districts were yet to be negotiated, but the most visible part of the park now had a finished A.T.[17]

17. PATC archives, Avery papers, Schairer letter, December 19, 1935.

When the CCC-built trail was in place, it was loudly praised by the PATC leadership. Avery noted to Lassiter in 1934, "I want to tell you how delighted we are with the new trail. We think that it is one of the most important assets of the Park and when it becomes known, should receive considerable praise."[18]

The next year, Schmeckebier, Avery's perennial vice president, wrote that the old trail followed mostly old woods roads, lacked scenic qualities, and had been put hastily on the ground. Now that the CCC had come through and built a graded trail, the hiking public would surely approve of this new type of construction. Comparing it with the Edmands Path in New Hampshire, he wrote, "I do not know that a graded trail is such a radical undertaking." As for the construction scars that attended the new CCC path, he argued that summer growth would quickly cover them over, and the trail would soon resemble the forest trail that was the ideal.[19]

The objective, to get the trail onto public land, had an unexpected downside. Once on public land, the government took over, the volunteers lost control, and the park began maintaining the new trail in 1934.[20] The park maintained the Appalachian Trail for several years, relegating the volunteers to side trails, but volunteers began easing back onto the Appalachian Trail, park records show. PATC kept volunteer work reports for the A.T. in 1940, so the assignment to sections was a bit muddled — apparently the people available for the job at the time got the task, whether or not they were government employees.

The park refused to blaze the trail, relying on a graded trail and concrete posts with metal bands at trail junctions for directional signs. (The park did not give PATC permission to blaze the A.T. until 1964. The job was done in a single day, involving several crews and many gallons of paint.[21])

The two sides argued back and forth about trail standards. The park wanted to convert some of the side trails into fire roads, called "truck trails," and the volunteers resisted. But, over all, the relation-

18. PATC archives, Avery papers, Avery to Lassiter, October 16, 1934.
19. Hunter Library, Sherman Collection, *op. cit.*, Schmeckebier memo of December 12, 1935.
20. PATC archives, Avery to Taylor, October 16, 1934
21. PATC *Bulletin*, October-December 1964.

ship worked reasonably well, partly because everyone was aware of Avery's relationship with Cammerer.[22]

Once the central district A.T. was finished, action moved to the southern district. Although Halstead Hedges had scouted a potential trail in 1922, no one but Hedges was really familiar with the terrain. Hedges had been traveling in the area for some years, providing charity medical help to the residents, and so was familiar with the area when he originally scouted a trail route. In 1930, Avery proposed to scout the trail himself and Hedges sent Avery his notes.

Avery was accompanied on this excursion by Myron Glaser, and it was Glaser who later described the remarkable scouting trip, over a route that today occupies forty-five miles. The two stayed in a hotel in Afton, a small town in Rockfish Gap at the southern end of the park. "Everyone at the hotel thought we were off to an impossible objective because the mountaineers who inhabited the area were reputedly unfriendly. Jarman's Gap, in those days, was the center of a corn liquor distilling area, and the opinion was that strangers...would not be very welcome."

Glaser's description of the start of the trip was vivid. "However, bright and very early we were off to a flying start. I say this with much feeling, because we had covered 6 miles before 7:30, at which time Myron conceded to a 5-minute rest." At Jarman's Gap, they followed Hedges' suggestion and left the ridgeline because of dense scrub oak and followed the Moormans River on the east side of the ridge, reemerging on the ridgeline at the ruins of the Black Rock Hotel. They encountered a local resident who had driven up the old Black Rock Hotel road, and they overnighted with him. The next morning, they continued north, encountering Appalachian settlements at Simmons Gap.

"I might say that many of the mountaineers knew Dr. Hedges. He has done them many a merciful deed, and they spoke of him affectionately as 'Dr. Hedge.'" Commenting on the conditions, Glaser wrote, "These people were eking out a hard, poor existence from the

---

22. See, for instance, an Avery letter to Taylor on February 8, 1934, regarding truck trails, in PATC archives, Avery papers, 1934.

This grainy photo was probably taken at Simmons Gap. Avery is on the far right, and Myron Glaser was probably behind the camera. [Source: Carolyn and Jack Reeder, Shenandoah Secrets: The Story of the Park's Hidden Past *(Vienna: Potomac Appalachian Trail Club, 1991), p. 73.]*

rocky slopes and since the disappearance of the tan-bark and chestnut crops, were faced with ruin."[23]

Hedges established a trail club in Charlottesville in 1932. It had ambitions to take over the trail from Rockfish Gap to Swift Run Gap, but, after correspondence with Avery in 1932, it was not heard from again.[24] The southern district was taken over by PATC.

Although the park was not opened officially until July 1936, President Hoover had ordered work to begin on Skyline Drive in 1931. The section from Thornton to Swift Run was opened in September 1934, and the section from Front Royal to Thornton in October 1936. The southern district was still not open in 1936, and that became a secondary issue during the tense 1935 ATC conference.

---

23. PATC *Bulletin*, April 1943, p. 34.
24. PATC archives, Avery papers, Box 3, Hedges to Avery, December 12, 1932.

The Rest of Virginia

Even though the PATC section officially ended in the south at Rockfish Gap, Avery didn't intend to stop there. He wrote to Judge Perkins in 1929 to propose a route from Rockfish Gap south to the Peaks of Otter, a collection of three high peaks (all just less than 4,000 feet) in the Natural Bridge National Forest. His route would then proceed down the eastern side of Roanoke along the Blue Ridge, following Roy Ozmer's scouting in southern Virginia (see pages 114-117). In his mind, he had a route planned all the way to the North Carolina border and intended to scout it himself.[25]

Avery contacted Harold M. Sears, the supervisor of Natural Bridge National Forest, in early 1930. Sears wrote Avery that the Forest Service had already been active in trail-building and recommended a route from Rockfish Gap to the Peaks of Otter, which had become a destination with a popular tourist hotel. Sears' trail route would use a combination of existing Forest Service hiking trails, local roads, and power-line rights-of-way.[26] The southern end of the proposed route was Apple Orchard Mountain — at 4,200 feet, the highest peak in the national forest. (Unfortunately, the map that Sears provided Avery apparently has not survived, so we don't know exactly where the Forest Service trail was.)

Avery began a solo hike from Rockfish Gap on June 19, 1930, carrying a heavy pack and pushing his measuring wheel. On the evening of the third day, he walked into Camp Kewanzee on Apple Orchard Mountain, having walked and measured seventy trail miles in three days. PATC had a large delegation at the camp, and the exhausted Avery was greeted as a hero.[27] His reputation as a super-hiker was firmly established.

Sears was at Kewanzee, too, and so was Ruskin Freer, a professor of biology at Lynchburg College. Freer had heard about Benton MacKaye's trail and was enthused by the idea. He and Avery had

---

25. PATC archives, Avery papers, Avery to Perkins July 31, 1929.
26. *Ibid*, Sears to Avery May 24, 1930.
27. Bates, *op. cit.*, p. 18; PATC *Bulletin*, July 1955, Kathryn Fulkerson, "Twenty-Five Years Ago," p. 72.

PATC at Kewanzee in June 1930.

been communicating for more than a year, and Freer planned to organize a trail club in Lynchburg.[28]

Sears wrote an article about the Appalachian Trail for the *Lynchburg News* of May 19, 1929, that sparked two members of the Lynchburg Lions Club, Fred Davis and Elmer Ayers, to urge Freer to organize a meeting at the local Lions Club. Davis and Avery agreed to hold a public meeting in Lynchburg on October 2, 1930. The Lynchburg group was led by Freer, Davis, Ayers, and Charles L. DeMott, a civil engineer.

Freer invited Avery to come to talk about the new trail. When Avery arrived, he brought a delegation: P.L. Ricker, Frank Schairer, Andy Anderson, Marian Lapp, and Kathryn Fulkerson. That evening, following the meeting with PATC, the Lynchburg group met at the YMCA and formally organized the Natural Bridge Appalachian Trail Club (NBATC). The new club immediately adopted the section from Rockfish Gap south to the Peaks of Otter. (NBATC surveyed, marked, and measured its entire section the following year.)[29]

28. PATC archives, Avery papers, Avery to Freer, May 20, 1929.
29. See "History of the Natural Bridge Appalachian Trail Club," excerpted from a publi-

The PATC delegation drove south from Lynchburg to Roanoke the next day, October 3. Avery already had decided to use Ozmer's scouted route along the Blue Ridge, instead of the various ridges farther west. In Roanoke, he had been in touch with two local trail advocates, Tom Campbell and S.L. Cole. (Cole was the same man who had guided Roy Ozmer along the eastern route.) They arranged a meeting with local community leaders at the Patrick Henry Hotel. A Mr. Malcolm, the city engineer, took them up in a light plane to see the proposed trail route from the air. The group stayed over in Roanoke and the next day piled into a car and drove south along the Blue Ridge to the town of Floyd, stopping at scenic points. That evening, they attended a meeting of "several hundred" enthusiastic trail supporters, a meeting that was brought together by Cole.

Cole, an evidently gifted organizer, had started the Southern Virginia Appalachian Trail Club. As noted earlier, this club organized satellite groups in Galax, Roanoke, Stuart, Hillsville, and Mount Airy.[30] Other clubs sprang up, more or less ephemeral. There was, for instance, the Mountain Club of Virginia, with Fred Davis of Lynchburg as president. Farther south was the Unaka Mountain Club, and still farther south was the Balsam Mountains Hiking Club.[31]

Cole's trail clubs lasted only as long as the planned route along the Blue Ridge and disappeared when the Appalachian Trail was moved west of Roanoke. But, Donald Gates of nearby Salem organized a more sustainable club in Roanoke (the Roanoke Appalachian Trail Club, RATC). It came officially into being in November 1932. Gates, a professor of economics at Roanoke College, had attended the 1931 ATC conference and began writing to Avery.[32] Avery was concerned about the condition of the A.T. along the Blue Ridge and urged Gates and NBATC to take on a greater load south of Roanoke.[33]

cation prepared as part of the club's 60th anniversary celebration, October 18, 1990, and PATC archives, Avery papers, Davis to Avery, September 11, 1930.
30. PATC *Bulletin* # 27, November 26, 1930; report by Cole.
31. ATC archives, Avery correspondence, 1936-1937, letter from Davis to Avery, no date shown (probably 1937).
32. *ATN*, July/August 1982, p. 12.
33. ATC archives, Avery correspondence: Avery letters to Gates and NBATC, March 10, 1933.

One of the Pinnacles of Dan.

The Blue Ridge route possessed numerous attractions. Top among them were the Pinnacles of Dan, Little Falls of the Dan River, and Lovers Leap, all of them significant tourist attractions today. The route went south, dipped for a few miles into North Carolina, and then moved back into southern Virginia, through the town of Galax. It then crossed the New River at Dixon Ferry and proceeded along the New River to Iron Mountain, where it turned southwest to Damascus, near the border with North Carolina.

Following the scouting trip by Roy Ozmer, a team of Cole, Campbell, and three others had thoroughly scouted and documented the proposed Blue Ridge route. Campbell and Cole appeared at the 1930 ATC conference to deliver their report, and disagreements about the precise route with Paul Fink and Ozmer were worked out at the conference. The conference authorized Cole to begin building the trail.[34]

Avery's earliest scouting hike had gone east of Roanoke, followed Ozmer's route, and joined the ridge line at Adney Gap. The Roa-

34. Three-page undated report by Cole and Campbell; PATC *Bulletin* #34, May 20, 1931.

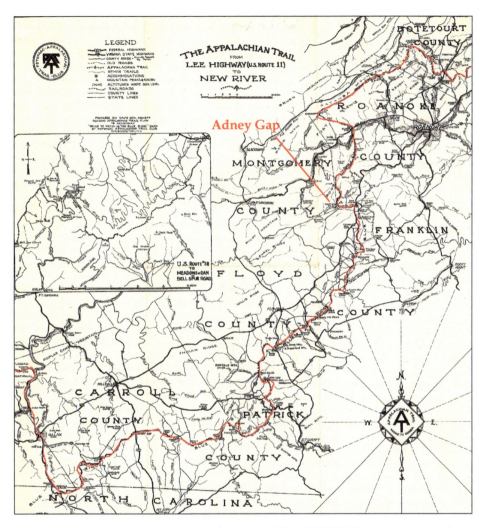

RATC's 1933 map by David Dick, printed by PATC: The route not taken.

noke club never built that route. Instead, the club built a trail that descended from the Blue Ridge, crossed the Shenandoah Valley near Daleville north of Roanoke, and ascended Tinker Mountain. That route passed two iconic overlooks, Tinker Cliff and McAfee Knob. (It was the spectacular McAfee that was the linchpin of this routing.) It continued southwest on Catawba Mountain to the small town of Bradshaw, where it turned east, descending the ridge line, recrossing the valley at Glenvar west of Salem, and ascending Poor Mountain, where it met Ozmer's route at Adney Gap.

In 1931, the irrepressible Avery and several PATC members walked the entire route scouted by the Cole/Campbell group. They hiked south along Ozmer's route, marking the trail. When they came to the Pinnacles of Dan, PATC veteran Charlie Thomas told of how he and one other (probably Schairer), as a joke, proposed that the trail be marked directly over one of the pinnacles, to get Avery's reaction. Myron didn't get the joke and ran his measuring wheel directly up over the mountain and down the other side.[35]

Had that route followed MacKaye's prescription, it would have continued south over Grandfather Mountain and on to Mount Mitchell, where it would have ended. Avery understood very early that the eastern route, while the most scenic, was unsustainable in the long run because it was entirely on private land. Ultimately, the route would have to be moved to the west, where the Forest Service was buying land for Jefferson National Forest. He also knew that the land had not yet been acquired in sufficient quantity and thus Ozmer's early route would be the Appalachian Trail for the foreseeable future.

In 1935, Avery learned that the federal government had decided to build the Blue Ridge Parkway. Beginning at Rockfish Gap, it would extend south, directly over the route of the Appalachian Trail. Just how far south it would go was not yet decided, but it was certain that the A.T. would suffer a fate similar to that incurred by the parkway's northern sibling, Skyline Drive in Shenandoah National Park. The parkway was just another in a series of skyline drives along the Appalachian chain that threatened the trail and caused huge controversy in the hiking community. Construction of the parkway began in 1938 and became a preoccupation for Natural Bridge and other clubs to the south.

Avery began planning to reroute the A.T. through Natural Bridge National Forest, to move it away from the proposed route of the Blue Ridge Parkway. In 1940, he proposed to M.C. Howard, the superin-

---

35. Earl Shaffer, *Walking with Spring* (Harpers Ferry: Appalachian Trail Conference, 1983), p. 57.

tendent of the Blue Ridge Parkway, that the relocated trail swing far to the east. South of Humpback Rocks (six and one-half trail miles south of Rockfish), the trail occupied a low ridge, and Avery proposed that it be relocated eastward, beginning at Reids Gap, onto a series of 4,000-footers known then as the Religious Range: The Priest, The Cardinal, and The Friar. It would rejoin the original route near Spy Rock. Everyone viewed this route as offering a far superior (although quite strenuous) hiking experience.[36] Although this was NBATC territory, it was assumed that the CCC would shoulder the main burden of rerouting the A.T. south of Rockfish, just as it had in Shenandoah National Park.[37]

South of the Religious Range (but north of Roanoke), much of the trail had to be relocated, and Avery complained in December 1939 to a Park Service landscape architect that, in the four years since it had been decided to build the parkway, work had not yet begun on the Appalachian Trail relocation over the Religious Range. "There seems to be a definite difference of opinion as to whose turn it has been to move. Your letter [November 29] indicates that everything is being held in abeyance while you were waiting to hear from the local club. Mr. Phelps was quite positive that the Club had carried out its commitments and that it was up to the Service to get these relocations under way."[38] In March 1940, he complained that not a single foot of new trail had been built. His constant prodding had an effect, and, by April, work had finally begun on sections north of the James River. The Forest Service finally got moving, and Arno Cammerer wrote to Avery in June that fifty-five miles of the section south of Roanoke had been marked.[39]

World War II interrupted the work, and, at the end of the war, the PATC *Bulletin* noted that the section from Reids Gap across The Priest

---

36. ATC archives, Avery correspondence, 1938-39, Avery to Howard, November 1, 1938; *ATN*, July 1939.

37. ATC archives, Avery correspondence, memorandum from Stanley Abbott, acting NPS director, to superintendent, Blue Ridge Parkway, February 20, 1940.

38. ATC archives, Avery correspondence, Avery to Edward H. Abbuehl, acting resident landscape architect, December 4, 1939.

39. ATC archives, Avery correspondence: Avery to Demaray, March 25, 1940; Cammerer to Avery, June 8, 1940.

to Montebello Fish Hatchery still was not finished.[40] The relocation was not completed until 1951.

South of Roanoke, the Ozmer route was no sooner in place than Avery began talking about relocating the trail onto the long-discussed western route from Roanoke to Pearisburg on the New River. The Forest Service planned to buy land farther west, on a series of ridges from Roanoke to the West Virginia border. This included Tinker, Catawba, North, Brush, Sinking Creek, Johns Creek, Potts, Salt Pond, and Big mountains and Peters Mountain on the border with West Virginia. Between 1935 and 1940, Jefferson National Forest had increased in size from 160,000 acres to 560,000 acres, and the Forest Service was building trails in its new domain.

Donald Gates, the president of the Roanoke club, wrote to Avery in 1933 about potential routes westward. The options were numerous, but any trail they might adopt should include the existing route along Tinker and Catawba mountains. Avery liked what he saw and wrote to Gates, "Your people have explored the routes and their knowledge and experience should control." He intended to go to Roanoke and take a look at the potential routes as soon as possible — this, when the Ozmer route was still barely marked all the way.[41]

By 1940, Avery was writing to David Dick, who had taken on the mantle of Roanoke A.T. Club leadership on trail scouting, outlining his thoughts about a possible route. He wrote that the Forest Service intended to build a fire road along Tinker Mountain north from McAfee Knob to Lambert Meadow, and that could become part of the A.T. He also suggested a trail from McAfee Knob southwest to North Mountain and Cove Mountain (where Dragons Tooth is), circling around through Miller's Cove to Brush Mountain. Avery then asked if the best route might be to continue south on Brush Mountain on a newly built Forest Service road.[42] World War II halted those discussions, with no more talk of the western alternative until after the war.

40. PATC *Bulletin*, October 1946, pp. 99-102.
41. ATC archives, Avery correspondence: Gates to Avery, January 18, 1933; Avery to Gates, January 25.
42. ATC archives, Avery correspondence: Avery to Dick, July 23, 1940.

McAfee Knob

South to North Carolina and Tennessee

The western border of North Carolina and the eastern border of Tennessee form a diagonal that runs from northeast to southwest. That is the spine of the Appalachians, and the border between the two states runs along the high points. Avery described the land from the New River (in southwest Virginia) to the Nolichucky (at Erwin, Tennessee) as a "real no-man's land.[43] Once it was decided to skip Mount Mitchell, it was a given that the trail would run through this remote mountain vastness.

North and south of Damascus, the trail would run along Iron Mountain (whose name is a *non sequitur*, because there was no iron in Iron Mountain). It would run past Roan Mountain but not over, because the Roan was entirely private land.

43. ATC archives, Avery correspondence, Report of the Chairman, April 1, 1935.

In the Unaka National Forest, south of Iron Mountain and Watauga Dam, was a spectacular series of balds called the Roan Highlands. It had more than 200 acres of Catawba rhododendrons, the largest field in the United States. The Roan also had forests above 5,000 feet of red spruce and fir; below that, beech and maple predominated.

The Roan was rich with resources, iron mining being the biggest money-maker. The Cranberry Mines, in the vicinity of Elk Park, North Carolina, was one of the first. General John Wilder established a number of mining operations, and, in 1882, a railroad was in operation from Johnson City, Tennessee, to Cranberry, North Carolina. Named the East Tennessee and Western North Carolina, it was commonly referred to as the Tweetsie. Wilder catered to tourists and built two large hotels: the Roan Mountain Inn on the Doe River near the new railroad depot, and Cloudland on top of the Roan. Wilder's operations were relatively benign.

That was not so with the timber companies. Moving south from New England, they discovered easy pickings in the southern mountains and began bringing down trees in large numbers.

Around the turn of the century, a new scourge visited the Roan. A 1902 report by the Department of Agriculture stated, "The effect of exposing mountain lands to the full power of rain, running water, and frost is not generally appreciated.... In the dashing, cutting rains of these mountains, the earth of freshly burned or freshly plowed land melts away like sugar." This report documented the harmful erosive effects of clear-cutting, poor farming practices, and fires. In 1901, an event called the May Tide wiped out whole towns and was followed the next year by a second destructive flood, just as violent.[44]

Environmental destruction was ameliorated by later Forest Service acquisitions, and the Roan became a favorite hiking venue. But, much of the Roan remained in private hands, and the trail largely bypassed the rhododendron gardens atop the mountain. The A.T. was not relocated over the Roan until a reroute of more than 70 miles was

---

44. Description and history of the Roan Highlands can be found in Jennifer A. Bauer, *Roan Mountain: History of an Appalachian Treasure* (Charleston, S.C.: Natural History Press, 2011). The quote is from page 60.

The Roan Highlands in the 1930s, by George Masa.

completed in 1952. Until then, it bypassed the Roan Highlands on a long, twenty-four-mile road walk maintained for many years by Paul Fink, a route that was eventually changed to a longer route — but a trail rather than a road (see page 307).

It would cross the Nolichucky River near Erwin and proceed to Spivey Gap, Sams Gap, Devils Fork Gap, Hot Springs, Max Patch, and Snowbird Mountain, finally arriving at Davenport Gap, named for a nineteenth-century surveyor, the eastern entrance to Great Smoky Mountains National Park. It would run past but not over Mount Guyot, named for the Swiss explorer and naturalist and professor at Princeton, who was the first to explore and map the area.[45]

Entering Great Smoky Mountains National Park, the trail first encountered Mount LeConte, a favorite climbing venue for hikers from

---

45. His manuscript, "Notes on the Geography of the Mountain District of Western North Carolina," was submitted to the government in 1863, apparently for military use during the Civil War. It lay unused in government files until rediscovered by Myron Avery in the 1930s and published by ATC. See page 102.

Paul Fink's road.

Knoxville.[46] Along the spine of the mountains in the Great Smoky Mountains National Park, it encountered Charlie's Bunion, named by Horace Kephart for Charles Connor. (On a trip to survey erosion damage in 1929, Kephart said the craggy formation had the "knobby appearance of Charlie Connor's bunion.") The strange rock formation had resulted from human activity — extensive logging had left much slash, and a fire in 1925 swept across the mountains, burning timber and sterilizing the soil to the extent that nothing would grow,[47] all subject to eroding rainstorms.

The only road across the park was at Newfound Gap, running east from Gatlinburg, Tennessee, to Bryson City, North Carolina. Just eight miles east of Gatlinburg was Clingmans Dome, at 6,643 feet the

46. Allen R Coggins, *Place Names of The Smokies* (Gatlinburg, Tenn.: Great Smoky Mountains Natural History Association, 1999), p. 107.
47. *Ibid*, p. 44.

highest point on the Appalachian Trail, named for Thomas Cling-man, a Confederate Army general and early Smoky Mountains ex-plorer.[48] (The road from Newfound Gap to the top of the mountain is the highest paved road in the eastern United States, and the moun-tain is the highest point in Tennessee.[49])

The southwestern boundary of the park was the Little Tennes-see River, without an obvious crossing point until Fontana Dam was built in the early 1940s to provide power for Oak Ridge National Laboratories, a federal scientific research center, part of the Manhat-tan Project. One could then walk across the top of the dam. (It is the highest dam in the eastern United States, and, when it was finished in 1944, it permitted a significant reroute of the Appalachian Trail.)[50]

The southern mountains are characterized by grass balds, high meadows populated by grasses, sedges, herbs, and wildflowers. They also sport "shrub balds," resembling the heaths of England with their low shrubs. Some of the most famous spots on the Appalachian Trail — Round Bald, Jane Bald, Grassy Ridge, Big Yellow Mountain, Hump Mountain, Roan Mountain — are grass or shrub balds.

Finding a route for the trail would involve locating it onto federal lands. In this, the A.T. was lucky, because many of the earliest east-ern national forests were in the South. Pisgah was the first national forest established under the Weeks Act of 1911, with its center near Asheville. Much of it was along the North Carolina side of the Ap-palachians and could provide public lands for the A.T.

The most promising national forest was Unaka, created in 1920. Its proclamation boundary ran all the way from a point south of Wy-theville, Virginia, to a point well south of the Nolichucky River and Erwin, Tennessee. The map on the next page shows the Unaka with its proclamation boundary in black. The green areas had already been acquired by the Forest Service, while everything else inside the proc-lamation boundary remained to be purchased. The Unaka was very large and spread out.

---

48. He was reputed to be the first person to measure its height.
49. Coggins, *op. cit.*, p. 48.
50. Leonard M. Adkins and ATC, *Images of America: Along the Appalachian Trail: Georgia, North Carolina and Tennessee.* (Charleston, S.C: Arcadia Publishing, 2012), p. 37.

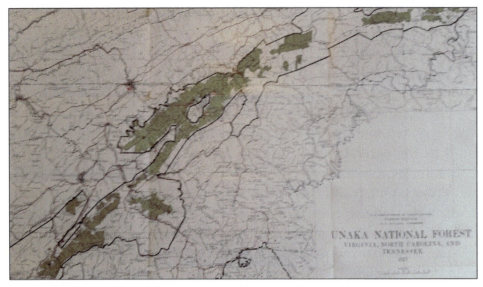

Unaka National Forest on the Virginia/North Carolina border.

In 1936, the extensive Unaka was divided into several national forests. The portion in Virginia became the Jefferson National Forest; in Tennessee, the Cherokee National Forest. The portion in North Carolina became part of the Pisgah, while the name Unaka ceased to be used. The resulting national forests provided federal protection for a long section of the trail.

Once beyond the Cherokee, the A.T. entered the Smokies, which provided national-park protection. South of the park, the trail would enter Nantahala National Forest, established in 1920. When it entered Georgia, it would be in the Chattahoochee National Forest, also officially established in 1920. Thus, technically, virtually no private land was crossed in the South. However, the Forest Service owned less than fifty percent of the land within the proclamation boundaries, and the rest of the land was private property, called inholdings, which would be of great concern for decades in the future.

Roy Ozmer's route, one remembers (see page 114), entered what would become the park at the Little Tennessee River and proceeded up to Silers Bald, then east to Clingmans Dome. While in the Smokies, he was on Smoky Mountains Hiking Club (SMHC) turf and did

Unaka National Forest, by George Masa.

not get on well with the club, mainly because his route planning did not accord with their idea of where the trail should be. But, Ozmer had the strong support of both Avery and Paul Fink. They accepted without question the contention of the Georgians that the southern terminus of the trail should be at Mount Oglethorpe in Georgia, not Cohutta or Lookout Mountain at Chattanooga in Tennessee, and that resulted in the arguments between Ozmer and the SMHC leadership in Knoxville. In this dispute, Fink sided with Avery, "I am heartily in accord with you in accepting Ozmer's revision of the A-T route." The terrain from Cohutta to Lookout Mountain was most uninteresting, he wrote.[51]

The dispute with SMHC leaders underlined an unusual disagreement between Arthur Perkins and Myron Avery. Perkins believed that local clubs should make local decisions and was temperamentally a compromiser on all the early disputes. Avery was a centralizer

51. McClung Collection: Paul M. Fink papers, Fink to Avery, July 28, 1929.

and believed that the route should be established at the ATC level, regardless of what local clubs felt. When Perkins visited Ozmer on one of the occasions when Ozmer was at home, laid up with back pains, he took the side of the Knoxville club. Avery wrote to Ozmer later, "The Judge told me that when he got into Knoxville some of the Smoky crowd seemed to resent you having blazed a route along the Smokies. They said it was their territory and you should have kept your profane foot out of it."[52]

The leaders — Perkins, Avery, and Fink — continued to struggle to find a mutually agreeable route through the South. Fink had earlier gone with Grandfather Mountain, but Avery had already moved the route westward, with Perkins' support. Perkins continued to favor the SMHC routing down to Cohutta in Georgia. The Knoxville group had laid out a route east of Newfound Gap, but they argued with Ozmer and Avery, still wanting the trail to include the entire length of the park, west of the gap. When Perkins effectively turned over leadership of ATC to Avery in 1931, no one had agreed on the route, and it was left to Avery to resolve the matter (see page 195).

In the late 1920s, a new and very influential player had entered the game. Vernon Rhoades was the Pisgah National Forest supervisor and had been named to the original ATC board, along with Paul Fink, in 1925. Rhoades suggested that the new trail use the existing Forest Service State Line Trail between North Carolina and Tennessee. Since the western boundary of the Pisgah was on the state line from a latitude opposite Elizabethton, Tennessee, all the way to the Pigeon River and the eastern boundary of the national park, this "State Line Trail" was probably that boundary. Today, that route would take in 185 trail miles, and the previous State Line Trail is probably most of that segment.

Forest Service officials in the South all supported MacKaye's long-distance trail and wanted it in their forests. W.H. Stoneburner, Unaka forest supervisor, wrote to Fink, "I am sure there will be no objection to designating the Trails on the Unaka National Forest as part of the Appalachian Trail System and am enclosing a map showing that part

52. PATC archives, Avery papers, Avery to Ozmer, October 20, 1929.

Vernon Rhoades, who in 1906 became one of the first graduates of Carl Alwin Schenk's forestry school at the Biltmore estate, went on to become one of America's most significant and distinguished foresters. After graduation, he worked for several years evaluating tracts of land for acquisition by the Forest Service. After the Weeks Act was passed in 1911, Rhoades began acquiring tracts to form what became the Pisgah National Forest (1916), the first national forest in the East. He also became one of two "Deep South" members (the other was Paul Fink) of the founding ATC board in 1925 and was one of the leaders in the creation of the Carolina Mountain Club. He and Avery worked together to establish a viable route for the A.T. in the South.

of the Forest where Mountain Top Trails have been completed."[53] The Forest Service's active enthusiasm for the trail played an absolutely key role in the success of the Appalachian Trail in the South. By the time Avery became involved, the die was already set.

Paul Fink, who knew more about the mountains in the South than anyone else involved with the A.T., remained convinced that the trail down the Blue Ridge should end at Grandfather Mountain in North Carolina and then switch over to the Unaka Mountains. Grandfather was close to the Unakas, and a connecting trail would be relatively short. At that point, the A.T. would be on federal land, where the Forest Service was already building trails.[54] (Today, a trail from Grandfather toward the west would hit the A.T. in only twelve miles.)

The leaders — Avery and Fink — continued to discuss the route. The matter was finally decided in a climactic meeting at Fink's home

---

53. McClung Collection: Rhoades to Fink, February 6, 1925, and Stoneburner to Fink, February 21.
54. ATC archives, MacKaye box, Fink to Harlan P. Kelsey, January 30, 1922.

in Jonesboro in January 1930. The group, minus Avery, decided once and for all to omit Grandfather and run the trail into the Unaka National Forest at its northern proclamation boundary near Byllesby Dam on the New River. This, Fink wrote to Avery, would eliminate both Grandfather and the Roan, a prediction that became only half true.[55] (Roan Mountain eventually was included on the A.T.)

South of Unaka, the trail would enter the Smokies. Although the new park had been authorized by Congress in 1925, little was known about the land at the time. Three pioneers — Fink, his hiking buddy Walter Diehl, and Horace Kephart — provided most of the information that was available in the 1920s.

Kephart and Fink

Horace Kephart, one of the pioneer advocates for the Smokies, was a librarian and a well-known writer on historical subjects. Working at a library in Saint Louis, Missouri, at the turn of the century, he became a clinically depressed alcoholic. He suffered from what would be termed today bipolar disorder, and, in 1904, he suffered a mental breakdown. During his worst period, he was hospitalized for four days. To recover his health, he struck out into the forest, disappearing for longer and longer periods of time. Eventually, he and his wife, Laura, agreed to a temporary separation, and she took their six children and moved to Ithaca, New York. In 1908, after the death of his father, he and his wife agreed to a final separation.

Kephart decided to live in the wilderness and try to restore his health. He disappeared into the North Carolina side of the Smokies and, in 1906, began publishing his findings and observations. His first book was *Camping and Woodcraft*, which Fink considered the best book on the subject ever written. Following that, however, was his most famous work, *Our Southern Highlanders*, which described the conditions in the Southern Appalachian highlands.

Published in 1913, it was an influential work that inspired much of the movement to create a park. Kephart threw himself into the park move-

---

55. PATC archives, Avery papers, Fink to Avery, January 24, 1930.

ment, and, in recognition of his influence, one of the peaks in the Smokies eventually was named after him. He died in an automobile accident in 1931, only a few days before the ATC conference was to open in Gatlinburg.[56]

Paul Fink was the second explorer of the southern mountains and, for the future A.T., the most significant. He began corresponding with Harlan Kelsey in 1922, and Kelsey once wrote, "So far as I am able to learn Paul Fink was the first person in the

From left, Paul Fink, Walter Diehl, and Myron Avery

south to be consulted about the A.T."[57] When Fink began hiking the region in 1914, there were no hiking trails, and what footpaths there existed were very primitive — just cow trails or narrow footpaths from one mountain cabin or grazing meadow to another. The states of North Carolina and Tennessee had sent surveyors to mark the state line, so there was a State Line Trail, not much more than a line of blazes on the border between the states.

Fink described the lower regions as beset by heavy timbering, occupied by moonshiners, with a few primitive trails with occasional blazes. William Johnson, an early president of SMHC,

Horace Kephart on the State Line Trail, by George Masa

---

56. PATC *Bulletin*, October 1946, p. 107. Some of this information was taken from a compact disc, Libby Kephart Hargrave (ed.), "An American Legend: Horace Kephart, His Life and Legacy."
57. ATC archives, Conference meetings, box 6-1-2.

wrote, "There was absolutely no trail along the top. Much of the travel was through brush, briers, or kalmia, not to mention downed timber."

Fink's book, *Backpacking was the Only Way*, described his early trips through the mountains. His first trip into the mountains was in 1914, with Walter Diehl, a young college graduate and later a member of PATC. Fink wrote that they had no idea how to backpack, carried bed rolls rather than packs, and wore street shoes and socks. Their gear improved when they adopted Army ruck sacks, and their outings became regular. Fink and Diehl, often joined by assorted companions, hiked all over the southern mountains — Roan Mountain, Big Bald, the Black Mountains, Rich Mountain, and, of course, the Smokies. Their first trips into the future national park began in 1916 with a hike to Mount LeConte.

In 1919, they tried to follow the state line in the eastern Smokies, reputedly the most difficult area to hike. On this trip, they followed the general route of the future A.T. But, without built trails, the going on all these trips was difficult in the extreme. Johnson described attempts to follow the state line, following crews that were blazing the line. "There were no maps. Neither were there any Park rangers to interrogate. The geographic knowledge of the mountaineers, beyond their restricted clearings, was limited indeed.... Grazing cattle at times left a trace of a route.... The State Line survey — when it could be followed — would indicate the route along the main ridge."[58]

Fink would try to follow that ridgeline, but the topography was so convoluted that he often followed branch ridges and, when he found himself heading downhill, would have to turn around and hike back up to where he had gone wrong. For Fink, the explorations were long and frustrating because the Appalachians in the Smokies spread out in all directions. Many places had hardly a central ridgeline at all.

---

58. Article by Johnson in the PATC *Bulletin*, October 1945, pp. 85-92. The best source for early Smokies exploration is Fink's *Backpacking was the Only Way* (Jonesboro, Tenn.: Research Advisory Council, 1975). The relationship between Kelsey and Fink is covered in ATC archives, Conference meetings, box 6-1-2, Guy Frizzell to Murray Stevens, January 20, 1955.

The Smokies

When Perkins and Avery were working on a trail route in the South, there were two hiking clubs in the area that had expressed interest in building the trail. The first was the Smoky Mountains Hiking Club (SMHC), which had been formed in Knoxville in 1924. The club became an active participant in the building and maintaining of a section of the A.T. through the park. The new club had strong leadership — Guy Frizzell, Harvey Broome, Jim Thompson, and Carlos Campbell. Dutch Roth led the club's first official hike on December 6, 1924. SMHC also had a wilderness bent and believed that the Smokies should be kept wild.

Benton MacKaye would live in Knoxville for about two years in the mid-1930s while employed by the Tennessee Valley Authority and exercised a strong influence on the club's later leadership. It was hardly coincidental that The Wilderness Society was established on an SMHC outing in 1934, partly as a revolt against Avery's dominance of ATC and Appalachian Trail management (see page 158).

The influence of MacKaye would lead to inherent conflicts between the SMHC leadership and Avery, who cared much less about wilderness than he did about a connected trail. It was paradoxical that Avery established close personal ties with the SMHC leadership. The club managed to work cooperatively with Avery, who they genuinely liked as a person and respected as a hiker and leader. (They had never seen anyone hike like Avery could — not even Paul Fink.)

Avery on Charlie's Bunion in 1937.

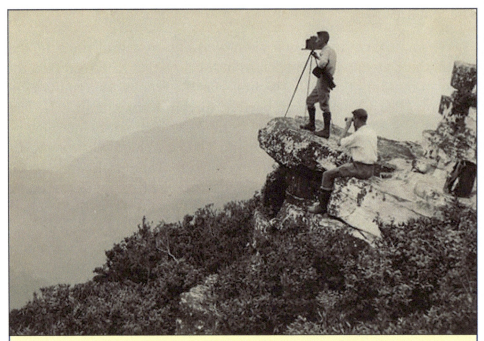

George Masa and Horace Kephart on the trail.

George Masa, born in Japan in 1881, came to the United States in 1901, settling in Asheville in 1915. A dedicated photographer, he began photographing the mountains around Asheville and measured long stretches of the Appalachian Trail with a measuring wheel. He died in 1933, only two years after the death of Horace Kephart, his close friend, hiking partner, and predecessor on the ATC board. Masa was the link between CMC and Myron Avery as long as he lived.

The other club was the Carolina Mountain Club (CMC), centered in Asheville on the North Carolina side of the Smokies. The tale of this club was much more complicated than that of SMHC, as the club rose, fell, and then rose again to become a major player of southern sections of the Appalachian Trail.

CMC was originally organized in June 1920 as the southern chapter of the Appalachian Mountain Club (AMC). Dr. Chase Ambler, who had been a leader in the campaign to secure the Weeks legislation, was its

Myron Avery (right) with leaders of the Smoky Mountains Hiking Club: Carlos Campbell, Dutch Roth, and Guy Frizzell.

first president. But, the relationship with AMC was beset by conflict over dues (see page 65) and CMC withdrew from AMC and now considers its origin to be in 1923, the year when it became fully independent.[59]

CMC did not at first enjoy smooth sailing. Within a few years, the club had become moribund, and, in 1929, Horace Kephart and famed photographer George Masa, spurred by the ever-present Avery, moved to revive the club. Only six people showed up for the initial meeting, but Avery continued to push Masa, and the following year Masa and Kephart tried again. This time, they drew nearly fifty people. Kephart, who was well known in those parts, was enlisted to chair the meeting, and he was supported by Vernon Rhoades of the Forest Service. Their new club was at first named the Carolina Appalachian Trail Club, after a naming convention that was becoming common along the trail. The new club conducted its first hike in February, and it drew fifty-six people. (Masa was surprised that sixty percent were women.)[60]

59. Carolina Mountain Club archives, University of North Carolina–Asheville Special Collections, "History of the Carolina Mountain Club," by Peter Steurer; article in the *ATN*, January 1964; PATC archives, Avery papers, CMC pamphlet.
60. Multiple sources cover the organization of what finally became CMC. See McClung Collection, Paul M. Fink papers: Kephart to Fink, October 2, 1929; Kephart to Fink, January 17,

BENTON MACKAYE'S FIRST SIGHT of the A in the SMOKIES
S·M·H·C·

The new club changed its name back to Carolina Mountain Club in 1937 and assumed responsibility for the entire distance from the northern boundary of the Smokies to the Virginia border. They also worked in Nantahala National Forest, but it was clear that such a small club lacked the capacity even to keep the trail through the Unakas clear, let alone going south of the Little Tennessee River into the Nantahalas. The Nantahalas awaited another savior.

The new club was an improvement over the old one but tended to wax and wane, depending on the leadership. In 1940, the club finally got a dynamic president. His name was Arch Nichols, and he became one of the most storied trail blazers in the South.

Myron Avery first went to the Smokies in 1929. On the way back from a trip to Mobile, Alabama, he stopped in Knoxville and met the SMHC leadership. He then spent three days hiking with SMHC and

1930; Masa to Fink, February 9, 1931; Kephart to Fink, January 2, 1920; also, ATC archives, Avery correspondence, 1930-1932, Masa to Perkins, January 8, 1931; and William A. Hart's article, "George Masa: The Best Mountaineer," in Robert Brunk (ed.), *May We All Remember Well*, Volume 1, 1997, pp. 249-275.

formed a close bond with the club's leaders. It was the first of several hiking trips in the national park, scouting a route all the way from Davenport Gap in the east to Gregory Bald in the west. Along with Fink and Diehl, he hiked the State Line Trail, following a route that had originally been blazed by surveyors.

Of course, considerable scouting had already been done, and Avery's trip was, in a way, to "certify" the route already selected. It was not that Avery was the first northerner that SMHC

Arch Nichols in 1983

had seen. Perkins and Torrey had already visited, and Fink had been on the ATC board since the organization was created in 1925. It must have been Avery's dynamic personality that fascinated SMHC. For his part, Avery was impressed with the Smokies crowd and commented to Perkins that "Fink certainly lived up to the glowing press notices."[61]

Avery and Fink worked together, long distance, to plan the trail route in the Smokies and, to a lesser extent, in the Nantahala, Pisgah, and Unaka forests. They went back to Guyot's descriptions of the area, matching places on the current map with those that Guyot had identified. Avery also worked closely with Masa and used Masa's photographs to add to the route description. Meanwhile, Fink held a series of planning sessions in his home in Jonesboro. Their correspondence was voluminous and detailed. Avery hiked various parts of the proposed trail in 1930, 1932, and 1933.[62]

Owing to the Park Service's penchant for control, trail-building in the Smokies was fraught with disputes. Harvey Broome complained to Avery in 1932 that the route they had selected in the eastern Smokies was in jeopardy because the Park Service had marked a horse trail

61. PATC archives, Avery papers, Avery to Perkins, July 24, 1929.
62. McClung Collection, Paul M. Fink papers.

Smoky Mountains Hiking Club's first thru-hike from Davenport Gap to Clingmans Dome (1932). Harvey Broome is second from left, kneeling; Guy Frizzell is at top right; and Carlos Campbell, at back center.

on the North Carolina side of the ridgeline, and that might become the A.T.[63] (It did not.) The Park Service decided in 1932 that volunteers would not be permitted to maintain the trail. Broome wrote Avery, "It was inadvisable for us to do any trail work in the Park area, that they preferred to do it on their own and were very particular as to how it was done."[64] That was typical of the early attitudes of Park Service rangers, who tended to look down on volunteers. The Park Service blew hot and cold on blazing, but mostly it disliked it and refused to do it. Marcus Book, the president of CMC, reported that the A.T. in the western Smokies was almost impossible to follow because the Park Service did not paint blazes.[65] And, as in Shenandoah National Park, actual construction of A.T. in the Smokies was by the CCC, not by volunteers.

The fiercest arguments were over shelters. A long-held agreement among ATC, the Park Service, and the Forest Service assumed that shel-

63. McClung Collection, Harvey Broome papers, Broome to Avery, September 22, 1932.
64. McClung Collection, Broome papers: SMHC Board Minutes, 1929-1959; Broome to Avery, July 26, 1932.
65. PATC archives, Avery papers, 1931, ATC letter report #2, October 1935.

ters were essential for long-distance hiking, and the unilateral action by the Smokies park superintendent not to build shelters agitated Avery and brought down the wrath of his friend Cammerer (see chapter 3.)[66]

The clamor over skyline drives eventually hit the Smokies. In 1932, Cammerer wrote to Dutch Roth of SMHC of a plan to build a drive along the ridgeline west of Newfound Gap, leaving the eastern Smokies still primitive. It would, he explained, be a tourist road, to terminate either at Cades Cove or Deals Gap. It was Park Service policy, Cammerer explained, to make the delights of nature accessible to those who could not put on a pack and hike long distances.[67] But, the threat mysteriously disappeared, and the Smokies, unlike Shenandoah, did not have to live with a crestline road.

West of Newfound Gap, the trail route was a muddle. The Georgians were advocating for the terminus at Burnt Mountain (later renamed Oglethorpe), a routing that would use Ozmer's proposal to go south from Silers Bald directly to the Little Tennessee. The Smoky Mountains Hiking Club wanted the trail to continue west from Silers Bald the entire length of the park, with an eventual terminus at Lookout Mountain in Tennessee. Paul Fink supported the terminus in Georgia and wrote to Dutch Roth, advising him to terminate A.T. markers at Silers Bald.[68]

Perkins, ever the compromiser, tried to wiggle out of the muddle by advocating both routes. The Georgians could have Oglethorpe, and the Tennesseans could have Lookout Mountain or, at the least, Cohutta. (He turned up his nose at continuing to Lookout Mountain, characterizing the route from Cohutta to Chattanooga as a "tourist road," nothing more.[69]) As for construction and maintenance, SMHC was already capable of building the Cohutta route, while the club that was languishing in Asheville should, it was felt, be revived and assigned to build the Trail from Silers Bald to the Georgia border.[70]

66. PATC archives, Avery papers, 1937: Avery to Cammerer, December 4, 1937; Cammerer to Avery, March 8, 1938.
67. Hunter Library, Sherman Collection, Cammerer to Frizzell, November 23, 1932.
68. McClung Collection: Fink to Roth, August 23, 1929. Silers Bald was named for Jesse Richardson Siler, who once owned the land and grazed livestock on the bald.
69. ATC archives, Perkins box, Perkins to Kephart, June 15, 1930.
70. *Ibid*, Perkins to Fink, January 8, 1930. *Q.v.* Hunter Library, Kephart papers, Perkins to Kephart, January 22, 1930.

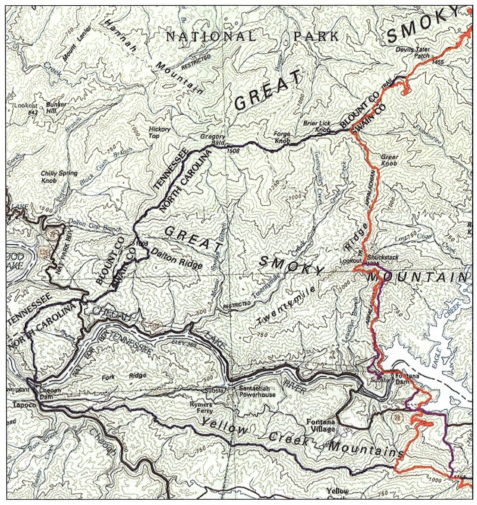

Competing routes out of the Smokies: Ozmer in red; SMHC in black at left.

Kephart, who was not at all enthused with the Cohutta terminus, urged that the Perkins compromise be adopted to solve the increasingly acrimonious dispute. Split the trail at Silers Bald, he wrote. A trail to Mount Oglethorpe could continue down the Ozmer route, over the Little Tennessee, and on through Nantahala National Forest. But, a second route also was possible: Continue the trail past Silers through the park, across Gregory Bald, down Twentymile Creek to Rymers Ferry, and across the river there. The problem with that route was that, as Roth and Carlos Campbell pointed out, Rymers Ferry had no ferry, and no plans were in place for one. So, they advocated continuing along the state line *via* Daltons Gap and Deals Gap to the river and crossing it below the old Cheoah dam at Tapoco. Then, they argued, build a trail that doubled back eastward along Yellow Creek Mountain, meeting the planned A.T. in the Nantahalas at a convenient spot, such as Cheoah Bald or Tellico Gap.[71]

Perkins approved the Kephart proposal.[72] At once, it would solve the problem of dual termini and give SMHC what it wanted — a trail through almost the entire length of the Smokies — but with a terminus at Oglethorpe. The problem, of course, was the need to revive a trail club in Asheville and convince it to take on the trail through the Nantahalas. In the short run, this did not happen. CMC decided to work on the trail north of the Smokies, not south. The trail from the Little Tennessee to the Georgia line became an orphan and remained so for many years.

Avery felt that, given the approved Kephart compromise, it was up to SMHC to find the route from Tapoco back to connect with the trail in the Nantahala National Forest. The route finally selected was the only logical one — from Tapoco along Yellow Creek Mountain, then eastward from there to Cheoah Bald, and then to Tellico Gap, where a trail already was in place.[73]

SMHC did, in fact, scout a new route from Tapoco, but the club had all it could handle with the trail through the Smokies. Harvey Broome was concerned that it was already over-extended.[74] The trail remained in this location until after Fontana Dam was finished in 1944. Then, the trail was rerouted from Doe Knob down past Shuckstack and over the dam — in general, the original Ozmer plan.

The Nantahalas

Farther south, the Nantahalas were in desperate shape. SMHC had done some trail scouting from Tapoco to Cheoah Bald, but it

71. ATC archives, Avery correspondence, 1930-1932, Kephart to Avery, April 4, 1931.
72. *Ibid*, Perkins to Avery, February 21, 1930.
73. McClung Collection, Broome papers, Avery to John Byrne (Nantahala National Forest supervisor), June 30, 1931.
74. *Ibid*, Broome to Avery, November 19, 1931; Fink papers, Fink to Avery, July 1, 1932.

made no long-standing commitments. Avery hiked the area in 1933, accompanied by Carlos Campbell, Dutch Roth, and Guy Frizzell, but that did not result in finding a maintaining club. A so-called Nantahala Hiking Club emerged, but its president, George Tabor, died in 1936, and the club collapsed. A nascent Kephart Hiking Club in Bryson City, North Carolina, scouted the trail route around Cheoah Bald, Swim Bald, Grassy Gap, and the Nantahala River. After Kephart died in 1931, nothing more was heard from it.

Avery wrote to his board of managers that the Forest Service declined to put much effort into trails in that area because, they contended, it was little used by hikers. Orville Crowder hiked through the Nantahalas in 1940 and wrote to Avery that he saw few hikers: "We need desperately an active maintaining organization for this section."[75]

The Nantahalas continued without any progress toward a trail organization until 1938, when an Episcopal priest from Franklin, North Carolina, wrote to Avery of his interest in the A.T. Avery wrote back, "I am sorry to say that Mr. Tabor is dead, and the small organization of which he was the principal figure disintegrated upon his death." Avery told the minister, A. Rufus Morgan, that the Wilderness Hikers club was now maintaining in the Nantahalas. (This never actually happened, but, in 1938, it appeared to Avery that that was the only hope down there.)

Two-and-a-half years went by without any word from the minister in Franklin. In January 1941, the correspondence renewed. Avery wrote to Morgan that the pressing need down there was to paint blazes, and he was hoping that Morgan would do the job. Morgan replied to Avery that he had hiked the A.T. in the Smokies and Nantahalas and was inclined to take on the blazing project.

Avery called Arch Nichols into action. Nichols was the president of the newly revived Carolina Mountain Club, and he was determined to see what kind of a man this Morgan was. Nichols, accompanied by Marcus Book, attempted to meet with Morgan, driving from Asheville to Franklin. They talked with neighbors and got glowing reports of the preacher's hiking prowess but couldn't find him. They drove

---

75. ATC archives, Avery correspondence, Crowder to Avery, October 23, 1940.

to the parish hall, and people said he was home, but, when they went to the house, he wasn't there, and neighbors thought he might be at the parish hall. They returned to Asheville frustrated, but Nichols was not going to give up and wrote to Avery, "We'll see if he can paint as good as he can walk."[76]

Nichols and Morgan finally linked up and got out on the trail together, and it turned out the minister could, indeed, paint as well as he could walk. Nichols wrote to Morgan after the trip, "I am sure I speak for the Appalachian Trail Conference Board of Directors [sic] as well as myself in thanking you for your enthusiasm and interest in our project. The hike with you last Saturday was a great pleasure for me." In letters to Avery, he referred to Morgan as "one of my C.M.C. strong-arm men...."[77]

The Rev. A. Rufus Morgan leading a sunrise service at the 1958 ATC meeting.

Avery tried to work out a division of labor between Morgan, who was a one-man trail club, and the Wilderness Hikers. He suggested two sections, totally about 17 miles, a large order by today's standards but much more usual in 1941.[78] The Wilderness Hikers never became a force, and Morgan did his own thing, eventually taking on an unbelievable 55 miles of the A.T., the longest section that any maintainer ever did. Crowder, who had just walked the Nantahalas, wrote Morgan thanking him that the "lost trail in the Nantahalas has fallen into such good hands."[79]

76. ATC archives, Avery correspondence, Nichols to Avery, March 4, 1941.
77. *Ibid*, Nichols to Avery, March 28, 1941.
78. *Ibid*, Avery to Morgan, April 11, 1941; to Morgan, April 5; Morgan to Avery, April 29.
79. *Ibid*, Crowder to Morgan, March 9, 1941.

Georgia

It is uncertain who finally decided that the Appalachian Trail would end in Georgia. The ATC conference in 1925 had decided that it would end at Cohutta Mountain, although no one on the board of managers had actually seen it. According to one writer, "That decision was based solely on a line drawn on a map, without any ground reconnaissance."[80] When, in 1929, Perkins and Avery commissioned Roy Ozmer to begin scouting a trail route in the south, it appears that Ozmer, who was from Georgia, decided by himself that it would begin in Georgia (see page 114). He met no objection from either Perkins or Avery.

Ozmer had held several meetings with Horace Kephart, also an advocate of a Georgia route. If the trail were to end in Georgia, where should it be? Avery seemed to have the answer — at Burnt Mountain, which, Avery wrote to Perkins, a Georgia state geologist had told Raymond Torrey was the most southerly mountain in the Appalachian chain.[81] (This was, of course, where Ozmer had begun his hike.)

In a long letter to Perkins, Avery discussed the Burnt Mountain issue. He concluded by advising Perkins, "I think in the final analysis we should be covered by the views of Fink and Ozmer.... My personal view is to have the route followed by Ozmer marked as the A.T. trail."

In 1929, a new figure had emerged. Everett B. "Eddie" Stone was the assistant state forester for Georgia and a passionate advocate for the Georgia route. Stone was a bulldog off his chain, a true force in the scrap over the southern terminus. He was in touch with Ozmer, Avery, and Kephart when the Ozmer hike was first discussed and advocated that it begin at Burnt Mountain.

Kephart visited Burnt Mountain in 1929 and supported the change from Cohutta. Writing to Fink, he described the "360-degree cyclorama" atop the mountain.[82] In late 1929, he and Masa made a pilgrimage back to Burnt Mountain and were greeted by Sam Tate, a developer who planned a large development on the mountain. He looked at this new

---

80. Frank Wright, "Anchor of the Deep South," *A.T. Journeys*, November/December 2005.
81. . GATC, *op. cit.*, Avery to Perkins, July 24, 1929.
82. McClung Collection, Fink Papers, Kephart to Fink, January 2, 1929..

trail as another amenity that he could trumpet in his advertisements — the southern end of a 2,000-mile trail! Tate didn't like the name of the mountain, though, and went to the Georgia legislature to get it changed to Oglethorpe. James Oglethorpe, the original founder of the colony, was a magical name in the state, and this, too, would surely lure buyers to Tate's development. The Tate group even erected a monument to James Oglethorpe.

The Oglethorpe decision, made at the Jonesboro meeting at Fink's home, received a passionate endorsement from Stone, who would have things no other way. The decision to adopt the Georgia route and the

Eddie Stone

Oglethorpe terminus owed much to his dedicated advocacy.

The decision was essentially confirmed by Perkins himself, who wrote to Avery in May 1930, "I think Oglethorpe is very much preferable because it adds a good many miles to the length of the Trail and brings it down to a point much more accessible."[83]

It only remained to change the ATC constitution, which still read "Cohutta." At the 1930 conference, Ozmer made the presentation for Stone, who was not able to attend, using photos by George Masa to depict the route through the Carolinas and Georgia. It was an easy sell, and the conference voted to change the terminus from Cohutta to Oglethorpe.[84]

Perkins cautioned Avery not to talk to MacKaye about the decision, with good reason. Privately, MacKaye criticized Oglethorpe. "The southern terminus, selected without my knowledge, is Mount

---

83. ATC archives, Perkins box.
84. Frank Wright, "Anchor of the Deep South," *A.T. Journeys,* November/December 2005, pp. 24-28.

The Mount Oglethorpe monument, by George Masa

Oglethorpe in Georgia. With utter respect for the great James Edward Oglethorpe and for the great State of Georgia, I want to say that nothing more inappropriate than a man-made monument could possibly be selected to mark the terminus of the wilderness footpath from Maine to Georgia — the Appalachian Trail."[85]

The selection of Oglethorpe was unfortunate. It was the wrong place for a number of reasons unrelated to a monument. The terminus rested on private property, not national forest land, and became subject to all the vicissitudes of private-property ownership. It made

Fashionable hikers of the 1930s.

the first fourteen miles of the Appalachian Trail a road walk rather than a hiking trail.

Just north of Oglethorpe was the then-titled Cherokee National Forest (now Chattahoochee–Oconee National Forest) with its spectacular waterfall at Amicalola (at 729 feet, the highest falls east of the Rockies), and a hiking trail to the summit of Springer Mountain. As early as the 1937 ATC conference, the subject of moving the terminus north came up. Nothing was done in 1937, but it was truly only a matter of time before someone pushed a different solution.

In 1929, Eddie Stone wrote to Avery about trail clubs. He had a copy of the PATC *Bulletin* and wrote that he hoped to organize a similar club in Georgia. Stone's assistant, Charles Elliott, was devoted to Stone, but their personalities were very different. While Stone was single-minded and as persistent as a Rottweiler, Elliott was easy-going and humorous, a friendly raconteur in a social setting. Together, they formed the team that established the Georgia Appalachian Trail Club.[86]

Stone talked to Elliott, and Elliott advertised a meeting in the local news media. They decided to begin in Gainesville, at the Boy Scout hall, but, at the appointed time, no one came. A second meeting netted only the janitor. It was a dismal start to a new adventure,

---

86. PATC archives, Avery papers, Stone to Avery, May 15, 1929. Krickel (note 84 above) has the best description of both individuals.

but a third meeting, held in Dahlonega, drew 30 people, and the new club was off and running. One of the attendees was a young newspaperman from Atlanta named Warner Hall. Hall was to become the lynchpin of the Georgia Appalachian Trail Club.

Elliott began advertising hikes, and those drew more people than did meetings. The hike leader was Hall, and his engaging and outgoing personality drew increasing flocks of people. A photograph of a group of hikers on Hall's first hike up Blood Mountain in 1930 shows twelve people crowding into the picture, including four women in dresses and furs. Some men wore coats and ties, as was the fashion for hikers in the early 1930s.[87] Blood Mountain is not an easy climb under any circumstance, and it must have been especially difficult in that apparel.

The new club obtained its first locked cabin in 1931, at Amicalola Falls, with funds donated by Sam Tate. Stone claimed to have marked 90 miles of the projected 130 miles in Georgia, and, as an attention-getter, he recruited three Boy Scouts to finish the job. Their odyssey was timed to end at Oglethorpe on the day that Tate dedicated the monument atop the mountain.

Another notable spot in Georgia was Neel Gap, at the foot of Blood Mountain. Formerly known as Frogtown Gap (or Walasi-Yi, Cherokee for the Great Frog), most of the land was owned by a Mr. Vogel, a Midwestern resident who had acquired large acreage there to provide wood for his tannery. (It was Vogel who donated the land for what is now Vogel State Park.) The state built a road through Neel Gap in 1930 — a Mr. Neel was the chief engineer for the project.

In 1933, the CCC built the Walasi-Yi Center in the gap as a lodge for its workers, and it was converted to an inn in 1937. The CCC — whether officially or through some volunteers "off the clock" is not clear in the historical record — also built the large stone shelter atop Blood Mountain, an enduring monument to CCC engineering and one of the most iconic shelters on the Appalachian Trail.[88]

87. Wright, *op. cit.*
88. Multiple sources: Larry Luxenberg. *Walking the Appalachian Trail* (Mechanicsburg, Pa.: Stackpole Books, 1994), p. 4; Shaffer, *op. cit.*, p. 16; interview with Georgeanna Seamon, owner of the store and campground at Neel Gap, September 21, 2014.

Warner Hall became the longtime president of GATC and the face of the club. One of the people who moved in his orbit was Dr. George Noble, an Atlanta physician and sculptor. Hall convinced Noble to sculpt the image of a hiker, to be placed strategically in locations on the Trail in Georgia to lend dignity to the section. The first bronze plaques were placed at Neel Gap, on Springer Mountain, and at Unicoi Gap. Curiously, no plaque was ever installed on Oglethorpe.

Hall was persuaded to be the model for the hiker on the plaque, and he is credited with creating the well-known phrase found on it: "A footpath for those who seek fellowship with the wilderness."[89]

Warner Hall posing for the Georgia bronze plaques.

Eddie Stone left Georgia in 1934. It was announced at the time that he had accepted a position with the Park Service in Washington, D.C. Hall wrote to Avery at the time, "The State forester who is making the change has never looked upon trail building as of much importance or interest, except possibly to a few boy scouts. He thinks our Georgia group is merely a small group of fanatics."[90]

Stone was either asked to leave or left out of frustration from the lack of support for his efforts from his supervisory chain. He battled supervi-

89. Dave Sherman e-mail to the author, November 18, 2015.
90. GATC, *op. cit.*, Stone to Avery, p. 63.

sors to get recognition for his trail. He opposed proposals to build skyline drives anywhere near his new trail. Stone must have been a thorn in the side of his superiors, much as he had been to anyone in the volunteer community who opposed his insistence that the trail run through his state all the way to Oglethorpe.

GATC in the early years was small and hard-pressed to maintain 120 miles of trail. Avery constantly chided the group about marking the trail. He understood that the group was too small to keep the trail clear constantly, but he insisted on frequent blazing to keep hikers on the trail. In 1934, he wrote, "After all, the only absolute reliance in marking is judiciously placed paint blazes. They stay. Even if your trail is overgrown, it can be easily followed." Galvanized markers would be too expensive to be used frequently. Paint was the only solution.[91]

The maintenance battle continued for years. GATC was based mainly in Atlanta, many miles from the A.T., and was constantly defending its maintenance records against Avery's criticism. Lovejoy Harwell, the GATC chair for trails and shelters, pleaded to Avery to acknowledge "some of the difficulties we are confronted with here in Georgia so that they [hikers] will not judge us too harshly when they find parts of the trail in such poor shape."[92]

The club was getting no help from the Forest Service, whose officials did not believe in the trail project through Georgia. Forest Service leaders complained that the trail was little used, and they, in turn, avoided putting resources into its maintenance. The Chattahoochee forest supervisor wrote to Avery in 1945, "As near as I can determine not a single person traveled the entire length of the trail in Georgia in 1944."[93] (What that had to do with trail maintenance remains a mystery, and 1944, being the last full year of World War II, was probably not a good example of missed hiking opportunities.)

---

91. *Ibid*, pp. 62-63.
92. ATC archives, Jean Stephenson correspondence, Harwell to Avery, October 27, 1939.
93. *Ibid*, C.K. Spaulding to Avery, March 31, 1945. Paul Pritchard, who headed ATC in the 1970s, complained that, during his time in ATC, that was still the case, and the Forest Service in Georgia was content with just a thin strip of trees on either side of the trail as environmental protection: Interview with Pritchard, May 12, 2014.

The Trail in the South

The South was Avery's territory. The Appalachian Trail in the North preceded Avery and was well-developed in many places. South of Delaware Water Gap, Avery was, alone, the undisputed leader. He was, in most cases south of the gap, not the original scout, but he managed the entire operation, personally walked every foot, and made routing decisions himself. He made the word "leader" a very meaningful term.

Avery's correspondence with the southern clubs was rarely infected with the sharp jabs, innuendos, and personal insults that characterized many of his letters to the New England leaders. His image in the South was very different than his in the North. Despite the occasional disputes that characterized his leadership, he remained a shining star to the southern clubs.

When the Blue Ridge Parkway threatened to wipe out the pre-World War II A.T., Avery proposed moving it from just south of here (Humpback Rocks), going east to the Religious Range. See pages 174-175.

Chapter 5

THE TRAIL THROUGH THE NORTH

The Appalachian Trail is a single integral unit. It is to be treated as such a unit. Its practices and standards are prescribed by the Appalachian Trail Conference. It is not a federation of fourteen different state trails.

— Myron Avery

The Appalachian Trail was started in the North, and, when Myron Avery began his work there, the trail was a *fait accompli* in many areas. The careful spadework necessary in the South was needed only in some places. Yet, in spite of that, the North was more challenging for Avery.

Avery, in typical fashion, began working in Maryland and Pennsylvania simultaneously from the Harpers Ferry footpath he had established. But, Pennsylvania was further along, because it already had a vibrant hiking culture and many trail clubs. In some ways, it resembled the situation in New York City, with its hiking culture and large number of clubs.

Pennsylvania

When one looks at the geologic map of the state, it resembles a rug kicked into folds. The folds slash the central part of the state from northeast to southwest. The ridges tend to be fairly low, seldom exceeding 2,000 feet in height, crossed occasionally by gaps. The ridgelines have been worn down to their base rock layer. The state is infamous for its rocky trails — sharp, pointed rocks sticking up through the dirt, with occasional large boulder fields. For hikers, the downside is constantly watching one's feet, but the upside is fewer steep up-and-down portions, and the ridges tend to be at a constant elevation.

The state was one of the first to develop a culture of forest conservation, owing partly to the presence of Gifford Pinchot, the leading conservationist in the country. Pinchot served as the first chief of the United States Forest Service, from 1905 until his removal in 1910, and was the twenty-eighth governor of Pennsylvania, serving from 1923 to 1927 and again from 1931 to 1935. Pinchot promoted scientific forestry: the controlled, profitable management of forests and other resources to the maximum benefit of the nation.

Locally, the "father" of Pennsylvania forests was Dr. Joseph Rothrock. In the last decades of the 19th century, the forests of Pennsylvania were being cut at an alarming rate. In 1895, Rothrock, a University of Pennsylvania professor, was appointed the first commissioner of the Pennsylvania Department of Forests and Waters. In 1897, the legislature began the state forest system by authorizing the purchase of "unseated lands for forest reservations." The fact that the state already had created a forest system was of major importance for the Appalachian Trail.

By the turn of the century, Pennsylvania had created two forests that were in the direct path of Avery's planned trail route. Mont Alto was the more southerly of the two and was important for being the location of Rothrock's forestry school, the first in the state. The more northerly of the two was Michaux State Forest, named after André Michaux, the French botanist who had been dispatched to the colonies by Louis XVI to gather plants for the Royal Gardens in Paris. Both state forests were created as a direct result of the depletion of forests by timber companies and Rothrock's insistent promotion of forest reserves. The two forests were separated by what is now U.S. 30 and Caledonia State Park.

Yet a third state forest was involved, that of Tuscarora. It was established in 1902 as the Rothrock Forest Reserve, and its importance here was that there were two competing routes for the Appalachian Trail west of Harrisburg. One of them would go through Michaux and Mont Alto; the other, along Tuscarora Mountain.[1]

Although many informal hiking groups operated in the state, the first one to organize a statewide club was the Pennsylvania Alpine Club, with chapters in various towns. The club was the brainchild of one Henry Shoemaker (1880-1958) from New York City. He was the son of Henry Francis Shoemaker (1845–1918), a railroad magnate, investment banker, and close confidant of future senator Charles W. Fairbanks. His mother, Blanche Quiggle, who was the sole daughter of railroad magnate and diplomat Col. James W. Quiggle of Philadelphia and Lock Haven, obviously had roots in Pennsylvania. Although he grew up in New York, young Henry summered in Pennsylvania and was intrigued with the state. After service in the State Department and the military, Shoemaker, a campaign write for Pinchot, became a stockbroker and still later published several local Pennsylvania newspapers, moving to an estate that he inherited in McElhattan, a town on the West Branch of the Susquehanna River in north-central Pennsylvania. He became renowned as a writer on the subject of Pennsylvania folklore.

Shoemaker, a strong conservationist, advocated the preservation of forest land and was distressed by the ravages of the timber and mining industries. It was his interest in conservation that moved him toward hiking, and, in 1917, he established the Pennsylvania Alpine Club. The club grew to more than 2,500 members across the state, and the Harrisburg Chapter built the Darlington Trail, which was to become the first designated section of the Appalachian Trail in Pennsylvania.[2] The club, dominant in the early years, disbanded in the late

1. Much of the information for this section was taken from an Avery article in *American Motorist*, April 1931.
2. One of the best accounts of early hiking in Pennsylvania, and of the Pennsylvania Alpine Club, can be found in Silas Chamberlain's master's thesis, *op. cit*. Shoemaker's biography was found at Wikipedia.org. Shoemaker formed a folklore group with Darlington.

1930s. Shoemaker's club was important more for its promotion of conservation than for its continuing importance in the trail movement.

Frank Schairer of PATC was dismissive of the Alpine Club's efforts, noting that, so far, it had only built the six-mile segment (the Darlington Trail) from the Susquehanna River to Lambs Gap. Judge Perkins, who attended an Alpine Club meeting in 1929, ridiculed the proceedings.

> *I am a good deal amused by the report of the meeting of the Pennsylvania Alpine Club. You know I was out there a year ago when they had a meeting.... As perhaps you can imagine, a mountain club which requires a Grand Chaplain, a Chief Guide, and a Chorister and a Poetess, is not exactly the kind of a club that we are used to.... Add to this the fact that all the members of the Alpine Club are members of the Pennsylvania Folklore Society, and you won't be surprised that they do a good deal more talking than climbing.*[3]

The club that came to represent the interests of hikers and trailbuilders was the Blue Mountain Eagle Climbing Club of Reading, Pennsylvania. That club evolved from a hiking group called the *Fussgangers* (a German word for walkers or hikers). The legend for the beginning of the formal club revolved around the discovery of an eagle's nest, ascribed to Dr. Harry Rentschler of Reading. Rentschler reported that he had found an eagle's nest on Blue Mountain near Shartlesville (a small town northwest of Reading), and the *Fussgangers*, led by a former mayor of Reading, decided to climb to the spot where Rentschler had seen the eagle's nest.

When they arrived, on June 15, 1916, there were no eagles. (Some say the nest was still there, but even that is uncertain.) But, they returned in October of the same year, inspired by Rentschler's eagle sighting, and formed the Blue Mountain Eagle Climbing Club. William Shanaman became president, and Rentschler was the secretary. Although Rentschler never became president, he was the true founder of hiking and trail building in Pennsylvania.[4]

---

3. ATC archives, Perkins Box, Perkins to Avery, May 5, 1929.
4. At least two accounts of the founding of the club are available: Rita Floriani, "Blue

From left, Harry Rentschler, Raymond Torrey, William Shanaman, and Judge Arthur Perkins.

The club, typical of hiking clubs in those days, was restricted to prominent businessmen and had a strong element of conservation, religion, and patriotism. They would hold religious services and sing "America." Shanaman remained president until his death in 1939. Daniel K. Hoch, who was to become prominent in the history of the trail, succeeded him and was president for another twenty years, 1939–1959.

The seminal event in the history of Pennsylvania's A.T. section occurred in 1926. That was the year that Eugene Bingham, chairman of the chemistry department at Lafayette College in Easton, Penn-

Mountain Club Celebrates 90 Years," in *A.T. Journeys*, September/October 2006, pp. 42-44; and Paul R. Lehman, *Blue Mountain Eagle Climbing Club, Keepers of the Appalachian Trail,* at berkshistory.org. An Eagle's Nest Shelter is today near the spot where the original eagle's nest was said to be found.

sylvania, established a new club, the Blue Mountain Club (not to be confused with the Blue Mountain Eagle Climbing Club).[5] Bingham, who had heard about Benton MacKaye's new trail project, contacted BMECC and asked them to join his club in building the new trail from Delaware Water Gap to the Susquehanna River.

BMECC leaders met with Bingham on October 30, 1926, after the annual hike to the spot of the eagle's nest. Bingham's club had already decided to build a 35-mile section from Delaware Water Gap to Lehigh Gap and urged BMECC to take on the rest of the project, the 102 miles to the Susquehanna River. Rentschler took the lead, and the club plunged enthusiastically into the project. The first work trip was recorded in Rentschler's diary:

Sky Line Trail - 1st training, Sunday, Nov. 21, 1926. Members: Wm. R. Shanaman, Truman Temple, S.I. Goss, D.K. Hoch, Nick Phillipson, H.F. Rentschler, E.D. Greenawalt, Wm. Burkey, John O. Baer and nephew, Clarence Rahn. Left Reading at 9 o'clock; parked machine at John O. Baer home, Mountain, 10:45. Proceeded up the mountain. The trail was started by placing a marker close to the Berks and Lehigh Co. marker. Proceeded westward for ½ mile on the Drech road...to the high point known as Baer's Ridge.[6]

In five years, BMECC was ready to open the twenty-mile section west of Port Clinton. This Berks section of the Appalachian Trail was formally dedicated on October 12, 1931. Present for the occasion (see page 156) were both Myron Avery and Benton MacKaye.[7]

As seen in that diary excerpt, the trail in Pennsylvania was known originally as the Sky Line Trail, so named by the Blue Mountain Club. Its proposed route from Delaware Water Gap to the Susquehanna followed Blue Mountain, moving along the relatively level ridgeline, through Lehigh Gap, Swatara Gap, and Manada Gap before reach-

---

5. Article in the *Lafayette College Newspaper*, April 26, 1926, according to an e-mail from Barbara Wiemann on August 19, 2012.
6. Rentschler diary entry provided by Barbara Wiemann on December 30, 2015. The site of the marker can be located with fair precision on the current Keystone Trails Association trail maps.
7. Floriani, *op. cit.*

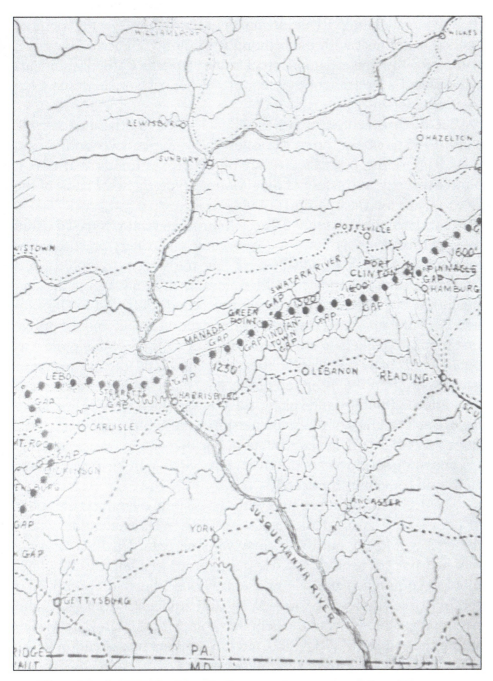

The original 1927 Sky Line Trail proposal, reproduced from Blue Mountain Club Bulletin #2.

ing the Susquehanna River just north of Harrisburg. At this point, it needed to connect with the Bishop Darlington Trail across the river, named for the Episcopal bishop of Saint Stephens Cathedral in Harrisburg and a prominent member of the Pennsylvania Alpine Club (see pages 24 and 87).

But, no direct connection was available. Hikers either had to walk south to Harrisburg, cross the river on an automobile bridge, and walk back north, or cross illegally on a railroad bridge that took it almost directly to the foot of Blue Mountain on the west bank of the river, where the Darlington Trail began.

Years later, the Indiantown Gap Military Reservation forced the trail off Blue Mountain because the area became an artillery practice range for the Pennsylvania National Guard. The trail was moved northward from Swatara Gap, up Second Mountain, then Stony Mountain, and finally to Peters Mountain, where it proceeded southwest to Duncannon. At Duncannon, it crossed over the river on an automobile bridge that permitted hikers to cross. One of the attractions of this route was public land. State gamelands already existed, and the expansion of gamelands from the inception of the state gamelands commission in 1919 afforded public lands along ridgelines, which were prime hunting areas. The areas of public ownership were spotty, and most of the ridge was still in private hands, but public ownership was expanding.

The route southwest of the river confronted a problem that was to confound trail clubs for decades.

The problems began in 1929 with the dispute over the route south of Lambs Gap. Avery had already decided two years earlier where the trail would go, but the Pennsylvanians regarded it as an issue that had not yet been closed. He pointed out in a letter to Bingham that the conference at Skyland the previous year had authorized a committee to resolve the issue. Avery and Anderson from PATC and two representatives from the Pennsylvania Alpine Club were to constitute the committee. [8] The ATC archives reflect no resolution to the issue — Avery probably went ahead on his own, based on concurrence from Perkins.

---

8. PATC archives, Avery papers, Avery to Bingham, February 28, 1929.

Rockville Bridge, the longest stone-arch bridge in the United States at the time.

South of Blue Mountain and the Darlington Trail was the Cumberland Valley: farmland and private property. It would be difficult to bring a trail down through that area, so the Blue Mountain Club proposed to extend it along Blue Mountain all the way to Doubling Gap (present-day Colonel Denning State Park), then hooking down past Newville and south of Car-lisle, a 30-mile road walk all the way to Pine Grove Furnace. From Pine Grove Furnace, Bingham's map showed it proceeding along South Mountain, through the new Michaux State Forest and Mont Alto State Forest, and into Maryland at Blue Ridge Summit. Bingham's proposed route took the trail all the way to the Potomac River east of Harpers Ferry. (The first part of this extension past Cumberland Valley later became the Tuscarora Trail.)

But, Bingham's solution was not adopted once Avery became the decision-maker. Avery had other plans.

Beyond the two original clubs, several others sprang up to take on sections of the new trail. First to form was the Batona Club in Philadelphia in 1928, by a group of nature enthusiasts. (Batona is Back to Nature abbreviated.) The original patron was the *Philadelphia Evening Bulletin*, which sponsored a lecture by Captain Albert Rodriguez, an outdoor enthusiast and member of the Dutch army. Rodriguez partnered with Benjamin Schneyer, a Philadelphia dentist, to begin Sunday hikes, and this eventually became the Batona Club.[9]

The Allentown Hiking Club was formed in 1931, under the leadership of Elwood S. Thomas, a member of the Allentown school board, who had visited Europe and was impressed with the vigor of

9. Chamberlain, *op. cit.*, pp. 33-34.

the European walking clubs. In response, the Allentown Recreation Commission, under the leadership of Irene Welty, issued a call for local citizens to meet at City Hall on December 2 to form a new club. The group began hiking immediately and agreed to take on a 7.5-mile section of the A.T.[10]

The Philadelphia Trail Club also began in 1931, and Avery assigned it a stretch of the Appalachian Trail near Harrisburg. That was soon changed to a section much closer to Philadelphia and was changed again several times. This was typical of maintenance assignments and sometimes seemed to be at the whim of Myron Avery, who closely (many felt *too closely*) managed maintenance assignments. The Philadelphia club produced some of the early leaders in long-distance hiking, including Charles Hazelhurst, George Outerbridge, and Martin and Mary Kilpatrick.

The York Hiking Club was founded in 1932 and would become the home club of Earl Shaffer (see chapter 6). Active in hiking, it did not become a maintaining club until late 1948, when the members participated in a work trip with PATC at Caledonia State Park to see what trail work would be like.

The Balkanized Pennsylvania clubs fiercely guarded their independence, though they all helped enthusiastically with various sections of the A.T. in their state. In 1956, they finally established a unified organization, the Keystone Trails Association, with the active encouragement of the PATC leadership. By that time, the Blue Mountain Club, which led the original charge, had disappeared, having ceased to exist by 1953.[11]

After a long roadwalk from the end of Kittatinny Mountain in New Jersey, the trail originally entered Pennsylvania at Portland on the Delaware River. This required another road walk on the Pennsylvania side of the river to Delaware Water Gap, where it reentered the forest and climbed Mount Minsi. Once on Blue Mountain (the same ridge as Kittatinny; different state, different name), it was originally

10. Allentown Hiking Club history, Wiemann e-mail message.
11. Smithsonian Museum of American History, Earl V. Shaffer Collection, minutes of the formative KTA meeting; Ralph Kinter statement.

on private property all the way to the Susquehanna. The Blue Mountain Club celebrated the completion of its section from Mount Minsi to Lehigh Gap in 1932 and marked the route with blue metal signs. The Blue Mountain Eagle Climbing Club had already completed its section from Lehigh Gap to the Susquehanna.

This long unbroken stretch of ridgeline was marred by a devastated moonscape around Lehigh Gap. That was the product of the New Jersey Zinc Company, which in 1898 built a plant to manufacture various zinc products in Palmerton, at the foot of the gap.[12] Effluvia from the zinc process killed every tree and every blade of grass on the hillside. Lehigh Gap was the most environmentally devastated section on the entire Appalachian Trail.

Farther west, the trail was maintained by a pair of brothers, Reuben and Jacob Runkle. The brothers, who recruited fellow farmers from the area, maintained the stretch from Indiantown Gap to Manada Gap, and they were so highly regarded that a monument was erected in their honor in 1937. BMECC President William Shanaman presided, and the monument still exists, although the Appalachian Trail no longer runs through Manada Gap.[13]

After crossing the Susquehanna, in about six miles, the Darlington Trail reached Lambs Gap and a major decision point. As noted, three trail plans had emerged. The Pennsylvania Alpine Club chapter in Altoona proposed to continue the trail along Blue Mountain to Sterretts Gap and then, jogging over a series of ridges, to Tuscarora Mountain. At Doubling Gap, there was the Eugene Bingham proposal of the roadwalk to Pine Grove Furnace.

The Pennsylvania Alpine Club intended instead to proceed southwest along Tuscarora Mountain all the way to the Potomac River at Hancock. Since Harpers Ferry remained the launching point for the Appalachian Trail south of the river, that would require a 64-mile walk on the abandoned Chesapeake and Ohio Canal towpath east to Harpers Ferry.

---

12. *ATN,* July/August 1996, pp. 14-15.
13. *"Appalachian Trail Marker Dedicated; Climbing Club Hikes to Manada Gap,"* May 5, 1937, *Reading Eagle.*

Avery intended to cross the Cumberland Valley and then go through Michaux and Mont Alto state forests and into Maryland on South Mountain. The disconnect between Avery and the Pennsylvanians troubled Perkins a great deal, and he urged Avery to meet with them and work out an agreement. In his correspondence with Avery, Perkins favored the South Mountain route, but his main thrust, as always, was to keep the peace.[14]

The Pennsylvanians were proceeding with their original plan, despite Avery's insistence on his own route, but there were defections. Henry Shoemaker eventually came around to Avery's route, and, in March 1929, even Eugene Bingham conceded that perhaps the South Mountain route would be acceptable.[15]

A route along South Mountain would have many advantages. As Schmeckebier pointed out to Avery, South Mountain in Pennsylvania had a great deal of history that was not present along Tuscarora Mountain. Pine Grove Furnace, at the approximate midpoint of the proposed A.T., was historic. Established in 1764 as the Pine Grove Iron Works, it manufactured stoves, fireplace backs, iron kettles, and munitions during the American Revolution. The iron works changed hands several times and was owned at one time by the infamous financier Jay Cooke, a railroad mogul whose financial failure brought on the Panic of 1873. The iron works closed in 1883, a victim of newer, competing technologies. In 1913, the 17,000-acre ironworks was sold to the state to become part of the new forest reserve, and part of it became Pine Grove Furnace State Park. Fuller Lake, named after Jackson Fuller, Jay Cooke's financial manager, became a popular swimming lake. In 1933, the Civilian Conservation Corps (CCC) set up camp there, building roads, trails, and facilities until 1941.

Barely two miles south of Pine Grove Furnace are the ruins of Camp Michaux, originally a CCC camp and, during World War II, a camp for German prisoners of war. Twenty miles south of Pine Grove Furnace was Caledonia State Park, where famous abolitionist Thaddeus Stevens built a charcoal iron furnace in 1837. A self-con-

14. ATC archives, Perkins Box, Perkins to Avery, November 21 and December 12, 1927.
15. *Ibid:* Bingham to Avery, March 4, 1929; Shoemaker letter, December 9, 1927.

tained village, Caledonia had the furnace, forge, rolling mill, stables, warehouses, blacksmith shops, sawmill, and houses for the workers and their families. Stevens died only three years after the end of the Civil War, and, like Pine Grove Furnace, the land was purchased by the state in 1903 as part of the new forest reserve system. Also like Pine Grove, it became a recreational park, and the Appalachian Trail was routed through the western edge.

As previously noted, Mont Alto Forest was the home of scientific forestry in Pennsylvania and rivaled Yale, Cornell, and the Vanderbilt's Cradle of Forestry in North Carolina as a center for American scientific forestry. The trail passed close to the former home of Joseph Rothrock. Outside the town of Mont Alto were acres of experimental forests, including a failed attempt to halt the spread of the chestnut blight.

At the Mason–Dixon line, Avery's trail route crossed through Pen Mar, an amusement park opened in 1877. At its height, it had seven hotels, and, during the weekends, trains arrived from Baltimore carrying vacationers. The emergence of the automobile started Pen Mar's decline, and, when a 1913 fire consumed the Blue Mountain House, one of its preeminent hotels, the end was near. Excursion trains stopped running in 1935, and the park closed in 1943 during World War II. (It was reopened as a county park in 1977 with picnic tables and roofed pavilions.) In the middle of the park was a magnificent overlook of Pennsylvania farms, the sort of feature that was highly valued by hikers. And, just north of Pen Mar, one of the original Mason–Dixon stone markers could still be seen a short distance off the trail route.

Perkins had given Avery running room for the South Mountain route, and, in 1929, following the ATC meeting in Easton, Avery and Andy Anderson drove to Sterretts Gap, just west of Cumberland Valley, in Anderson's car. They drove on roads along Blue Mountain, looking for a logical place to cross the valley. Avery picked Lambs Gap, on the Darlington Trail, and wrote to Perkins that he had found the way south.[16]

---

16. ATC archives, Perkins Box, Avery to Perkins, May 12, 1929.

Moving south, Avery and Schairer marked the Appalachian Trail across Cumberland Valley, from Lambs Gap to the Chambersburg–Harrisburg Pike, more than ten miles, in December 1930. The route through the valley was entirely on roads and entered Michaux State Forest southeast of the town of Boiling Springs.[17]

Next, Avery began working with Pennsylvania authorities for concurrence for the new trail on public land. In July 1930, he began an exchange of letters with Joseph Illick, the Pennsylvania state forester, requesting permission to work directly with foresters in Michaux and Mont Alto. Illick immediately authorized the project and told Avery to work with the foresters to select a specific route. Illick noted, however, that there were no funds to build the trail — it would have to be built by "private organizations." That was all Avery needed to start scouting the route.[18]

Avery formed a bond with foresters Tom Norris of Mont Alto and Tom Bradley of Michaux. The foresters suggested a preliminary route using old roads. The irrepressible Avery was out on the suggested route, accompanied by Schairer, almost immediately, hiking from Pen Mar to a point just north of the Big Flat fire tower. "We were extremely pleased with the route selected. It is Appalachian Trail caliber in every way," Avery wrote to Bradley.[19]

In February 1931, the official route through the two forests was marked by two parties of state foresters. One group began walking north, and the other walked south. Later in the month, a busload of forty-five enthusiastic PATC members invaded Mont Alto Forest to walk twelve miles of the new trail, led by Tom Norris.[20]

The interaction between PATC and the two groups of foresters was very smooth, and, before the end of 1931, a route for the A.T. was established all the way across Pennsylvania. It was one of Avery's most successful and enduring partnerships, probably because he let

17. ATC archives, Avery correspondence, Avery to T.G. Norris of Michaux, December 23, 1930. White blazes can still be seen along the old route.
18. PATC archives, Avery papers, Avery to Illick, July 28, 1930, and Illick reply to Avery, August 1.
19. ATC archives, Avery to T.G. Norris of Michaux, *op. cit.*
20. *Gettysburg Star Sentinel*, March 14, 1931.

the public officials lead. He could be very engaging when it suited him (and when it benefited PATC).

The first route through southern Pennsylvania was mostly on dirt roads. When it followed existing trails, it was primitive, not much more than a marked path with overhanging vegetation removed, much like the original A.T. through Shenandoah National Park. Later on, in 1933, the CCC established a camp at Old Forge in the Mont Alto Forest and began building a graded trail.[21]

The Maryland A.T. (see below) was placid compared with Pennsylvania. Avery had a life-long talent for scrapping with people, and his donnybrooks with the Pennsylvania clubs were memorable. Avery's problem in Pennsylvania was trying to impose order and discipline on the various clubs when they had already built the trail and were unamused at a late-stage interloper. They could hardly have been enthusiastic about the creation of ATC, which now claimed jurisdiction over their route.

Meanwhile, the Pennsylvania clubs forged ahead with trail construction, and, by 1931, Avery was in the middle of the matter. In the early days, he seemed to be working in harmony with the clubs, but many clubs competed for trail sections, and Avery felt that it was his role to work out the responsibilities. He also wanted to ensure that the clubs were following his guidance on trail construction and maintenance. He sniped constantly at the standards of trailwork in Pennsylvania and gradually sapped the goodwill that he had earlier established.

Having walked the entire trail in Pennsylvania, Avery criticized the Blue Mountain Club for poor maintenance. To E.M. Zimmerman, one of the club founders, he wrote, "Frankly, I see a complete collapse in maintenance from the Delaware [to Lehigh Gap]. The activities of the B.M.C. [Blue Mountain Club] seem equally finished." Zimmerman was in no mood to accept criticism. "I didn't suppose even an 'admiralty lawyer' would lay himself open to so palpable a charge of slander.... If bad dreams of our section are keeping you awake nights, you

---

21. Chamberlain, *op. cit.*, p. 207.

can turn over and go to sleep. We'll do our part."[22] Avery replied that he had recently walked the Blue Mountain section, and, "now you can sell me and the rest of the world many things, but you can't make me believe that the Trail can be followed. Why at Little Gap for the first ¼ mile east, it can't be followed at all. No connection in the gap how to go west. Across from Wind Gap west to the power line, when Torrey and I were there, was almost impassable." [23] Avery had correctly detected that the Blue Mountain Club was in decline and worried that he would have to find other clubs to maintain the BMC section.

Avery began changing section responsibilities and moving trail clubs around, often without telling the dispossessed club. In 1934, unhappy with a BMECC section, he arbitrarily assigned that section to the Philadelphia Trail Club. When Rentschler discovered this, he informed the Philadelphia club that BMECC intended to keep the section. A confused Philadelphia club member (presumably Martin Kilpatrick, although the letter in the file showed no signature), replied that he knew nothing about the BMECC responsibilities but had just been assigned this section by the chairman of ATC.[24] (That would be Avery.) Rentschler complained to Avery, who was unmoved. In reply, he sent a long and acerbic letter to Rentschler. If BMECC could not properly maintain their section, Avery stated, then he would send a crew from PATC to show them how to do trail maintenance. "To say that this section was in order before the Philadelphia club trip indicates an utter lack of comprehension as to what a trail should be."[25]

Avery's tendency to intervene in matters large and small in Pennsylvania was just part of his personality. He switched club responsibilities around with kaleidoscopic speed, sometimes apparently on a whim. He dictated maintenance standards, instructed clubs in even the smallest detail, and insisted that his standards be followed to the letter. If a club did not comply, Avery would move that club to

22. ATC archives, Avery correspondence, Avery to Zimmerman, November 1, 1933; Zimmerman to Avery, November 10.
23. *Ibid*, Avery to Zimmerman, November 13.
24. *Ibid*, Rentschler to Kilpatrick, May 31, 1934, and unknown (probably Kilpatrick) to Rentschler, unsigned and undated.
25. *Ibid*, Avery to Rentschler, June 18, 1934.

a shorter section or even move it out of maintenance responsibility altogether. He would then assign another club to that section, sometimes without informing the losing club. The clubs in the state had a difficult time keeping up with Avery and were perpetually unhappy with their relationship with him and ATC.

Avery and Rentschler eventually reconciled, and, when it was over, everyone seemed reasonably happy with the outcome. But, Avery in Pennsylvania reflected the way he operated in other states. It was a character flaw that caused animosity for many years.

Maryland

The trail in southern Pennsylvania moved past Pen Mar and climbed High Rock Road, where it began its 40-mile trip through Maryland along South Mountain. Unlike much of Pennsylvania, this was private land, and that produced much trouble in later years, as landowners began discovering a hiking trail through their properties. But, in the early years, the support of state foresters eased the way to a preliminary trail route.

Avery contacted Maryland State Forester F.W. Besley and Cyril Klein, the city forester for Frederick, in 1929 to ask their advice about a trail route on South Mountain. (This, it hardly needs be pointed out, was prior to having located a route in Pennsylvania. Avery already had Pen Mar in mind as the place where the trail would cross the Mason–Dixon Line.) Besley contacted Klein, they rounded up three other forest rangers, and, in four days, they had blazed a route from Weverton on the Potomac to Pen Mar.

PATC crews surged into the forest in 1931 but did not apparently follow the Besley–Klein route in all cases. In the December 1932 issue of *Appalachia*, Avery reported that the route through Maryland had been marked with string and rags and was then cut on subsequent work trips. On one trip, he reported, five volunteers had cleared and marked ten miles to "boulevard" proportions.[26]

---

26. PATC archives, Avery papers, series of letters between Avery and Besley, 1929.

It seemed, in the early 1930s, that Avery was everywhere at the same time. This was especially true in the mid-Atlantic region from Delaware Water Gap (marking the dividing line between New Jersey and Pennsylvania) to Damascus at the border between Virginia and Tennessee.

New York and New Jersey

The trail situation in New York was divided by the Hudson River, in more ways than one. West of the River was much public land, and trails had strong support from the Palisades Interstate Park Commission (PIPC). East of the river, private property seriously impeded hiking on the A.T.

Moving west from the river, one climbed magnificent Bear Mountain and hiked through the glorious Harriman State Park lands, offering dense forests and scenic vistas preserved in perpetuity by the Harriman family. At N.Y. 17, hikers crossed into the Sterling Forest lands owned by industrialist and politician Abram Hewitt. A letter from Hewitt's representative stated, "I am very glad to able to say that Mr. Hewitt has no intention of closing this property to parties of walkers now that it will shortly be included within the game preserve boundaries. It has ever been his wish to preserve both the forests and the game therein for the enjoyment of all."[27] Hewitt's declaration exemplified the spirit of public service of many of the rich landowners along the Hudson in New York.

West of Route 17 were a few tracts of private property, and each presented its own set of problems. A landowner near Lake Mombasha (north of Sterling Forest), Franz Kloiber, had put up a barbed-wire fence across the trail. When Joe Bartha from the New York–New Jersey Trail Conference went to see Kloiber, he discovered that Kloiber didn't object to hikers crossing his land. The fence was to keep his cattle in, not keep hikers out. Kloiber left the fence but clipped the barbs off the wire crossing the trail so that hikers would not tear their clothing.[28]

---

27. Quoted from Raymond Torrey, "The Long Brown Path," a newspaper column published in the *New York Post* — N.Y.-N.J. TC archives, unknown date in 1930.
28. *Ibid*, February 9, 1938.

The A.T. moved along the western ridge line of beautiful Greenwood Lake. Entering New Jersey, hikers encountered a trail that was mostly on private property, and the trail between Greenwood Lake and High Point State Park was rerouted often as the Trail Conference struggled with private-ownership issues. In many places, it was on road shoulders. Many of those problems could be surmounted only through governmental action. It was fortunate that New Jersey took on the challenge of protecting the trail much earlier, and with greater effect, than other states. Its Green Acres acquisition program was employed often to establish a trail corridor.

South of High Point, along Kittatinny Ridge, the land was in large tracts. Typical was the land around Sunfish Pond, part of the Buckwood tract of the Worthington estate. Hikers were permitted to cross, but, after several incidents of hiker misbehavior, the owner threatened to close the tract. That was solved by a unique solution — hikers would have to present identification, indicating membership in either ATC or a trail club. When notified of this, Avery was in favor because he thought it might result in an increase in ATC support.[29]

In Stokes Forest, south of High Point, a hiking permit was required by a revocable license. On many, if not most, private tracts, camping was prohibited, but hikers could still cross the land. Some tract owners (Buckwood was a good example) prohibited blazing. Pierson Lumber Company permitted hikers to cross its land after paying a charge of 10 cents, a situation that paralleled the crossing of the Bear Mountain Bridge, which also charged a small toll.[30] Newspaper columnist and conference leader Raymond Torrey performed what was described as "heroic" efforts to maintain good relations with landowners, and, in his columns, he encouraged hikers to be good citizens.[31]

So, with one artifice or another, hikers had an easier time of it west of the Hudson. The land east of the river was almost entirely private property, and the Trail Conference had to deal with constant shifts in

29. *Ibid*, October 27, 1937.
30. N.Y.–N.J. TC archives, Trail Conference minutes, 1935-1940, unknown date.
31. ATC archives, Jean Stephenson correspondence.

the trail route as its permissions with landowners changed.

Torrey enlisted Murray Stevens in 1926 to do some preliminary scouting. What Stevens found presented a difficult problem. After crossing Bear Mountain Bridge, the eastbound hiker would climb steeply on public land to Anthony's Nose, a military reservation (preserved in 1939 as the first installment of what became Hudson Highlands State Park). Next came private land west of Clarence Fahnestock State Park (which was created in 1929). No public land was available at all east of Fahnestock.

Stevens mapped out a trail

Bear Mountain Bridge

route, negotiated with landowners, and, with the help of fellow Appalachian Mountain Club members, had marked out a tentative route by 1928, but most of the trail east of Fahnestock was on road shoulders.[32] Occasionally, willing landowners were found, but that was relatively rare. Torrey reported in 1938 that no shelters were available for the entire 105 miles of trail east of the Hudson into Massachusetts, while nine shelters were in place from the Hudson to the Delaware.[33] In all, it was almost sixty miles alone from the Hudson to the Connecticut line, mostly on road shoulders.

At the far eastern end of New York, the A.T. had to connect with Ned Anderson's Connecticut section. The connection was made more difficult by a private-property problem. Anderson had been given permission for the trail to cross a large tract, but, when the landowner died, his daughter, a Mrs. Bonos, put the land up for sale, and

32. *ATN*, May/June 1990, pp. 1-13.
33. Torrey column, *op. cit.*, March 10, 1938.

she did not want it encumbered with a hiking trail. That necessitated a long reroute from River Road up to Schaghticoke Mountain so that the New York and Connecticut sections could reconnect.[34]

Torrey was the unifying force in New York and New Jersey. Working with Avery until a falling-out in 1935 (see chapter 4), Torrey provided direction to the trail programs in his area, and he often had to bring trail clubs in line with ATC policy. Despite his leadership, not all the trail clubs involved in creating trails in New York were easily controlled.

Blazing was the subject about which hikers argued fiercely, and not everyone agreed with a standard color. Under intense pressure from ATC, the Trail Conference finally agreed to reblaze its sections of the A.T. white, to conform with other trail sections. Having made the decision, the Trail Conference then had to enforce it. With many small clubs in its confederation involved with trails and only short sections of the A.T. to maintain, the Trail Conference had great difficulty controlling the activities of the clubs. The enforcement authority that ATC later attained was, in those days, Myron Avery hammering at club leaders to do the right thing.

Once the A.T. was blazed white, hikers complained that some of the side trails were also white, and trail junctions sometimes became debating matches — which white-blazed trail should hikers take? Complicating that was that some of the clubs were painting out the blazes of other clubs, something William Hoeferlin, the Trail Conference mapmaker, called "trail wars."

In December 30, 1937, Torrey wrote in his column, "Further reports on the 'Trail war in the Ramapos,' from Joseph Bartha and Paul H. Schubert, disclose more of the blackening out of the blue blazes on the Seven Hills Trail by the mysterious trail eradicator who seems to be at large." In his January 20, 1938, column, Torrey reported that the "trail eradicator" was caught, and it turned out to be one Keson Nurian. Nurian defended his activities as retaliation for others painting their own blazes on coaligned trail sections that he had originally built. Torrey, who was as particular about trail standards as Avery,

34. ATC archives, Stephenson correspondence, Avery to Allis, May 23, 1944.

was incensed. The matter was illustrative of the problems involved in managing a trail that went through fourteen states and countless (and ever-changing) trail-club responsibilities.

Legions of stories abide about Torrey's combative personality, and one story, told by Frank Place, was of first meeting Torrey on a hike. "Near the mountain we met an elderly, beetle-browed man who abruptly addressed us thus: 'You ought to be in church.' Torrey came back: 'Are you the one who desecrates nature by painting texts on the rocks?' 'Yes,' said the stranger. 'Then you ought to be in jail,'" was Torrey's retort.[35] Torrey also had a famous confrontation with parks czar Robert Moses,[36] in which Moses tried to choke Torrey and later threw a smoking stand at him. The combative Torrey was smaller and no match for the enraged Moses.[37]

Raymond Torrey remained *the* central figure in hiking trails in New York until May 1938, when Avery reported that Torrey was sick. For a time, he seemed to be recovering, but the recovery was only temporary. Torrey died of a heart attack on his birthday, July 15, 1938. He was only 58 years old, and his death stunned the New York hiking community. A memorial was placed on Long Mountain in Harriman State Park, which had one of his favorite views, reading, "In Memory of Raymond H. Torrey, A Great Disciple of the Long Brown Path, 1880–1938."

New England

New England was a completely different problem for Avery. There, he was dealing with a mature trail and mature trail organizations that had been on the ground, in some cases, for decades. They already had their organizations, their trail plans, their leaders, and their methods of doing things. Avery was stepping, somewhat fear-

---

35. ATC archives, scrapbook #8, article about Torrey by Place, unknown publication, around 1940.
36. Robert Moses, unelected head of parks, urban renewal, highways, and other authorities, dominated New York City politics and the city's very configuration for more than four decades.
37. Robert Caro, *The Power Broker: Robert Moses and the Fall of New York*, pp. 316-18 (New York: Alfred A. Knopf, 1974).

lessly, into a situation in which he was unwelcome. New Englanders were not looking for leadership — they already had it. Who was this upstart from Washington, they wondered? Avery might have thought that he had come to help, just like in the South. New England neither needed nor wanted help. It was a recipe for trouble.

The plan for the Appalachian Trail in New England had been laid out originally by Ashton Allis. In 1921, he had proposed, quite independently of MacKaye, to extend the Long Trail south into Massachusetts, along the Berkshires and Taconics, down to the Hudson Highlands at Mount Beacon, then across the Hudson over the Beacon–Newburgh ferry to Storm King. (The Bear Mountain Bridge was still some years in the future.) Once across the river, it would use a trail that Will Monroe proposed from the Hudson Highlands to the new Ramapo–Dunderberg Trail. From there, it would proceed across Bear Mountain State Park land, down along the west of Greenwood Lake into the Wyanokie Plateau of New Jersey and on to Delaware Water Gap.[38]

Connecticut

Trail development was mature in New Hampshire and Vermont and likewise in New York, but the connecting link through Connecticut and Massachusetts had yet to be made when Avery got involved. Plans had been developed, but they were controversial.

Originally, Connecticut wasn't even in the plan. Allis proposed to bypass Connecticut completely, routing the trail along the border but entirely within New York until it got abreast from Massachusetts.

In contrast, Albert Turner laid out a route that included Connecticut, through Macedonia Brook and Kent Falls state parks west of the Housatonic River and Mohawk and Cornwall state forests along the eastern side of the Housatonic. When Allis and Torrey scouted a route, they walked south from Mount Everett, over Bear Mountain, and into Connecticut, contrary to Allis' original idea. Finally, Perkins laid out a route that bypassed Bear Mountain and stayed on the

---

38. *ATN*, September/October 1985, pp. 7-11.

Sitting, Myron Avery (center) and Ned Anderson atop Wildcat Falls in Connecticut in 1941. A note on the back of the photo in an Avery family album says, "Just found the maps were wrong again." Behind Avery are Howard Evans and George Helmke of the Housatonic Trail Club. (Photo by Frederick S. Best.)

western side of the Housatonic. So, by the end of the 1920s, several proposed routes were on the table.

In Connecticut, the still-undefined trail was taken over by a new enthusiast, Ned Anderson. Anderson became a legend among hiking enthusiasts in the state, almost single-handedly scouting and routing the trail. He was the Rufus Morgan (see chapter 4) of the north.

Originally from Hartwell, Ohio, Nestle K. "Ned" Anderson grew up in New York state. Eventually settling outside Sherman, Connecticut, Anderson became a dairy farmer. He also drove the local school bus and organized the Boy Scouts in Sherman and got them involved with the A.T. Anderson was a classic community organizer, and his wide-ranging connections were beneficial when he needed volunteers.

His connection with the Appalachian Trail resulted from a chance meeting on the trail with Judge Arthur Perkins in 1930. Perkins suggested that Anderson contact Avery, and the two became coworkers on the Appalachian Trail in Connecticut. Anderson had such a gentle personality that Avery warmed to him instantly, and they were friends until Avery's death in 1952. It was one of those rare times when opposites seemed to attract — the manic, hard-driving Avery and the mild-mannered, soft-spoken Anderson.[39]

Anderson began scouting and marking the trail in his home state, a not-inconsiderable task given that the Trail in Connecticut was then 70 miles long. For maintenance, he formed the Housatonic Trail Club and also used his Boy Scout troop. The trail in Connecticut ran through much private property, and it was up to Anderson to negotiate free passage. His disarming personality made him many friends and helped get permissions to cross.

By 1931, Arthur Comey of the New England Trail Conference suggested that Avery go to Connecticut and see for himself what was happening there. So, in May of that year, Avery traveled to Connecticut and began hiking from Bear Mountain Bridge, seventy-eight miles through eastern New York and as much of Connecticut as had been marked. Anderson accompanied Avery on the Connecticut portion, which at that point had been completed to Kent Falls on the Housatonic. It was then that Avery and Anderson formed their bond.

The other major figure in Connecticut trail development was Edgar Heermance, who led the Connecticut Forest and Park Association's Trails Committee. Heermance was a genuine trail pioneer, who began Connecticut's statewide trail system. His appearance was singular. The Watermans described Heermance as "a scarecrow-like figure — tall, lean, intense, bespectacled, and bushy-browed retired minister."[40]

---

39. Doris Tomaselli, *Ned Anderson: Connecticut's Appalachian Trailblazer, Small Town Renaissance Man.* (Sherman, Conn.: The Sherman Historical Society, Inc., 2009).
40. Watermans, *op. cit.,* p. 433.

In Connecticut, all hiking trails were blazed blue, but the Appalachian Trail was supposed to be white, so the problem was how to integrate the A.T. with the rest of the trail system. At the first meeting of the committee on December 27, 1929, ATC Chairman Perkins, a resident of Connecticut, laid out the general outlines of the Appalachian Trail in the state and discussed the uniqueness of the A.T. That did not, however, lead to an agreement on blazing.

In 1930, the same year that Anderson and Perkins made a connection, Heermance wrote to Perkins that he had become acquainted with Ned Anderson and regarded him highly — so highly that he and Perkins both left the Appalachian Trail through Connecticut to Anderson's judgment and field work.[41]

Avery was initially impressed with Heermance's dedication. In ATC Letter No. 2 in 1934, he noted that Heermance had been elected chairman of the New England Trail Conference, and Avery believed that Heermance would lead a revival of interest (and work) on the Appalachian Trail. "Under Professor Heermance's direction, a very enthusiastic revival of activities of the New England Trail Conference promises to be very productive."[42]

However, as Avery's combative instincts took over, this sunny relationship lasted but a relatively short time. In 1940, an argument over blazing erupted, agreements collapsed, and Anderson wound up in the middle. In line with the blue-blazing scheme for the rest of Connecticut, Heermance thought that the Appalachian Trail would, of course, be blazed blue. The mild-mannered Anderson was perplexed by the growing animosity between Heermance and Avery and wrote to Heermance, "Truly, Mr. Heermance, I cannot understand the feud between Mr. Avery and you.... Please do not give up the A.T. as one of the Connecticut system."[43]

Heermance and Avery continued arguing about the blaze color, finally leading Avery to make one of the most significant policy statements ever made for the Appalachian Trail. "The Appalachian Trail

---

41. ATC archives, Avery correspondence, Heermance to Perkins, October 23, 1930.
42. ATC archives, Stephenson correspondence, October 1, 1935.
43. Tomaselli, *op. cit.*, p. 558.

is a single integral unit. It is to be treated as such a unit. Its practices and standards are prescribed by the Appalachian Trail Conference. *It is not a federation of fourteen different state trails.*"[44] (Emphasis added.)

Eventually, Avery and Heermance came to an agreement of sorts. The Appalachian Trail would be handled as a different category, not managed by the Connecticut Forest and Park Association. It was to be the sole responsibility of ATC (and, of course, blazed white).

Massachusetts

The situation in Connecticut was simple compared to Massachusetts. Several routes were proposed for the state, with little effort to decide which route would be selected. Several trail groups already were anxious to work on the trail, with no central authority able to establish policy. Into this morass stepped an unwitting Myron Avery in 1931.

The Taconic link to the Appalachian Trail had been problematic from the first. The original Torrey–Allis proposal to bypass Connecticut completely and switch the trail from New York over to Massachusetts once north of western Connecticut[45] was just one of the early trail plans that did not survive on the ground.

The first route through the Taconics was plotted by Walter Pritchard Eaton, a writer (but not a doer). It was after Eaton made his proposal that a new group was formed, the Berkshire Hills Conference, headed by Franklin Couch. By 1931, the group had built a nearly complete trail system through western Massachusetts. Other groups were involved, especially the enthusiastic Williams College Outing Club, which was very active in building trails over Mount Greylock. The Williams section then connected to the north with the Long Trail, thus providing a link to a completed trail through Vermont and New Hampshire.[46]

At that point (1931), the Berkshire Chapter of the Appalachian Mountain Club (AMC) joined the effort and began sending work

44. *Ibid*, p. 59.
45. Hunter Library, Sherman Collection, Torrey to Governor Franklin D. Roosevelt, February 14, 1926.
46. Watermans, *op. cit.*, pp. 498-502.

parties. Now, two trail clubs were working on the same section. Arthur Comey tried to calm the waters, appointing Harland P. Sisk as a mediator. Sisk promptly set out his own understanding of the trail route, following in general the present trail route over Greylock.[47]

Greylock was already in public ownership and had been since 1898. Revered as the highest point in Massachusetts, it had been made a state park in order to conserve a watershed that had been badly cut over. South of Dalton, the trail ran through the Whitney Estate, a large private estate owned by Asa Whitney, a former secretary of the Navy under President Grover Cleveland, that had been turned over to the state for public use in 1915. Most of the rest of the route was over private land or followed public roads.[48]

Because of "trail wars" in Massachusetts, Comey urged Perkins to get Avery, with whom he still had decent relations, to go up to Massachusetts as soon as possible. [49] Avery responded immediately and hiked the entire route in 1931. He was not pleased. The trail was overgrown in many places and difficult to follow throughout. He felt that the Berkshire Hills Conference should be fired. "The inactivity of the rest of the Committee...," he commented to Perkins, "has convinced Sisk and myself that it is not worthwhile to bother with them."[50]

So Avery "fired" Couch and his group (without, it appears, informing Couch[51]) and appointed the AMC Berkshire Chapter to replace them. Explaining his decision, Avery lashed out at the former group. "The scheme of coordination of Massachusetts work through the activities of the Secretary of the N.E.T.C. has proved an absolute failure.... But for the activity of the Berkshire chapter this situation would be as hopeless as last year. To them all praise." After noting that the trail over Greylock was in poor shape, he urged Comey to

---

47. A map in the ATC archives (box 3-4-1, Avery maps) shows the route over Greylock on the west side, with ski slopes on the east. The issue of trails and commercial ski interests clashing was worked out in later decades.
48. ATC archives, Avery correspondence, H.P. Sisk, "The Appalachian Trail in Massachusetts, April 10, 1931."
49. *Ibid*, Comey to Perkins, June 26, 1931.
50. *Ibid*, Avery to Perkins, December 4, 1931.
51. *Ibid*, Anderson to Avery, December 9, 1931.

formally request that the Berkshire Chapter of AMC be given complete jurisdiction over Massachusetts.[52]

In early 1933, Avery finally informed Couch that his organization had been replaced. He based his decision on poor maintenance and accused the Couch group of being inactive, thereby losing its claim to the Appalachian Trail in their state. This, in Avery's opinion, ended the matter.[53] The Watermans comment that, once the trail route had been cut to Avery's satisfaction, the Berkshire Chapter of AMC left the scene,

Arthur Koerber presents Max Sauter with honorary membership at the ATC meeting in 1967.

believing, apparently, that their role ended with trail construction.[54] And, since the Berkshire Hills Conference had been "fired," no one was left to keep the trail clear.

After 1936, the situation was saved by the emergence of the Mount Greylock Ski Club under Max Sauter and Metawampe, the faculty outing club of Massachusetts State College, under John Vondell. Sauter and Vondell became members of ATC's board of managers and longtime pillars in New England ATC matters.

Vermont

Since the time of James Taylor, the Green Mountain Club had pushed its trail and cabin system much further along. The headquarters was at Sherburne Lodge, a rustic and picturesque facility at Sherburne Pass. Completed in 1923, it was built astride the Long Trail itself. Coming off Pico Peak, the white blazes ran right through the lodge.

In 1929, the club decided to fund a small summer crew of paid workers to complete the trail. Wallace Fay was the first crew chief,

52. *Ibid*, Avery to Comey, May 25, 1932.
53. *Ibid*, Avery to Couch, January 17, 1933.
54. Watermans, *op. cit.*, pp. 498-502.

Roy Buchanan (sitting) and the early Long Trail Patrol.

but, in 1931, a college professor named Roy Buchanan assumed leadership. This dynamo pushed trail construction on to the Canadian border and added thirty-seven new shelters approximately every eight miles. The diminutive Buchanan, who was only 5 feet, 2 inches, tall, hurled himself into the task and was the inspiration for GMC for as long as he continued to work (which was well into his eighties).[55] He was one of the great trail-builders in East Coast trail history.

In 1933, the national movement toward mountaintop roads (the so-called skyline drive movement) hit GMC and the entire state of Vermont; see chapter 4. The idea was viewed by some as a commercial plus and as a badly needed, Depression-era jobs program. Colonel William Wilgus of Ascutney became the principal supporter and got the backing of the governor, Stanley Wilson. The proposal reached Washington, where it met with a mixed reception. Skyline drives were known to be favored by President Roosevelt who, wheelchair-bound, wanted to see nature on his own but could not just go off into the woods. But, Secretary of the Interior Harold Ickes was not as favorably disposed, and mixed messages came out of Washington.

---

55. Nuquist, *op. cit.,* p. 49. The Watermans also cover the Long Trail Patrol on pages 458 and 469-472.

The Wilgus plan encountered stubborn opposition from an influential portion of the Vermont population. Acting GMC President Herbert Congdon wrote, "The most difficult thing to bridge is the deep gulf that lies between some of us in the matter of taste. To those of us who love the forests through which our Trail passes, the idea of having hordes of people, convenient hot dog stands and the like, is abhorrent. Yet there is a very large number of people who think those features are the only things lacking to make our mountains perfect!"[56]

Each time the matter came up, the GMC trustees voted it down. But, the allure of commercialization split the club, and Wallace Fay proposed a compromise that would have had the road but farther from the Long Trail than the original proposal. Although much of the leadership of GMC, including Fay, Mortimer Proctor, and L.B. Puffer, was in favor of this compromise, they never had the support of the rank-and-file members.[57]

Wilgus campaigned up and down the state, trying to enlist chambers of commerce. Vermonters remained adamantly opposed. Novelist and Nobel laureate Sinclair Lewis, one of their most prominent residents, wrote, "The peculiar charm of Vermont is that, though it has adequate highways, it also has isolation, and it would be criminal to gash a great parkway through it."[58] A resolution favoring a parkway was introduced into the state House of Representatives but was voted down, 126–111. In Washington, Ickes took a position in opposition to the president: "I think we ought to keep as much wilderness area in this country of ours as we can. It is easy to destroy wilderness; it can be done quickly, but it takes nature a long time…to restore for our children what we have ruthlessly destroyed."[59] The matter of skyline drives devolved to town meetings. It was decisively defeated all over the state, and the proposal was dead.[60]

---

56. Vermont State Archives, Box 241/3, *Long Trail News*, September 1933.
57. *Ibid*, Box 225/17. An article in the *Burlington Free Press*, January 14, 1935, reported that the club members voted down the Fay/Proctor/Puffer compromise.
58. *Ibid, Long Trail News*, November 1933 issue.
59. *Ibid*, Box 241/4, *Long Trail News*, April 1933 issue.
60. *Ibid*, April 1936.

In 1937, the federal government was considering the idea of creating a national park in Vermont. It would have been established around the northern and central Green Mountain peaks and would have had little impact on the trail, and GMC never took it up.[61]

The culture in Vermont is resoundingly different from the other forty-nine states. Vermont residents think of themselves as a separate nation, and they are not prepared to join the Union culturally. The stubborn opposition of Vermonters to skyline drives and national parks was symbolic of this attitude. Vermonters fiercely protect their Green Mountains.

That paralleled their attitude toward the Appalachian Trail. Phil Stone, one of Avery's top lieutenants in the Potomac Appalachian Trail Club (PATC), returned from a visit to Vermont in 1940 with the strong feeling that Vermonters valued the Long Trail but placed no value on its association with the Appalachian Trail.[62] That contrasted with trail clubs in the South, which valued their association with the A.T. and competed for management of trail sections. Vermonters, recalcitrant to the last, just shrugged. The Long Trail mattered — the coaligned Appalachian Trail did not.

New Hampshire

The trail system in New Hampshire was a product of decades of planning and work dating back more than 100 years. When the Appalachian Trail project came along, it confronted a settled situation and an organization that dated back to the years following the Civil War. Of all the nuts Avery felt he needed to crack, New Hampshire was the hardest, and the one least amenable to ATC oversight.

Because AMC had developed its own set of trail standards, and Avery contended that the Appalachian Trail was not fourteen different state trails, conflict was inevitable. For instance, AMC refused to blaze its sections of the A.T., notwithstanding ATC policy that all parts of the trail would bear white blazes. As for alignment, Wil-

---

61. *Ibid*, July 1937.
62. ATC archives, Stephenson correspondence, Stone to Avery, September 25, 1940.

AMC trail crew in 1924.

liam Fowler, president of AMC, contended that the A.T. in the White Mountains was not even a single route. It could be many different routes through the mountains, and AMC did not propose to select anything in particular.[63] His position stood in direct opposition to Avery's conception of the Appalachian Trail. In his mind, it was a single, defined route and could not be a tangle of parallel hiking trails.

A messy dispute arose in 1940 over conflicting policies on guidebook publication. Jean Stephenson, ATC's editor and guidebook publisher and Avery's right arm, wrote an article for *Appalachian Trailway News* insinuating that AMC policy was to ensure that hikers would buy AMC trail guides. Avery jumped into the middle of the dispute,

---

63. *Ibid*, Fowler to Avery, November 1, 1941.

and acrid letters flew back and forth between him and Fowler. That became part of the dispute over marking the route of the A.T. in New Hampshire.[64] ATC eventually won all these disputes, and the trail really did become a single integral route, but it did not start out that way.

The connecting link from the Connecticut River at Hanover to the Long Trail was built and managed by the Dartmouth Outing Club (DOC), which initially took a position on the Appalachian Trail that echoed that of GMC. To them, the connection with the Long Trail mattered much more than any tenuous association with the A.T. After Avery completed his first hike from Sherburne Pass to Lyme–Dorchester Road in New Hampshire, he commented to Comey about DOC that "they are frank to say that they are not yet wholly sold on the Appalachian Trail idea."[65]

The latent hostility between AMC, the senior trail organization in the country, and the upstart ATC continued for years. Within AMC, some felt that things were rigged in Washington. Ronald Gower, one of Fowler's top associates, wrote, "The underlying situation…points to the necessity of a thorough housecleaning in the high command of the A.T. Coming down to personalities, Avery made a good driver to force through the completion of the AT. Now that phase is over, it needs a smooth operating diplomat who will make people want to work with and for him."[66] Gower certainly had a point but didn't get his wish.

Although the idea for the trail began in New England, centralization did not mesmerize the New Englanders. As local interests took over, the push for a trail along the entire Appalachian spine waned. The vision of James Taylor, Benton MacKaye, Allen Chamberlain, and Ashton Allis was no longer a New England vision. It had been absconded by the mid-Atlantic crowd.

AMC operated mainly in New Hampshire. When the subject of Maine came up, AMC backed off. Comey wrote to Avery as early as 1931 that AMC would not go north of Grafton Notch, in the far southwestern corner of Maine.[67]

---

64. Appalachian Mountain Club archives, Boston: Fowler to Stephenson, October 25, 1940; Avery to Fowler, October 28; Fowler to Avery, November 1.
65. ATC archives, Stephenson correspondence, Avery to Comey, June 20, 1932.
66. *Ibid*, Gower to Fowler, November 12, 1940.
67. ATC archives, Avery correspondence, Comey to Avery, December 10, 1931.

Maine

Maine was the last state to be brought into the realm of the Appalachian Trail. It was not until later in 1925 that it was even on the list and became the fourteenth Appalachian Trail state by virtue of the decision to take the trail all the way to Katahdin. (Not that it was ever far from builder's minds, with Major Welch pushing the "Maine to Georgia" motto as early as 1923 and Judge Perkins himself tacking up A.T. signs on Katahdin in 1927.) This decision left more than 280 miles to build, with no plan and no organization to pursue one.

Although every A.T. state has its uniqueness, Maine, like Vermont, was another country. In the case of Vermont, the uniqueness was cultural — in the case of Maine, it rested on the environment. The lands of the A.T. were remote, and the trail habitat was a vast forest. Towns were small and widely spaced, and the sense of remoteness for hikers was the most vivid memory of their transit. After leaving Monson, northbound hikers confronted the roadless 100-mile wilderness, where resupply was nonexistent and backpackers were advised to carry ten days' worth of food.

The hinterland, where the trail was to be cut, was the domain of the timber companies. In the nineteenth century in particular, massive timber harvests were the norm, and the land was almost entirely owned by such companies as Great Northern Paper, Brown Forest Products, and others engaged in the same trade. Ownership was measured in thousands of acres. When hikers started scouting the trail, they were on the lands of large companies.

The backwoods of Maine are called the "unorganized territories," and 10 million acres were owned by those timber companies. When Maine split from Massachusetts in 1820 to become a new state, Massachusetts kept much of the land and sold it off at auction to compensate the veterans of the War of 1812. The state allocated two lots in each township to be set aside for the support of schools and churches, but, since most of the area was never incorporated, the lots were eventually sold to the "dominant landowner," generally a timber company, "in perpetuity."

[In 1970, by virtue of a successful lawsuit, the scattered tracts were consolidated into large tracts, and the A.T. went through much of this land. In 1972, Maine created local Land Use Cooperative Committees (LUCCs) to decide on how the consolidated tracts were to be used. The A.T. was zoned as a PRR (Protected Recreation Resource), and the Maine Appalachian Trail Club argued strongly for a wide corridor but ended up with only 200 feet.]

As in the South, the vast timber cut produced huge piles of slash, and forest fires ravaged the state. Bedeviled by these fires, Maine hired fire wardens to spot and combat fires. The fire wardens were some of the first people that trail advocates encountered, and they found them to be significant friends in their desire to build trails. Fire wardens, after all, needed trails to get to fires, so they were natural allies. The wardens were also well known to timber companies, and it was understood that wardens could come and go on timber company properties.

So, too, could trail builders. In discussing the need to cross timber-company lands with Walter Greene in 1932, Avery wrote, "By having the fire wardens take the initiative, there is a cover of State action, which would be most useful in getting the trail out over the four mountains."[68]

Avery developed a close relationship with Helon Taylor, a fire warden in western Maine, who once wrote, "I never had to get permission or anything to cut a trail. In fact, I could cut a trail wherever I wanted."[69] In 1933, Taylor began scouting for an Appalachian Trail route along the slopes of Bigelow, and, in 1934, he ran the trail along the crest of the Bigelows to The Horns and completed marking the A.T. all the way to Sugarloaf, almost 50 miles. He was an incredible hiker and could walk four miles an hour over the very difficult landscape in Maine. He enjoyed a wide reputation for his physical ability and, in 1950, became supervisor of Baxter State Park, continuing in that position for seventeen years.[70] Taylor achieved legendary status

---

68. Maine State Library, Avery files, Avery to Greene, June 21, 1932.
69. Rima Farmer interview with Helon Taylor, *ATN*, July/August 1987, pp. 18-20.
70. Farmer, *ATN*, July/August 1984, pp. 18-20.

York's Long Pond Camps, some buildings of which still exist — one of many sport camps along the early trail.

both among volunteers and Maine state employees. (He claimed that Avery could out-hike him, which, given Avery's shorter stature, just adds to the Avery legend.)

Another distinguishing characteristic of Maine was the sport camps. Located principally on lakes in northern Maine, they provided excellent overnight facilities for hikers, as well as sport fishermen, recreational boaters, hunters, and the like. When the route of the A.T. was first laid out, the location of sport camps was considered, so that hikers could hike from one camp to another and never have to carry a full pack. The camp owners encouraged the A.T., which would provide more business. Walter Greene — a Broadway actor who, with Taylor, laid out large parts of the future A.T. in the state — connected Avery with the camp owners, and the location of sport camps was a major factor in the location of the trail. For their part, many of the camp owners built short trails in the vicinity, some of which became part of the A.T. or side trails to overnight accommodations.

Maine trails tended to be significantly more difficult than those farther south. It wasn't just the steep climbs that hikers often complained about — it was the tread itself. Maine trails were full of roots and rocks, and even hikers with a vivid memory of the rocks on the Blue Mountain section of the A.T. in Pennsylvania, and the mud and roots in Vermont, were surprised by the difficult treadway in Maine. Experienced backpackers who averaged three miles per hour in other states often had to be satisfied with half that speed in Maine. On the plus side, owing to the long, cold winters, low-lying bushes and grasses in Maine tended to grow more slowly, and trails that had to be maintained several times a year in the mid-Atlantic might get by with a clearing operation once every two or three years.

In 1925, the same year that ATC decided that Katahdin would be the northern end of the trail, the redoubtable Arthur Comey of Massachusetts and the New England Trail Conference (NETC) scouted the proposed trail from Old Speck, through Grafton Notch, to the summit of Old Blue. In 1929, he completed the scouting trip all the way to Katahdin. The trail route that Comey scouted (see page 89) accorded generally with the route of the A.T. today, although his description of the hike to Arthur Perkins was rather vague the farther north and east he went. Many of the place names on Comey's report would be familiar to hikers today.

That incredible feat was accomplished without an existing trail. In some places, he followed logging roads, but in others it was an out-and-out bushwhack. Comey wrote to Perkins, "The route would not be feasible now for one not used to banging through brush and blow-downs for long distances with pack, and with no adequate maps (though these are coming within a few years)."[71] Comey's hiking accomplishments took second place to no one, not even Avery.

Comey did not want the trail to go beyond Grafton Notch until a capacity was developed in Maine itself. He wrote to Perkins, "It is my opinion that no lasting progress can be made in Maine except through local Maine action. When they come to believe that a through trail will help them they will open it. At present there would

---

71. Maine State Library, Avery files, Comey to Perkins, August 27, 1929.

be so infinitesimally few through hikers that the opening of the trail for outsiders would be too previous."[72] This verdict, coming from the secretary of NETC and the most accomplished hiker in New England at the time, would be difficult to contradict. Avery, never one to dodge a fight, was the first to challenge Comey, and that was the basis for his entry into the state of Maine.

Avery's battles with Comey originated with the route selection. Maine was Avery's home state, and he believed that no one could exceed his grasp of the terrain. They argued especially about place names, and Avery sent letters to Comey challenging his understanding of the names of prominent features. Finally, Comey had enough and wrote in exasperation to Avery: "Thank you for sending me copy of your letter of Oct 24th to Mr. Perkins, for the valuable information on Katahdin contained therein, although mixed with the sort of scurrilous remarks without which so far I have been able observe you are unable to write any letter at all."[73]

Avery also could issue backhanded compliments. In 1934, following the ATC meeting in Rutland, Vermont, he wrote to Comey, "You are certainly doing things this year. I am becoming proud of you."[74] It is hard to know if Avery was serious.

A number of hikers, many of them state employees, hiked long sections of what would become the first Appalachian Trail route through Maine. An early adventurer was George Dillman, a New Yorker who set out to hike the supposed route all the way from Greenville to Grafton Notch, the western section of the trail. Without a marked trail, Dillman must have done what Comey had done earlier — bushwhacked major stretches. Dillman sent his account to Avery.[75]

However, the most significant trail blazer of them all was Walter Greene. The New York actor spent his summers at a vacation cabin in Sebec, and, in 1931, he and Avery began corresponding. Avery introduced him to Perkins thus: "He has been, over a dozen times, over ev-

72. *Ibid.*
73. *Ibid,* Comey to Avery, November 4, 1927.
74. *Ibid,* Avery to Comey, July 3, 1934.
75. *Ibid,* 1932, Dillman to Avery, various dates.

ery foot of the route he outlined on the map for me. I know of no one better qualified to select the most favorable route between Sowadnahunk and Greenville."[76]

Seeking to move the trail off roads, Avery became convinced that he needed to hire someone to build the trail over the rugged Chairback range. In 1932, he proposed to engage Maine fire warden Harry Davis and his son, Lyman, to build this section. In the summer of 1932, Avery contacted

Walter Greene (left) with Myron Avery

both the Maine Development Commission and the New England Trail Conference, looking for funds. After a huge struggle, he finally got a small amount of money to pay the Davises. But, according to a letter from Avery to Davis in January 1933, it appears that the project fell through.[77] Lyman seemed to have lost interest in the project and did not complete it. (Once he took a look at the Chairback range, he probably felt underpaid.) In any case, the most difficult section of the trail in Maine still remained to be completed in 1933.

It was Greene who decided that the low road was not the best road and, in 1933, single-handedly built the trail over Chairback, Columbus, Third, Fourth, and Barren mountains, considered by many the most rugged chain traversed by the Appalachian Trail in Maine. An article in the *Appalachian Trailway News* stated, "The fact that Walter Greene was 61 when he performed this herculean feat makes the project one of the great accomplishments in the annals of trail-blazing."[78]

Greene was pleased with his new route over Chairback and named one overlook "Monument Cliff," now known as Monument Ledge:

---

76. *Ibid*, Avery to Perkins, April 4, 1932.
77. *Ibid*, Avery to Harry Davis, January 19, 1933.
78. *ATN*, September/October 1991, p. 12.

Myron, I can't really describe the grandeur of the view from here. I honestly believe it will be the finest on the trail. The cliff is sheer with no trees to obscure the view. Long Pond lies at one's feet and the sweep of the valley to the north is so broad one can see North West and East. Mountains looming everywhere. The Saddlerock being very impressive. Katahdin is seen distinctly in the gap between two mts., directly north to the West, in the distance there are some wonderful peaks, no doubt around Moosehead. How I wished for a movie sweep of it. I feel this spot will become famous in time. Monument cliff is a good name for it.[79]

Greene and Avery could engage in heated arguments by letter, disagreeing, for instance, about the role of sport camps on the trail. (Avery wanted shelters and camping spots located along the trail, but Greene

The view from Monument Ledge today.

---

79. David B. Field manuscript, *History of the Appalachian Trail in Maine: The Early Years.*

wanted to protect the business of the sport-camp owners.)[80] But, their correspondence was voluminous and generally free of acrimony, and Greene, in particular, wrote long pages describing the route he was scouting. In places, it was almost a turn-by-turn description of his progress, written in a hand that was virtually illegible, apparently, to anyone but Avery. Greene — not Comey, not Dillman, and certainly not Avery — was the scout that laid out the trail in Maine. (But, he needed the organizing genius of Avery to make the trail actually happen.)

Despite the fact that Avery did not make an ATC-related appearance in Maine until 1933, his draft of a Maine guidebook followed in the main the route that was eventually selected. He was working with many of the sport-camp owners, who were reporting local trail construction. He was also working with Robert Stubbs, a Maine forest supervisor who developed the forty-nine-mile route from Blanchard (120 trail miles south of Katahdin) to Dead River. It was Stubbs who had put Avery in touch with Harry Davis.

And, despite arguing with Greene about sport camps, Avery kept in touch with many of the camp owners. He often consulted with them on the best route through their territory and, according to a local newspaper, included twelve sport camps on his proposed trail route.[81]

Comey, who felt strongly that no work should be done on the trail in Maine until local clubs could be formed, made sure that AMC was not a participant in the project northeast of Grafton Notch. Avery opposed Comey's position on this (as on many other things) and wrote to Perkins in 1932,

> In the first place I have the very decided conviction that scouting without leaving any permanent record of the route is not advancing us very much in that region for when the Trail is unmarked this activity has to be done over again…. Comey and I rather disagree about the procedure in Maine. He doesn't want to do any marking until these location organizations spring up like mushrooms. He

---

80. Field, e-mail to the author, January 2016
81. Maine State Library, Avery files, series of letters in 1932 and 1933.

wants to continue scouting, which I consider now useless to the project but a very pleasant vacation.[82]

He wrote to Greene in September of the same year that the trail in Maine was an ATC trail and was connected in no way with AMC, which had decided (arbitrarily in Avery's view) not to do anything in Maine. He criticized Greene for posting signs on side trails indicating that this was an AMC side trail. AMC, he insisted, was not involved with the A.T. in Maine.[83]

Avery was ready to push ahead in Maine without the assistance, or even the blessing, of AMC. It was typical of his latent animosity to AMC, revealed in his ventures in other New England states. He would go to Maine and would find others to work with him on that project. With Greene, Stubbs, Taylor, and others, he seemed to have plenty of partners.

In August 1933, Avery began his long-planned transit of the trail south from Katahdin to Blanchard, 119 miles. With him were Al Jackman, Frank Schairer, Shailer Philbrick, and others, including Marion Park. They carried the first sign up to the top of the mountain, ascending *via* the Dudley Trail and descending *via* the Hunt Trail, marking the northern terminus of the Appalachian Trail. Avery, of course, also pushed his measuring wheel. The very next day, at Daicey Pond, they began walking south.

Jackman wrote a vivid description of this historic day in the PATC *Bulletin* for October 1933:

On August 19, a party consisting of Myron H. Avery, J.F. Schairer, E.S. Philbrick and A.H. Jackman, climbing Mount Katahdin, placed one of L.F. Schmeckebier's artistically decorated signs upon a white cedar post lugged up for the purpose, nailed a metal A.T. marker below the sign, and painted the farthest-north blaze on the Appalachian Trail. The post was then properly embedded in a rock cairn on Monument Peak (elevation 5,267 feet), a cup of water christened the new landmark, pictures were taken as Avery concluded his speech

82. Field manuscript, *op. cit.,* Avery to Perkins, April 4, 1932.
83. *Ibid,* Avery to Green, September 9 and October, 1932.

Al Jackman, Myron Avery, and Frank Schairer in 1933 after mounting the first A.T. Katahdin summit sign. (Photo by Shailer Philbrick)

of dedication (probably the shortest dedicatory speech on record, compassed in three words: 'Nail it up') and the party started working south along the Hunt Trail.

The next day, the foursome was joined by Greene. When they ended their hike, Philbrick continued south, accompanied by Elwood Lord and several fire wardens, marking another 55 miles from Blanchard to a point in the Bigelow Range. The Philbrick party used the trail route scouted by Stubbs.[84]

---

84. *Ibid,* Avery to Frank Phillips, a Maine game warden, November 9, 1933. Philbrick, an engineering geologist, worked for the Army Corps of Engineers for 30 years and later taught geology at Cornell University.

Later in that trip, Avery (left), Greene (hat), Philbrick (back), and Schairer ride the waves and air laundry to the next trailhead.

Avery had originally planned to mark all the way to the Kennebec River, but storms delayed the group for two days, so they stopped at Blanchard, just west of Monson. They took a day to explore Jo-Mary Lake, adding eight miles on this side trip over an old abandoned trail.[85]

After that trail trip, only the 85-mile section from Bigelow to Grafton Notch remained to be finished. According to Dave Field, the trail in 1935 was just more than half on roads, mostly old logging roads, abandoned railroad grades, and telephone-line rights of way. Very little of it was through uncut forest, and hikers went through long stretches of cleared land. Most of the route was, after all, owned by timber companies.[86]

85. Maine State Library, Avery files, Avery to Neil L. Violette, Forest Commissioner in Augusta, September 6, 1933.
86. Field, *Along Maine's Appalachian Trail* (Mount Pleasant, S.C.: Arcadia Publishing, 2011), p. 37.

Avery believed that he could recruit trail workers from among local outdoor groups and college outing clubs. His first attempt, in 1932, was with a group from Portland, the Eastern States Mountain Club. The president, Arthur Fogg, continued a dialogue with both Avery and Comey through 1934 but was vague about actual plans to

Avery in 1942 pointing to the Bigelows from Sugarloaf. One of those peaks later would be named for him.

get out and work on the western portion of the trail (the part that interested Comey). Finally, Comey commented to Avery, "I am of course delighted that the Eastern States Mountain Club now finds it will interest it to explore, *etc.* They have been a feeble group, but actual trail work may vivify them."[87] On June 10, Fogg wrote back to Avery about a scouting trip on the western portion of the A.T. on Old Blue and Elephant. They walked the section but did not do any work. Visits to Portland to talk to Fogg's group served only to discover that the group was interested in ski trails, not hiking trails.

A more productive relationship developed with the Bates College Outing Club. An Avery feeler to the college in 1934 elicited an enthusiastic response from W.H. Sawyer, the faculty advisor, stating, "The Bates College Outing Club would welcome the opportunity to work on this last link in the Katahdin to Atlanta Trail."[88] On July 13, Sawyer sent a long and detailed report of a scouting trip west of Saddleback — there is no evidence that they did anything but walk the route and assess its con-

87. Maine State Library, Avery papers, Comey to Avery, May 25, 1934.
88. *Ibid*, Sawyer to Avery, June 7, 1934.

dition.[89] Avery answered enthusiastically on July 18, commending the report in its thoroughness, although there was some question as to whether or not Sawyer and his friends actually knew where they were. Much of what

Professor W.H. Sawyer, Jr., with Bates College Outing Club members in 1934.

they scouted had already been scouted by the Portland group. Finally, on October 5, the *Lewiston Sun* (the college is located in Lewiston) gave a glowing report on a trail-blazing trip over a route. It was somewhat exaggerated — most of the real work was done by the Civilian Conservation Corps (CCC).[90]

But, after a slow start, Bates College did provide a continuing source of trail workers, the only college group that was sustainable. For many years, it maintained a section of the A.T. and helped redesign its trail section in the 1970s when much of the trail in Maine was relocated. The college insisted that its entire

Avery wheeling a stretch of Maine trail.

89. *Ibid*, Sawyer to Avery, July 13, 1934.
90. Field, in an e-mail to the author in January 2016, contends that the Bates group did not fulfill its commitments.

student body become members of the Outing Club,[91] making Bates College the most sustainable contributor to A.T. maintenance.

Several other ventures with college outing clubs were false starts. Colby College, the University of Maine, and other schools were contacted, some of them by Sawyer himself. The replies tended to be mumbled and noncommittal, and no other club was convinced to take on trail-maintenance responsibilities.

Relationships with professionals were far more productive. The connection with both Stubbs and Taylor began a very significant association on their portion of the Appalachian Trail. In 1934, the two Maine employees began working together. Along with a game warden named Phillips, they formed a team that did the preliminary work from Bigelow westward. In an unpublished article in 1937, Myron Avery credited Stubbs with developing the route between Blanchard to Bigelow and Taylor with the extension from Bigelow to Sugarloaf.[92]

The Maine Appalachian Trail Club (MATC) was Avery's one notable success in building a local club in Maine, and that was an important one. In 1935, it was announced that a club had been formed and that Walter Greene was the president. The list of officers included such PATC leaders as Frank Schairer, Jean Stephenson, and Marion Park. Every leader came from somewhere besides Maine. Stephenson took a special interest in the new club and effectively ran it for many years, despite coming to Maine only in the summer months. In the 1960s, a new and vibrant club was to develop around a new leader, Dave Field (see page 495).[93]

Avery ran many work trips in Maine. It was part of his role in supporting operations in Maine, his home state. He and Jean had to take the train to Maine whenever something A.T. needed to happen in that state, with little local involvement until after World War II.[94] In one sense, Comey had been right — building a local constituency proved

91. Field e-mail, April 8, 2018.
92. ATC archives, Avery correspondence: ATC board meeting, November 7 1936; "Afoot Along the Two-Thousand-Mile Appalachian Trail," Avery unpublished article, sometime after 1937.
93. See chapter 10.
94. Interview with Steve Clark, former Maine A.T. Club president, August 13, 2014.

difficult, and, in the early years, the leaders were all imports.

In 1934, plans were laid for the CCC to become engaged in trail work in Maine. James Sewall, the CCC forester, worked with Avery and Stubbs to plan a program for the newly formed CCC camps, and they began operation in 1935. Trail crews went out from camps in Millinocket, Greenville, Flagstaff, and Rangeley, working all the way from Katahdin to Grafton Notch. Mostly, they improved existing trails and built many shelters on the western/ southern half of the trail. (The eastern/northern half was still dominated by the sport camps, and it was felt that no more overnight facilities were needed

CCC Director Robert Fechner during the 1939 ATC meeting near Katahdin.

east of the Kennebec River.) The Rangeley crew built new trail sections in the Bigelow Range, a new trail up Saddleback, and a section from Saddleback to Andover–South Arm Road.[95]

They faced obstacles. The CCC was not permitted to work on private property except under certain circumstances, and, since most of the A.T. in Maine was on timber-company land, every project was prefaced by a struggle to get permission from the companies and thus clearance from federal officials.[96] But, in the end, they got the permissions they

95. There are various sources for CCC work on the A.T., some of them contradictory. In 1936, Myron Avery's article, *In the Maine Woods*, discusses CCC projects in Maine.
96. Maine State Archives, Avery papers, February 16, 1940: E.G. Amos, Chief, Division of Hazard Reduction, U.S. Department of Agriculture, New England Forest Emergency Project, Boston, CCC Plans, Work Projects, Maine, to Myron Avery. Dave Field discussed this in an e-mail to the author in January 2016.

A typical Adironack-style lean-to in Maine.

needed, and work went forward. Stubbs in the far south and Helon Taylor in the Bigelow Range guided CCC crews in their respective areas, working with Avery to decide where the CCC was needed most.

The task registered a few temporary failures. The existing crossing of the Penobscot River had been deliberately destroyed in 1932 by a logging company, because it was blocking its log flow. (A more vivid example of the dominance of lumber companies in that area could hardly be imagined.) Sewall had planned for the CCC to build a new cable bridge, but, when funding was cut, he had to discard that plan. The Penobscot crossing awaited future years.

The CCC program also had to contend with the vagaries of federal funding. Part way through the year, Sewall informed Avery that the budget had been cut, and two of the CCC camps had to close for the 1936 season. Despite those temporary setbacks, the CCC program in Maine managed to push on. In 1936, the CCC had six crews of fifteen workers each, and their shelter construction put the A.T. on a solid footing, with fourteen new Adirondack structures. In 1938, CCC crews worked to clear the very extensive damage from a hurricane that closed the A.T. for long stretches throughout New England. According to an article by Jean Stephenson in the *Portland Sunday Telegram*, a single two-mile stretch suffered more than 2,000 blowdowns.[97] Avery pressed to obtain permissions from the timber companies and was almost never turned down.[98]

On Katahdin, ATC was dealing with Percival Baxter, the former governor of the state. Baxter, described by the Watermans as an "eccentric millionaire" from Portland, had been first mayor of Portland and later governor. Unable to convince the legislature to purchase the land around Katahdin, Baxter began buying the land himself, and, in 1933, he donated the initial expanse of private land, 5,700 acres, to the state to establish a state park. For Baxter, this was just a "starter kit," and the park eventually encompassed more than 200,000 acres.

In January 1934, Baxter wrote to ATC, asking if its maps and guidebooks gave proper credit to his name. In doing so, he cited the legislation that had created the park in 1931. Possibly viewing this as a sensitive matter, Avery handled the answer himself, pointing out passages in the Maine guidebook naming Baxter Peak and crediting Baxter himself with the donation of land. Baxter seemed mollified and later in the year went with a group of AMC hikers on a tramp of the eastern section of the trail to Blanchard.[99]

But, three years later, Baxter was blindsided by a bill, the work of Avery himself, that would convert the state park to a national park as part of a larger national program. The problem, in Avery's view, was that the environment within the park was deteriorating due to misuse, and the Maine state legislature had not appropriated the funds that would be necessary to keep the park up. Avery contended, "Due to the lack of supervision over the area, the *laissez faire* policy prevail-

97. Hunter Library, Sherman Collection, newspaper article on December 8, 1940. This works out to a blowdown every five feet or so.
98. Best sources for the CCC role are Field, *Along Maine's Appalachian Trail*; Avery's correspondence from the Maine State Library; and the Watermans, *Forest and Crag*.
99. ATC archives, Avery correspondence, Baxter letter to ATC, January 23, 1934; Avery letter to Baxter, January 30.

ing" (a reference to the lack of state funds for maintenance) and "the failure to provide facilities for the increasing number of people going to this area...which are close to irreparable damage to the locality, the situation at Katahdin has been a matter of grave concern to all who know the region."[100] Baxter became the principal opponent of the bill and was supported by AMC and The Wilderness Society, two of Avery's main antagonists. The bill did not pass.

Avery's relationship with Baxter was made more difficult by the personalities of the two men. Each worked the problem of protecting Katahdin in his own way, and they were not men inclined to compromise.

Because there were, at first, no trail clubs on the ground in Maine, Avery had to find money himself. Greene was constantly after him for money to finance his scouting trips, and the issue of finding money for Harry and Lyman Davis persisted. Even Shailer Philbrick expected financial support for his trail scouting from Blanchard to the Bigelow Range. Avery needed blazing paint and A.T. markers for Taylor and other workers. That did not include the funds that Avery needed to finance publication of the guidebook for Maine.

All those demands left Avery constantly scrounging for funds. He managed to get small amounts from the Maine Development Commission and the Maine Forestry Department and also went after NETC for money. (There appear to have been no overtures to AMC — perhaps because Avery knew his relationship with that organization was not good, and perhaps because he wanted to keep AMC out of Maine completely.)

That became a struggle without complete resolution. At one point, the NETC board authorized $100, but Avery only received a check for $50 and suspected Arthur Comey, then the chairman of NETC, of managing to reduce the amount at the last minute. He wrote to NETC, "Your chairman seems to adhere to the theory that outside organizations should refrain from activity and that spontaneous germination will occur in Maine and presto: a local group will have opened and marked in Appalachian Trail fashion, some 200 miles of

---

100. ATC archives, scrapbook #1, Avery letter, March 23, 1937.

Trail in the Maine wilderness. I regret extremely his attitude. I consider it unfortunate."[101] It was just another in a set of long-running disagreements with Comey.

Avery also struggled with publicity. He felt that the best advertisement was large numbers of hikers. In 1934, a large AMC group under Ronald Gower hiked from Katahdin to Blanchard (a railhead — perhaps a reason why so many hikes began or ended there). That same year, the Pennsylvania hiking group of George Outerbridge, Charley Hazelhurst, and the Kilpatricks did the same hike and sent back their detailed trail critique to Avery. (They were generally pleased with the experience.) Avery's most successful recruitment was his 1935 PATC group. This hike became an annual event until the gas crisis of World War II and the wartime commitments of such military personnel as Navy employees Avery and Stephenson themselves prevented most travel.

By 1936, only two sections of the Appalachian Trail remained incomplete: the first, a two-mile stretch over Sugarloaf in Maine; the second, a stretch between Davenport Gap and the Big Pigeon River in the South. When this was announced at an ATC board meeting in November 1936, considerable competition sprang up between the Maine group and the southerners to see which one could close its gap first. The gap in the South was closed first, and, on August 14, 1937, the gap over Sugarloaf was finally completed by the CCC. Avery announced this, but qualified it: "As applied to the Appalachian Trail, the word 'completed' will always be an entire misnomer. The Trail, as such, will never be completed. As long as the project exists, there will exist the ever-present problems of maintenance and of developing a greater utilization of the Trail's attractions."[102]

The great 1938 hurricane that hit New England in September closed long sections of the Appalachian Trail. More than fourteen inches of rain fell in Hartford, Connecticut, in just more than a week. The storm did most of its damage in Connecticut, Massachusetts, and New Hampshire. The White Mountain National Forest lost an

101. Maine State Library, Avery papers, Avery to NETC, July 5, 1932.
102. ATC archives, Avery correspondence, Letter Report No. 5, January 2, 1937.

estimated 200 million board-feet of lumber. Some trails were closed and never again reopened.[103]

Because the forests in Maine were controlled by timber companies, other setbacks were common. In 1939, the Barren–Chairback Range was logged for the first time since Walter Greene built the trail, and Seaboard Paper Company obliterated the trail. The path was relocated in 1950 along a new tote road along the northerly slopes of Fourth and Barren mountains and was finally restored to its original ridgecrest location in 1956.[104]

Wartime

In 1939, the U.S. Maritime Commission, to which Avery was the legal counsel, was transferred to New York City. Avery moved his family to Tarrytown, close enough to commute into the city, and became special assistant to the U.S. attorney for New York, responsible for civil and military shipping litigation. But, he also had been a naval reservist since 1928 and was placed on active duty in 1942. This brought him back to Washington, D.C. As a naval officer, first a commander and later as captain, he worked on base rights agreements, settling airplane accidents, and related matters. During his wartime service, his family continued to live in Tarrytown, and Myron commuted by train on weekends.[105]

The 1939 job transfer to New York had a profound effect on Avery's connection with PATC, although not immediately. He did not resign, and his passionate following in the club noted with relief that he kept the door open to continue as president. The club members had never had another president and seemed unable to imagine anyone else leading the club.

A year later, however, the club got very unwelcome news — Avery sent a resignation letter. (Although his residence in New York might

103. Watermans, *op. cit.,* p. 550.
104. Field, unpublished history, "The Relocation Era"; interview with Field, August 12, 2014.
105. *ATN,* July/August 2000, Robert Rubin, "The Short Brilliant Life of ^Myron Avery." Also, author's interview with Hal Avery, September 10, 2013.

have factored into his decision, also involved was an obscure dispute with Paul Bradt, a world-renowned climber who headed the club's new mountaineering section.) Jean Stephenson, his devoted follower, wrote a protest letter to Avery, and the club refused to accept the resignation. But, Avery stuck stubbornly to his decision, and so L.F. Schmeckebier, one of the "immortal six," eventually succeeded him.[106] Schmeckebier's principal role in the club was as sign-maker (see page 125). Avery left a leadership vacuum.

Captain Avery in 1940.

Avery the leader cut an awesome figure, and those who did not know him personally often feared him. He came across to them as the distant figure of the chairman with the gavel, but he did make attempts to humanize himself. After a board of managers meeting in December 1939, he wrote to Max Sauter, "I think formalities should be a thing of the past and while 'Dr. Mr. Avery' was bad enough, 'Dear Sir 'is still worse. From hence forth it will be 'Max' and 'Myron.'"[107] It was symptomatic of Avery's more convivial relationship with his board.

The last board meeting before Pearl Harbor was held in June 1941 at Bear Mountain. After Pearl Harbor in December, men and women began joining the war effort, and trail matters took second place. In the January 1943 issue of the *ATN*, Avery announced that no conference would be held in 1943 and officers elected at Bear Mountain would continue to serve *de facto* until the end of hostilities. Work trips, he wrote, could be justified, but pleasure outings were strongly discouraged because of the need to conserve such resources as rubber and gasoline.[108]

Avery essentially had shut down ATC until the end of the war.

---

106. PATC archives, Avery papers, 1940. Avery's resignation letter was dated June 11, 1940, and Stephenson's letter informing him that his resignation was not accepted was dated the same day.
107. ATC archives, Avery correspondence, December 1939.
108. GATC, *op. cit.*, pp. 127-28.

Because of gas rationing, trail construction came to an end any-place that could not be reached by public transport. PATC was in a relatively good position, because public buses ran to Rockfish Gap, Chester Gap, Thornton Gap, Weverton (*i.e.*, Harpers Ferry), and Pen Mar. Other spots on the trail could not be reached for work trips, and some of the bus commutes were lengthy. The bus commute to Chester Gap for a work trip, for instance, was a two-day affair.

Some trail sections were closed by the Army for the duration of the war. Anthony's Nose along the Hudson in New York was occupied by the Army, and the Bear Mountain bridge manager informed Avery that explosives could be hidden in knapsacks and used to sabotage the military effort there. In Pennsylvania, the sixteen-mile section from Swatara Gap to Manada Gap was closed due to heavy-artillery practice. A three-mile section south of Pine Grove Furnace was closed because of its proximity to an Army prisoner-of-war camp. In Virginia, the A.T. near the Pinnacles of Dan was closed because the trail was too near the Danville power plant.[109] (One assumes that sabotage was the consideration there, too.) Some of the closures appear hysterical today but did not seem so at the time (and were decidedly less draconian than the internment of Japanese-Americans).

The loss of CCC assistance in 1942 was a not-unexpected blow. Letters from forest supervisors poured into Avery in early 1942, documenting the rapid closure of the various camps along the Appalachians. In the Jefferson National Forest, the forest supervisor had been relying on the CCC to construct the very large relocation caused by the construction of the Blue Ridge Parkway south of Rockfish Gap (see page 174). He had been counting on the seven-mile Three Ridges–The Priest relocation, which had been agreed on by ATC and the forest in the mid-1930s. First, a massive forest fire in the area destroyed the flagged reroute in May 1942. Then, the CCC camp that had been tasked with the relocation was closed in July.[110] The new route remained un-

---

109. *ATN,* January 1942.
110. ATC archives, Stephenson correspondence, Acting Blue Ridge Parkway Superintendent Stanley Abbot to Avery, July 28, 1942.

finished. The New England hurricane of 1938 had closed eighty miles of the Dartmouth Outing Club section.

Fires, the closure of the CCC program, and finally the war took a considerable toll. Three years after the end of the war, Avery lamented in 1948, "As to trail maintenance, we shall have, I fear, an interrupted Trail for many years."[111] Earl Shaffer, who did his thru-hike that same year, was to confirm that grim assessment. The good news was that, once finished with his historic hike, Shaffer helped to put some of those sections back in operation.

The trail route in Maine — remote, isolated, and owned mostly by logging companies — was especially hard hit. Helon Taylor reported to Avery in 1943 that the trail over Columbus and Chairback mountains had been skinned down to brush by logging companies. Avery negotiated desperately with the companies to restore the trail, with some success. But, the slash was horrific, and ATC had no control over events.[112]

During the war, twenty-five percent of the male members of PATC were in service, and at least sixty-five percent of the trail workers were women. They could still go in trucks, and some of the transportation was by flatbeds. It must have been an adventure for groups of maintainers, mostly women, to ride out to the A.T. on flatbed trucks, bundled up against the cold in winter. (No one, apparently, fell out of a flatbed.) But, for PATC, the principal work-trip transportation was the Red Beauty, a covered truck to haul volunteers to the trailhead.

Clubs up and down the A.T. announced to Avery that they were suspending operations for the duration of the war. In the South, the trail became very overgrown, where it was not actually wiped out by natural or man-made disasters. Two women, Marene Snow and Carolyn Allen, paid GATC dues to ATC themselves so that the club did not lose its accreditation, but club activities were suspended.[113] In 1942, Arch Nichols went into the Army, and the Carolina Mountain Club promptly suspended activities. On August 25, Roy Buchanan wrote to Avery, "The Long Trail patrol has had troubles this year. In fact, there isn't any Pa-

---

111. *ATN,* January 1948.
112. Maine State Library, Avery papers, 1943, series of letters among Taylor, Avery, and logging company employees.
113. Krickel, *op. cit.*

trol so it would be more accurate to say that a non-existent Patrol has no troubles."[114]

Despite the wartime restrictions, Avery was still able to organize a major work trip from Kokadjo to Katahdin. In

PATC's "Red Beauty" for work trips in 1944.

September 1944, he brought seventeen enthusiastic PATC members to northeastern Maine, where they put in a week of work, clearing forty-nine miles of trail.[115]

In some areas, the A.T. was being used as a tote road for timber companies hauling out dead chestnut trees. Arch Nichols reported that a section of the trail between Hot Springs, North Carolina, and Rich Mountain had been converted to a lumber road. Both of these uses violated the 1938 agreement (see page 137), but instituting uniform practices and enforcement over a 2,000-mile trail was surely problematic. Not all of the forest rangers knew of the agreement, and practically none of the lumber companies had ever heard of it.

After World War II, the Maine Appalachian Trail Club appealed to the Forest Service to help clear the neglected path. After that, maintenance became an increasingly volunteer job, as it had become in other parts of the trail. (The "great relocation" of 1970–1990, involving 164 miles of new trail in Maine, was done entirely by volunteers.[116])

---

114. ATC archives, Stephenson correspondence.
115. Maine State Library, Avery papers, Avery to Raymond Rendall, September 21, 1944.
116. Field, *Along Maine's Appalachian Trail*, p. 91.

Avery awarded the Legion of Merit in February 1947 by Rear Admiral C.S. Colclough, Judge Advocate General.

The Trail in 1948

As the war came to an end, the Appalachian Trail was in pieces. Blue Ridge Parkway construction had obliterated portions of the trail south of Rockfish Gap, and the Park Service had not had the manpower or budget to build its promised relocations of the A.T. In 1947, Avery took the unusual step of closing the trail near Bear Wallow Gap north of Roanoke.[117] And, the trail had in places been used as a haul road by timber companies, with little oversight by a stretched Forest Service.[118] Avery complained to anyone who would listen that the 1938 agreement was being ignored (see page 137).

Following the war, in 1947, he unleashed a general blast about trail conditions to Newton Drury, National Park Service director. Citing the Trailway Agreement (see page 137), he wrote, "The maintenance and marking of the Appalachian Trail in both parks [Smokies

---

117. ATC archives, Avery correspondence, Avery to Sam Weems, Superintendent of the Blue Ridge Parkway, August 7, 1947.
118. For instance, ATC archives, Avery correspondence, Avery to Mr. Cochran, Supervisor of the Jefferson National Forest, June 5, 1946.

and Shenandoah] is far from a credit to either the Trail Conference or the National Park Service."[119]

The Blue Ridge Parkway issue in Virginia had long nagged at Avery, who predicted that the trail would eventually have to be moved west of Roanoke. In 1947, Jim Denton, the new president of the Roanoke Appalachian Trail Club, wrote to Avery, "Several of our members and I have discussed the advisability of relocating the trail and are ready to do the preliminary scouting."[120] Avery did not know Denton; he was more familiar with the generation that he had recruited to establish the Roanoke club. But, he had long been thinking about a trail route west of Roanoke. With the troubles related to the Blue Ridge Parkway, he began to think that the time had come.

Not all the news was bad. The Eastman Kodak plant in Kingsport, in northern Tennessee, had several outdoor clubs, and, in 1943, Frank Oglesby, a chemist at the plant, had proposed that the employees form a hiking club. The new Tennessee Eastman Hiking and Canoeing Club held its first hike on April 28, 1946. Avery heard about the new club, first from Paul Fink and then from Oglesby.[121] At their invitation, Avery went down to Knoxville in November 1946 and encouraged the members to become involved with the Appalachian Trail. A young man named Stanley Murray was one of the most enthusiastic volunteers. At the time, the Carolina Mountain Club had a section between the Nolichucky River and the Smokies. TEHC, as it was abbreviated, began helping them with the northern section, between Spivey Gap and the Nolichucky. In 1947, TEHCC accepted Arch Nichols' invitation to take over the section.

The Roan Hiking Club (which no longer exists) maintained the Appalachian Trail on Holston Mountain from Winner, Tennessee, north to Damascus, Virginia. Paul Fink was maintaining a 25-mile road walk from Winner to Limestone Cove. So, in 1947, the Kingsport club met with the president of Roan Hiking Club and agreed to take over its section. TEHC originally required members to be Eastman

---

119. PATC archives, Avery papers, Avery to Drury, February 6, 1947.
120. ATC archives, Avery correspondence, Denton to Avery, February 22, 1947.
121. *Ibid*, Fink to Avery, September 11, 1947; Oglesby to Avery, January 9, 1947.

employees but eventually rescinded that requirement. The club produced some dynamic leaders and, like PATC, became influential far beyond its borders.[122]

In the Avery days, everything was centrally controlled. ATC published the guidebooks and tried to exercise some control over shelters. In 1939, ATC published a plan for shelters on the A.T. and hoped that individual clubs would conform. The centralization trend was strongly resisted in New England, much less so in the South. Avery did battle with both Shenandoah National Park and Great Smoky Mountains National Park, and he was known to call in Arno Cammerer of NPS when he needed reinforcements. Until 1942, the CCC built most of the shelters on public land, although the federal government insisted that lease agreements be signed before doing any work on private land.

In those early, chaotic years, A.T. clubs would spring up and then disappear in fairly rapid succession, sometimes not informing ATC of their demise. The situation was especially fluid in the Nantahalas, where Rufus Morgan operated almost as a one-man club for many years. At one time in the late 1930s, reputedly up to 50 clubs had some role in the Appalachian Trail. It was all that ATC could do to keep a list of the clubs and hope for the best.

A control freak like Avery must have had a hard time with all that, and lack of control was a reason why sections of the trail were poorly maintained for long periods of time.

The first ATC board of managers meeting after 1941 was in 1948, and the first general membership meeting was at Fontana Village in June of that year.

By the end of the Avery era four years later, there was a connected trail, but much of it was on private property, and long stretches were on road shoulders. Much work remained to be done, and ATC would be searching for a leader to replace their creator. The business was unfinished.

---

122. *ATN*, January/February 2005, p. 13; TEHCC Web site, March 2013.

Daniel Hoch's Legislation

In an otherwise obscure letter to ATC members in 1937, Myron Avery called attention to the precarious nature of the Appalachian Trail. Technically, it would be complete once the short section in Maine was finished, but it would always be under threat. Since it crossed state boundaries, the only solution, Avery wrote, was for federal protection.[1]

In 1942, Avery finally saw his chance. Daniel K. Hoch, the president of the Blue Mountain Eagle Climbing Club and a member of the board of managers of ATC, was elected to Congress. Avery lost no time writing to the new congressman about a plan that he had been thinking about. "It may well be that, in your position, after the war you could accomplish something in the way of perpetuating this project through federal ownership."[2]

Daniel Hoch (left) in 1950s at Clarks Ferry Bridge relocation with Earl Shaffer and Murray Stevens.

Although the war had not yet ended, the impetuous Avery could wait no longer, and, in December 1944, he sent Hoch the draft of a bill to protect the Appalachian

1. ATC archives, Avery correspondence, Letter Report No. 5, January 2, 1937.
2. ATC archives, Stephenson correspondence, Avery to Hoch, June 22, 1942.

Trail. His draft proposed not only to protect the A.T. It also proposed a national system of foot trails. This revolutionary idea, far ahead of its time, made it into the so-called Hoch Bill, H.R. 2142, introduced on February 13, 1945. In the short time between Avery's letter to Hoch and the introduction of the bill, Avery had expanded the proposed federal system of foot trails from 5,000 to 10,000 miles.

The Forest Service was to administer the system, but, rather than an independent piece of legislation, the bill was introduced as an amendment to the Federal Aid Highway Act of 1944. By doing this, Avery avoided the need to dip into the Forest Service appropriation, and thus the Forest Service was more likely to support the legislation. The money would come from the highway funds.

The bill stated, "All trails of such system shall be constructed, developed, and maintained in a manner which will preserve as far as possible the wilderness values of the areas traversed by the trails of such system." Avery tried to link the bill with both physical fitness and "as a part of the basic training of our youth for service in the armed forces."[3] Although it authorized the Forest Service to acquire lands for trail protection, it contained only $50,000 per year for three years, a paltry sum even by the standards of 1945.

Having worked with Hoch to get the draft legislation before Congress, ATC launched a "full court press" to get it passed. Avery and Jean Stephenson pushed it in every communication with members of the organization and trail-maintaining clubs. Avery asserted, somewhat hyperbolically, that, "if this battle is not won, then all else is useless."[4] They contacted individual board of managers members and individual members from every corner of the trail. The bill met with the expected support from the trail clubs, although AMC, while not pleased with the bill, was dissuaded from taking any action pro or con.[5] The A.T. was the only trail specifically mentioned, but Avery wrote to Clinton

3. Hearings before the Committee on Roads, U.S. House of Representatives, Seventy-Ninth Congress, First Session, on H.R. 2142, October 14, 1945.
4. GATC, *op. cit.*, p. 131.
5. ATC archives, Avery correspondence, Avery to Allis, April 11, 1945.

Clark, who headed the Pacific Crest Trail, that he hoped for support from the Pacific Coast since it was very likely that the PCT would benefit if the legislation passed.[6]

Issues had to be worked out. The Forest Service was concerned about the use of federal money for trail maintenance on private lands. Avery viewed the solution to this as the outright purchase of the private lands through which the Appalachian Trail ran. And, he was very nervous about its relationship with the National Park Service (NPS). Since much of the trail ran through NPS land, could the two agencies work together? Their relationship was often more competitive than collaborative.

The relationship with NPS was indeed a difficult problem. Conrad Wirth (acting NPS director) wrote to Avery, "We would question the advisability of having another agency construct and maintain trails in National Park Service areas."[7] Avery tried to explain away the problem, and Wirth professed to understand, but, in the end, the Department of the Interior opposed the bill. For its part, the Forest Service was just as nervous and determined to avoid conflict with the Park Service.

Hearings on the bill took place on October 14, 1945. Testifying for the bill were Hoch, Avery, Harlean James, and L.F. Schmeckebier. In addition to wilderness preservation, which Avery probably assumed would not be of much interest to the Committee on Roads, he emphasized physical fitness and preliminary military training. The chairman, Rep. J.W. Robinson, stated that this looked like a job for the individual states and wondered why the federal government would have any interest at all. He further objected to the idea that the federal government should be empowered to exercise condemnation authority within the states. (This was a strange argument from a committee that oversaw roads, for which condemnation frequently had to be exercised.)

Harlean James defended the concept of the trail by citing the precedent of the Blue Ridge Parkway and wondered why cars had

6. *Ibid*, Avery to Clark, February 15, 1945.
7. *Ibid*, Wirth to Avery, March 9, 1945.

such precedence over walkers. Hoch tried to defend his bill by listing the organizations that were in favor, including the American Planning and Civil Association, American Forestry Association, and American Nature Association. His arguments centered on preserving nature, and all the organizations that were in favor of it were connected with nature in some way.

All that was a weak argument when presented to hard-bitten members of Congress whose interest was in building roads. Robinson opened his remarks by noting that the bill had an unfavorable report from both the Federal Works Agency (FWA) and the Bureau of the Budget. FWA stated, "It is not apparent that there can be any substantial need for such trails. The extension and improvement of public highways which have taken place throughout the State would seem definitely to make any such system of trails unnecessary and to limit any need that may exist for them." (Build more highways — that was the best way to get Americans closer to nature.)

It was pointed out that the Department of Agriculture and the Department of the Interior, which would have to administer such trails, were opposed to the bill. The Forest Service, which was part of the Department of Agriculture, was hesitantly in favor but obviously had no interest in pushing the point. The National Park Service, not wishing to publicly oppose their close friend Avery, stayed diplomatically out of the fray.

It was all window dressing. Conrad Wirth wrote, "I might add that when I called Congressman Robinson on October 25 he told me that Congressman Hoch is thoroughly satisfied now that he has had a hearing and that he realized that the bill would not receive favorable action. Congressman Robinson gave Congressman Hoch a fine 'pat-on-the-back' and he feels that the hearing will be of value to him with his constituents and that's all he could possibly expect." Hoch had, in fact, been concerned that no hearing at all would be held.[8] Both Hoch and Robinson were defeated for reelection, so Daniel Hoch was not around to push his bill in subsequent congresses.

---

8. Hunter Library, Sherman Collection, Wirth to Demaray, October 26, 1945.

Not even MacKaye supported the bill. When he learned of it, he drafted a different bill, as a wilderness belt, an old MacKaye plan for wilderness preservation. MacKaye sent it to Howard Zahniser of The Wilderness Society, who shopped it around as an anonymous proposal. When Avery received it, he was cool to the idea, sensing that it was intended to be a competitor to the Hoch bill. (In that, he was absolutely right.) Larry Anderson wrote that this was the first draft of what would become the Wilderness Act.[9]

The Hoch bill, so to speak, was not completely dead after the war. Hoch was no longer in Congress, but Avery wasn't giving up. The bill was reintroduced in 1948 by Representative Francis Walter, also from Pennsylvania. It had been redrafted to avoid the conflict between the Forest Service and Park Service: "Provided, that where such trail system shall cross property under the jurisdiction of any Federal agency other than the United States Forest Service or any State or municipal agency, nothing in this bill shall affect the previously existing jurisdiction of the Federal or State agency or confer on the Forest Service any jurisdiction with respect to such areas that did not previously exist."[10]

The redrafted bill added the nascent Pacific Crest Trail as the second national trail. No political will existed for it in Congress, and the bill never came to a vote on the House floor. It continued to languish well into the 1950s.

---

9. Anderson, *Peculiar Work*, pp. 95-96.
10. ATC archives, Avery correspondence, Avery to Hoch, January 30, 1947.

Chapter 6

EARL SHAFFER AND MURRAY STEVENS: THRU-HIKING PRECEDES THE END OF THE AVERY ERA

My advice in a nutshell is: Travel light, be careful, keep moving, and eat plenty.

— Earl V. Shaffer, 1955

Although the Appalachian Trail exercised a fascination for hikers, and several had walked the entire route in sections, no one until Earl Shaffer in 1948 had ever walked it from end to end in the same year and reported such a feat.

Myron Avery was the first person to have walked the entire trail, completing it in sections in 1936. A few others completed the trail in section hikes by the outbreak of World War II: George Outerbridge, Mary and Martin Kilpatrick, and Charles Hazelhurst, all Pennsylvanians. (Mary was the first woman to walk the entire trail.) Orville Crowder (see page 133) was credited in some quarters (including Shaffer: see *Walking with Spring*) with walking the entire trail, but Jean Stephenson, who was keeping track, did not include Crowder's name on her list.[1] The list kept from at least 1968 onward, however, showed him as the fifth to complete, in 1939.

As for thru-hikes (as they came to be known), no one before Shaffer had reported even attempting a thru-hike, but that did not mean there had been no later claimants. In 1994, an aging Boy Scout, Max Gordon (not his name at the time of the remembered hike), stepped forward to report that a troop of Boy Scouts thru-hiked the trail in 1936. According to his casual report, BSA Troop 257 of the Bronx did the deed, inspired by one Harry "Pop" O'Grady, a leader in the area Scout council. A local veterans group (one would sup-

Earl Shaffer at the end of his first thru-hike.

pose World War I vets) sponsored the hike, meeting the Scouts at points along the trail. The boys were mostly 16 and 17 — at 15, Gordon was the youngest. Gordon stated accurately that there were only two uncompleted sections, from Davenport Gap to the Big Pigeon River and between Spaulding and Sugarloaf mountains.[2] Anyone else associated with this venture was presumably dead, and no corroboration was ever produced despite extensive explorations of the story by ATC and at least two persons who did not have Max's real name to go by. Lacking documentation, ATC did not credit the purported accomplishment permanently.

The Long Cruise

Like Outerbridge, Hazelhurst, and the Kilpatricks, Earl Shaffer was a Pennsylvanian. Born in York, he was the son of a Pennsylvania

---

1. ATC archives, Avery correspondence, 1944-45, Stephenson to "Ruth" at MCM, November 4, 1944.
2. *ATN*, November/December 1994, p. 9.

Dutch mother and an Irish-Welsh father. His father was a tradesman, including silk-weaving and cabinet-making. His mother died at 39 of uncertain causes following gall-bladder surgery. When Earl was five, the family moved to a seven-acre farm near Shiloh, about three miles northwest of York, and there Earl grew up. He graduated from high school in 1935, at 16, with excellent grades, having skipped a grade in grammar school. It was the depth of the Depression, and, since the family was not wealthy, he never attended college, taking on odd jobs, including farm labor and carpentry, where he showed good promise. He was very bright and "knockout handsome."[3]

The family had a tradition of hiking, and the Shaffers would often hike with the Winemiller boys from a neighboring family. Walter Winemiller was closest to Earl's age, and they became close friends. Earl's first experience with camping came when he was 16 or 17. He rode his bicycle to Pine Grove Furnace for a sleep-out. (It was not an entirely happy experience for Earl, who lacked a sleeping bag on a memorably cold night.) On another occasion, he and his younger brother, Evan, hiked for a week on the Appalachian Trail, starting at Snowy Mountain fire tower near Caledonia State Park in southern Pennsylvania.[4]

Earl was drafted into the Army in April 1941. World War II raged in Europe, and the country was swept by the anxiety of war, but Pearl Harbor was still eight months off. Walter chose to enlist in the Marines, and both wound up in the Pacific. Earl did not have a direct combat job, working instead as a radio repairman and communications technician, setting up communications systems in battlefield areas. Walter, on the other hand, was part of a line combat unit that hit the beach at Iwo Jima, near the end of the Pacific War. He was killed in the assault. Earl was devastated.

Three years after the war ended, Earl had still not recovered. Like many GIs who had been through harrowing combat experiences or had lost close friends, he was trying to adjust to a new reality. In

---

3. The most thorough source on Earl's life is David Donaldson and Maurice J. Forrester, *A Grip on the Mane of Life: an Authorized Biography of Earl V. Shaffer, 1918-2002* (Gardners, Pa.: Appalachian Trail Museum, 2014).
4. *Ibid*, p. 41.

his account of his thru-hike, he wrote, "This was the threshold of my great adventure, long delayed by World War II and without my trail partner, who had been killed on Iwo Jima. Those four and a half years of army service, more than half of it in combat areas of the Pacific, without furlough or even rest leave, had left me confused and depressed. Perhaps this trip would be the answer."[5] (In today's parlance, he was probably struggling with post-traumatic stress disorder, or PTSD.)

Planning his trip, he wrote to ATC for maps and guidebooks but never received them — it was discovered later that the Post Office had sent the materials to the wrong address, and they came back "Moved — left no forwarding address."[6] So, he started out with only road maps that showed the general route of the Appalachian Trail but nothing specific. It is a wonder that he even found the trail. Shaffer was 30 years old when he began his hike.

Riding buses, he arrived in Jasper, Georgia, on April 3, 1948, searching for the southern end of the trail. He carried a war-surplus rucksack containing the possessions that he would need for a 2,000-mile walk. He had a rain hat, compass, sheath knife, hand axe, sewing kit, snake bite kit, cook set, T-shirts, Navy turtleneck sweater, Mountain Cloth pants, wool-cotton socks (which he used as gloves, since he didn't wear socks), Birdshooter 9-inch boots, and food that he expected would last him for a week.[7]

Like many hikers before him, he did not carry a sleeping bag, which most hikers considered heavy, and instead slept in a blanket, with a poncho as a rain cover. The blanket was large, felted wool of a type that was used in paper mills to squeeze water out of the paper and was thus termed a "paper mill blanket." Shaffer wrote that he spent $250 on his gear, an expense that was completely covered by a $300 bonus that the War Department had decided, rather late, to award GIs for their service.

---

5. Earl V. Shaffer, *Walking with Spring* (Harpers Ferry, W.Va.: Appalachian Trail Conference, 1983), p. 8.
6. Donaldson and Forrester, *op. cit.*, p. 142.
7. Shaffer, *op. cit.*, p. 8.

No one in Jasper seemed to know where Mount Oglethorpe was, but the resourceful Shaffer managed to find it, and, just before nightfall, he finally arrived at the mountain. He described the scene in *Walking With Spring*:

> *The board sign was battered and weather beaten, its posts held up by a heap of gathered stones. A wintry wind gusted across the bleak and isolated summit, rustling brown leaves among the scraggly grass and muttered through the surrounding trees and brush. Midway in the clearing stood a tall white shaft of native marble, honoring the founder of the state of Georgia.*

He had found the southern end of the trail, and, with this inauspicious start, began one of the great, history-making hikes.

It was a hike that he and Walter had talked about many times, and here he was, ready for the trail and ready to record it. Shaffer carried a notebook to write down his experiences and a camera to photograph them. He was an amateur poet and writer, and he hoped to publish his works. Although not a world-class writer, his writing skills were more than adequate for the task, and his powers of observation were acute. That made his hike all the more historic.

The trail was poorly marked in many places and, in others, not marked at all. "The Long Cruise," as he termed it, got off track many times, and Shaffer wrote of walking the wrong direction for hours and having to backtrack to find the route. In many places, he bushwhacked until he happened across a paint blaze, and, on other stretches, he walked road shoulders for long distances to get around private property. In North Carolina, he walked the Yellow Creek Mountain section to Tapoco and into the Smokies over Gregory and Parson balds, not knowing that the trail had been rerouted down Shuckstack and over Fontana Dam.

In Virginia, he came to a place where a sign stated that the trail was closed, just south of The Priest, for the very good reason that the Blue Ridge Parkway had obliterated the original trail route, and, owing to the war effort and lack of funds, the Forest Service had not yet built the reroute. Not knowing just what to do, he continued on through the unfinished route, bushwhacking for hours until he once again found the A.T.

He stopped to talk to people along the way, encountering quite by chance John Vondell in Massachusetts and Joe Dodge (the AMC White Mountains backcountry manager and legendary trail maintainer) in New Hampshire. In New England, he walked for days trying to follow a trail obliterated by the 1938 hurricane. Arriving, finally, at Katahdin, he insisted on carrying his pack up to the top, because it had been with him all the way, and he didn't propose to change the process on the last day.

He cooked over an open fire and kept his blanket and poncho near it for heat. For food, he specialized in "pan bread," which he called "wonder bread" because he wondered what the next evening meal would be like. He would take oatmeal, corn meal, and flour mixed up into a batter that he would bake in a pan over the fire. He foraged for berries, apples, and other fresh things to stay healthy. He often had to hike off trail to find stores and shop for food.

When he arrived in Holmes, New York, Shaffer sent a letter to ATC announcing where he was, what he was doing, and that he intended to continue to Katahdin. ATC was meeting at Fontana in June 1948 when it received Shaffer's letter. This was the first anyone at ATC had heard of Shaffer or his plans, and it was greeted with initial skepticism. The *Appalachian Trailway News* had recently published an article that such a hike was considered to be impossible, especially considering the condition of the trail following World War II and the long-term lack of maintenance.

Avery sent Shaffer's report to the board of managers, with his own extensive comments.[8] He was astounded at the barriers that Shaffer had to overcome and was unstinting in his praise. "We have never before had an appraisal of the entire route based upon observations over such a short period of time.... Mr. Shaffer, as a stranger, was able to make his way from Georgia to Maine in an extraordinarily short time with a high average rate of daily travel." (Shaffer

---

8. ATC archives, Avery correspondence, Avery letter, November 23, 1948.

averaged more than 16 miles per day.) After his death, Shaffer's claim was challenged because he had to go off the long-neglected trail in so many places. But, the conclusions of Avery and Stephenson have always carried the day at ATC.

Shaffer was determined to advertise his hike and wrote several accounts for various publications. In an article in the *Appalachian Trailway News* for January 1949, he noted that the most useful piece of gear that he carried was a gunny sack that a store owner in Tapoco gave him to stow groceries. He used it to put leaves in and keep his feet warm and to stow his cook set in. When asked what he did when it rained, he wrote, "The answer is simple: I kept on going."

Shaffer was elected to the ATC board as corresponding secretary in 1952 to handle the volume of incoming questions. He remained at that post until Florence Nichol took the job in 1958.

He intended to publish a book and began writing an account of his hike almost as soon as he got back home, sending copies of the draft to ATC's editor, Jean Stephenson, who circulated it to board members. They helped him with editorial changes, misspellings, and typos. But, publisher after publisher rejected the book. When he sent it again to ATC, he never even got an answer, despite offering it fifty percent of the profits. Finally, in 1981, he self-published and had 500 copies printed. Thurston Griggs, another board member, got a copy, and asked ATC to reconsider. *Walking With Spring* was finally published in 1983 and has been kept in print ever since. All profits went to ATC.[9]

In 1949, both *National Geographic* and *Reader's Digest* published articles on Shaffer's thru-hike and the Appalachian Trail. ATC was unprepared for the publicity, and Avery complained that his small volunteer staff in Washington would be overwhelmed by the queries.[10] The articles did result in a dramatic increase in use of the A.T. It was paradoxical, then, that the next thru-hike would be completely uninfluenced by all this publicity.

---

9. Donaldson and Forrester, *op. cit.*, pp. 176-78.
10. ATC archives, Avery correspondence, Avery to Hoch, August 28, 1949.

Espy

In 1951, a twenty-four-year-old Georgia Tech graduate decided to thru-hike the trail. Gene Espy was from Cordele, Georgia, an agricultural area known for its watermelons. Unlike Shaffer, Espy was too young to serve in World War II. He graduated valedictorian of his high school class in 1944 and attended Georgia Tech on a scholarship.

He first heard about the Appalachian Trail from a school teacher and later took a backpacking trip in the Smokies. Unlike Shaffer, he did not decide to hike the trail to work off emotional issues. Instead, he claimed, he thought it would be fun. As he wrote later, "The motivation for my thru-hike was purely to have a fun vacation, and to be right in the middle of the natural beauty God created."[11]

Espy did not know about Earl Shaffer's thru-hike when he put on his pack and headed for Oglethorpe, but his selection of gear was similar, and his recorded expenses were almost identical. Like Shaffer, he used a World War II Army rucksack, but, unlike Shaffer, he carried a sleeping bag, tent, Primus gas stove, and an inflatable pillow. Included in his gear was a hatchet, steel-wool soap pads, canteen, Boy Scout aluminum cook kit, pocket knife, miner's carbide lamp, Kodak camera, compass, Band-Aids, sewing kit, plastic poncho, ground cloth, two T-shirts, clothesline, Maine guide books from L.L.Bean, mosquito netting, and a Bible. His pack weighed 45 pounds, heavier by five pounds than that of Shaffer, but was equipped with more creature comforts.

Espy began somewhat later, on May 31, and ended at Katahdin on September 30. Like Shaffer, he was met at Katahdin by reporters eager to record his experiences. And, like Shaffer, he met Joe Dodge in New Hampshire. (Dodge seemed to be everywhere on the trail.) And, also like Shaffer, he hiked at the same speed, averaging 16.5 miles per day. He had to bypass bad stretches of the trail that had still not been cleared from the results of wartime and the 1938 hurricane.

That same year, two other hikers completed end-to-end hikes. Chester Dziengielewski of Naugatuck, Connecticut, hiked from north

---

11. Gene Espy, *The Trail of My Life: The Gene Espy Story* (Macon, Ga.: Indigo Publishing Group, Inc., 2008), p. 55.

Gene Espy at station at Katahdin base with ranger Fred Pittman in 1951.

to south, the first southbounder, finishing on October 10, just ten days after Espy. He had actually started his hike the year before, but quit at Delaware Water Gap, and returned the following year. (So, technically, his was a "section hike.") On the way, he met Espy and also encountered southbounder Bill Hall from Ohio, as they both passed Clingmans Dome. They hiked the rest of the way together, thus becoming the third and fourth hikers to complete the hike after Shaffer. Finally, in that eventful year of 1951, Martin Papendick of Flint, Michigan, started at Katahdin on June 25 and reached Oglethorpe on October 25.[12] Shaffer had started a trend of sorts.

Mildred Ryder on her A.T. hike.

The thru-hike became a special art form for hikers, and 1951 marked the beginning of a surge in long-distance hiking. Among other notable thru-hikes, perhaps the most ignored was one by Mildred Norman Ryder, later known as Peace Pilgrim. A self-described spiritual teacher and nonviolence advocate, she began a

---

12. *ATN,* January 1952.

thru-hike on April 26, 1952, at Mount Oglethorpe. On the way, she and her companion "flip-flopped" directions and detoured to do the Long Trail, but still completed the hike in October 1952. Peace Pilgrim thus became the first woman to thru-hike the trail.

That same year, George Miller, at 72 the oldest thru-hiker to that point, completed his thru-hike.

Most of these early thru-hikers were oblivious of the others. Espy, for instance, didn't know about Shaffer until he had completed his hike. Dziengielewski didn't know about Bill Hall until the two happened to meet on the trail. In those days, no official record of thru-hikes was kept as reports came in, beyond mentions in the *ATN*. It seemed somewhat odd that the movement should have started so spontaneously. But, once it got rolling, it became almost a cult activity.

In 1956, the *Appalachian Trailway News* reported the most attention-getting thru-hike of all. Emma Gatewood, who went by Grandma Gatewood, from Ohio, had completed a thru-hike from Oglethorpe to Katahdin. She had actually begun the hike the year before in Maine but got lost in Baxter State Park and was the subject of an extended search-and-rescue operation. When they found her, the unsympathetic rescuers told her not to try that again.

The next year, she did try it again but in the somewhat friendlier environs of Georgia. The *ATN*, not acknowledging Peace Pilgrim (despite ATC's having a set of postcards sent by Dick Lamb as he and Mildred hiked), reported that Gatewood was the first woman thru-hiker. It was all the more remarkable because she was 67 at the time, just five years junior to

Emma "Grandma" Gatewood (left) after her failed 1955 thru-hike attempt, in Sugarloaf, Maine, with Marilyn Bell Simpson.

Grandma Gatewood in 1964 (family photo) and her 1956 ATC membership card.

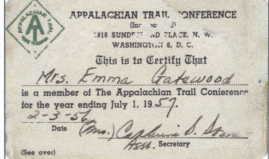

Grandma Gatewood with Ed Garvey and other early thru-hikers at a 1972 ATC meeting.

George Miller, the oldest male thru-hiker. She did it again in 1958, and, in that same year, Dorothy Laker became the third woman thru-hiker.[13]

Grandma Gatewood became a cult legend, partly because of her hiking style, partly because of her background, and partly because she was more "newsworthy" than the run-of-the-mill backpacker. She didn't have a pack but carried her belongings in a sack slung over her shoulder. She didn't have hiking boots but wore tennis shoes. She had no maps, no guidebooks, and no information — in that sense, she was no better off than Earl Shaffer, but a lot older. Shaffer had been a robust 30 — Grandma Gatewood was more than double Shaffer's age.

She was from Gallia County, Ohio, and had grown up poor. A 2014 biography revealed that she was abused by her husband and, after she divorced him, refused even to tell her children where she was, for fear that he would find out. In many ways, one can speculate that she was going through an emotional crisis similar to that of Earl Shaffer. She confronted the trail completely unprepared.[14] Another woman thru-hiker, Dorothy Laker, did her first of two in 1957.

Restoring the Trail

As Myron Avery had stated, the trail was not really "finished" in 1937. Managers faced the constant threat of reroutes forced by private-property owners closing their land to hikers, and, in many places, a better route should be found because of new realities on the ground.

That was the situation with the trail coming south out of Great Smoky Mountains National Park. The problem was, where to cross the Little Tennessee River? The course of least resistance had been to cross over the automobile bridge at Tapoco, a solution that also accorded with the Smoky Mountains Hiking Club's insistence that the trail be routed over the entire distance in the park, rather than using Ozmer's proposed route heading south at Silers Bald.

---

13. *ATN*, January 1956, p. 10; January 1958, p. 9.
14. The most thorough single source on Grandma Gatewood is Ben Montgomery, *Grandma Gatewood's Walk: The Inspiring Story of the Woman Who Saved the Appalachian Trail* (Chicago: Chicago Review Press, 2014). Some related correspondence is among Ed Garvey's papers in the ATC archives, along with a tape of an interview with her elsewhere in the holdings.

But, in 1944, the federal government built a great dam at Fontana on the south side of the Great Smoky Mountains National Park, part of the Tennessee Valley Authority effort to provide more electricity during World War II.[15] Two years later, Hal Miller, an assistant director of publications for a government contractor, sent a letter to Myron Glaser, one of Avery's associates in PATC, suggesting that the trail could now cross the river over the dam. Bring the trail in the park down Shuckstack Ridge, past the fire tower, and straight on down to the dam, he suggested.

Avery passed the suggestion to Guy Frizzell of Smoky Mountains Hiking Club (SMHC), but Frizzell was already thinking about this. SMHC was in favor of a route that would approximate the one that Avery had in mind. Avery wrote to John Stanley, the district ranger for the Nantahala National Forest in August 1946, but, even as he wrote, SMHC volunteers were in the forest, laying out the new route, roughly as originally envisioned by Roy Ozmer and other Georgians (see chapter 3). ATC approved the new trail in January 1947, but it was already a *fait accompli*.[16]

The big rerouting effort took the trail south over Shuckstack and to the Little Tennessee River, crossing over the top of the dam. Avery's decision to hold the first post-war ATC conference at Fontana in 1948 highlighted this major reroute. That was the conference that first received Shaffer's letter, predicting that he would arrive at Katahdin on August 1. (It was actually August 5. He didn't know about the lasting hurricane damage in New England from a decade before.)

Avery addressed the conference about the precarious condition of the trail. Some sections were still virtually closed because of lack of wartime maintenance. Others had been obliterated by timber cuts (despite the 1938 Trailway Agreement pledging not to do that); rerouting promised but not completed by the National Park Service to compensate for the loss of trail to the Blue Ridge Parkway; closure of parts of the trail by private landowners; and the 1938 New England hurricane. All had combined to place the trail in jeopardy.

---

15. It was the highest dam in the eastern United States and fourth-highest in the world.
16. ATC archives, Avery correspondence: Miller to Avery, May 20, 1946; Avery to Frizzell, May 7; Frizzell to Avery, June 4; Avery to Stanley, August 15; Frizzell to Avery, September 24. Also, *ATN*, January 1947, p. 6.

Despite the failure of the Hoch bill (see page 271), Avery renewed the call for public ownership. Writing in 1948, he stated, "Those of us who have labored on the trail on privately owned lands know all too well the hazards of a trail system which depends on the whims of a landowner. For years it has been apparent that the only solution is to bring the trail into public ownership."[17]

Meanwhile, Avery and ATC continued to struggle to get the trail back into serviceable condition. The trail was obliterated by truck trails to fire towers, timbering haul roads, and even the construction of a Federal Communications Commission aircraft radio facility. The Forest Service in particular had trouble coming up with a budget that would permit implementation of the Appalachian Trailway Agreement, and, in some cases, timber companies, evidently oblivious to the fact that there was such an agreement, just continued their former practices. (They were obviously not being watched very carefully.) The agreement was only as good as the funding from Congress and getting rangers educated to support it in the field.

The biggest problem was the long section of trail south of Rockfish Gap that had been closed by construction of the Blue Ridge Parkway. Following the war, the George Washington National Forest informed Avery that they did not have enough money to put the trail back in shape after timber cuts. After stating that there was "keen competition for the use of allotted funds," the George Washington National Forest supervisor wrote, "Demand of National Forest timber is heavy. Much of this mature and overmature timber can be made accessible only by the construction of so-called timber access roads. Projects of this nature are receiving high priority. Other roads and trails...are not considered as urgent for immediate construction as timber access roads." The national housing boom that followed the war was having an effect, and building the new trail over Three Ridges and The Priest kept falling below the cut line in his annual work plan.[18]

A year later, the Forest Service superintendent notified Avery that the trail route over the Religious Range had finally been scouted and

17. ATC archives, Avery correspondence, quote from an ATC news release June 26, 1948.
18. *Ibid*, R.F. Hemmingway, forest supervisor, to Avery, January 4, 1949.

flagged, largely through the help of volunteers, and he was asking for volunteers to help approach landowners to permit a crossing of inholdings. Apparently, Avery indicated that ATC volunteers could do this, both for the Three Ridges–Priest gap and for a trail gap further south, between Black Horse Gap and Bearwallow Gap.[19] By June, Avery notified the Forest Service that ATC had certified the new trail route — he, Fred Blackburn, and Vic Howard had hiked the last thirteen-mile section of trail and pronounced it fit to walk on.[20]

In Maine in 1948, the Bates College Outing Club reopened a section from Saddleback to Andover Hill Road that had been closed since the war. Also in Maine, the Maine State Highway Department restored the Nesowadnehunk Bridge that had been destroyed by a timber company wanting to get their logs downstream so they could go to market.[21] On the minus side, the Barren–Chairback Range was logged by the Saint Regis Paper Company, obliterating the trail and forcing another relocation to the north slope of the range. In New York, the Army gunnery range at Anthony's Nose remained closed despite the end of the war, and the same was true with a range near Indiantown Gap. Those closures lasted for years.[22]

The seven-mile Three Ridges–Priest section finally was opened officially in 1951. At the ceremony, Avery announced that the final blaze had been painted by an anonymous volunteer, chosen by lot and never to be identified. To Avery, this marked the final link in a 2,000-mile chain. The trail was whole again.[23]

Sign marking the restoration of a complete A.T. in 1951. (Photo by Sadye Giller)

19. *Ibid*, Earnest Karger, forest supervisor, to Avery, February 8, 1950.
20. *Ibid*, Avery to Sam Weems, June 26, 1950.
21. *ATN*, September 1950, pp. 38-39.
22. *Ibid*, p. 36.
23. *ATN*, January 1952, p. 11.

The Leadership Change

Myron Avery's legendary work ethic had alarmed his friends as early as 1942. In that year, Marion Park, one of his closest associates in PATC and longtime ATC secretary, wrote to him that

> I have one more thing that I wish to say. I do wish that you would not work so hard. You are always preaching at me about working too hard and that I should try to take things easier, but it seems to me that this time I should urge the same on you. In spite of all your troubles and worries on the Maine work trip, I think the change did you good. You did not seem nearly so nervous and overworked at the end of the trip as you did on our way there. I am really very seriously urging you not to do so much. You are the one who makes the wheels turn so far as the Trail work is concerned and if you get sick, what will happen to the Trail project? Aside from the Trail, I should be very much worried if you got sick and am very much worried about you now. _Please_ take life a little easier and let up on yourself some.[24]

Only six years later, in July 1948, Jean Stephenson sent an ominous letter to an associate. "While returning from the Appalachian Trail Conference at Fontana Dam, N.C., Mr. Avery experienced an accident which will require his hospitalization for a month or more."[25] Whatever this "accident" was, it had occurred at the end of a series of hikes following the conference. Avery was in a hospital in Franklin, North Carolina, but, by the end of July, he was back in Washington. A letter in his file referred to an "illness."

It wasn't, however, an "illness"; it was a heart attack, for him the first of several. Avery's health was sliding downhill, and it would never recover.

Myron worked out regularly at the YMCA, often running laps. He watched his diet, ate fish frequently, and never drank or smoked in his life. He could be described as a health nut but was undoubtedly aware

24. Maine State Library, Avery papers, Park to Avery, October 29, 1942.
25. ATC archives, Avery correspondence, 1948-49, Stephenson to Professor Baldinger, July 7, 1948.

of a family history of heart trouble. His sister, Evelyn (age unknown), died from a heart condition in 1941, and a brother, Bob, died of a heart attack at 68.[26]

Up against this was Avery's lifestyle. In the words of his son, Hal, "Myron was completely committed to everything he touched. He had a regular phone in the house, and also one that connect to the Admiralty, and it was death if you touched that phone." In other words, Myron the admiralty lawyer was on duty at all times, and that was just his regular job. He would work on PATC/ATC business in the evenings after work, and he was known to have dictated forty letters in a single evening. In those days, government employees worked five full days with a half-day on Saturday. Myron was always on a trail somewhere whenever he wasn't at work

Marion Park, ATC's longtime secretary.

or at a meeting somewhere in the East. The intensity of his life is hard to imagine.

Myron slept poorly, and, once Hal turned 16, the son was often deputized to drive his dad to work because Myron was too sleepy to operate a motor vehicle. The combination of lack of sleep and a frenetic lifestyle, plus a family history of heart trouble, proved to be a lethal combination in the long run.

In those days, there was no real cure for a heart condition. Bed rest was prescribed, and, in many situations, that bed rest was done in a hospital. Myron spent several sessions in various hospitals. Hal tells of one hospital stay in which he was posted in his dad's bedroom and told to "go get someone" if Myron stopped breathing.

---

26. Interview with Hal Avery, September 10, 2013.

Avery and his wife, Jeannette, in an undated photo.

In those later years, Avery appeared to age considerably, as the photograph at left, taken on an unknown date with his wife, shows. In April 1952, he wrote to Paul Fink about his problems:

...[P]robably Walter Diehl has told you something of the Avery disabilities during the past year. I made a good recovery from my Fontana troubles in 1948, but 1951 turned out to have much in store for me. Last June, I blew the 'circulator tubes' and had the usual hospital experience. That was quite an affair. Then I went to the Maine woods to rest and recuperate but developed pulmonary troubles, which pulled down my strength tremendously. I came back and returned to work in September but my intestinal system cracked up, also. As a result, I became exhausted and depleted to the point that I resigned my professional activities at the beginning of the year 1952. Hospital and Sanitarium tours have not improved the situation very much. At the present time, it is a matter of whether the medics will decide to remove any of the worn-out parts.[27]

All this was out of public view. Only close associates knew of Avery's true condition. Thus, it must have come as a shock to the ATC membership when it learned *via* the January 1952 *ATN* that he would not continue past the upcoming conference at Skyland. Although Avery signed all the conference paperwork, when the conferees assembled in June, Avery was not there. He was too sick to travel.

---

27. ATC archives, Avery correspondence, Avery to Fink, April 28, 1952.

In his final report to the conference, Avery delegated the chairmanship of the conference to Murray Stevens of New York, and, at the business meeting, the conferees elected Stevens as the permanent chairman to succeed Avery. Avery again emphasized the need for permanent protection of the Appalachian Trail by government involvement.

ATC had never known another leader. His presence was still so magnetic that almost thirty percent of the delegates came from PATC, where he was not just the president, he was an icon. The conferees memorialized their former chairman since they had no other. "Now, therefore, be it resolved that this Twelfth Appalachian Trail Conference...acknowledges that no words are adequate to express the feelings of this Conference but that all who know the story of the Appalachian Trail will cherish in their hearts the privilege which was theirs of being associated with Myron in the common objective and accomplishments of our Appalachian Trail."[28]

Murray Stevens understood what he had gotten himself into. Living in New York, he could not exert the physical presence in Washington that Avery had, and it was unlikely that he could dictate up to forty letters in a single sitting. In his letter to Avery, he wrote, "I warned them all that the days of 'Let Myron do it, he won't mind' were over, and told them that my major policy was one of 'decentralization,' which according to my definition, meant less work for the chairman and more work for everyone else."[29]

Nor did Stevens have the support of Myron's devoted volunteer secretarial staff — Marion Park, Kathryn Fulkerson, Florence Nichol, etc. — swirling about his desk, taking care of his correspondence like true executive secretaries. For the first time, ATC hired secretarial help for Stevens, with an annual budget of $200 per year, and authorized transportation expenses for the chairman.[30]

Now retired from public life, Myron took his younger son, Hal, on a trip in July 1952 to do some research into his family background. That took them to Nova Scotia, directly across the Bay of Fundy from

---

28. PATC *Bulletin*, July 1952, p. 66.
29. ATC archives, Avery correspondence, Stevens to Avery, June 3, 1952.
30. ATC archives, Conference meetings, Box 6-1-2.

Lubec, and they checked into the Annapolis Royal Hotel. The next day, they were on the grounds of Fort Anne National Historical Park when Myron complained of not feeling well. They stopped and got out of the car, whereupon Myron fell to the ground. Hal rushed to the door of a house on the road where they were. It happened that a doctor lived in the house and was home at the time. He went out to examine Avery and pronounced him dead at the scene. In his opinion, Myron Avery was dead the moment he fell, from a massive heart attack.[31] He was only 52.

After death, Avery was accorded many eulogies. Ed Garvey, who went on to significant leadership roles in ATC, characterized Avery as "drive, drive, drive!.... It is generally conceded that the constant driving of one man, Myron Avery, was the primary force which resulted in the completion of the 2,000-mile Appalachian Trail. It is true that Avery ruffled a few feathers in his efforts to create the trail. No one will deny, however, that he was guided by a sense of urgency that undoubtedly accomplished the almost impossible job of creating the Trail."[32]

One anonymous writer, undoubtedly Jean Stephenson, wrote somewhat poetically of Avery's significance:

> It has been said that every achievement is but the lengthening shadow of one man. As Myron Avery, facing into the sunset, follows the trail over the hills into the land from which there is no return, we can see the long shadow of his erect and vigorous figure stretching back over mountain and woodland until it changes imperceptibly into a footpath from Maine to Georgia and Georgia to Maine, a path where all may find once again the oneness of a man with Nature and feel with him 'joy because the Trail is there,' and share his 'peace because the Trail is good.'"[33]

In 1953, the Maine legislature named the east peak of Bigelow Mountain after Myron Avery. It became Avery Peak, with an Avery

---

31. Interview with Hal Avery.
32. PATC *Bulletin*, July/September 1965, p. 43.
33. *ATN*, September 1952, p. 35.

Memorial Lean-to.[34] ATC created an Avery Memorial Fund, used to finance the guidebooks for a period. It was an appropriate purpose — Myron loved guidebooks.

The Avery family plot in Lubec, Maine, where both Myron and Jeannette are buried. She outlived him by 36 years.

In an Avery family photograph album kept by Myron's granddaughter, this is labeled, "Dad's last picture."

---

34. PATC *Bulletin,* July 1953, p. 82.

Murray Stevens and the near-term future of the Appalachian Trail

Murray Stevens, who succeeded Myron Avery at the ATC conference in 1952, was confronted with the slow-rolling crisis that Avery, in his final message to the conference, had identified — that of private ownership.

Stevens was not unfamiliar with the problem. He was a member of the New York Chapter of the Appalachian Mountain Club (AMC), and his trail section ran from the Hudson River to the Connecticut line. Stevens had worked with Ned Anderson to link the New York and Connecticut sections, surmounting private-property issues along the way, but that success was not replicated in most other parts of his section. East of the Hudson, the trail confronted built-up areas, with towns and roads and very little public land east of Fahnestock State Park. (See chapter 5.) It was the hardest of the hard and sensitized Murray to the problem that Avery had left him.[35]

Stevens' tenure, from 1952 to 1961, was a time of turmoil for the Appalachian Trail. Created it was, but it rested on a bed of sand. Estimations of private property ranged from forty-five to fifty percent, and the location of the trail was so poorly defined that no one knew for sure what figure was accurate, or where, exactly, the trail tread lay. ATC and the component clubs were working on various solutions to the private-property issue, and several were implemented, in addition to a change of terminus from Oglethorpe to Springer. The trail reroute south and west of Roanoke placed the trail on Forest Service land (albeit encumbered by inholdings) and solved one of the most pressing issues, but there were many others. State or federal ownership was the most permanent solution, but no one knew precisely how to go about it. As Stevens assumed his chair, the alarms of Avery were still ringing in his ears. His mission was clear.

ATC also was making little progress in its program to build shelters every eight to ten miles on the trail. In 1955, Stan Murray of the Tennessee Eastman Hiking and Canoeing Club reported the loss of seven shelters in its section — two to old age, three to fire, and two

---

35. For Murray's background, see the Watermans' *Forest and Crag, op. cit.,* p. 493-95, and *ATN,* July/August 2000, Robert Rubin, "Murray Stevens."

Murray Stevens was born in Brookline Village, Massachusetts, in 1894. His family moved to New York when he was 10 and decided to stay. He graduated from Princeton in engineering in 1916 and joined AMC after service in World War I (like Major Welch, in the Army Corps of engineers). Stevens became associated with the A.T. route east of the Hudson, one of the most difficult stretches of trail because of the lack of public land and the opposition of landowners in the area. He and Avery became acquainted at the ATC meeting in Easton in 1929 and remained close until Avery died. When Avery lived in New York during World War II, he worked with Stevens on that section of trail.

Sadye Giller, Marion Park, and Murray Stevens (right) at the 1955 Clarks Ferry Bridge dedication.

to closure by landowners. This led to renewed requests to the Forest Service and National Park Service to help build new shelters on public land. ATC had some success in Maine and in the South, but little progress was made in Connecticut, Massachusetts, New Jersey, and New York because of private-property issues.[36]

Private forest land was being lost at a rapid pace, and nowhere was this moving faster than in the mountains west of Washington, D.C. PATC was losing trail miles and shelters. In 1954, for instance, where U.S. 50 crosses the first ridge of the Appalachians, the owner of the land on which the trail and Ashby Gap Shelter sat unceremoniously booted the club off his land, not even permitting them to retrieve the wood from the shelter. This was to happen again and again on the trail from Harpers Ferry south to Shenandoah National Park.

---

36. *ATN*, September 1955, pp. 37-38; *ATN*, September 1961, pp. 47-48.

Roanoke club members on a break during the 1958 meeting (left to right): Charlene Campbell, Tom Campbell, Molly Denton, Jim Denton, Preston Leech, and Sally Nelson.

To counter the threat, the club reconstituted its conservation committee. Originally established to study the problem of the Chesapeake and Ohio towpath, the committee was asked to begin looking into the landowner issues south of Harpers Ferry. The committee, chaired by Phil Stone, represented a seminal moment in the history of the trail — a recognition that something had to be done and fast.

The 1958 ATC meeting was held at the idyllic Mountain Lake resort in south-central Virginia. Just fourteen miles east of Pearisburg, it was nestled into a cove below Potts Mountain, and the new Jim Denton-scouted route of the trail ran along the ridge above the resort. The conference had some big decisions to make, all of them related to the private-property issue. It also was at this conference that ATC officially approved the southern-terminus change from Mount Oglethorpe to Springer Mountain. It also approved the scouting and construction of a new trail, called the Big Blue south of the Potomac River and the Tuscarora north of it. This new trail would be a potential new route of the Appalachian Trail should private-property concerns force the trail off its existing path.[37]

37. ATC archives, Conference meetings, Box 6-1-2, Mountain Lake file.

During the 1958 conference, Seymour Smith of Connecticut and Murray Stevens hike up to the War Spur Trail, left, while Earl Shaffer serenades hikers outside a Pearisburg outfitter, right.

A report there by the PATC conservation committee resulted in a long roundtable discussion, chaired by Murray Stevens, entitled, "Can Permanent Stability of the Appalachian Trail be Attained?" Phil Stone was joined by Jim Cragon (affiliation unknown), Jean Stephenson, Jim Denton from the Roanoke club, and Sam Wilkinson of the New York–New Jersey Trail Conference. Stone began the discussion by reading from a report by his committee that focused on the troubled fifty-six-mile section from Harpers Ferry to the Shenandoah park.

The conferees had available Stone's very detailed study of land use along the trail. He included every aspect, including subdivision, farms, homes, road access, ownership, and topography. The study posed questions: Could easements (instead of the current method of handshake agreements) work? Could volunteers work with landowners, or did it have to be public officials? Was the power of eminent domain a requirement?[38]

Stone was convinced that government ownership was the only answer, but he did not know whether it should be federal or state. Jim Denton disliked the state solution, contending that Virginia would never accept responsibility for the trail — Virginia officials regarded it as a long, thin park that would be impossible to govern. If even one state opted out, the project would run aground. In Denton's opinion, only federal ownership would work.

Carl Chauncey of the New England Trail Conference was pessimistic about the prospects for public ownership in New England, because all the land had been populated for decades, and ATC would just have to accept some road-walking. Cragon was hopeful that the trail had been in certain places for so long that a right-of-way could be legally established, similar to British common law concerning the public's right to walk. Jean Stephenson held out hope that easements might be the answer in some cases. Some felt that ATC would have to get into the land-buying business — raise money and buy the most threatened tracts.

Sidney Tappan of Maine was pessimistic. He wrote to Carl Chauncey that he did not believe the trail would ever be stable. Referring to the burgeoning timber industry in Maine and the movement for skyline drives in many areas, Tappan wrote, "The odds are very much against us and have been from the moment of its inception, but let's keep up the fight which has only begun."[39]

With so many proposed options and no final determination, Jean Stephenson moved that the committee be continued at the ATC level, and Stevens appointed permanent members and a chairman.

The committee continued to meet, and the problem continued to fester. It was still there when Stevens handed over the ATC gavel in 1961. "I believe," he wrote, "that the only solution for the Trail is in public ownership." Then, in the same report, he added a new and interesting idea — that a "greenbelt" of public lands be purchased, with

---

38. *ATN*, May 1959, pp. 23-24.
39. ATC archives, Conference meetings; Tappan to Chauncey, May 14, 1958.

the Appalachian Trail as the spinal column for this sylvan belt. Was he remembering Benton MacKaye's proposal for a greenbelt?

In his final report, Stevens stated that the trail was mostly on public roads all the way from High Point in New Jersey to Greylock in Massachusetts. Why not build a bypass of that entire area, routing the trail up into the Shawangunks, over to the Catskills, across the Hudson on the Rip Van Winkle Bridge, over to the Massachusetts state line, and up the Taconics, rejoining the original route at Greylock?[40] Thus, Stevens added new ideas to the problems that he had inherited and was passing on to his successor.

Through the Stevens' term of office, the power relationship between PATC and ATC continued largely as before. Myron Avery was no longer alive, but his influence lived on, and ATC was not yet entirely in the lead. That was one of the things that the incoming chairman, Stanley Murray of Kingsport, Tennessee, intended to change.

ATC itself required a stronger voice in its relationship with PATC. In 1954, ATC was renting the basement of the PATC headquarters in downtown Washington for $150 per month.[41] That represented the true power rela-

The PATC/ATC building at 1916 Sunderland Place.

---

40. ATC archives, Murray Stevens paper, 1961 annual report. See also *ATN*, September 1964, p. 45.
41. PATC *Bulletin*, April 1954, p. 58.

tionship between the two organizations. In 1947, PATC had purchased a three-story townhouse at 1916 Sunderland Place in Washington. The top two floors were already rented when the club took over, so PATC took the main floor and donated the basement to ATC. It was small, just a single room measuring thirteen by nineteen feet, crammed to the ceiling with files. Finally, in 1955, the renters departed, and PATC took the second floor. ATC was given the third floor, which doubled their space, and PATC increased the rent. It took several more years for ATC to find its own headquarters. That project awaited new leadership.

Moving the Trail: Pennsylvania

Avery knew that the Appalachian Trail was not in the optimal location, and, under Murray Stevens' guidance, ATC began moving large sections. One of the first was in Pennsylvania, under the leadership of Earl Shaffer.

What drove the relocation was Indiantown Gap. Originally a Pennsylvania National Guard post, the U.S. Army took it over during World War II, began artillery practice, and, for safety, evicted the hikers. This resulted in a long road-walk.

A relocation would solve other problems, too. Originally the trail continued south through Indiantown Gap, through Manada Gap, and along Blue Mountain to the Susquehanna River, where it came to an abrupt end. Hikers could see Blue Mountain continuing along the ridge across the river, but there was no way to get there except to walk six miles on roads to a point north of Harrisburg where they could cross the river on an automobile bridge, then trudge another six-mile road walk back to Blue Mountain and climb up the ridge, continuing on the Darlington Trail.

Shaffer's reroute began at Swatara Gap, northeast of Indiantown Gap. The new trail crossed north over a series of low ridges: Second Mountain, then Sharp Mountain, then Stony Mountain, and finally across Clark's Valley to Peters Mountain. The relocation continued along Peters Mountain to the Susquehanna, where it conveniently met the river at the

Clarks Ferry Bridge. It continued south on road shoulders to the town of Duncannon, where climbed up to Hawk Rock on Cove Mountain, and along that ridge to Dean's Gap on Blue Mountain. It crossed Cumberland Valley on the Avery–Schairer route and finally joined the old trail at Center Point Knob.

Stevens' annual report to ATC in 1953 described the new route. It was a historic, fifty-eight-mile reroute, and it was dedicated in 1955 at the Clarks Ferry Bridge. Daniel Hoch and Murray Stevens attended (see page 270).[1]

Earl Shaffer was not done. He became the prime mover and, in some cases, the only worker on four shelters. He built Darlington Shelter out of stone, working by himself. For the Thelma Marks Shelter, Mountain Club of Maryland (MCM) provided some assistance dragging chestnut logs (highly prized because of their long-term sustainability) to the work site. He built what became known as the Earl Shaffer Shelter on Peters Mountain entirely on his own. Finally, he built an Adirondack-style log lean-to north of the Susquehanna, a shelter that was eventually replaced by Clarks Ferry Shelter.[2]

Shaffer argued that a new trail club should be established in Harrisburg, and a state-wide hiking organization should be formed. In 1954, the Susquehanna Appalachian Trail Club was established, pushed by Shaffer, Ralph Kinter, and George Gruber.

Shaffer also played a key role in bringing the disparate trail clubs in Pennsylvania together at last. The idea came up at a joint PATC–MCM meeting in the Catoctin Mountains in October 1955. The forward-thinking Fred Blackburn of PATC was the prime mover of the idea, which quickly caught the imagination of the Pennsylvania clubs. They formed a steering committee then and there, with Blackburn, Mel Brinton, W.R. Roessler of MCM, and Shaffer. The committee held its first formal meeting on January 21, 1956, in Harrisburg, chaired by Murray Stevens, which gave it enhanced status.

1. ATC archives, Stevens papers, Stevens annual report.
2. Donaldson and Forrester, *op. cit.*, pp. 204-208.

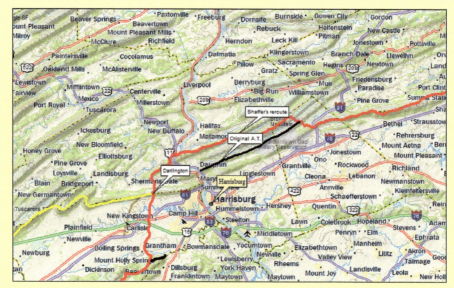

The Shaffer relocation

The new organization, naming itself the Keystone Trails Association (KTA), was officially established on April 15. Any trail organization in Pennsylvania could join, but most that did were A.T.-maintaining clubs. The original members were the Susquehanna Appalachian Trail Club, PATC, MCM, Williamsport Alpine Club (the remnants of the Pennsylvania Alpine Club), a Boy Scout troop, and the Horseshoe Trail Club. The rest of the trail-maintaining clubs soon joined.[3]

One of the most important reasons for KTA was an unusual one — guidebooks. At the time, the A.T. in Pennsylvania was divided into two guidebooks: one published by the New York–New Jersey Trail Conference, covering the trail from Delaware Water Gap to Duncannon, and one published by PATC that covered the southwest part of the trail from Duncannon south to Pen Mar. Jean Stephenson, whose fiefdom had always included the ATC publications program, was opposed strongly to a single issue for Pennsylvania, as was Ralph Kinter, who was elected the first KTA president.

3. PATC *Bulletin*, October 1956, p. 27; January 1957, p. 85; Smithsonian Museum of American History, Shaffer Collection, Box 25, folder 16.

It was a recipe for conflict, and Kinter could not get along with the rest of the KTA officers. He was defeated after a single year, and George Spring, who favored the consolidated guidebook, replaced Kinter. It took another ten years for the new guidebook to be published, but the most important product was not the guidebook itself, it was KTA and the unification of the formerly disunited Pennsylvania clubs.[4]

Moving the Trail: The Roanoke Reroute

The planning for the longest reroute in A.T. history began before World War II with correspondence between Avery and officers of the Roanoke Appalachian Trail Club. It had been Avery's strong feeling all along that the trail in Virginia would eventually have to be moved from the Blue Ridge route, which was entirely on private land and road shoulders. It was also due to conflict with the future Blue Ridge Parkway, which was to use approximately the same route as the trail. The war interrupted Avery's plans, but, immediately after the war, Jim Denton, the new president of Roanoke Appalachian Trail Club, contacted Avery to renew the planning. Avery did not know Denton but overcame his own personal doubts and asked Denton to chair a committee to design the reroute.[5] It was a wise choice. (See chapter 4.)

Denton was faced with an awesome task. He was to take the Appalachian Trail from its earlier route that followed the original path that Ozmer had scouted (see page 114). In subsequent years, the A.T. had to be rerouted west of Roanoke so that it could include Tinker Cliffs and McAfee Knob. It was near McAfee that Denton began his reroute. At that point, it turned west and continued over several ridges ultimately to Peters Mountain, on the Virginia–West Virginia border, and then south to Pearisburg, Virginia. From there, he had to go south and then east again to rejoin the existing trail on Iron

4. Maurice Forrester, "The First Ten Years of KTA: 1956-1965;" interview of Forrester by Deborah Smith, unknown date.
5. *ATN*, May 1949, pp. 15-16.

Mountain. Today, that route is 188 miles, almost four times the length of the Shaffer reroute in Pennsylvania. It was about nine and a third percent of the total length of the A.T.

Jefferson Forest Supervisor A.R. Cochran told Denton that any route through the forest was okay with him as long as it didn't intrude on active logging operations. The original plan was to have it continue down Big Walker Mountain and cross the New River at Ripplemead, but that route confronted some very difficult issues. It was a dry ridge for many miles and created a very difficult hiking environment, and private land owners dotted Forest Service land. The Forest Service tried to erase the most difficult inholdings, to no avail.

Ultimately, the Appalachian Trail had to be moved off Big Walker. Denton's new route proceeded almost due west over Catawba Mountain, Cove Mountain, Brush Mountain, Sinking Creek Mountain, John's Creek Mountain, Potts Mountain, and Big Mountain. It eventually hit Peters Mountain, the ridge that formed the border between Virginia and West Virginia. That route included an overlook of Burkes Garden, the highest valley in Virginia, about sixty-six trail miles south of Pearisburg. Murray Stevens announced at the ATC meeting at Mount Moosilauke, New Hampshire, in 1955 that the entire route had been laid out, but it took another twenty-five years to complete the construction.

The original work led by Denton was done by the Roanoke club, an organization with only sixty members.[6] The reroute was finally officially completed in 1980-1981.

Moving the Trail: Roan Mountain

Another major reroute was to Roan Mountain, on the border between North Carolina and Tennessee. The original Appalachian Trail continued south from Damascus, Virginia, on Holston Mountain on the Virginia–Tennessee state line. It dropped abruptly off the mountain and became a twenty-four-mile road walk,

6. ATC archives, Avery correspondence: Denton to Avery, March 15, 1950; 1950-52, Denton to Avery, April 10, 1950; *ATN*, May 1950; *ATN* September 1951.

maintained for many years by Paul Fink; see page 179. (This portion of the early A.T. is shown on the map at right in red.) The new A.T. would leave the trail at about the midpoint on Holston Mountain, follow an existing trail along the top of Cross Mountain, to Iron Mountain to Watauga Dam, and across the valley east of

The Roan Mountain relocation: Fink's road route in red, the new A.T. in black.

Hampton. It would eventually cross U.S 19E a few miles west of Elk Park, then up Hump Mountain. It would then follow the ridge from Hump to Cloudland and from Cloudland to Carvers Gap.

The catalyst for the reroute was Stan Murray of the Tennessee Eastman Hiking and Canoeing Club, who surfaced the new route at the ATC meeting in 1952. Both Cherokee and Pisgah national forest supervisors approved the route, with a seventy-two-mile trail that Murray described as "some of the most beautiful scenery to be found in this part of the country."[7] The new trail was dedicated on June 1, 1954. The dynamic Murray was to succeed Murray Stevens as chairman of ATC in 1961.

Saving the Towpath

In 1948, the Appalachian Trail bypassed Harpers Ferry, arguably the most historic place on the trail. After 1936 floods washed out a highway bridge, hikers had been using a ferry to cross the Potomac River. The arrangement frustrated hikers who, arriving at the ferry slip, had trouble hailing the ferry operator on the other side. A new bridge across the Potomac at

---

7. ATC archives, Murray correspondence, Murray to TEHCC members, undated [spring 1952].

Sandy Hook, Maryland, offered hikers on the towpath a way across that did not involve the ferry operators, and a bypass route was constructed on the Virginia side, up steep Loudoun Heights and joining with the existing trail farther south.[8]

In 1950, the National Park Service recommended to Congress that the Chesapeake and Ohio Canal towpath, which had formed part of the Appalachian Trail since it was opened, be paved over. It would make a wonderful scenic parkway, it was argued. As the proposal gained more traction, PATC became alarmed. In 1953, the club created a conservation committee and began running demonstration hikes along the towpath to advertise its scenic and historic qualities that could be damaged by being paved. But, the paving proposal just gained steam, and, in 1954, the prestigious *Washington Post* commented favorably about the idea.

That was when Supreme Court Justice William O. Douglas, a lifetime climber and hiker (including on the A.T.), stepped in

to save the towpath. Douglas led a hike along the entire 186-mile distance from the western end, Cumberland, Maryland, to the eastern terminus in the District of Columbia. Thirty-four people began the historic hike, and nine, including PATC's President Grant Conway, finished, becoming the "immortal nine."

Justice Douglas, an A.T. 2,000-miler, and his wife, Cathy.

8. *ATN*, May 1948, p. 69.

Logistics arrangements for the hike fell through at the last minute, and PATC rushed in to provide meals and overnight accommodations. After the hike was completed, the *Post* partially recanted its support for the parkway. The following year, the National Park Service quietly shoved its original proposal into a desk drawer, and, in 1971, Congress created the Chesapeake and Ohio National Historical Park, thus saving a small but important three-mile segment of the Appalachian Trail.[9]

Moving the Southern Terminus

The original southern terminus at Mount Oglethorpe had been adopted based on a recommendation by Roy Ozmer in 1927 that that mountain represented the southern end of the Appalachian chain. This mysterious recommendation was accepted by Avery, Kephart, and Perkins with very little discussion. At the time, no mechanism for "certifying" routing options for the trail existed.

By the mid-1950s, the problems of the section from Oglethorpe to Amicalola Falls State Park were unavoidable. The route was entirely on road shoulders and private property, and developments were intruding on the fourteen-mile section south of Amicalola. The trail was not through a mature forest environment that MacKaye had envisioned but was characterized by timbering operations and chicken farms and houses that had moved into the Oglethorpe area. Development pressures seemed to demand a route change, and the free-range chickens disgusted hikers as they walked along the road coursing down the mountain.

Hearing the complaints, the Georgia Appalachian Trail Club (GATC) decided in early 1956 to discontinue the Sassafras Shelter, only three miles from the end of the trail, and, at the same time, appointed a committee, headed by former president

9. PATC *Bulletin,* October 1953, p. 117, and April 1954, p. 9; *ATN,* May 1954, pp. 22-23, and September 1956, p. 42.

Larry Freeman, to study and recommend what to do about Oglethorpe.[10]

Freeman's committee was decidedly unimpressed with the environment around Oglethorpe and presented an unambiguous resolution to the club: "That the GATC recommend to the A.T. Conference that the southern terminus of the Appalachian Trail be located at the summit of Springer Mountain, and that the present Trail running north from Amicalola Falls State Park to Springer, which passes the Benton MacKaye shelter at Frosty Mountain, be retained as a blue-blazed trail, while the portion of the Trail extending south from Amicalola Falls be abandoned."[11]

Murray Stevens visited GATC the following year, made a trip to Springer, and supported the GATC position. He took that opinion to the 1958 ATC meeting at Mountain Lake, Virginia. Then-GATC President Henry Morris, attending the conference, made the official presentation of GATC's position, that the A.T. terminus be changed to read "Springer Mountain" instead of Oglethorpe.[12] And so it came to pass that the southern terminus was moved twenty-one miles northward. By a single stroke, ATC and the clubs changed the southern terminus that had existed for more than thirty years.

The "southern end" of the Appalachian Mountains is in fact in dispute. Some geologists contend that it actually ends in Alabama, Flagg Mountain being most frequently mentioned. (Others argue the chain ends in Peru, geologically speaking.) ATC has held consistently with Springer — not for geological reasons, but for historical justification. It has been there since 1958, and there it shall stay, according to ATC and the act of Congress establishing the Appalachian National Scenic Trail.

---

10. GATC, *op. cit.*, p. 172; *ATN*, January 1956, May 1956.
11. GATC, *ibid*, p. 181; *ATN*, January 1957.
12. GATC, *ibid*, pp. 183-184.

Chapter 7

STAN MURRAY AND THE NATIONAL TRAILS SYSTEM ACT

In choosing the location for a new trail, the first thing to know is that every inch of ground, however wild looking, belongs to some-body.

— Ron Strickland, in *Pathfinder:*
Blazing a New Wilderness Trail in Modern America

At the ATC meeting in 1952, Frank Oglesby from the Tennessee Eastman Hiking and Canoeing Club introduced a twenty-eight-year-old club member who had an idea. He proposed a seventy-two-mile reroute of the Appalachian Trail to take it off roads and place it onto Roan Mountain. The young man, Stanley A. Murray, was passionate about the Roan and thought that he could accomplish the reroute in just three years. Some of his own club members were incredulous, but Murray was undaunted.

Murray, like Myron Avery, grew up in Maine, in his case in the seaport town of Rockland. The town is about 150 miles down the coast from Lubec, Avery's birthplace and final resting place, and the coincidence of two Maine men heading ATC less than a decade apart is striking.

Born in 1924, Murray was at the University of Maine studying chemical engineering when World War II broke out and served in the

A young Stan Murray

Army for three years, working at Oak Ridge National Laboratories in Tennessee. (On the day the atomic bomb was dropped on Hiroshima, Japan, in 1945, he was awarded a certificate of appreciation for his work in developing it for the Manhattan Project.) After graduation, he got a graduate degree in engineering from the Massachusetts Institute of Technology. He then went to work at Tennessee Eastman in Kingsport, Tennessee. It was a job that he kept for the rest of his working life, eventually becoming a division chief. He hiked often, both from Oak Ridge and from Kingsport, and his favorite hiking area was the Roan Highlands. When he became chairman of ATC, he brought his love of the Roan to Washington.

Stan Murray was a very different person from Myron Avery. He did not have the fiery temper or the argumentative nature. His temperament was more like Murray Stevens — he has been described as quiet but determined, thoughtful, and serious. He was good at long-range planning, and he came to ATC at a time when planning was critical. His predecessors, Myron Avery and Murray Stevens, both believed that the only way to save the A.T. was federal protection. It was clear to Murray that this was his mission, and he managed to shove everything else aside in pursuit of a solution.

Kingsport was a long drive from Washington, and like Stevens, he did not have the coterie of volunteer secretarial pool that Avery could draw from. He would dictate his correspondence on a Dictaphone, and, once a week, a secretary would type it up and send it out. He often did commute to Washington (and later, to Harpers Ferry), usually accompanied by his wife, Judy, to the Potomac A.T. Club)/ ATC headquarters. Sometimes they would sleep on the floor of the ATC office at PATC, and Judy remembers sleeping on the fire escape once.

Stan soon struck up a close friendship with Walter S. Boardman, new executive director of The Nature Conservancy (TNC) and an A.T. 2,000-miler, and he and Judy would often stay with the Boardmans in downtown Washington. The trips to Washington were especially frequent when he was pushing for federal legislation in 1966–1968.[1] That was when he was in almost daily communication with Boardman. The Nature Conservancy was one of the prime sponsors of federal protection after his retirement.

Paul Pritchard, ATC's second hire as executive director, noted Stan's vision. "The clubs still considered that ATC was just going to be a loose confederation, but Stan had a vision. He felt it was going to be more than that."[2]

Since ATC had no staff when he became chairman, Murray in 1961 inherited a group of volunteers who came entirely from PATC but were ATC volunteers and even board members at the same time. It was a group of longtime club members who came to PATC in both capacities in the evenings to open the mail, answer correspondence, mail out maps and guidebooks, greet customers, and answer the phones. The secretary was Fred Blackburn; the treasurer was Sadye Giller; Jean Stephenson handled guidebooks; Egbert Walker made the maps; Florence Nichol was editor of the *Appalachian Trailway News* (*ATN*) after 1964, succeeding Jean; the archivist, former special assistant to Myron Avery, and secretary for fourteen years before Blackburn was Marion Park; the office manager was Ray Gingrich. This was the way it had always been done, because ATC was PATC, and PATC was ATC.

After Murray Stevens succeeded Avery in 1952, little changed at first. But, when Stan Murray replaced Stevens, Stan realized that the

---

1. Interview with Judy Murray and Jay Leutze, September 25, 2014.
2. Interview with Paul Pritchard, May 12, 2014.

organizations needed to pull apart. When in 1963 he launched his push to get federal legislation, he began moving toward a professional staff. In 1966, Ed Garvey, then the organization secretary, reported to the board of managers that the job was too big for a volunteer and said it was time to hire someone at least to take care of the mail. The board decided to bring on a part-time "secretary" with a $2,500-a-year honorarium. Searching for a candidate, they found Lester Holmes.[3]

Holmes (1905–1984) was a retired Army lieutenant colonel, the type who never quite shed the military mindset, with all its pluses and minuses. An Iowa native, he had attended the University of Iowa and entered the Army soon after graduation. He first got involved with the A.T. in 1950, when he was working with Boy Scouts at Fort Monroe, Virginia. After retirement, he moved to Frederick, Maryland, and joined PATC in 1966.

Once Holmes was hired part-time, the need for paid staff just kept increasing — the membership had increased five-fold in two years, a corollary to Murray's push for federal protection, and there was a need to manage the additional revenue coming in from membership dues and to maintain more frequent contact with the maintaining clubs and trail districts. In 1968, the year that the National Trails System Act was passed, Murray proposed that the board make Holmes' position full-time at a salary of $6,000 per year.[4]

For a time, Holmes staffed ATC alone. But, with a move to Harpers Ferry in 1972, all the PATC volunteers that had kept ATC afloat were no longer available, so all new people were needed. It was expensive to replace a herd of volunteers with paid staff. By 1974, the paid staff had increased to eight full- or part-time positions. The staffer with the greatest impact was Jean Cashin, who had been hired as the office manager, replacing volunteer Ray Gingrich. By that time, Holmes' job title had migrated to executive secretary and later to executive director.

Holmes and Murray had very different personalities and enjoyed a somewhat bumpy relationship. Holmes' correspondence contained at

---

3. *ATN,* January 1967, p. 3.
4. ATC archives, Murray files, Murray letter to executive committee, June 18, 1969.

least a tinge of the Army way. Complaints came in about the way he handled the staff and volunteers, with longtime treasurer Sadye Giller and Gingrich exchanging memos to Murray about the situation. Ruth Blackburn was finally asked to look into it. She sided with Holmes, and the matter went quietly away, but Les retired the next year, 1975.[5]

Holmes continued to work at ATC as a volunteer, setting up the archives, and acquiring MacKaye's book collection, knapsack, and furniture after his death.[6]

In those days, Ed Garvey was Murray's most influential associate. As the finance officer for the National Science Foundation, Garvey was, like Avery before him, a driven man, and he kept an eagle eye on the financial books. Argumentative and acerbic at times, his forceful personality shaped ATC for years. One never took Garvey lightly.

In 1964, Murray asked Garvey to succeed Fred Blackburn as ATC secretary. Commenting on the scope of his responsibilities, Garvey once wrote, "It seemed that the secretary was responsible for just about everything that had not been assigned to someone else," a statement that was probably true. The secretary had been the bulwark of ATC, especially after Avery died and his successors did not live in Washington. The secretary was the physical presence and represented ATC at many levels.[7]

At the time, the board met every three years for about two hours at the time of the general meeting. It was a legacy of the Avery years, when decisions came from one man and the board simply ratified his policies. Garvey concluded that, if ATC were to function as the superior organization, its board of managers simply had to meet more often. He talked to Murray and got him to agree to annual meetings.

Now that the board met in the years between triennial conferences, it could actually make decisions as a corporate group, rather than as one person setting forth an agenda. Soon thereafter, Garvey talked Murray into general membership meetings every two years

---

5. *Ibid*, Murray to George Zoebelein, February 10, 1974.
6. *ATN*, July/August 1984.
7. This paragraph, and those that follow, are drawn from a letter from Garvey to Ron Tipton on December 16, 1994.

instead of every three, and the first biennial conference was in Shippensburg, Pennsylvania, in 1972.

When Garvey took over from Blackburn, the entire ATC membership was only 850 "Class D" (individual) members. (That was a significant increase from a 1961 total of 350.) Believing that was entirely too small an organization and provided too little money, he went on a membership campaign. With Garvey in the saddle, membership more than tripled to 3,000. It had been Garvey who spearheaded the drive to hire a staff and to name Holmes as the first employee.

Being a finance officer by profession, Garvey was in a constant hunt for money. The way he grew the ATC revenue was largely through increases in membership, but he also hiked the price of just about everything. And, he got the board members to agree to limit their terms in office to six years, a reform that he regarded as the most significant thing that he accomplished. (The board might have disagreed with him.) Others tended to feel that Garvey's greatest accomplishment was to create a new committee on trail standards in 1963.

Garvey had an enduring influence on the future of ATC. His vision was to create an organization that was creative, well-financed, and entirely independent of PATC, his club. The move a decade later to Harpers Ferry was the watershed, after which ATC attained true independence and freedom of movement. That accorded perfectly with Garvey's vision, and its importance was as much psychological as it was financial. ATC had finally cut loose from reliance on PATC. That did not remove PATC from a central position in the trails movement, as Murray's reliance on PATC volunteers to push for federal trails legislation was to demonstrate.

Murray struggled to manage the far-flung organization and did not entirely succeed. Like Avery and Stevens before him, he never did rein in the independent New England organizations. He had several acrimonious disputes with AMC (not a typical Murray reaction), and he stated at one point that AMC was the only trail-maintaining organization that did not cooperate with the others.[8] In 1966, he wrote, "For some number of years, I have been rather painfully aware that

---

8. ATC archives, Les Holmes correspondence, 1967-74, Box 1-4-4, public-relations folder.

some of the larger and older clubs of New England have not felt quite the strong association with the Appalachian Trail Conference. This is something I have made it my personal objective to remedy."[9] He was not the first ATC chairman to feel this way or the last.

New clubs, in addition to Tennessee Eastman, sprang up in the 1960s. PATH (Piedmont Appalachian Trail Hikers) took over a section of the trail from the overextended Roanoke club and also got a trail section from the Mount Rogers A.T. Club. In North Carolina, the Nantahala Hiking Club was founded, partly through the efforts of Rufus Morgan. Finally, Nantahala had a club to replace the one that had collapsed more than 30 years earlier.

In 1964, Murray began to poke more thoroughly into the history of the organization, and several things puzzled him. One of them was the role of Myron Avery, who, he mused, was probably responsible for the completion of the trail, and his role seemed to have been either overlooked or forgotten completely. He had been talking to Jean Stephenson, who educated him about Avery and his influence on the trail.

The other thing that puzzled him was the loss of contact with MacKaye. Benton MacKaye had been absent from the Appalachian Trail for decades, so Murray wrote to MacKaye in February 1964: "I have frequently wondered over the fact that the inheritance of correspondence and duties I acquired with my present position in the Appalachian Trail Conference did not include any contact with you." He continued on to discuss the threats to the integrity of the trail, and his thoughts about the need for federal legislation to protect it.

MacKaye, now finally back in touch with the trail that he had inspired, answered immediately, approving Murray's plans to try to get federal protection. He read Murray's draft and urged that the word "primarily" (for hiking) be removed from the bill, since what he wanted was an exclusive hiking trail, with no other user groups. He also expanded on the idea of wide swath of protection, urging that the very name be changed from an "Appalachian Trailway" to a "wilderness way."[10]

---

9. ATC archives, Murray files, letter to Ben Rolston, March 20, 1966.
10. ATC archives, Murray files, 1952-74, letter to Garvey, August 2, 1964; Hunter Library, Sherman Collection, Murray to MacKaye, February 20, 1964.

In 1967, MacKaye at last reconciled with PATC. The peacemaker was Ruth Blackburn, who wrote to MacKaye inviting him to visit the club and attend their annual dinner. In reply, MacKaye praised the role of PATC in creating the trail, calling it the arch between the ends of the footpath. He inserted some points about keeping the path primitive and expanding the zone of wilderness.[11]

Now that he was fully connected to his old organizations, MacKaye related to Murray some of the early history of the idea of the trail. He recounted the role of Charles Harris Whitaker, the editor of the *Journal of the American Institute of Architects*, the first person to whom he had broached the subject of a skyline trail the length of the Appalachians. He wrote about the role of Clarence Stein and also covered the roles of Harlean James, Paul Fink, and Raymond Torrey. As for crediting the origins of the trail in the mid-Atlantic, he named L.F. Schmeckebier, Francois Matthes, and Halstead Hedges but did not mention Avery. The reconciliation with PATC did not include the club's creator.[12]

Threats

When Stan Murray succeeded Murray Stevens as ATC chairman in 1961, the matter of threats to the trail was already the principal topic of conversation. At the ATC conference at Delaware Water Gap that year, a small group of trail leaders huddled with Murray in a side room of the Glenwood Hotel. Present at the gathering were Ed Garvey, Ray Fadner, Lloyd Felton, Frank Schairer, Jean Stephenson, Phil Stone, Grant Conway, Egbert Walker, Jim Denton, and Sam Wilkinson. (All, except for Murray, Felton, and Wilkinson, were from PATC.) They spread out maps and studied the options.

The best option, it appeared, would be to reroute the A.T. around the most threatened area in northern Virginia from Harpers Ferry to Shenandoah National Park. The new route would leave the park in the north district, jump over several ridges to one far to the west, and then turn north, rejoining the existing A.T. near Duncannon,

---

11. PATC archives, MacKaye to Ruth Blackburn, March 22, 1967.
12. *Ibid,* MacKaye to ATC, June 4, 1967.

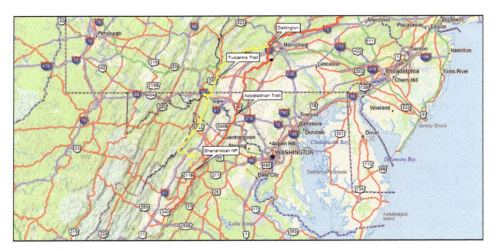

The idea for the reroute around northern Virginia

Pennsylvania. It would be a stop-gap, strategic withdrawal from developed areas. (If development continued marching westward, of course, it would only be temporary.)

When the new trail route arrived at Great North Mountain, it would move northeast along the ridge. Next in line was Sleepy Creek Mountain, and then north of the Potomac was Tuscarora Mountain, Rising Mountain, and finally Blue Mountain. In between those ridges were valleys with houses and farms. South of the Potomac was some national-forest land, but north of it was almost entirely private property.

Murray's first move was to appoint Frank Schairer to head an *ad hoc* committee to study the problem and undertake an initial route investigation. He wanted PATC, KTA, and Mountain Club of Maryland (MCM) to provide members. He specifically told Schairer that he wanted Jim Denton, formerly of the Roanoke club, to be the representative from PATC.[13]

Schairer's prestige was necessary to get things started, but Avery's former sidekick was old and soon left the leadership. The committee quickly morphed into a younger group that would undertake route planning. Murray appointed Lloyd Felton of MCM to chair the committee. He wanted it to be a centralized ATC creation, not a de-

---

13. ATC archives, Murray files, letter to Schairer, November 17, 1962.

centralized creature of the trail clubs, and insisted on appointing the members himself. Al McDonald of the Batona Club was to provide the leadership for the new trail north of the Potomac. McDonald, in turn, appointed Martin Brillhart of the York club to scout the northern section, to where Pa. 16 cut across Tuscarora Mountain, and Felton himself scouted south of that point. In Maryland and Virginia, Denton was to do the scouting. Murray consulted with PATC President Grant Conway, who strongly ratified the choice of Denton.[14]

Murray expressed his vision to Conway: "When completed, this blue-blazed trail would provide additional hiking opportunities in the area whose growing population is rapidly becoming conscious of outdoor recreation. The Appalachian Trail would remain intact in its present location. Yet we would all know that in the event of an irreparable break on its present route the A.T. could be promptly moved to this other trail already in existence." He insisted that the new trail not be called the "Alternate A.T."[15]

It was a struggle to get everyone on board. The Keystone Trails Association (KTA) wanted to name its own representative, but Murray, fearing that they would name someone hostile to the concept, went to a KTA meeting and made clear that he was the appointing official.[16] MCM, fearing that the Appalachian Trail would eventually completely abandon its section, initially was opposed to joining the committee.[17] But, Murray plowed ahead and eventually got everyone in line. It was, post-Avery, a rare example of ATC's taking the wheel. Under Stan Murray, it would become increasingly common.

"Denton" was the very same Jim Denton who had been president of the Roanoke Appalachian Trail Club (see chapters 4 and 6). He had moved with his wife, Molly, to Front Royal, Virginia, and, by the early 1960s, had become a leader in PATC. With his extensive trail scouting experience, he was the obvious choice to lead this new effort.

---

14. Much of the history of the Tuscarora Trail has been documented by Tom Floyd, one of its principal creators, in an unpublished book entitled, "Diary of a Trail." It has been submitted to PATC for publication.

15. ATC archives, Murray files, Murray to Conway, date unknown.

16. ATC archives, Murray files, Murray letter to George Spring, October 2, 1962, and letter to Jean Stephenson, October 12.

17. *Ibid*, Eunice Winters to Murray, February 23, 1962, and Murray to Winters, April 3.

Martin Brillhart, although joined occasionally by Earl Shaffer, scouted his section of the new trail basically alone. It was his decision to leave the A.T. at Dean's Gap and proceed along Blue Mountain and then continue to Rising Mountain and finally Tuscarora Mountain. Unlike early scouting of the Appalachian Trail route that used forest roads and paths roughed out by forest rangers, Brillhart had to contend with virgin territory. No other help was available.

When the route across Tuscarora Mountain reached Pa. 16, Lloyd Felton took over. He scouted along the top of the mountain, contending with sharp rock faces typical of orogenies, often called "devil's backbones." Assuming that the trail would cross the Potomac on the highway bridge in Hancock, he routed the trail off the southern end of Tuscarora Mountain, along Coon Ridge, and hit the Chesapeake and Ohio Canal towpath ten miles east of Hancock. It then coaligned with the towpath to Hancock. South of the Hancock bridge, trail-scouting was Jim Denton's job.

Denton was assisted by Woody Kennedy, a PATC member who worked for the U.S. Geologic Survey Map Division and thus knew the ridges by heart. But, according to Tom Floyd, the two were mismatched as scouts. Denton was focused and determined and, with his powerful, strapping physique, could hike long and hard, rarely stopping for food or water. Kennedy had an easy-going temperament and rolly-polly physique and loved to stop for long lunches, building a fire and having some wine before continuing on, much to the frustration of Denton. It was this odd combination of hikers that scouted the route until they came to private property.

Coming out of Shenandoah National Park at Mathews Arm Campground, the trail that Denton and Kennedy adopted was actually scouted and selected by the National Park Service. Exiting the park, it used road shoulders and dirt roads to the Shenandoah River, crossing on a low-water bridge. Across the river, it then entered George Washington National Forest. Rolling over two ridges, Massanutten East and Massanutten West, it had the advantage of being on forest land virtually all the way. After crossing Massanutten West, it entered the Shenandoah Valley and private property. After a long stretch of road-walking through the valley, the trail reached Great North Mountain, which was also on national forest land. It moved northeast along that ridge until it got to Va. 55. North of that was almost entirely private land. Denton looked it over and gave up. According to Tom Floyd,

> *He stood on high points and surveyed fields and hills and great mountains to the north, all of which he considered inaccessible. He drove roads beyond Capon Springs but came back 'thoroughly discouraged' by prospects on to the Potomac River, 70 miles of mostly farmlands and privately owned mountain properties, many closed off by iron gates or chains. The ultimate success of the endeavor, Denton knew, would depend on finding cooperating landowners through this sector, but he doubted that it could be done. Accordingly, he made his report and then stopped further scouting."*[18]

The Pennsylvanians, who had done their job, considered the discouraged PATC and decided that they should stop their work until something developed south of the Potomac. At the time, Stan Murray was busy working on federal legislation and thought it might be best to bide time until he knew what, if anything, was to happen in Washington. So, work on the new trail stopped. It was in pieces. North of the river, it had been named the Tuscarora Trail, although Tuscarora Mountain was only one of the ridges (and not the longest one) on which the trail was placed. North, it was blazed orange. South, it was blazed blue, and, at the suggestion of the Park Service, was called the Big Blue Trail. So far, it had been scouted, but the trail had not actually been built.

In New Jersey and New York, Murray and the New York–New Jersey Trail Conference were still discussing a possible reroute into the Shawangunks, up the Hudson on the Long Path, and then across the Hudson and on to Connecticut, bypassing some difficult sections with private-property problems. That effort, too, went on hold, awaiting word from Washington.[19]

---

18. Floyd, *op. cit.*, p. 16..
19. *ATN*, September 1964, p. 37.

By the mid-1960s, development was overtaking the trail. As the population in the East expanded toward the mountains, it seemed impossible to stop the growth. Stan Murray reported on the increasingly perilous state of the trail. The public's desire for skyline drives just seemed to be increasing. Second-home development in the mountains had become very popular, and ski resorts were opening up in many places. The increase in interstate highways was requiring more inventive solutions for A.T. crossings. Industrial development was often obliterating the trail — hikers would come to a clearing in the forest and find a huge bulldozer sitting in the middle of their trail. Murray concluded, "It does not take a very big crystal ball to see that some degree of public support, recognition, and protection will be required."[20]

The parkway issue was the oldest threat and had begun with the construction of Skyline Drive in Shenandoah National Park three decades earlier. In Pennsylvania, the state was studying a proposal to pave over Blue Mountain with a skyline road, and the Blue Mountain Eagle Climbing Club established a study committee to deal with the threat. Murray recommended that they push the provision in the 1938 Trailway Agreement for no roads within a quarter-mile of the trail. Jean Stephenson, however, felt that, in Pennsylvania, because of state game lands, the hunting community was probably strong enough to fend off parkway proposals.[21]

In 1963, the Kennedy administration opened up a "scenic roads study," a proposal to build 2,150 miles of Appalachian roads to stimulate growth in the economically stunted region. Each state was requested to make its own study. That represented a huge issue for the Appalachian Trail. Murray wrote to the governors of the various Appalachian Trail states, pointing out that highways should be compatible with outdoor recreation and should not disrupt wilderness areas. He urged that their studies take into consideration the A.T. and its values as a wilderness environment.

---

20. ATC archives, Murray files, address to the triennial meeting, June 27, 1964.
21. ATC archives, Murray files, Box 6-6-3, Stephenson to Murray, December 12, 1965; Box 6-6-4, Murray to George Spring, March 1, 1966.

Harley Webster, a congressional staff member who would later work for The Nature Conservancy, one of the most powerful environmental organizations in the country, wrote to the assistant special counsel to the president, pointing out the problems that such a road network would cause with the A.T. and speculating about ways to reconcile these new proposed roads with the trail.[22] (See page 334.)

In Vermont, the proposal for a skyline drive through the Green Mountains, thought dead in the 1930s, came up again, with the governor in favor. Ben Rolston, president of GMC, gave the task of fending off the revived proposal to Shirley Strong, and she wrote to David Levin, director of the scenic roads and parkway study, opposing the parkway proposal. (Strong proved to be an extraordinarily effective advocate for GMC.)

At ATC, Ed Garvey met with Levin on August 16, discussing the problems that this program would create for the Appalachian Trail. Levin appeared sympathetic, but, in view of the fact that many state governors were in favor, the best strategy for ATC, he advised, was to wait until the bill became law and then deal with the problem state by state.[23] This not-very-encouraging advice proved unnecessary, as the bill never became law.

The greatest threat to the trail was in the South. A proposal to extend the Blue Ridge Parkway south into Georgia had the support of Richard Russell, one of the most powerful members of the U.S. Senate. GATC went into discussions with Chattahoochee National Forest officials to be prepared for a possible reroute of the A.T. in many places. The rangers agreed on a general plan for rerouting, and the Forest Service agreed to build the new trail sections. But, as Murray wrote, "While we are all happy to have arrived at something we can live with, I should restate for the record that these agreements... are to the Georgia Appalachian Trail Club and the Appalachian Trail Conference second best to no interference from the parkway at all."[24]

---

22. ATC archives, Murray files, A.T. easement and ownership file, Webster to Lee White, November 14, 1963; Murray to various governors, 1964.
23. *Ibid*, Garvey to Murray, August 18, 1965.
24. *Ibid*, Murray to Chattahoochee National Forest, April 13, 1964.

Ski slopes also threatened the trail. A ski development outside of Rangeley, Maine, on the slope of the iconic Saddleback Mountain, harmed the view from the trail, which ran over the top of the mountain with a view directly down onto the ski slopes. It alleged, not very convincingly, that it would not disturb the trail corridor itself, and subsequent events were to negate these reassuring words.[25]

In Vermont, political pressure to protect ski developments was so strong that Senator George Aiken urged that the committee considering federal protection for the trail give him "your assurance that nothing is intended that would have an adverse effect on this source of cash income to my state."[26] Aiken's solicitous consideration for ski resorts did not accord with the sentiments of most Vermonters, who repeatedly voted down all proposals that violated their Green Mountain sanctuary. The unique culture of Vermont reappeared again in the history of the Appalachian Trail.

Strip mining was an issue, too, particularly in the South with its marketable deposits of various minerals. In Appalachia, people needed jobs — in some ways, the region had not come very far from the Depression. The Forest Service understood the need to protect the trail but sometimes yielded to pressures from politicians to put people to work. Mining was one threat, and timbering was another. The Forest Service was under constant pressure, and trail protection sometimes lost out.

Housing developments provided yet another source of worry. In 1968, a landowner in North Carolina north of Allen Gap requested that the Appalachian Trail be moved off his land so that he could subdivide and sell housing lots. Murray contacted the Forest Service to see if they could buy the land, possibly with money from The Nature Conservancy up front. He subsequently learned that the price was too high — far above what the Forest Service thought the appraisal value would be.[27] (The federal government was not allowed to pay

---

25. *Ibid*, letter from Bronson Girscom to Murray, February 21, 1968. For the completion of this story, see chapter 11.

26. *Ibid*, *Burlington Free Press*, March 14, 1967.

27. *Ibid*, letter from District Ranger Thomas E. Fraser to Murray, May 15, 1968.

a price above the fair market value as determined by an appraisal.) This, and other such projects, damaged trail values.

The biggest controversy over development threats at the time was the infamous Big Bald matter. A large landowner, one Pearl Ramsey Buck, had long permitted the A.T. through her property and had agreed to keep the land wild and not develop it. But the A.T., lacking governmental protection, was subject to the vagaries of landowners, and, in 1964, she changed her mind and sold the entire tract to C.P. "Bud" Edwards, a developer from Kingsport and owner of the Bald Mountain Development Corporation. The land was east of U.S. 23 as it snaked through Sams Gap. A portion of it, called Wolf Laurel, would consist of hundreds of home sites, a dude ranch, a hunting preserve, and ski slopes. Edwards planned lodges, stores, and all the amenities of a community of vacation homes. The A.T. ran directly through some of the tracts and along the edge of others. It would present the most immediate threat to the trail.

Murray alerted the ATC membership to the threat at the ATC meeting in September 1964, and he worked to oppose the development. He hinged his plea on a new road that would be built to service the development. In his letter to the Tennessee Department of Highways, he cited the Appalachian Trailway Agreement of 1938 that prohibited incompatible developments within a quarter-mile of the trail. "The road presents some conflict with the Appalachian Trail which… is a wilderness footpath, remote as possible from the signs and influences of modern civilization."

Although Murray tried to work with Edwards, he was getting nowhere. In March 1966, Arch Nichols of the Carolina Mountain Club (and the Forest Service) wrote to Representative Roy Taylor (see page 352), who was sponsoring the bill to provide federal protection for the A.T., addressing the development and stating that it would require a twenty-mile reroute of the A.T., from a spot near Erwin, Tennessee, to Big Butt Mountain north of Devils Fork Gap on the state line. Concerned that his development plans would be sidetracked, Edwards, who was well-connected politically, immediately also contacted Taylor.

Murray's chief concern was that Taylor might turn against the legislation and slow-roll it until Edwards got his houses on the ground. Taylor, instead of backing Edwards, sought a compromise. Writing back to Nichols, he proposed that the solution was to pass the legislation and then use the authority to purchase land for an A.T. reroute around the development. Since the trail was at that point along the state line, both Tennessee and North Carolina would be involved and would presumably support the reroute of the trail to avoid both the new road and the development.

Murray was convinced that the development on Big Bald would result in a diminished trail experience. "I believe we all recognize that the bald will have lost some of its original charm and any sense of remoteness from the activities of the mechanized world will be lost."[28]

Taylor continued to work with both state planning and highway departments. He received reassurances from both state governments that the Appalachian Trail would be protected. But, portions of the trail unquestionably would have to be rerouted, and the compromise outcome, achieved only through Taylor's intervention, did not entirely satisfy anyone.[29]

Farther north, another threat resulted in a happier outcome. The problem affected Mount Greylock in Massachusetts. From Williamstown, just south of Vermont, the Appalachian Trail ran straight up Greylock and then straight down the other side, from north to south. The land was in the possession of the Greylock Reservation Commission that had been established in 1898 to manage the Mount Greylock State Reservation. But, in 1953, the state legislature set up the Mount Greylock Tramway Authority to build and operate a tramway to the top of the mountain. It would be funded with state bonds, and, until they were paid off, no other competing enterprises were to be set up. The Tramway Authority would control 4,000 acres (half the protected area) and was permitted to set up ski slopes, a mountaintop restaurant, and a hundred-foot metal tower to support the tramway cables.

---

28. *Ibid*, Murray to Taylor, March 22, 1966.
29. The Big Bald records are in the Murray files at the ATC archives, Box 6-6-3.

The objective was to make Greylock a first-class tourist attraction for the state.

A fierce antidevelopment reaction emerged, something that it seems only New Englanders could manage. Citizens formed the Mount Greylock Protective Association and sued the Tramway Authority. This mountain belonged to the citizens of Massachusetts, they contended, and they were not going to sell it, loan it, or lease it to any tourist organization. The lawsuit was successful, and Greylock was saved. The legislature transferred Greylock from the Mount Greylock Reservation Commission, now thoroughly discredited, to the Department of Natural Resources.[30]

Back down south, what would become known as the North Shore Road controversy emerged. When Fontana Dam was constructed on the southwestern end of Great Smoky Mountains National Park, it created a large reservoir behind it that flooded land that held cemeteries of mountain residents displaced by the national park. The Tennessee Valley Authority had promised to replace an original road with a new thirty-mile road, running along the lake shore to Forney Ridge, where it would climb the ridge, approach the main crest near Silers Bald, and parallel the Appalachian Trail for about three miles. It would cross under the trail in a 1,200-foot tunnel being built expressly to keep the trail and road separate.

But then park officials stepped between the residents and TVA. The park opposed the new road because blasting could expose rock that was extremely acidic and could leach heavy metals into streams that fed into the lake. The road controversy got involved with local politics, and the pressure to build it was considerable. The park stood firm, and it was never built beyond the eight miles north of Bryson city. Instead, the park agreed to transport family members to the gravesites by motor launch once or twice a year. A geologic issue (and a large cash settlement payment to Swain County in this century) thus had the side effect of protecting the trail.[31]

---

30. *ATN*, September 1965, p. 7, and May 1966, p. 21.
31. Bolgiano, *op. cit.*, p. 145; ATC archives, Murray files, Murray letter to board of managers, December 1, 1965.

Other roads threatened the trail in various spots. New Hampshire Route 25 was widened, damaging a section of the A.T. When interstates were built, beginning in the late 1960s, every crossing produced its own set of problems for the Appalachian Trail. Interstate 81 in Virginia, the Pennsylvania Turnpike, Interstates 84 and 87 in New York — each presented a problem for a trail that was not legally protected. The only possible savior was the Appalachian Trailway Agreement, which seemed to be less and less relevant every year as development continued.

And then, of course, the odd bulldozer appeared. Sometimes a road was permitted by a local government unaware of the federal-state "restriction." An example of that was a road built in the Roanoke watershed. "The Manager of city of Roanoke Water department….has stated that if he had known what would happen no crossing permission would have been given."[32] Even in the best of times, word did not get out to everyone.

One barrier to snowmobiles.

Sometimes, the battle to discourage incompatible uses became almost comic. In 1969, CBS News proposed that the Appalachian Trail become a venue for a snowmobile race from Maine to New Jersey. Murray tried not to say no but did point out the Trailway Agreement specifying foot travel, and the obvious barriers, such as boulders, fences, and the like. He did not bring up the Lemon Squeezer.[33]

Incompatible use was a problem for a trail that had no legislative protection. In parts of both the Smokies and Shenandoah National Park, the superintendents authorized equestrian use. Even the Forest Service allowed horses in places, contending that there was no rule against it.

---

32. ATC archives, Murray files, Box 6-6-3, letter from Tom Campbell to Murray, February 20, 1965.
33. ATC archives, Holmes papers, 1967-74, Murray letter to Holmes, Art Koerber, and Sam Wilkinson.

Trail maintainers adamantly and publicly opposed the use of horses. Grant Conway, president of PATC, wrote in *The Washington Post*, "Unlimited numbers of steel-shod quadrupeds would scrape furrows and only partially refill them with their droppings in return."[34] A donkey owner, querying the possibility of taking her donkey on the A.T., received the following answer from Fred Blackburn: "There is no regulation prohibiting you from taking a donkey on the Appalachian Trail. It is, however, a foot trail, and there are some obstacles, such as fences, that might make your progress difficult."[35]

The Crisis

In the mid-1960s, PATC began having significant access problems with the trail south of Harpers Ferry. The center of the problem was a fourteen-mile stretch between Snickers Gap, where Va. 7 crossed the mountains, and Ashby Gap, where U.S. 50 goes over the mountains. A similar, but not quite so critical, problem arose from Ashby Gap south to Manassas Gap, where Va. 55 (and later Interstate 66) crosses through the mountains in a narrow gap. At the time, no public landownership was immediately south of Harpers Ferry, and road improvements were bringing second-home enthusiasts in large numbers.

From Snickers to Ashby, a dirt road along the ridgeline was paved by the state. That became infamous Route 601, the center of the controversy. Landowners, expecting to buy solitude, found a hiking trail running through their back yards. It was not what they thought they were getting. Some were okay with it, but not all.

The problem was made much worse when, beginning in 1965, they started hearing rumors of some sort of federal legislation that would protect the trail. It would include, they heard, condemnation. But, if the trail were not on their land, condemnation could not be used. "No trespassing" signs began popping up. The PATC *Bulletin* began reporting landowner trail closures. By July 1966, five closures were known, and, at that point, the club formed a committee on landowner problems.

---

34. *ATN*, January 1963, p. 6; date of the article in *The Washington Post* not given.
35. ATC archives, Murray files, Box 3-2-4, Blackburn to Mrs. L. W. Potter, March 19, 1958.

The committee achieved some success negotiating with some owners, but others resisted, and the crisis only deepened. "Our problems with landowners," the committee reported, "come directly from publicity on these bills [various House and Senate bills proposing federal ownership, potentially through condemnation.]"[36] Ruth Blackburn blamed an opportunistic realtor in Berryville, just west of the Appalachian Trail. Landowners were getting notices, and, according to Ruth, the theme was the same: Get the trail off your land.[37]

With all the problems inherent in a volunteer-created trail on private land, Avery's prediction of 1937 was fast coming true. This was not a half-mile nature loop in a local park. It was a 2,000-mile trail through fourteen states and countless jurisdictions. Almost half of it was on private property. Without some sort of protection, its future was limited, and the end was in clear view.

Advancing toward the Act

The idea of federal protection of the Appalachian Trail had a long history. MacKaye and then-Governor Franklin D. Roosevelt exchanged letters on federal protection of the trail in 1926. In 1934, Robert Underwood Johnson of AMC suggested to the then-president that there should be a "continuous reservation" of land in Appalachia to support this new trail.[38] In 1941, Avery proclaimed at the ATC meeting at Bear Mountain, "Experience in trail maintenance indicates more clearly, each year, that public ownership is the only assurance of the perpetuity of such a trail route."[39] Avery reiterated this at the ATC meeting at Fontana in 1948 and continued this theme for the remaining years of his life.

In 1958, Congress became involved with the need for outdoor recreation facilities across the country and created the Outdoor Recreation Resources Review Commission (ORRRC). Chaired by Laur-

---

36. *Bulletin*, July-September 1966, p. 69.
37. ATC archives, Murray files, Blackburn to Murray, March 18, 1966.
38. ATC archives, MacKaye box. The Johnson-Roosevelt letters are at Western Carolina University, Hunter Library, Sherman Collection.
39. *ATN*, September 1941, p. 45.

ance Rockefeller, one of the most prominent conservationists in the country, its recommendations were of major significance. Hiking was high on the list, because it was a simple activity that was very popular and not very costly. The ORRRC study resulted in Congress' creating the Bureau of Outdoor Recreation in 1963 and the Land and Water Conservation Fund in 1964, both of which had major impacts on the Appalachian Trail.

Two clubs had an outsized influence on Stan Murray's thinking on this topic. First to act was the New York–New Jersey Trail Conference. Under the leadership of President Harry Nees, it passed a resolution in May 1963 urging ATC to pursue federal ownership of the trail.[40]

Closer to Washington, Grant Conway, the president of PATC, appointed a trail preservation committee to stave off private-property ownership of the trail corridor in northern Virginia. His first thought was to purchase land, and, since PATC had financial resources unavailable to most trail-maintaining clubs, Conway asked the club's history committee to begin researching land titles. If landowners could not be convinced to allow the trail, the club would begin buying the land.

According to Tom Floyd, Murray read about this new committee in the PATC *Bulletin*. "He read it, and reread it, and then he sat back and pondered its significance. Events were outpacing the Appalachian Trail Conference. The time had come for him to lead."[41] This began a series of letters between Murray and Conway that led to the formation of ATC's own committee. PATC's John Oliphant, a lawyer, was named to chair the new committee, and its membership included mostly PATC leaders.

The Revelation

By Stan Murray's public account, the touchstone for the drive for federal protection began in Maine. On August 20, 1963, after a day of

40. ATC archives, Murray files, N.Y.–N.J. TC resolution, February 6, 1963.
41. Floyd, *op. cit.*, pp. 14-15.

hiking in the Chairback Range, Murray sat down at a cabin on Long Pond with Sidney Tappan of Massachusetts and Jean Stephenson and Sadye Giller of the ATC board (and PATC). By lamplight, they talked about the problems the trail was experiencing and decided that the time had come for ATC to seek federal help.

While still in Maine, Murray wrote to Walter Boardman of The Nature Conservancy. "I am writing this from a beautiful spot on the Maine seacoast, sitting on some ledges and looking straight into the Atlantic Ocean. I have spent the last two days with Jean Stephenson, Sadye Giller and Sidney Tappan at Chairback Mountain Camps." He wanted to meet with Boardman as soon as possible to discuss federal protection of the trail.

However, Murray went to Maine with a purpose, and the idea of launching a drive for legislation did not originate at the camp — it was merely confirmed there. In Murray's file at ATC is a letter, in Murray's hand, dated August 8, 1963, twelve days before the meeting at Long Pond, and it is a draft of federal legislation, almost identical to that which was finally introduced in Congress the following year.[42] So, no one else but Stan Murray gets the credit for the genesis of that draft.

That touched off a hurried series of meetings in Washington. At an October meeting, a committee was appointed to draft legislation. Chaired by Boardman, it included John Oliphant (who had chaired the earlier committee), Conway, Ed Garvey, and Frank Wallick. Working with this core group, Murray commissioned PATC to mount a lobbying effort — to be, in effect, his eyes and ears in Washington, since he lived in Tennessee. The committee met on October 12 to discuss the draft (presumably Murray's draft) and to talk about who they should get to introduce the legislation. Various senators were mentioned — Saylor of Pennsylvania, Saltonstall of Massachusetts, Byrd of Virginia, McIntyre of New Hampshire, O'Brien of New York, Russell of Georgia, Hayden of Arizona. Aside from Hayden, all were from Appalachian Trail states.

---

42. ATC archives, Murray files.

No one thought to mention Gaylord Nelson of Wisconsin. Although no one on the Senate Interior and Insular Affairs Committee represented any of the fourteen Appalachian Trail states, Nelson's state was physically the closest. And, in the House of Representatives, no one thought of Roy Taylor of North Carolina.[43]

After the October meeting, Murray worked confidentially with a small group of ATC leaders. Most critical in the group was its leader, former congressional staffer W. Harley Webster, who had the ear of the White House. Murray wanted to keep things quiet, so that the baby would not be strangled in its bed.[44]

The group began working with the Bureau of Outdoor Recreation (BOR) and presented drafts of the legislation that they wanted made into presentable language. Webster, now the assistant director of BOR, tipped off the effort to Lee White, legislative counsel to the president, on November 14, 1963. Webster noted to White that a bill was before Congress on a system of Appalachian road networks, a residue of the Kennedy proposals (see page 324), and he wondered what effect this might have on proposed legislation for the trail. This was clearly an effort to get the White House on board and keep competing legislation at bay.[45]

Murray was concerned that the volunteer component could disappear if the trail became a federal responsibility. He urged Webster to keep ATC in the legislative proposal. The problem of keeping a balance between government and the volunteer organizations was a continuing theme in the negotiations.

As the attention swung toward federal protection, the times could not have been more favorable. The Congress that was about to convene two months after President Kennedy's assassination has been hailed by many as the "Conservation Congress." It was to pass the Wilderness Act, the Land and Water Conservation Fund, the Wild and Scenic Rivers Act, and others.

In the larger context of the policy times, this was all part of Lyndon Johnson's Great Society legislation that included the Voting

---

43. *Ibid*, minutes of the October 12 meeting.
44. *Ibid* and Dave Sherman e-mail of June 10, 2013.
45. *Ibid*, Webster to Murray, November 14, 1963.

Gaylord Nelson, the unexpected pick by ATC to introduce legislation to protect the Appalachian Trail, was born in Clear Lake, Wisconsin, in 1916. A lawyer by profession, he fought in World War II in the Battle of Okinawa. Returning from the war, he was elected to the state senate in 1948 and served there for a decade before becoming governor in 1958. After serving two terms in the statehouse, he was elected to the U.S. Senate in 1962. He served in the Senate until 1981. Nelson was a strong conservationist and founded Earth Day in 1970. He was also associated with many social issues and was a noted opponent of U.S. participation in the Vietnam War. This got him cross-ways with President Johnson, who held Nelson's opposition to the war against him as long as he was president.

Speaking at the 1993 ATC meeting in Georgia

Rights Act, Medicare, and Medicaid. It, and the federal legislation passed during the Great Depression, were the two periods of the most significant social legislation the nation has ever seen. The times were ideal for federal involvement in trails, more than at any other time in American history.

The Land and Water Conservation Fund (LWCF) Act was of greatest moment for hikers. Funded from off-shore oil leases, it set up a fund to be used for conservation and recreation, sixty percent by the states and forty percent by the federal government. On the state side, two-fifths was to be apportioned equally among the states, and three-fifths would be held by the secretary of the interior to be administered as a grant program on the basis of need. To be eligible, states had to write a "comprehensive plan" for outdoor recreation and submit it to BOR. Each state was to name a liaison officer for LWCF.

Murray realized the implications immediately. The Appalachian Trail needed to be in those plans in order to be eligible for funding. And, if a federal act were to be passed protecting the Appalachian Trail, it needed a funding source. Here was a funding source! He urged board representatives from the fourteen states to make contact with BOR, and he set about naming state representatives to contact their LWCF representative and ensure that their trail section was in the state comprehensive plan.[46]

Each state did this differently. Virginia, for instance, formed a new organization, the Virginia Trails Association, as an advisory group in formulating a state trail plan. John Oliphant was the first chairman of the committee. The Georgia Appalachian Trail Club, the sole maintaining club in that state, urged the Forest Service to use the money to purchase inholdings, to give their trail section a buffer from the proposed Blue Ridge Parkway extension.[47]

Contacts with BOR had been made, and legislation was being drafted, using Murray's early draft as a starting point, but no senator or representative had yet been identified to introduce legislation. Then, out of the blue, came Gaylord Nelson, the senator from Wisconsin.

What brought Nelson into play was a most unexpected and unorthodox event. Nelson was attending a congressional fund-raiser in northwest Washington sometime in late 1963 when he was buttonholed by Dr. Cecil Cullander, a member of PATC. Cullander suggested that Nelson sponsor this new legislation that was in draft form at BOR, and Nelson, a strong conservationist but not a hiker, decided to take Cullander up on the matter. According to Nelson, "He knew I was interested in conservation, and we got to talking. He was concerned about permanently protecting the Appalachian Trail because so much of it was on private lands. I thought, well, hell; I might as well introduce a bill to preserve the Appalachian Trail."[48]

Nelson already had developed an interest in hiking trails and had proposed a 1,500-mile hiking trail in his native Wisconsin. He called Dr. Edward Crafts, who then headed BOR, and requested that BOR draft a piece of legislation to protect the trail. Stan Murray was al-

---

46. *ATN*, January 1965, p. 4.
47. ATC archives, Murray files, letter from Gannon Coffey (President, GATC) to J.K. Vessey, Regional Forester, December 8, 1964.
48. Interview with Gaylord Nelson, December 12, 1983, with Dave Sherman, Ron Tipton, and Ed Garvey. According to a comment by Garvey during the interview, Cullander was an active volunteer but was never noted to be in a leadership position.

ready in the office talking with Crafts when Nelson's call came in, so he became a collaborator with BOR and Fred Madison, Nelson's legislative assistant.[49]

We know little of Cullander today. He was a dentist and a member of the National Parks Conservation Association as well as PATC but was not a leader in the club and is not mentioned in any other context than the contact with Nelson.

Grant Conway, the president of PATC, at the same time was planning to contact Nelson because of Nelson's position on the Interior and Insular Affairs Committee, but he had apparently not informed Murray and had viewed this venture as something that he alone would do. When he reached Nelson, he found out, to his evident chagrin, that Nelson had already been contacted by Cullander, was in touch with BOR, and planned to introduce legislation. His plan that would have backdoored Murray backdoored him also. Jean Stephenson wrote to Murray acquainting him with the facts as she understood them, so that eventually everyone was on board.[50] (Jean viewed Grant as something of a loose cannon. He was certainly a major figure in the history of PATC.)

So the parties, finally together, proceeded with drafting the legislation. Crafts asked if ATC wanted to take the first crack, and, of course, Murray, who had already done so, left his draft with Crafts. A great deal of discussion followed about particulars, because these would surely shape the trail. Murray was for a soft beginning, initially suggesting only the purchase of easements and leases, but he did eventually come around to the idea of condemnation, even though he feared that landowners who had given the clubs verbal permission to put the trail on their land might revoke that permission. (There proved to be some validity for that view.) The final copy of the draft was handed to Nelson by Crafts on May 2, 1964.[51]

---

49. The records are unclear on this point. Nelson, in his oral interview years later, stated that he first handed the drafting of the legislation to his own legislative staff, but the drafting ultimately wound up at BOR.
50. ATC archives, Murray files, Stephenson to Murray, May 27, 1964; Murray letter to Webster, January 25, 1964.
51. *Ibid*, various dates.

The bill that Nelson introduced on May 20 (S. 2862) was, when compared with later versions, limited in scope and effect. It dealt only with the Appalachian Trail and no other trail projects, although senators and representatives from other parts of the country looked at the bill with considerable envy and began planning to tack things onto Nelson's bill. Its purpose was close to MacKaye's ideal and, in fact, drew MacKaye's concurrence, if not outright praise. It was to be a trail for foot travel only, "through natural or primitive areas." It was to be "administered, protected, and maintained so as to retain its natural scenic character in keeping with the purposes of this Act, excluding therefrom all inconsistent and nonconforming uses wherever this can be accomplished in the public interest." MacKaye himself probably would have written it this way.

It established the Appalachian Trail as a federal interest and directed the various federal jurisdictions through which it went to cooperate. But, outside of existing public lands, it contained only a "willing seller" provision. Condemnation was not an option in the legislation. Essentially, the bill looked a lot like the 1938 Trailway Agreement, a term that was directly quoted in the bill. The difference with the 1938 agreement was that it would be a law, not a memorandum of understanding.

The first step had been taken. A bill to federalize the trail had been introduced into the Senate. It was a weak bill, but, given the mood at the time, members of Congress and senators alike viewed it with great favor and wanted to tag their own trails onto it. Western senators were insisting that the Nelson bill include trails in their states. Murray noted, "Those present [at the meeting with BOR] unanimously concurred that it would be a mistake to so broaden the bill now."[52] What was not contemplated at the moment was intervention by the White House.

Congress adjourned without action on the Nelson bill. This was not unexpected, and Nelson's legislative staff already had prepared to reintroduce the legislation in the new Congress. It was placed on the floor of the Senate on January 19, 1965, as S. 622. The language

---

52. *Ibid*, Murray letter to board of managers, Box 5-5-2.

was identical to S. 2862. So far, no equivalent bills had been introduced in the House.

Senators hopped onto the bandwagon. As with S. 2862, senators from every trail state but one cosponsored Nelson's bill. Nelson's subcommittee on parks and recreation was part of the Senate Committee on Interior and Insular Affairs, chaired by Henry M. Jackson of Washington State. Jackson was a strong proponent of the legislation, so Nelson had a friendly path to enactment, assuming the House would go along.

Hearings on the bill did not come until September, at which time Murray, Garvey, Harry Nees (from New York–New Jersey), Conway, and Tom Campbell (from the Roanoke club) all testified. The focus of the testimony was on volunteers. It was volunteers who had created this trail, and members of Congress were urged to pass legislation that would include mention of the role of volunteers. Nelson himself underlined the volunteer contribution:

> *As Congress finally stirs itself into action to preserve what little is left of this Nation's great misspent heritage of natural beauty, it is only just that special recognition be given to those valiant citizens who have for many years been carrying on this national task from their private resources.... The entire Nation owes them a very great debt of gratitude for their service in developing and protecting this trail.*

In his testimony, Murray underlined the volunteer nature of the enterprise: "[T]he entire project developed and matured without government sponsorship, without foundation support, and without a profit motive."[53]

The volunteer component became the linchpin behind the legislation. It was a consistent theme.

The matter of funding became another important issue. How Nelson's legislation was to be paid for was not contained in the bill. Daniel Ogden, assistant director of BOR, made light of the matter. He

---

53. Hearings before the Subcommittee on Parks and Recreation, Committee on Interior and Insular Affairs, September 16, 1965.

stated that LWCF revenues would a sufficient funding source.[54] This proved to be a completely erroneous prediction.

In February, Sam Wilkinson of the New York–New Jersey Trail Conference proposed a statute that would protect landowners from liability suits in case of injury on the trail on their land. Murray was concerned that this could begin a discussion that ATC could not afford. ATC could not afford blanket liability coverage. Avery had looked into this years ago, Murray wrote, and concluded that it was better to let sleeping dogs lie. He asked for Jean Stephenson's opinion. Jean, a lawyer, answered that a landowner was not liable for injury to a "trespasser," or to someone who was there merely by permission. This seemed to quiet the discussion, but Murray was still agitated about the potential for ATC getting sued, even though there was no record of such a lawsuit by a landowner. He felt that the liability problem strengthened the need for federal protection.[55]

The White House gets involved

Soon after the Nelson bill was reintroduced, it ran into trouble. Stewart Udall, the secretary of the interior, indicated that his department was not releasing its report to the Senate. Something was up. The something was the White House.

Lady Bird Johnson had taken an interest in the trail, part of her fascination with "natural beauty." As the nation's First Lady, she decided that her cause would be beautification. It was an aspect of the environment, and, after the 1964 election, she decided to do something about it.

Today, people think of the beautification campaign as planting flowers along the nation's highways and removing junk cars and billboards from view. Her vision was far broader than that, and she intended to act on it.

Nash Castro, a naval aviator in World War II, was serving as regional director for the National Park Service in Washington when he was called to the White House. Having served in the Kennedy White

---

54. *Ibid.*
55. ATC archives, Murray files, Murray to Wilkinson, February 7, 1965.

House as executive vice president of the White House Historical Association, he was known to Mrs. Johnson, and she appointed him to work with her on the beautification idea. Working with Castro, she convened a Committee for a More Beautiful Capital and began planting pansies on the National Mall. Dogwoods and azaleas followed.

The First Lady's influence extended to the Rockefellers and other moneyed families. She was concerned with pollution, urban decay, recreation, mental health, and the crime rate. She pressed for the revitalization of Pennsylvania Avenue and the preservation of Lafayette Park. She visited historic sites around the country, accompanied by Castro. And, in the area of recreation, she was known to be a big supporter of the Appalachian Trail. (Because of that, she was made an honorary member of PATC.)

On February 8, 1965, Lady Bird's beautification campaign became part of her husband's Great Society program. Lyndon Johnson sent a message on beautification to Congress and requested several pieces of legislation to protect the environment and restore its beauty. He also noted his various executive authorities to improve the environment and add new recreation areas. It was a very ambitious plan, something that only Lyndon Johnson could push.

In late 1963, members of the Johnson White House did not believe that legislation was necessary to protect the Appalachian Trail.[56] But, by 1965, this had been completely reversed, most likely due to Lady Bird's influence on the president. In his message on natural beauty, Johnson seized on the idea of protecting the Appalachian Trail and proposed expanding it into a broader system:

> *I am requesting, therefore, that the Secretary of the Interior work with his colleagues in the Federal Government and with state and local leaders and recommend to me a cooperative program to encourage a national system of trails, building on the more than hundred thousand miles of trails in our National Forests and Parks.*

---

56. Nelson interview, *op. cit.*

He added, "In the back country, we need to copy the great Appalachian Trail in all parts of America."

Following his message, the White House Conference on Natural Beauty took place on May 24 and 25, 1965. Murray attended, along with about 1,000 other people. (Lyndon Johnson never did anything small.) Mrs. Johnson opened the meeting, and Laurance Rockefeller chaired the meeting. Senator Nelson also attended and spoke about the Appalachian Trail.[57]

Much speculation ensued within ATC about how the proposal for a national trails system, modeled after the Appalachian Trail, got into the beautification message. All fingers seemed to point to Stewart Udall. Udall, a westerner, was apparently the first in the administration to insert the idea of broadening the bill to include some trails in the west. A strong lobby for this existed in such states as California and Colorado. Udall, in a speech out West, pledged protection of western trails.[58] Plans for a new bill proposing a national trails system released by Udall's office in July 1965 referenced Johnson's natural-beauty speech.[59]

The Nelson proposal had been effectively hijacked by the White House. One writer on the subject stated that, when Nelson inquired about why Udall's message to the Senate was delayed, "he was discretely advised that LBJ 'likes the concept, and he'd like to be the one who gets the credit for it.'"[60] That made perfect sense — it was how the president had operated in many arenas.

In an oral-history interview, Nelson reinforced this idea that Johnson wanted the credit — it was just one more item that he could add to his lengthening list of Great Society accomplishments. In the background, it was known that Johnson was upset with Nelson for his public opposition to the Vietnam war, although Nelson stated in his interview that he did not believe Johnson held a grudge against

---

57. *ATN*, September 1965.
58. ATC archives, Murray files, Murray to Garvey, June 7, 1965.
59. Department of the Interior news release, July 6, 1965.
60. Donald Dale Jackson, "The Long Way 'Round: The National Scenic Trails System and How it Grew. And How it Didn't," *Wilderness*, Summer 1988.

Stewart Udall, born in 1920, was from Arizona, where he went to college and became a lawyer in Tucson. He took on social causes early, helping to desegregate various public facilities years before the case of *Brown v. Board of Education* directed desegregation in 1954. In that year, he was elected to the U.S. House of Representatives for three terms. When John F. Kennedy was elected president, Udall became his secretary of the interior and was the

only such secretary that Kennedy and Lyndon Johnson ever had, not leaving that post until 1969. As secretary, he pushed aggressively for new national parks and monuments, federal land protection, and environmental legislation. It would be difficult to find an interior secretary in American history with greater impact.

him.[61] In 1965, it was the political kiss of death to oppose the president on this issue, so there were several reasons for LBJ to want to take leadership of the trail bill.

The Bureau of Outdoor Recreation asked Don Shedd, from its Atlanta office, to study the Appalachian Trail proposal and write a report as a baseline for its proposal for a national system of trails. Shedd's report, published in October 1965, was a watershed for the trail — its history and prospects. It was well understood that the Appalachian Trail bill would be expanded into a national trail system bill, and it would be important to examine the model to understand how it could become a national system.

Shedd did not write his report in a vacuum. Stan Murray recalled later, "In the summer of 1965, Don Shedd of the Bureau of Outdoor Recreation tracked me down while I was on vacation in Maine. He

---

61. Nelson interview, *op. cit.*

explained that he had been given the full-time assignment of preparing the section of the report that related to the Appalachian Trail. So we sat down and talked about the Trail, its philosophy and concept, its problems and what might be done about them."[62]

In characterizing the Appalachian Trail, Shedd called it "the longest marked pathway in the world." He first focused on the volunteer nature of the enterprise but quickly got down to hard facts. Only thirty-four percent of the trail was then on federal land — if the Nelson bill were to pass, there would be much work to do. Another twenty-three percent was on state or local government land, which provided some form of protection, provided that those governments cooperated with the Department of the Interior and continued to protect the trail. The problem came with those portions of the trail that were on private property. In 1965, that number was forty-three percent, just more than 866 miles.

No matter whose land the trail was on, conflicting uses abounded. Commercial and residential developments, wholesale timber-harvesting, intersecting and parallel roads, horses and motorized vehicles all represented well-known threats and were the reason why legislation was needed.

How would one protect the trail? The Nelson bill, in Shedd's opinion, needed some modifications to improve protection. Easements were nice and could protect a wider zone, not just the 200-foot-wide footpath. But, the bill needed some form of condemnation authority, and it needed specific language that would make clear that acquisition would take place outside of federal lands. In the hearings, Nelson stated that was his intent, but Shedd advocated that the language be changed so that there could be no doubt. If there were any wiggle room, some landowners would wiggle out.

In dealing with the states, Shedd wrote, "The concept of the States' playing a pivotal role in recreation planning is absent from the bill." The states, he wrote, should be full partners in the process. "It is recommended that the Secretary of the Interior...establish a set

---

62. ATC archives, Conference Meetings, Murray report to the 1967 conference in Cashiers, N.C.

of regulations to be adopted by the State governments in fulfilling their memorandums of understanding." Most of the land acquisition should be done by the fourteen states. (This was a view that seemed to captivate federal planners and was pursued vigorously until, by 1978, it was clear that the states were not, and did not intend to be, partners in the process.) Shedd's view made it into the final 1968 law.

How would the states participate in the process? According to Shedd, it would vary from state to state, depending on circumstances. In some places, as with the Mahoosucs in New Hampshire, land should be acquired by an expansion of national forest lands. And, national forests should move to acquire inholdings to protect trail segments. In northern Virginia, a special case, Virginia should take urgent action. Only two states already had programs that had special promise: New Jersey with its Green Acres program and Pennsylvania, which had moved to acquire lands to protect the Appalachian Trail on Blue Mountain. Shedd concluded, "There is a need for exploration of the avenues by which State agencies can provide the necessary protection services for Trail lands currently held in private ownership."

He was also critical of the almost complete lack of discussion of the role of volunteer organizations. By this, he clearly meant ATC and the component clubs. "The Department [of the Interior] believes that the Appalachian Trail Conference should continue in its present role as the principal guardian of the Trail.... But nowhere is there authorization for the federal government to accept assistance or advice from the Appalachian Trail Conference or any other part of the private sector in the formulation of any policies." He felt that it was strange that ATC had so unreservedly supported Nelson's bill, since it was left out of the legislation.

Murray had come out strongly for the Nelson bill because, as he admitted, it was the first proposal to protect the trail, and he would accept anything rather than see the trail disappear. But, he was glad that Shedd wanted to strengthen the bill, and, on this matter, he and Shedd wrote a long series of letters back and forth to ensure, in the minds of both, that ATC was there, where it should be.

On the subject of the width of the protected zone, Shedd concluded that there could be no uniformity. "Uniformity," he wrote, "is out
of the question. There are too many variables." One could use the
1938 Trailway Agreement as a guide — that document specified a
footpath four hundred feet in width, with a zone of a mile either side
of the trail (later a quarter-mile) where incompatible uses would be
prohibited. In many areas, that would be impractical. He suggested
that condemnation be restricted to the footpath and four hundred
feet and that it not be used outside of that zone.

Murray disliked the four-hundred-foot standard. He was already
thinking about a far wider protection of the trail environment and
wrote, "Such a conception is not at all that held by Conference leaders over the years. Should industry, real estate, and commercial es-
tablishments build up to within 200 feet of the Trail over long lengths
of it, because the land was not protected in any manner, we would
indeed end up a watered-down version of the Appalachian Trail....
Beyond this another zone is needed in order to preserve the 'remote
for detachment,...lonely for contemplation' features."[63]

What of the role of ATC? Despite Shedd's advocacy of the role of
volunteers, he admitted, "the Trail Conference...is neither staffed nor
funded to acquire lands, to develop facilities, to manage the resource,
to protect the land from fire and acts of nature, or to provide for the
Trail the guarantee of perpetuation that it needs. This must be done
through State and Federal protection." That was why legislation was
needed. To regularize the process of consultation with volunteers, an
Appalachian Trail council should be in the legislation.

That drew a strong rebuke from AMC. Francis Belcher, the executive director, wrote that the report placed too much emphasis on
federal control and not enough on the states. "I would hate to see the
Appalachian Trail become a child of federal bureaucracy."[64] MacKaye
was also concerned with the role of the feds, that if the federal government became the body of the trail, it would lose its volunteer soul
and become just another federal bureaucracy. "The Trail itself, that

---

63. *Ibid*, Murray files, Murray to Shedd, October 30, 1965.
64. *Ibid*, Belcher to Murray, October 29, 1965.

thing ought to be run by the clubs, not by government. That is the soul — the clubs represent the soul."[65]

How was the acquisition of land to be funded? Shedd advocated that wording should be inserted to authorize appropriations. Many people expected, he wrote, that the Land and Water Conservation Fund would pay for acquisitions. This was chimerical, he contended. LWCF could not possibly pay for all the land that was needed. And, it was unrealistic to expect federal agencies to pay for the land through their regular appropriations. Provision for funding needed to be in the bill.

On the matter of trail construction, Shedd recommended that the trail width and height should be four-feet-wide by eight-feet-high. That was a good start and was a standard already in use. Shelters should be located away from the trail, another standard that most volunteers already adhered to. He also recommended that a graded trail be employed only in high-use areas, something that was more debatable. Finally, the slope should be less than ten percent and avoid switchbacks. (Trail maintainers today might ask how this was to be done on steep slopes.)

Shedd's report introduced many ideas that were ultimately incorporated into the final legislation. It was a ground-breaking report that set a standard for BOR to use in crafting the legislation.

Even as the Shedd report was being presented, Udall was already pushing for a national trail system and had appointed a four-member steering committee to study the issue and propose new legislation that would take the Appalachian Trail concept and broaden it to the whole nation.

BOR was requested to take the lead, and Udall indicated that three classes of trails were being considered:

• Scenic and historic trails of national significance, five hundred miles or more, passing through several states, with overnight accommodations.
• Specific-area trails on public lands.

---

65. Hunter Library, Sherman Collection, MacKaye note, unknown date in 1965.

- Regional and local trails near metropolitan areas, for day-use recreation.[66]

The New Bill

On October 1, 1965, Gaylord Nelson sent forward a new bill. His bill introduced the idea of a system of national trails, but it did not mention any specific trail (not even the Appalachian Trail) or any particular type of trail. Like its predecessor, it did not contain provisions for acquisition by condemnation. Aside from the idea of a national trails system, it was more limited than S. 622.

The new bill came out of the blue. Ed Garvey sent a memorandum to the ATC board of managers, informing them and stating that it "caught all of us by surprise, including the Bureau of Outdoor Recreation. It appears that Senator Nelson introduced this bill completely on his own." Nelson's legislative aide told Garvey that the intent was not to stop progress on S. 622 — this bill was in addition to it. Nelson was clearly trying to stay ahead of the administration. The news release by his office stated that the bill included both the Appalachian Trail and the Pacific Crest Trail, but neither trail was mentioned in the legislation. The entire episode was evidently done so quickly that his own office did not know what was in the proposed legislation.

ATC was not in favor of broadening S. 622. Murray wrote to Nelson on June 18 urging that the bill be kept limited. He feared that passage would be delayed by consideration of other trails farther west, and it could jeopardize passage of a bill that appeared to have widespread support. The other trails were conceptual, and, other than the Pacific Crest Trail (PCT), no shovel had yet hit the ground.[67]

In March 1966, Udall took the lead on the Appalachian Trail bill. On March 31, he sent the president the draft of a bill that expanded S. 622 into a true national trails system. The Appalachian Trail was specifically named, and other trails were named in a "study group": the Chisholm, Continental Divide, Lewis and Clark, North Country,

---

66. *ATN*, September 1965, p. 35.
67. Hunter Library, Sherman Collection.

Oregon, Pacific Crest, Potomac Heritage, Santa Fe, and Natchez Trace trails. Aside from the Potomac Heritage Trail and the Natchez Trace, all were in the central or western states.

Focusing on national scenic trails, the legislation contained the vague definition of "an extended trail which has *natural, scenic, cultural or historic qualities*[68] that give the trail recreation use potential of national significance." The arbiter of this was to be, not surprisingly, the secretary of the interior.

The secretary also was empowered to decide on a precise route for the trail and on a unique marker for each national scenic trail. The matter of a marker was of concern to ATC, and Benton MacKaye pointed out that the A.T. already had a unique marker, devised in 1922 by William Welch. (In all other respects, MacKaye was very pleased with the legislation — his long-held dream of a protected trail might possibly come true.)[69]

The bill established that the secretary of the interior would administer the Appalachian Trail, in cooperation with the secretary of agriculture (because of the office's jurisdiction over national forests). That meant that the trail would come under the jurisdiction of the National Park Service. That key provision became the most important change in the legislation, because it gave the trail designated leadership. Volunteers at ATC were nervous about the implications — would it take away their role, and would their trail become simply an administrative entity of the National Park Service? And, what would be the relationship between the Park Service and the Forest Service? Those very difficult relationships remained to be worked out.

Their concerns were softened somewhat by a provision that created an advisory council to help administer the trail with one member from each federal agency concerned, one from each of the fourteen states, and one from each "private organization that, in the opinion of the Secretary, has an established and recognized interest in the trail." How far down this would go was left unaddressed. Would it

---

68. This phrase was to survive all drafts and defined the trail qualities that the A.T. was supposed to encompass.
69. ATC archives, MacKaye files, MacKaye to Garvey, April 25, 1966.

include only ATC, or would the participating clubs also have representatives? In view of the number of trail clubs then belonging to ATC, the advisory council might become unwieldy.

The bill placed a heavy emphasis on cooperative acquisition. Acquisition in fee simple was stressed, and the willing-seller process was preferred. It included other methods of acquiring authority to cross private land, such as leases and cooperative agreements. Land could be donated, or an exchange agreement could compensate a private landowner with an equivalent amount of federal land in another location.

And, for the first time, condemnation was included: "Provided further, That the Secretary shall utilize condemnation proceedings without the consent of the owner to acquire private lands or interests therein pursuant to this subsection only in cases where, in his judgment, all reasonable effort to acquire such land by negotiation have failed." Condemnation usually was associated with highway construction and had never before been used to acquire recreational trails. This, the most revolutionary part of the legislation, stayed in the bill all the way to enactment.

The bill introduced the further idea of other types of trails. "Federal park, forest and other recreation trails" and "state and metropolitan area trails" were the other types of trails that appeared in the draft. The Land and Water Conservation Fund was integral to the funding of those new trail categories.

In his message to President Johnson, Udall discussed what it might cost to buy the land needed for the A.T. from private landowners. He estimated that $4,665,000 would be needed, along with $2,000,000 in development costs. Noting that 866 trail miles were on private land, that amount of money would be sufficient to acquire an average of twenty-five acres per mile of trail. "The twenty-five acre per mile acquisition in fee would permit a right-of-way averaging 200 feet in width." This, then, became the federal standard for trail corridor protection and did not include the acquisition of any lands to protect the trail values that the legislation espoused.

That, too, became a matter of great concern to ATC. Still, it was better than not having a protected path, and Murray was for getting half a loaf as opposed to none at all. Acquisition costs were spread out over five years. All the financial estimates and length of time to acquire the lands proved to be gross underestimates — they were not even close.

Congressmen raced to introduce the Udall bill immediately after Johnson's budget message in January. Competition was particularly hot in the House of Representatives. Within days of the budget message, the following bills were introduced, all identical in language:

H.R. 12204, by Frank Down of New York
H.R. 12391, by Phil Philbin of Massachusetts
   (a friend of Benton MacKaye)
H.R. 12708, by Nathaniel Craley, Jr., of Pennsylvania
H.R. 14222, by L. Mendel Rivers of South Carolina

Others were introduced within a few days of each other. In the Senate, Henry M. Jackson introduced the administration bill, S. 3171, while, in the House, Representative Roy A. Taylor of North Carolina introduced it as H.R. 12393 on January 27. It was Taylor who proved to be the congressman most responsible for shepherding the bill through Congress. He worked almost daily with Stan Murray and the ATC committee that was working on the passage of the legislation. How he was picked to shepherd the bill through Congress is unknown today, but he proved to be the right man for the job.

ATC had great concern about the administration's decision to intervene. To Walter Boardman, the issue was confused mightily by the existence of Nelson's S. 622, limited to only the Appalachian Trail, and the new administration-sponsored bills that named the A.T. brought in the idea of a whole system of trails, not all of them hiking trails. To have a competitor to the Nelson bill was confusing enough, but to bring in all these local trails would introduce opportunities for individual interests to object, and all might fail because one met insurmountable objections.[70]

---

70. *ATN*, September 1966, p. 35.

Roy A. Taylor was a U.S. representative from western North Carolina. Born in 1910 in Washington state, he graduated from Maryville College in Tennessee and Asheville University Law School. He served as a member of the North Carolina general assembly from 1947 to 1949 and 1951 to 1953. After that, he served almost eighteen years in the U.S. House of Representatives, beginning in 1960. Taylor was a strong proponent of environmental legislation in Congress and is still revered in his district for his advocacy of environmental causes and forest protection. It happened that the Appalachian Trail ran through his district, and he took an early interest in the trail. Taylor became the principal sponsor of federal protection for the trail. No one had a greater impact.

Murray, too, favored sticking with the simpler Nelson bill, even though Udall's proposal contained provisions for condemnation. Murray and BOR went back and forth on condemnation. Murray wrote to BOR, "I would like to suggest that we start off by preparing a bill specifically and exclusively for the Appalachian Trail." That was not what the administration wanted, and, in the end, BOR stuck with the broader bill.

Nelson's bill did not advance. Wayne Aspinall, the chairman of the House Interior Committee, was on board with the administration bill and declined to hold further hearings. Boardman, Murray, and even the assistant secretary for fish and wildlife all urged Udall to accede to the Nelson bill, to no avail.

Amid the kludge of bills in Congress, the one that became the spearhead was the one pushed by Roy Taylor. Murray and his committee needed Taylor because Taylor's bill had become the focus of the administration's energies, so they trod softly. They did not want to alienate Taylor, while trying to soften the impact that Taylor's other interests would have on the Appalachian Trail. Eventually, Murray had to abandon work in support of Nelson's bill and throw his full support behind Taylor.

Late in the year, BOR released a seminal report, "Trails for America," to support the administration's interest in a national system of trails. That report served as the public underpinning for the administration's trails program. And, it took the program further than any other document before it, listing the Appalachian, Pacific Crest, Continental Divide, and Potomac Heritage trails as the first proposed national scenic trails.

Working with Taylor

In introducing the bill on February 6, 1967, Taylor delivered an inspiring message about the Appalachian Trail. Acknowledging that the bill promoted a broad-based national trail system with several different kinds of trails, he drew attention to the A.T., the cause that had generated the legislation.

The Appalachian Trail is one of the truly great achievements of volunteers in American outdoor recreation.... The trail program I propose here today is a truly cooperative program, which will welcome the efforts of all. Those many citizens who have counted their volunteer labor on the trail as their greatest outdoor experience can be assured that we intend, in this legislation, to guarantee them the continued opportunity for such creative contributions to the outdoor recreation heritage of our Nation."

Stan Murray and Ed Garvey sent identical written statements in support of the bill to both the Senate and House. Their testimony emphasized, first, the role of volunteers, and, second, the public nature of the enterprise. "Any person may use any portion of the Trail at any time, without charge, registration, or any other acknowledgement of use.... The Trail provides an outdoor recreation experience of high quality. A trip on the Trail is seldom forgotten."

But, the need for protection was great. "The Appalachian Trail in its finest sense is a fragile entity.... Unwelcome interruptions have cropped up with disturbing frequency in recent years. Typical are newly bulldozed roads, logging devastation..., colonies of summer homes, lakeside developments on hitherto unoccupied jewels in the wilderness, and newly erected gates across the Trail with well-lettered signs reading 'Keep Out.'" Concluding their concern, they stated, "We are running out of places to go."[71]

Directly addressing the potential downside of government ownership, they concluded, "The Conference Board is of the opinion that the present bill H.R. 4865 provides adequate safeguards that such things as just mentioned will not happen. It is our fervent hope that they will not happen." Finally, addressing the concern that the Appalachian Trail would just become another national park, with roads, entrance stations, ice-cream stands and visitor lodges, they cited the purpose statement in the bill, that "national scenic trails shall be administered, protected, developed, and maintained to retain their *natural, scenic, cultural and historic features*...and the primeval environment." That, they felt, was what would make the trail different from Yosemite, Yellowstone, or Shenandoah. They were willing to accept government control of the entire trail in order to guarantee its continued existence and were reassured by the wording in the bill that it would stay the same as the trail that the volunteers had created.

Working with Taylor, Murray was still nervous about the scope of the legislation. Writing to Walter Boardman in 1967, he said, "I find it difficult to believe that the Nationwide System of Trails bill will ever pass in 1968 unless most of the trails are confined to the study group.... I am not very optimistic. There seem to be just too many broad questions that have arisen that the BOR had not anticipated or worried about."[72]

In his private correspondence with Taylor, Murray made his position, and the position of ATC, clear. "The risk which the Conference has been prepared to take in supporting H.R. 4865 is the risk of mismanagement by the federal and state agencies which administer the Trail lands. We have been prone to accept this risk, for several reasons: to continue as we are without federal protection is even less

---

71. ATC archives, Murray files, statement to Congress, March 7, 1967.
72. *Ibid*, Murray to Boardman, October 30, 1967.

attractive; [and] our 29-year experience under the Appalachian Trailway Agreement has in general been quite good."[73]

The bill seemed very popular but did run into opposition from some quarters. In Maine, Percival Baxter opposed any federal control of any trail in the state and was adamant about it. (Baxter seemed adamant about anything he addressed.)[74]

The only downside to the relationship with Roy Taylor was with his broad scope of interests for his constituency, not all of them compatible with the Appalachian Trail legislation. For instance, it was Taylor who pushed for the proposed extension of the Blue Ridge Parkway into Georgia. Breaking off from the existing parkway just west of Asheville, Taylor's home, it was to go south into Georgia, right on top of the existing A.T. The proposed ridgetop road, supported also by Udall, would be 180 miles, all the way to Kennesaw Mountain outside Atlanta. Although only 43 miles would be in North Carolina (Taylor's district) and 137 miles in Georgia, it was Taylor who was the most prominent advocate.[75]

Taylor had sponsored the legislation to survey the route of the proposed parkway in 1961, his first year in Congress. Murray was immediately concerned, and his legislative committee began corresponding with Taylor. Rather than opposing the parkway extension outright, Murray and his legislative committee decided to use the same approach that Myron Avery had with Skyline Drive — to get the government to move the trail out of the way of the parkway. (That required acceptance of the road, a decision that Murray came to only very reluctantly.) In 1967, Taylor assured John Oliphant that the trail would be moved before the bulldozers appeared. "At the meeting [an executive session of the House subcommittee on national parks and recreation], we also agreed to place a provision in the committee report stating that if and when the National Trails Bill is passed…that the provision of that bill will govern over the Blue Ridge Parkway Extension Bill."[76] And, in 1968, Taylor stated publicly, "The Ap-

---

73. *Ibid*, Murray to Taylor, March 15, 1967.
74. *Ibid*, Baxter to Taylor, July 7, 1967.
75. Roy Taylor papers, University of North Carolina–Asheville Special Collections.
76. *Ibid*, Taylor to Oliphant, August 8, 1967.

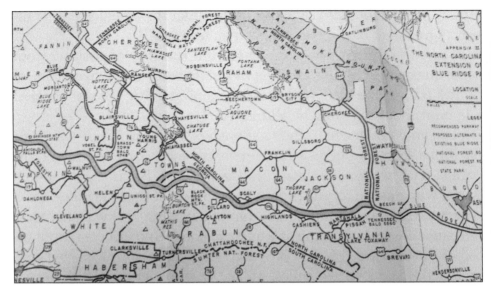

The proposed Blue Ridge Parkway extension from Asheville (lower far right) to Dahlonega, Ga., at far left.

palachian Trail group is now satisfied with the bill."[77] Still, Murray was very concerned about the parkway extension because it would change a remote part of the trail into one that would lose its primeval nature.

Taylor also supported extension of "the road to nowhere" from Bryson City to Fontana Dam. In a letter to Udall, he urged that $3.5 million be promptly released "to keep the bulldozers pushing toward Monteith Branch."[78] ATC opposed the road extension but kept quiet on the issue so that it could retain its close relationship with Taylor. To get the legislation passed, one had to make compromises. In the end, neither the Fontana Road nor the Blue Ridge Parkway extension was ever built.

Taylor's other causes were aligned more closely with ATC's interests. He was a sponsor of the national scenic rivers bill and supported building a center at the Cradle of Forestry in the Pisgah National Forest. (Murray sent a letter of support for the center.[79]) Over all, the closeness of ATC with Taylor was a huge plus for the trail.

---

77. *Ibid*, prepared statement of July 9, 1968.
78. *Ibid*, Udall to Taylor.
79. ATC archives, Murray files, Murray to Taylor, January 30, 1968.

Taylor proved to be an adroit manager and headed off all objections to the trails bill. But, he was realistic and informed Murray that the bill was unlikely to pass in 1967. He needed time to address all the detractors and either allay their concerns or simply ignore them.

That made Murray nervous — he was always nervous — that waiting another year could cause other issues to override the trails bills, so that, in the end, nothing would be done. Still, he waited — he had no choice, really. Final passage of the bill was held up, waiting for Taylor to get all the ducks in line. Taylor, an expert in the legislative process, appeared unconcerned about the delay.[80]

Entering 1968, Taylor was still working out some objectionable passages in the bill that, he told Murray, did not relate to the Appalachian Trail. (The problems were with western members of Congress, and the proposed Continental Divide Trail was one of the contentious matters.)

Wayne Aspinall argued with Stewart Udall about the number of trails that should be authorized in the bill. Aspinall, probably closer to the push and pull of the legislative process, wanted only the A.T. and PCT. Udall still pushed for the whole package — that is, those that, in Aspinall's bill, were in the study category. Over the winter and spring, the arguments in Congress about which trails would be authorized and which would be placed in the study category were holding up a final mark-up in both House and Senate.[81]

The legislation had other problems. The trails bill was moving through Congress during the height of the Great Society concentration on conservation, and many competing bills seemed to take a higher priority with the administration. Dear to Lyndon and Lady Bird Johnson's hearts was a project to save the redwoods in California, but Congress had many others on its plate, including a bill to create a federal program to preserve "wild and scenic rivers" and another to protect the North Cascades in Washington. Murray worried that the trails

---

80. The back and forth between Murray and Taylor is well-documented in the ATC archives' Murray files, Box 5-2-1. Murray's nervousness, and Taylor's confidence, can be sensed in reading those letters.
81. See, for instance, ATC archives, Murray files, Boardman to Murray, January 22, 1968, and Taylor to Murray, November 14, 1967.

bill would get lost in the pile of competing legislation, and, if it were shifted to the following year, it was a new Congress, and everything would have to be started again. Murray again suggested to Boardman that he make an attempt to pull the Continental Divide Trail from the bill, but to no avail.[82] The push to get the bill through Congress was becoming frantic, but Taylor appeared imperturbable.

The pulls and pushes were just part of a messy legislative process, and the Senate bill (S. 827) was finally marked up in the Senate on the first of July. On July 15, the full House committee marked up its trails bill.

After having been passed by both the House and Senate, the bill was sent to a conference committee to reconcile the differences. On the last day, Murray asked Ed Garvey to sit outside the committee room and wait in case Taylor should come out of the room with more questions for Murray. Garvey would then make a pay-telephone call to get the two on the line. Taylor never emerged from the committee room, and Garvey's wait was unnecessary.

Although the House and Senate bills were generally the same, they had some differences. A key omission in the House bill was the absence of an advisory committee. Murray had pushed Taylor to include it, to no avail. So, he wrote to the conference committee, urging that the advisory council, which was in the Senate bill, be retained.

He also asked that the legislation include the words "and shall be administered so as to retain and improve natural, *primitive,* and scenic qualities of the areas through which the Trail passes."[83] The language, which MacKaye was so insistent be part of the legislation, never appeared in the final act. Instead, national scenic trails were defined as "extended trails so located as to provide for maximum outdoor recreation potential and for the conservation and enjoyment of the nationally significant *scenic, historic, natural, or cultural qualities* of the areas through which such trails may pass."

The word "primitive" never appeared. But the words that did appear, "*scenic, historic, natural or cultural*" became the phrase that judges would

---

82. ATC archives, Murray files, contains numerous letters involving Taylor, Murray, and Boardman.
83. ATC archives, Murray files, Box 5-2-1, undated letter.

use to decide which properties must be included in the trail corridor. Imprecise wording such as this gave the secretary a lot of discretion in interpreting the meaning of the act, and courts generally deferred to his judgment in lieu of any other directions found in the act. The phrase came to define what the Appalachian Trail was and would be.

The act as finally passed was much longer than the one that began in 1964. In eight turgid pages, it described national scenic trails, of which only two were finally authorized, the A.T. and the PCT. It then provided a long list of "study trails," including Continental Divide, Potomac Heritage, Old Cattle Trails of the Southwest, Lewis and Clark, Natchez Trace, North Country, Kittanniny, Oregon, Santa Fe, Long, Mormon, Gold Rush, Mormon Battalion, and El Camino Real. Some of those had never appeared in earlier drafts and were evidently the product of special or local interests. Some have never become national trails at all.

Recreation trails were also included but were of a very different character, being entirely within public land and designated by the federal official involved. Another category that had not appeared in earlier versions was the "connecting or side trail." These would provide access to a national scenic or recreation trails, and, by implication, the administering agency of the scenic or recreation trail would be the approving authority. These "connecting or side trails" could become, in some cases, blue-blazed trails leading to the A.T.

The advisory council appeared in the act, so that various groups would be consulted about the two authorized trails (A.T. and PCT). In this regard, ATC was specifically mentioned: "Provided, That the Appalachian Trail Conference shall be represented by a sufficient number of persons to represent the various sections of the country through which the Appalachian Trail passes." That removed any ambiguity as to what "private organizations" the act referred to. It did not establish a specific number from ATC but implied that at least some of the trail clubs would be providing members. The word "volunteer" did not appear in the legislation, but this provision did more than anything to allay the fears of volunteer organizations that they might be forgotten.

When considering the forty-three percent of the trail that was on private land, it would be up to the individual states to acquire the land or rights for the trail to cross. However, were the states not to act within two years, then the federal government was to acquire the land or rights-of-way. In the case of the Appalachian Trail, this would be the

Secretary Udall and Chief Justice Earl Warren are behind the President, with Mrs. Johnson to his right, Senator "Scoop" Jackson (hidden) to Warren's left. Next to Mrs. Johnson is Senator Ernest Gruening (Alaska); to the right are Senators Frank Moss (Utah) and Clinton Anderson (New Mexico). At the very back is future House Speaker Thomas Foley (Washington)

President Johnson greets Stan Murray on October 2, 1968.

parent departments of the National Park Service or the U.S. Forest Service. Among volunteers, it was widely supposed that the states would act and that there would be no requirement for the federal government to intervene. That was to prove completely unrealistic.

President Johnson signed the act on October 2, 1968, and S. 827 became law as Public Law 90-543. In fact, he signed four pieces of conservation legislation at the session: the Redwoods National Park Act (what Mrs. Johnson had on her schedule as the purpose of the event), the Wild and Scenic Rivers Act, the Cascades National Park Act, and the National Trails System Act. The room was crowded with invited guests, among them Stan Murray. Several PATC members were also invited, including John Oliphant. One searches photographs in vain for the face of Gaylord Nelson. He was not on the invitation list. The White House sent a signing pen to MacKaye, who could not be at the ceremony.

Rather than being watered down through the legislative process, the bill was strengthened as it went along. The early, relatively toothless proposal to acquire land only through willing-seller purchase and scenic easements was strengthened by condemnation authority. (Murray seemed happy with the willing-seller limitation, but he did note, "Many knowledgeable persons state that scenic easements are about as costly as fee title and far less satisfactory from the standpoint of control."[84])

---

84. *Ibid*, Murray to Boardman, May 27, 1968.

AREAS AUTHORIZED FOR ESTABLISHMENT OR STUDY BY ACT OF CONGRESS 1961-1968.

After signing four conservation bills, including the NTSA and the Wild and Scenic Rivers Act, Secretary Udall (left) discusses with President Johnson the proposed expansions of protected federal lands and waters, in the East Room of the White House.

The role of the states in earlier bills was backstopped by the provision that, should the states fail to act, the federal government would step in. That was an essential provision because fourteen states could go off in fourteen different directions, and some might fail to act at all. Experience showed how difficult it was to get the states to move together.

A survey would be necessary to document the route. Once it was finished and published in the *Federal Register*, the states would have two years to acquire the corridor. Should they not acquire the entire corridor, the National Park Service was tasked with acquiring any additional land needed.

Curiously, in Murray's archived files that had been inventoried at this writing, no correspondence with the Senate committee that considered the bill appears. S. 827 became the bill that became law, reconciled with

Taylor's House bill, H.R. 4867. Yet all the correspondence, and all the contacts, were with Taylor, and none with Jackson. (ATC *was* given a copy of a bill autographed by Senators Jackson and Nelson.)

Murray, who lived in Tennessee, had assembled an impressive team in Washington to push the ATC interests. The committee chairman, Walter Boardman, was assisted by Grant Conway, Ray Gingrich, Frank Wallick, John Oliphant, and Ed Garvey. Managing the effort from a long distance was a significant achievement but could not have been done without his troops on the ground. On the day of the signing, he wrote to all Conference members that this was a "truly red letter day in the history of the Appalachian Trail."

The impact of Stan Murray on the Appalachian Trail was second only to Myron Avery. Like Avery, he was single-minded and determined. Unlike Avery, he had a talent for dealing with people on their own terms. Avery and Murray were as different as different could be, but their accomplishments were both historic.

The Murray era represented a watershed in the development of the Appalachian Trail. He managed to accomplish what Avery said must happen, but a betting man, in 1945, would have placed his money on the trail eventually disappearing. It was inconceivable that the federal government would step forward to protect a hiking trail, almost half of which was on private land. Unlike in England, American common law had no tenet preserving a person's right to walk on another's land. It was just not in the American cultural tradition.

That Congress would pass such legislation was simply mind-boggling. No one could have predicted it.

For the Appalachian Trail
Conference, Archives
Henry Jackson
Gaylord Nelson

90TH CONGRESS
1ST SESSION

S. 827

IN THE SENATE OF THE UNITED STATES

FEBRUARY 3, 1967

Mr. JACKSON (for himself and Mr. NELSON) introduced the following bill; which was read twice and referred to the Committee on Interior and Insular Affairs

A BILL

To establish a nationwide system of trails, and for other purposes.

1 *Be it enacted by the Senate and House of Representa-*

2 *tives of the United States of America in Congress assembled,*

3   STATEMENT OF POLICY

4 SECTION 1. (a) The Congress finds that in order to pro-

5 vide for the ever-increasing outdoor recreation needs of an

6 expanding population and to promote public access to, travel

7 within, and enjoyment of, the National and State parks,

8 forests, recreation areas, historic sites, and other areas,

9 existing trails should be improved and maintained and addi-

10 tional trails should be established both in the remaining

II

Chapter 8

IMPLEMENTING AND AMENDING THE ACT

As a project, the Appalachian Trail is symbolic of American ingenuity and perseverance: People work together to build something they felt needed building. The trail project was like an immense barnraising in which scores of volunteers from all parts of the East Coast spent over fifteen years to build more than 2,000 miles of trail.

— Peter Dunning, ATC staff member

Shortly after the act was passed, Murray formed a committee on implementation, with Ed Garvey as chairman. All the members were based in Washington. At the same time, Murray moved ahead to bring the clubs into the task. A trail had been authorized and legislation enacted to acquire the corridor. But, where was the trail?

Volunteers on the ground could take you there, and trail clubs made maps showing the route, but, before satellites and GPS technology, where it was precisely on the surface of the Earth was still inexact. The act required the secretary of the interior to select the route and to publish that route in the *Federal Register*. He was to consult with the states, local governments, "private organizations" (that would be ATC), and landowners. The route would be established by an aerial survey. Once the route was established, "substantial" relocations required an act of Congress. (The history of the A.T. is full of relocations, but Congress has never been asked to authorize any of them.)

In a letter to trail clubs, Murray asked each one for feedback on where the trail was. He needed to know where each section was, where it began and ended. The volunteer management system had created it, but no system was in place to know exactly what they had created or precisely where it was.

Just as important to Murray was, where *should* it be? It was located wherever the volunteers had obtained permission for it. No one had ever addressed the question of where they would like it to be. The facts on the ground were what they had. Murray asked them if the trail should be moved. "The recommendation there is, 'Think big.' This will be our one and only opportunity to get sufficient land protected for the A.T. so that we can continue to call it a wilderness trail. Include all acreage that had been included under the 1938 Trailway Agreement. Mark in pencil the approximate boundaries of the right-of-way that should be protected, then submit the plan to the conference vice chairmen. ATC would submit the maps to the Department of the Interior."[1]

So, the federal government began working on a process for establishing where the trail actually ran. The Park Service hired Aero Services to fly light planes over the trail corridor and take photographs. Using marked maps that the trail clubs had provided to ATC, Les Holmes sent them to the company. Volunteers were then tasked to go out on the trail and place white sheets at key points along the trail to guide the pilots.

Aero Services took more than 800 photos and made eighty-five segment maps covering the whole trail. But, in many places, the pilots, flying at 9,000 feet, could not see the sheets. Flying in June, with the tree leaves out, made the job even harder, and many of the overflights had to be repeated in the fall. After repeated overflights taking several months, the trail route was published in the *Federal Register* on October 9, 1971. With that, the trail route had been identified as best as the technology of the time would permit.[2] The clock was ticking, for the states and for the National Park Service.

1. Roy Taylor papers, UNC–Asheville Special Collections, Box 20, undated Murray letter to trail clubs. The ATC Archives include the flyover negatives and prints.
2. PATC *Bulletin*, January-March 1971, pp. 3-4; *ATN*, September 1969, p. 16; Roy Taylor papers: Holmes to Nichols, September 22, 1969, and Nichols to Holmes, November 17, 1969; Appalachian Trail Land Acquisition Office files, Martinsburg, W.Va.; Dave Sherman e-mail, May 2015.

Volunteers laying down white cloth and paper to mark the route for the aerial photographers.

The act had placed the burden on the fourteen states to acquire the corridor, and they now had two years to do it. Most people agreed that the states would act, and Sally Fairfax wrote, "It has become accepted that the states bear the primary responsibility for outdoor recreation and that the role of the federal government should be confined to coordinating and stimulating the state effort." Citing several congressional acts dating back to 1936, she made a convincing case for state leadership in this area. Fairfax believed that the states, having been tasked with acquisition of the corridor, had no choice but to proceed. And, for his part, Murray predicted, "I believe that we will never see this privilege of the federal government to acquire land after two years exercised because I believe every Trail state will participate in the program."[3] They were both wrong.

Continued on page 371.

3. Sally K. Fairfax, "Federal-State Cooperation in Outdoor Recreation Policy Formation: The Case of the Appalachian Trail," doctoral dissertation, Duke University, 1973, p. 56.; *ATN*, May 1968, p. 19.

Ed Garvey

Hikers tend to be introverts, studies have shown. They also tend to be intellectuals. (Are these related?) The typical hiker, in that construct, is an office worker, teacher, or college professor who can't wait to get away from the office and out on the trail every weekend.

And then there was Garvey. A very few Appalachian Trail pioneers were extreme extroverts — Myron Avery was an obvious exception. Edward B. Garvey was another, and his personality was so extroverted that he sometimes seemed to be everywhere at the same time. (People used to say that about Avery. In a way, he was almost an Avery clone.)

Ed Garvey was born in 1914 in Farmington, Minnesota, the oldest of five children from a Catholic family. (Catholicism played a big role in his life.) His father ran a general store. Ed joined the Soil Conservation Service (SCS) as an auditor in 1935 and in the mid-1940s moved to the Washington, D.C., area, still with the Soil Conservation Service. In 1959, he switched agencies, joining the National Science Foundation as its finance officer.

He joined the Potomac Appalachian Trail Club only a few months after Avery died in 1952. He soon began volunteering at PATC, which at the time had an office in downtown Washington. That brought him in contact with ATC, which had its office in the same building. In those days, volunteers moved freely between the two organizations. In his PATC life, Ed became the supervisor of trails in 1959, serving until 1965, and eventually served as president of the club from 1972 to 1974.

But, his presence in ATC became more important. He joined in 1962 and, in two years, was elected to the board of managers as secretary, succeeding Fred Blackburn.

His reforms of ATC set the organization on a professional course (see chapter 7). He was Stan Murray's right-hand man in the area of administration. Garvey, always the green-eyeshades man, kept a close eye on the money. He was just the right person for the time — ATC was a loose and scattered organization and needed someone like Garvey to lasso it.

Murray came to rely on him more and more for congressional relations, too, since he lived in Falls Church, a Virginia suburb of Washington. When Murray needed someone to go to the Capitol, Garvey was often his person. Ed Garvey could not be turned away by opposition. He could confront anyone. He was a better advocate than a negotiator.

He was incredibly focused and kept detailed notes on everything that interested him. This included ATC finances, but it could also involve the miles per gallon on his hiking trips, itemizing the food that he purchased, notes on weather, *etc.* He followed baseball avidly and kept programs and box scores from games he had attended. His mind was omnivorous.

Garvey also had a flair for publicity. When, in 1970, he decided to retire and thru-hike the Appalachian Trail, he publicized the impending event far and wide. What if he failed? It would be the most public failure of a thru-hiker ever. But, of course, he didn't fail — he succeeded in hiking the entire trail that same year.

People would come out to the trail in hopes of encountering the famous Ed Garvey. When they did, they would struggle to keep up with him, despite the fact that it was him carrying the full pack, and they carried nothing but a day pack. Sometimes hikers volunteered to carry his pack for a ways, and even very fit hikers marveled at how difficult it was to carry Garvey's pack.

Often, they would gratefully retire at the next trail crossing, leaving Ed to push on without them.

Following his thru-hike, he published *Appalachian Hiker: Adventure of a Lifetime*, in 1971. It was a sensation, the first best-selling description of a thru-hike. The book sold 50,000 copies and became the standard by which all other books of the same genre were measured, selling more copies than any other A.T. book prior to the 1998 publication of Bill Bryson's *A Walk in the Woods*. But, in many ways, it was different from those that followed.

The first portion of the book was a how-to for a prospective long-distance hiker. He discussed gear, especially packs — he carried a Kelty external-frame pack, which (partly because of Garvey) became for a period the national standard for overnight hiking. He recommended that hikers hold their pack weight to no more than 35 pounds. He talked about sleeping bags, comparing the benefits and downsides of various types. (He strongly favored the down-filled, mummy type.) He covered boots with the same attention to detail. And food — he loved to talk about food. His greatest culinary invention was Citadel Spread, which he laid out in great detail so that others could duplicate. (But, it didn't sound particularly appetizing.) Like the marshmallow, it was ageless:

Peanut Butter + Bacon Grease + Honey Mix well.
Add Powdered milk, and stir until mix gets crunchy. Put in pint plastic freezer containers. It will keep in refrigerator indefinitely; it keeps for at least three weeks unrefrigerated.

The 1970s being the height of the back-to-nature movement, the trail was overrun with young people without any knowledge of trail etiquette or a sense of decorum. Garvey laid out his rules for hiking the trail, and, on the trail, he obsessively picked up litter, documenting his daily haul in his ever-present notebook. He insisted on proper behavior at shelters and campsites. He also recommended that hikers be properly attired — short sleeves were okay, but shorts did not work for Ed. His appearance on the trail was quite dapper, with his trademark chapeau and long pants. Garvey represented Mr. Hiker and became the model for hikers.

Garvey loved causes and pursued them with the same single-minded vigor that he adopted for packs and food. One of his causes was the double-offset blaze. That was necessary, he contended, so that hikers would know that a turn was coming up and which way it would go. (ATC struggled with the idea for years, finally deciding *not to decide* at the 1995 biennial conference, tabling a Garvey resolution.) The most famous photo of Garvey (page 367), on his first book's cover, had him standing next to a tree with a double blaze (but, curiously, not offset).

He obsessed about shelters (see page 422), considering them the most valuable facility on the A.T. He got into a memorable dispute with the superintendent of Shenandoah National Park, who for a time removed all shelters in his park because of perceived misuse. (Garvey contended that education was the way to fix the problem.) He wrote long dissertations about maintaining good relations with landowners who permitted the A.T. to be on their land and admonished any hiker who might leave a speck of litter behind. Garvey was a titan of the Trail, the most famous hiker of his day, and the most single-minded about its improvement. He didn't just hike — he set out to improve where he hiked. There has never been another one like him.

The Park Service immediately saw an out. After the act was passed, Phil Stewart, who was in charge of land acquisition, refused to move, saying that the states would take the action. Fairfax noted, "Quite reasonably, the Park Service did not wish to be in a position of owning and managing a series of isolated strips of land spread out over a 2,000-mile Trail. It did not want to be responsible for land in areas where it had no personnel and no way of adequately supervising the facilities. The Park Service very soon decided that its goal was *not* to acquire any of the Trail outside of National Park boundaries."[4]

---

4. Fairfax, *ibid*, p. 76; interview with Charles Rinaldi, November 7, 2014.

When one thinks about it today, the position of Stewart and Fairfax sounds eminently reasonable. What sort of a "park" was this? It had no entry stations, no boundaries, and no law enforcement, and almost half of it was on tracts not connected and on private land. How could the Park Service manage such an ill-defined linear park?

No such thing had ever been created, and the Park Service wanted no part of it. It was someone else's job. And, why pay for something when you can get somebody else to pay for it?

Now that the preliminary work had been done, ATC began the process of appointing coordinators to work with each state on route selection and corridor acquisition. The act-authorized Appalachian National Scenic Trail Advisory Council (ANSTAC) submitted the pertinent material to each state through regional coordinators.[5] The clubs were expected to be the contact points with their respective states, a reinforcement of the decentralized nature of the enterprise. It was clear that everyone expected the states to immediately take up their role in the process.

Funding for state acquisitions was to come from the Land and Water Conservation Fund, supplemented by appropriated state funds. The Bureau of Outdoor Recreation was to administer the grant program. Each state had to write a comprehensive plan that would include the A.T. if they expected to use LWCF for the trail. (See chapter 9.)

The challenge for ATC

After years of struggle, the Appalachian Trail was finally and officially a government responsibility. Although the triumph seemed complete, Stan Murray knew the road ahead and the work that had to be done to actually bring the trail into public ownership. As Murray had worked with Congress to pass the act, so, too, he now had to work with the states and the federal government to acquire the corridor. No one, not even Murray, realized how long it would take and how hard it would be.

---

5. ATC archives, Murray files, correspondence, 1972-75; Rauner Library, Dartmouth College, MacKaye Collection, Box 197, folder 8.

Many viewed ATC as a weak partner in building a relationship with federal agencies. In her 1973 doctoral dissertation, Sally Fairfax thought that ATC was ineffectively organized and unable to work with either the clubs or the federal government on an equal footing. But, if ATC were unable to carry the ball, few other options were available. By 1968, nearly 50 clubs, almost all of them small and weak, were in play with only a local outlook — they took care of their section, but that was about all. PATC was by far the strongest club south of AMC land but could not, and should not, represent the volunteer force.

Fairfax concluded, "This combination of circumstances has made effective coordination of the nonfederal participants almost impossible."[6] The organization was spread out, met only occasionally, and its meetings, to Fairfax, resembled a "huge pep rally," lacking in substantive discussions.

Fairfax was too pessimistic. ATC was changing rapidly. The Garvey reforms were in full swing. ATC had moved to Harpers Ferry the year before she published her paper. Murray had hired a staff and had extricated his organization from the controlling influence of PATC. And, Murray (with considerable help from PATC volunteers, it must be admitted) had managed the process of negotiating the legislation with Congress. The profile of ATC that had prevailed in earlier years was fast becoming archaic.

Murray reassured the volunteers that their role would continue unchanged. He wrote to them in January 1969, "The Trail clubs will continue in their present roles of custodians and stewards of their assigned Trail sections. All levels of government have not only asked that the work of the volunteer groups continue, but have expressed dismay at any thoughts to the contrary."[7]

Following the passage of the legislation, ATC signed an agreement with the Park Service providing for cooperative management of the trail. But, other than providing for close cooperation, little in the agreement was either new or obligatory on either party. The Park Service seemed to hold out hope that ATC and its member clubs would

---

6. Fairfax, *op. cit.,* p. 65.
7. *ATN,* January 1969, p. 3.

take the lead and that the states would acquire lands to protect the trail, since they did not intend to do it themselves.

The Park Service also signed an agreement with the Forest Service regarding administration of the trail. The agreement simply provided a mechanism for establishing procedures for developing regulations. The well-known competitive atmosphere between the Park Service and Forest Service was unaffected by this brief memorandum of agreement (MOU). Sally Fairfax was very dubious that the two agencies could work together to achieve anything. She wrote, "Two of the agencies, the Park Service and the Forest Service, are so deeply entrenched in their distinct positions regarding land management generally that common understanding and a unified approach to trail policy are almost impossible to achieve."[8] She was wrong about ATC, but right about the Park Service and Forest Service, although the three became staunch A.T. partners in time.

The rivalry between Forest Service and Park Service, which went back decades, extended to an interpretation of what the 1968 legislation actually meant. The Forest Service interpretation was that the act meant what it said — it could protect up to twenty-five acres per mile of trail. The Park Service discussed only the protection zone extending a mile on either side of the trail, a number that was in the 1938 MOU. It was clear that the Park Service was ignoring the requirement that it acquire in fee simple the twenty-five acres per mile of trail. Further, the Forest Service proposed to acquire corridor lands using the five million dollars authorized in the legislation, while the Park Service contended that money was for use by the states. This interpretation was consistent with NPS determination not to acquire any new corridor property.[9]

The two agencies went their separate ways — the Park Service to take no action and the Forest Service to work on inholdings. The Forest Service purchased whole tracts up and down the trail, bringing more trail miles into public ownership. Weeks Act money was finally drying up, so they would have to rely more on LWCF money, and,

---

8. Fairfax, *op. cit.*, p. 132.
9. Shelley Smith Mastran, *Mountaineers and rangers: A history of the federal forest management in the Southern Appalachians, 1900-81* (Washington: U.S. Department of Agriculture Forest Service, 1983), p. 165.

since this was administered by the Park Service, the Forest Service was reluctant to be beholden to their rivals in government, but it was the only way to get all those tracts.[10]

States Lag

Following the overhead flights of small aircraft to identify and mark the trail route, and its publication in the *Federal Register* on October 9, 1971, the National Trails System Act gave the fourteen states two years to acquire the trail corridor. This bizarre formulation went against almost two hundred years of experience. Thinking about it today, it is surprising that it was not viewed as "dead on arrival." Perhaps the experience of the Great Society legislation created optimists when there was little cause to be optimistic.

The National Trails System Act was silent otherwise about how the states would go about acquiring the corridor — it was up to each state. Virginia's statute, for instance, contained provisions for gift, purchases, or easements but did not provide for condemnation, and that was typical of the fourteen states. Serious questions were raised about the effectiveness of easements, since, over time, they generally proved to be more expensive to manage than outright purchase and had to be closely monitored to prevent violations of the terms of the easement. They always carried the threat that a new owner could take the state to court to try to void the easement. Land swaps could be brought into play but could only be used in isolated cases.

The states approached the task with an initial burst of enthusiasm. New Jersey, with its Green Acres Program, was already at work protecting its portion of the trail, and an early result was the protection of Sunfish Pond, which had formerly been on the Worthington Tract until the state had taken it over.[11] Plans to turn the pond into a pumped-storage facility met local resistance — Justice William O. Douglas (an A.T. 2,000-miler) led an event there with more than 1,000 people to publicize the threat, and the utility that had purchased the area succumbed

10. Dave Sherman e-mail, March 2014.
11. N.Y.–N.J. TC *Trail Walker*, September/October 1973.

Goodloe Byron (left) and ATC's Les Holmes, above the Potomac River.

to local pressure and did not follow through. The area ultimately was purchased by the state of New Jersey.[12] Massachusetts was another state that became proactive. The state legislature passed protective legislation and laid plans to protect the corridor outright.

Another state to move quickly was Maryland. In 1970, state Assemblyman Goodloe Byron (soon to be a U.S. representative) introduced legislation protecting the trail and directing the state Department of Forests and Parks to acquire the corridor. The director, Spencer Ellis, was a member of ANSTAC and promised fast action, but the program soon hit snags. The trail in Maryland was over South Mountain, and many South Mountain landowners were hostile to the trail. A landowner just north of the bridge over Interstate 70 refused to sell, and condemnation proceedings were begun. Paula Strain, the PATC president, noted that things were moving backward.

A landowner destroyed a shelter that had been on his land, and two expensive dwellings were being built within the hundred-foot protection zone for the trail.[13] (In 1974, Ruth Blackburn could see some progress in Maryland, but it soon stalled. The Board of Public Works,

12. Dave Sherman e-mail, July 17, 2016.
13. *ATN*, January 1972, p. 6.

which was evidently not on board with the trail project, said that the acquisition would be too costly, and progress came to a halt.) When the state began appraising property on the mountain preliminary to purchase, a group of residents formed a committee and opposed any state acquisition. The state lost its nerve, budgetary pressures became too great, and Maryland became the first state to slink away from the Appalachian Trail.[14]

Some years later, Dave Sherman, an active trail worker in Georgia who went to Washington with the Carter administration and served for decades in both the Park Service and the Forest Service, summed up the experience in Maryland. In a letter to Donald T. King, who ultimately headed the NPS land-acquisition office in Martinsburg, West Virginia, he wrote, "Beyond any doubt, the worst State...is Maryland. It stands out on your maps and in your reports as the one where Trail values have yet to be adequately protected, and where more work remains to be done than anywhere else.... The best you can do here is take over the remainder of the program from that State as soon as possible."[15] It was quite a disparaging comment, given that Maryland had fewer trail miles than almost any other state and that it had begun its campaign with good intentions.

In Pennsylvania, the trail corridor that needed to be acquired was mostly a simple straight line along Blue Mountain, but the situation was very complex. The state was progressive in the area of land and environmental protection, and proposals to protect the trail began as early as 1964 with a project by Keystone Trails Association to establish what land was still in private hands and how much it would cost to protect it.

In 1971, Dr. George Goddard, secretary of the Department of Forest and Waters, proposed a project to protect the trail. But, when he asked for land-ownership information on Blue Mountain, ATC and its component clubs in Pennsylvania still had no reliable information. Bills were introduced into the legislature, and two of them were passed in 1974, setting up a Pennsylvania Scenic Trails System that, of course, included

14. PATC *Bulletin*, July–December 1971, p. 13.
15. Hunter Library, Sherman Collection.

the Appalachian Trail. However, an amendment reduced the acquisition requirement from twenty-five acres to two acres per mile, and no money was included for even this paltry amount. In practice, no acreage was acquired specifically for the A.T.[16]

Part of Blue Mountain — Pennsylvania state game lands — was already in public ownership, but the Game Commission attitude toward the trail vacillated. The funding came largely from the federal government, through Pittman–Robinson Act funds to acquire hunting properties. Some on the Game Commission interpreted that as prohibiting any use except by hunters, the National Trails System Act notwithstanding. And, some private property owners on Blue Mountain opposed the trail. The result was that, after a promising start, Pennsylvania did not become a leader in the trail project.[17]

The experience in New York was no better. In 1968, even before the National Trails System Act (NTSA) was passed, a bill was introduced to acquire the corridor for the A.T. The bill was passed, but Governor Nelson A. Rockefeller vetoed it on a recommendation by the Division of Land and Forests of the Conservation Department. The division contended that the Palisades Interstate Park Commission and the Taconic State Park Commission already had the authority to acquire land outside their present park boundaries in the five counties east of the Hudson. Sam Wilkinson wrote to Murray that the division was reluctant to extend its authority and, anyway, had no money to pay for the acquisition.[18]

New Hampshire was another state that paid lip service to the Appalachian Trail. It passed an act supporting the NTSA but made no appropriation to acquire property. The director of parks seemed keenly interested but was frustrated by lack of legislative support.[19]

---

16. Letter from Art Humphrey of Keystone Trails Association to Murray, February 2, 1964 (with e-mail from Barbara Wiemann to the author, April 22, 2016); PATC *Bulletin*, June 1974; Smithsonian Museum of American History, Earl Shaffer Collection, Collection 820, Box 25, folder 16.
17. ATC archives, Murray files, Box 6-6-5, Kimmel to Murray, January 26, 1969; Fairfax, *op. cit.*, pp. 98-99.
18. *Ibid*, Wilkinson to Murray, May 2, 1965.
19. ATC archives, Murray files, Box 5-3-5, undated interview by Ann Satterthwaite with George Hamilton.

The southern end of the Long Trail in Vermont was part of the designated A.T., but the Vermonters, conforming with their heritage, declined to get involved. All of the A.T. in the state coaligned with the Long Trail was in the Green Mountain National Forest, and, of the estimated 72 miles, 38.5 were across inholdings that needed to be acquired.

Ann Satterthwaite, a longtime A.T. lands activist, interviewed three of the top Vermont officials for land acquisition. "The three of them wanted to let me know in no uncertain terms that they were not interested in the Appalachian Trail," she recalled. "In general, they were not interested in having any trail designated as a National Scenic Trail in the state of Vermont.... They would like to have the Feds stick to their own business and not interfere with state activities."

A similar interview with the Green Mountain Club yielded a similar result. "Lane [Gardner Lane, executive secretary of GMC] was very clear in telling me that he and the Green Mountain club were opposed to the idea of a national scenic trail, for two reasons — one, it brought in too many people, and two, the idea of anything with governmental connections would scare landowners."[20] The Vermonters folded their arms. Shirley Strong wrote, "National Scenic Trail designation only adds another layer of administration and red tape, more publicity at national level, no protection really except as state acts to protect it anyway."[21]

Connecticut passed a trails bill, but the official most responsible for its implementation viewed the legislation as weak and full of platitudes. Landowners expressed concern about marijuana parties at shelters and general misuse of the trail, but some would cooperate if assured of no vehicular use, no hunting, and adequate patrolling and police protection on the trail, a hope that would not be fulfilled by the state.[22]

Maine was a special case. Virtually the entire trail corridor was on timber-company lands. Some of the companies had already taken

20. *Ibid.*
21. *Ibid*, Satterthwaite interview with Benjamin Hoffman, head, Land Acquisition Unit, Agency of Environmental Conservation, and Gardner Lane, undated; Vermont State Archives, Box 226/41, letter from Strong to Advisory Council, July 27, 1971. It is interesting to note that Shirley Strong moved to Washington and became a key member of PATC and served on the ATC board.
22. ATC archives, Murray files, Box 5-3-5, undated interviews, Satterthwaite with Joseph Hickey and Theodore Brampton.

steps to protect the trail but had no requirement to do so, and many had permitted what was termed in the federal legislation "incompatible use," especially ski resorts and logging camps. Already ski resorts were planned or in place for Bigelow, Sugarloaf, and some of the peaks in the Mahoosucs. The Maine Appalachian Trail Club (MATC) was taking the beginning steps in working with timber companies, and the position of Dave Field, a professor of forestry at the University of Maine, was becoming an important relationship. Field had generally good relations with the companies and had begun planning for a major reroute of the trail through the state. The companies trusted Field — he spoke their language and knew what issues the companies faced. To a significant extent, he was one of them.

But MATC, in working with the companies, had competition. The Appalachian Mountain Club (AMC) was working with the same companies at the same time, and a good deal of animosity had built up between the two organizations. Letters from two AMC leaders, Francis Belcher and Art Koerber, to MATC President Jim Faulkner in 1967 tried to assert primacy in the negotiations, to which Faulkner replied with a strong letter demanding that AMC get out of his territory.[23]

PATC was becoming less engaged with MATC as the local club built up its strength, but Jean Stephenson was still involved, and she spent time negotiating with the timber-company representatives during the legislative process, trying to convince them that the bill did not threaten their interests and that they should not come out in opposition. Their concern was with the condemnation clause, but Jean told them that it should not be regarded as a threat to their interests — it could only be used in case an individual landowner would simply not agree to sell. In Maine, the generally cooperative relationship with the trail would remain, she contended.[24]

Once the bill was passed, the Maine forest commissioner negotiated memoranda of understanding with Great Northern Paper, Oxford Paper, International Paper, and Prentis and Carlisle.[25] So Maine,

23. ATC archives, Murray files, Box 6-6-4, several letters from Koerber and Belcher in the spring of 1967; Faulkner to Belcher, March 12.
24. *Ibid*, Austin Wilkins (forest commissioner) to Faulkner, May 13, 1969.
25. *Ibid*, Stephenson to Murray, March 16, 1967.

which was the last state to sign the Trailway Agreement of 1938 (it took twenty-eight years), was one of the few states that was actually working on implementing the legislation.

MATC took a global look at the corridor to determine the optimum location.[26] Much of the trail had been located on old logging roads — Walter Greene's trail over Chairback was one of the exceptions — and, with the very large tracts owned by logging companies, Maine had more flexibility than other states. The club in ensuing years relocated more than half of the trail in its state, and the Maine case became one of the real success stories. It answered Murray's question, "Where *should* the trail be?"

North Carolina, Roy Taylor's home state, passed no legislation appropriating money to acquire the trail corridor. Without money to acquire property and without a state agency specifically tasked with buying the land, the acquisition program was hollow.

Tennessee was one of the more progressive states. As soon as the NTSA was passed, the state passed its own legislation, creating a state scenic trails act and designating seven trails as part of the system, the Appalachian Trail being one of the seven. Eminent domain was one of the acquisition methods that was in the legislation. Tennessee put its money behind its trails system and was one of the few states that achieved anything.

Virginia had more trail miles (about 550) than any other state, and it was the state where the crisis in trail protection had come to a head. Consequently, it had the most complex process of any state. At the ATC meeting in Shippensburg, Pennsylvania, in 1970, Paula Strain of PATC called a meeting of all Virginia delegates to discuss how the process would work in their state. The committee drafted legislation making the Appalachian Trail a state scenic trail. The governor, Linwood Holton, a conservative, initially opposed the legislation, but PATC enlisted the help of *The Washington Post* to publicize the crisis in northern Virginia, where landowners insisted that the trail be completely removed from the Blue Ridge. In January 1971, the *Post* sent a photographer to take pictures of hikers standing in snow, looking at no-

---

26. Field, *op. cit.,* Maine A.T. history, "The Relocation Era."

trespassing signs across their trail. Three days later, the *Post* published an editorial entitled, "The Appalachian Trail — What is its Future?"

A special session of the legislature convened on the same date, January 6, with heavy lobbying in Richmond from PATC and other trail clubs. Under considerable pressure, the legislature eventually passed a bill making the A.T. a state scenic trail and gave PATC complete exemption from state property tax. The act omitted some key provisions. It did not contain condemnation authority — only willing-seller and easement provisions — and it did not contain funding. That would presumably be taken care of by the LWCF, which was an inadequate source to protect the mileage in Virginia. [27] Ben Bolen, the director of the Department of Conservation and Economic Development and a longtime friend of the Appalachian Trail, placed funding in his budget, but somehow it never made it to passage.

Follow-on legislation to take care of those "small details" was necessary but never happened. What did happen was that the division of state parks of the Department of Conservation and Economic Development was tasked with implementing the legislation. The legislature funded a single position within the division for the Appalachian Trail, but it was assumed that volunteers would continue to do much of the work, given that a single position could accomplish little. Volunteers would, Bolen hoped, collect land records from county land offices, go out and contact landowners, and negotiate settlements.[28] That, it was discovered, was unrealistic, and PATC, for one, informed the division of parks that this was well beyond the expertise and time commitment of volunteers.

Stan Murray pointed out the impossibility to Bolen, with typical Murray understatement:

I have certain reservations as to the complete success of this program as it's now outlined. I have worked with various Trail clubs for nearly 20 years and can assure you that they are dependable and

---

27. PATC *Bulletin*, January-March 1971, pp. 3-4; *The Washington Post*, January 3 and 6, 1971.
28. ATC archives, Murray files, Holton letter, January 4, 1972; Murray memo from a meeting in Lynchburg with A.T. clubs, January 25, 1972.

diligent in their assigned tasks. It must be admitted, however, that with a few exceptions their expertise resides chiefly in Trail location, clearing, and marking. The business of landowner negotiations will undoubtedly be new for most of their members....[29]

Working on a solution, the division of parks proposed that the state establish gateway parks at the state borders. Those parks would welcome incoming hikers and provide services, including camp-grounds, a hiker store, and various educational functions led by rangers. Given the conditions at the time, a heavy emphasis would be placed on avoiding misbehavior at shelters and camp sites and avoiding littering. Law-enforcement rangers would be present, but no interpretive rangers, as were common in national and state parks. The state also would do a comprehensive trail-management study, a recreational-impact study, and a trail-development study.[30] The proposal was imaginative but was opposed by the National Park Service officer at the meeting, who argued that it looked too much like a developed park and not a primitive hiking trail. It also depended on funding, which never came except in such isolated areas as Grayson Highlands State Park.

Meanwhile, the crisis south of Harpers Ferry continued unabated. Following the passage of the NTSA in 1968, sixty landowners from Va. 7 to U.S. 50, a distance of only fourteen trail miles, signed a letter expressing their opposition to a trail anywhere on their mountain. The state set up meetings with the landowners in May 1971, but the meetings accomplished nothing and were adjourned without result. PATC, in desperation, decided to build a new route off to the west, between the Blue Ridge and the Shenandoah River.

The club was supposed to wait for the state to purchase the trail corridor, but little was happening in Richmond to reassure the PATC leadership that this would actually happen. At the ATC Lynchburg meeting in 1972, the state urged PATC to begin purchasing land, be-cause the state would be too slow, and land prices would surely spike.

29. ATC archives, Murray correspondence, 1971-72.
30. "The Appalachian Trail: Pathway for the Future; a Planning Proposal," Virginia Division of Parks, January 9, 1974.

So, the club began collecting money to purchase threatened tracts. Several scattered tracts were purchased between Route 7 and the northern boundary of Shenandoah National Park, buttressed by occasional land donations by friendly landowners. Given the many tracts that remained, it was an effort that was doomed to failure. The club needed help from somewhere.

The one positive note from Richmond was the purchase of almost 2,000 acres of land on the east side of the ridge for a wildlife-management area by the Commission of Game and Inland Fisheries. This tract, which was to

Hikers face trail closures in northern Virginia.

become G. Richard Thompson Wildlife Management Area, protected more than six miles of the trail and came at a critical time. The option to purchase the tract was announced at a meeting in Lynchburg.

The States and the Money

The assumption in Congress was that the states could work together to create a 2,000-mile trail. It was also assumed that all the states would be on board, with no gaps in the trail. Yet another assumption, reading from the legislation, was that each state legislature would agree to fund what had become a federal project. [Annual Land and Water Conservation Fund (LWCF) appropriations were insufficient to provide the level of A.T. funding needed. The National Trails System Act of 1968 *authorized* $5 million for A.T. land acquisitions but did not specify who would use that money.]

Also assumed: Fourteen states would create a trail that had the same standards of construction and maintenance, corridor width, and rules for use. It was assumed that all this could happen in two years.

The states were assumed to leap to the task, despite knowing as they did that, if they simply delayed for two years, the federal government would have to take it on.

The response of the fourteen states varied widely, as we have seen. Some, like New Jersey, quickly established programs for state trail protection and land acquisition for the corridor, but most of the states were quite vague about what they would do and how they would do it. State involvement had no uniformity (as one might expect from different jurisdictions).

It was assumed that the LWCF would be the great grab bag, where states could get their trail money, working through the Bureau of Outdoor Recreation. LWCF was a fifty-percent match, so the state requesting money had to be ready to put up the match, should its request be approved. And, the A.T. was not the only suitor out there looking for money. Each state had to decide how it wanted to use LWCF money, and the A.T. was not always at the top of the list. Uncertainty soon crept into the process — uncertainty that would have been eliminated by line-item federal funding.

The availability of LWCF funds fluctuated from year to year (and federal administration to administration). In 1974, Russell E. Dickenson, the director of the National Park Service, asked James Watt, director of the Bureau of Outdoor Recreation, outright what priority the Appalachian Trail would have. By that time, Watt, who had not been particularly friendly to the trail in earlier years, had become something of an advocate and told Dickenson that he would give it the highest priority in allocating Interior LWCF funds.[31]

In 1976, six states applied for LWCF money; Interior was making available from its $8,000,000 contingency reserve and had specifically allocated $1,000,000 for the Appalachian Trail.[32] But, splitting a million dollars across six states (Virginia, Massachusetts, Connecti-

---

31. PATC archives, Niedzialek Box 18, Dickenson to Grant Conway, May 10, 1974.
32. *Potomac Appalachian*, June 1976.

cut, New York, New Jersey, and Pennsylvania) was hardly enough to complete the acquisition process, considering that those states in 1971 had to acquire a corridor for 866 trail miles.

Other questions related to management of lands acquired by the states: Should the state get involved in law enforcement on what was supposed to be a national park? If the National Park Service was not actively involved, who was responsible? Should ATC and the clubs take it on? Peter Dunning of ATC broached this idea,[33] but private, volunteer organizations enjoyed no such legal standing.

When the act was passed, 43.3 percent of the trail miles (measured on flat maps) was in private hands. The following depicts the 1971 situation:

State	Miles: Federal	State	Private	Total
Maine	0	20	260	280
New Hampshire	71	9	74	154
Vermont	26	19	89	134
Massachusetts	0	55	28	83
Connecticut	0	24	32	56
New York–New Jersey	0	94	65	159
Pennsylvania	0	154	60	214
Maryland	0	7	30	37
West Virginia–Virginia	254	62	146	462
Tennessee–North Carolina	255	8	80	343
Georgia	76	0	2	78
Total	682	452	866	2,000
Percentage	*34.1*	*22.6*	*43.3*	*100*

Although the states gave lip service to protecting the trail, eight of the fourteen states had not allocated any funds for land acquisition. By mid-1973, 680 miles still remained to be acquired. Now that the period of state acquisition had passed, an enormous burden awaited the National Park Service and the Forest Service.

Competition for money was intense. In 1973, the Forest Service was told to emphasize timber production, and "funds for hiking and other multiple uses, authorized by law, are to be deferred indefinitely." The Bureau of Outdoor Recreation, true to its title, was emphasiz-

33. ATC archives, Dunning correspondence, letter to John Oliphant, June 6, 1973.

ing funds for ball fields, swimming pools, *etc.* LWCF funds were, in fact, underused, with a carry-over of $750,000,000.[34]

The biggest problems were in the North. The southern states were in better shape, because the national forests protected most of their trail mileage. Much of the lands remaining to be acquired in the South were inholdings in the national forests, and that proved to be a more manageable problem than in northern states, where there were fewer national forests and more private land to be acquired.

In 1966, the Mount Rogers National Recreation Area was created, which protected seventy-four miles of the trail. The trail was rerouted into that area east of Interstate 81, taking it off the much older Iron Mountain route that had survived from Avery days. That placed the route along the ridge of the highest point in Virginia. (The route on the flank of Mount Rogers provided bragging rights, but no view from the top.)[35] The original plan concocted by local U.S. Representative Pat Jennings was to make the area a "National Forest Wonderland," whatever that meant — evidently intense development, including a sixty-three-mile long scenic highway, campgrounds, and reservoirs. The Forest Service began by designating the Mount Rogers Scenic Area in 1961 and gradually expanded the area. That required the acquisition of large tracts of land through condemnation, a process that the Forest Service had avoided in other areas that it administered. NRA administrator Keith Argow dutifully pushed land acquisition through condemnation, but local opposition eventually put a halt to the process. In the end, the Mount Rogers NRA became a less developed area but did protect the Appalachian Trail. A unique aspect was the presence of a large group of wild ponies in adjacent Grayson Highlands State Park, a marvel and highlight for hikers on the trail.[36]

---

34. *Potomac Appalachian*, September 1973.
35. *ATN*, May 1972, p. 35.
36. Mastran, *op. cit.*, p. 151; Hunter Library, Sherman collection, USFS proposal, March 1, 1963; interview with Keith Argow, July 26, 2016.

The Park Service Gets Involved (or Not)

It was evident to many that the bizarre provisions in the National Trails System Act that split the responsibility for corridor acquisition among the various states, leaving the National Park Service as an observer for several years, were not going to work. In October 1972, a Washington, D.C., television channel stated outright that the process was going to be too cumbersome, and the federal government would have to step in — this only a year and a half after the trail routing appeared in the *Federal Register*.

Behind the scenes, however, the Park Service already had decided that it would not act, then or in the future. Park Service official Edward Gray, then chairman of the Appalachian National Scenic Trail Advisory Council (ANSTAC), wrote in April 1972, "There seems to be no reasonable basis for the National Park Service to consider land acquisition along the trail route in the foreseeable future." His rationale appeared sound. A series of fragmented acquisitions would create only short, disconnected local segments, and it would make management of these fragments impossible. He concluded, in his memo to the southeast and northeast regional offices, "There is no justifiable need to seek funds for Appalachian Trail right-of-way at this time.... So the Council and the Conference agree that the States should continue to be encouraged to fulfill the intent of the legislation as to the acquisition of lands or interest in lands, it would seem that we could go forward to the Director with the recommendation that no funds be sought."[37]

In October 1973, Murray, vice chairman of ANSTAC, tried to pin Gray down on the Park Service responsibility to acquire the corridor, given that the states had failed to meet their deadline. He never got a straight answer. Instead, all ATC got was several years of evasion. A. Heaton Underhill of the Bureau of Outdoor Recreation, concluded that, in the words of his daughter, Pamela, "The NPS was not interested in the Appalachian Trail one iota; did not think that it was worthy of being part of the national park system."[38]

37. Department of the Interior/National Park Service memo from Edgar L. Gray to Southeast and Northeast Regional Directors, April 14, 1972.
38. Interview with Pamela Underhill, Heaton's daughter and retired manager of the Ap-

Dave Sherman, a longtime senior employee of both the Park Service and Forest Service, felt that the project would take a lot of resources, and, since those had not been allocated by Congress, the issue would be ignored.[39] Thurston Griggs, a redoubtable volunteer in Pennsylvania and Maryland, characterized the trail project as "an enormous powerline right-of-way."[40]

The project did not even have a manager until 1974, and then only because one David Richie from the Boston office was put on it part-time. The project began then, with one part-time person without a staff. At first, Richie hoped that volunteers would do the field work, contacting landowners and trying to obtain agreements of one kind or another. In Pennsylvania, owing to an intense controversy surrounding the trail route through Cumberland Valley, he proposed to hire Griggs, but Thurston wanted to remain a volunteer and did not take a paid position.

Richie began the task with the firm belief, as did everyone else in NPS, that it was a state task, and it was foolish for the Park Service to try to manage the effort. In 1975, Richie continued to push Charles H.W. "Hank" Foster of ANSTAC to begin visiting the states most in need of help, in his estimation: New York, New Jersey, and Pennsylvania.

But, as time went on, Richie moved toward a more active role. That seemed to reflect his frustration in dealing with the staff of the Washington and regional offices. As ATC moved more decisively toward outright rebellion against NPS, Richie was becoming more of an ally.

Still behind the scenes, ATC continued to try to push NPS toward a more active role. Grant Conway, one of PATC's top agitators, got Deputy Director Russell E. Dickenson in 1974 to agree to assign more staff to Richie's office and to revive ANSTAC, which had been terminated during the Ford administration. Ed Garvey, Conway's colleague in the agitation department, went before the House interior appropriations subcommittee to appeal for funding.

palachian Park Office of NPS, March 7, 2014.
39. Sherman e-mail to author, March 2014.
40. ATC archives, Laurence Van Meter papers, Thurston Griggs, "Cumberland Valley: Location for a National Foot-Trail."

All those efforts to push NPS toward more active involvement did not get outright opposition — instead, they just got more evasion. Dickenson finally did acknowledge that NPS had responsibility for administration of the trail,[41] but that did not in his eyes include land acquisition. That was the most expensive, and most difficult, part of the task. If NPS could get the states to do it, it would save a lot of money in its budget.

Finally, in 1976, the secretary of the interior announced that the Park Service would make available grants (on a 50/50 matching basis) from his $1-million contingency fund for corridor acquisition.

Paul Pritchard, executive director of ATC, made the grand announcement. "This is a first-time achievement for the Conference. It represents some long hours by all involved, including the staff of the advisory council chairman and the staff of the Conference."[42] Compared with previous accomplishments, that might have been singular, but, considering that it required hundreds of millions of dollars to ultimately acquire the corridor, one must withhold outright enthusiasm. It was a watershed only in comparison with previous (lack of) watersheds.

Congress had acted in 1968, and, by 1974, it was clear to congressional staff members that the will of Congress was not working on the National Park Service. Cleve Pinnix, a lead staff person on the House national parks subcommittee, met with the Park Service staff to discuss their inaction. In his words,

> I remember a meeting where the Park Service staff looked us straight in the face and said, 'Well, there was never any intention that there would be federal land acquisitions under the original act....' There was a fair amount of tension between the subcommittee members and the agency folks, because, from our perspective, they were not carrying out the intent of Congress."[43]

---

41. PATC archives, Box 16, informal chronology dated May 4, 1974, signed by Conway and Garvey.
42. Carolina Mountain Club archives, Box 17, Pritchard letter to club presidents, March 16, 1976.
43. ATC archives, Ronald Brown interview with Cleve Pinnix, May 23, 2007.

That, of course, got back to the committee chairman and would have consequences for the Park Service when Congress began holding committee hearings in 1976 on the lack of corridor acquisition.

George Zoebelein, then chair of ATC, wrote to Secretary of the Interior Thomas Kleppe in 1976, "The Department of the Interior has not yet purchased a single acre of land or obtained a single easement for the protection of that right-of-way."[44] His answer, by an assistant secretary, was, "It should be kept in mind, however, that the National Trails System Act gave first priority to protection of the Appalachian Trail through cooperative agreements and through acquisition of a right-of-way by the States."[45]

The turn of the political clock brought Jimmy Carter to the White House, and Cecil Andrus, the new secretary, answered Zoebelein on February 23, 1977, in a very different way: The federal government must get involved, and additional funds ($1 million being obviously insufficient) needed to be appropriated. A new era was dawning, and this was the opening bell. Much more was to follow.

The Forest Service

Rangers had been buying trail corridor tracts for years, but the process established in the National Trails System Act was new, and the rangers stepped back to survey the task. The agency had, at the outset, a strong predisposition to purchase land. It did not want to deal with land that was "less than fee," because it would not have full control. Dale Arnold, a senior Forest Service ranger, was blunt: "Lands, or interest in lands, are not acquired, *i.e.*, conveyed, by a cooperative agreement. They are acquired by deed."[46] He did not believe that federal funds could be used to construct a trail on lands based on agreements or permits. It might be possible to begin with some sort of lesser agreement, but, ultimately, the land had to be owned, not leased or crossed by cooperative agreement.

---

44. ATC archives, Zoebelein papers, Zoebelein to Kleppe, September 20, 1976.
45. *Ibid*, [illegible signature] to Zoebelein, October 1, 1976.
46. Hunter Library, Sherman Collection, Arnold to Byron Amsbaugh, November 21, 1969.

In September 1969, all the Appalachian Trail forest supervisors in the southern region met in Washington to discuss the task ahead. They found it daunting, but not impossible. They preferred full-tract acquisition to buying strips. They discussed trail standards, and many, especially those from New England, opposed rigidly enforcing Forest Service trail construction standards on volunteer clubs. The trail had been created by volunteers, but, now that it was to become a federal resource, its character should not change. Subsequently, agreements were signed between the Forest Service and Park Service that laid out how they were to work together to acquire the corridor, and the Forest Service established a process for land acquisition.[47]

Many rangers remembered the 1938 Trailway Agreement that demanded land preservation of a mile on either side of the trail (for federal agencies), and Arnold recommended that those more distant tracts could be acquired by a conservation easement in order to preserve a primitive, sylvan environment, or to preserve an outstanding view. (In this, Stan Murray concurred and continued to reference the 1938 agreement as the guiding principle in land acquisition.[48]) The Forest Service should examine the trail segment by segment, to determine the nature and extent of the land interest needed. An orderly process should ensue, including surveys, appraisals, landowner negotiations, and so forth. But, the end result should always be a purchase.

Arnold believed that a 200-foot width for the protection of the trail was all that was called for.[49] But, after acquiring the narrower corridor, the Forest Service had to go back and increase the size of some of the acquisitions and, in some cases, buy whole new tracts after 1978 legislation set a new standard of 125 acres per mile. The Park Service, not having acquired any corridor land at all, did not have that problem.

---

47. Forest Service document signed by Philip B. Etchison, Group Leader, Land Ownership — undated, but prepared originally around 1978.
48. ATC archives, Dunning Box, Murray to Ken Sutherland, Recreation-Lands Staff Officer, White Mountain National Forest, November 29, 1973.
49. Hunter Library, Sherman Collection, Arnold memo to Byron Amsbaugh.

The corridor width of 125 acres per mile that Congress adopted[50] was no accident. Instead, mathematics underpinned the number. If one multiplies the number of feet in a mile (5,280) times 1,000 feet (the nominal width of the trail corridor), the result is 5,280,000 square feet. Divide that number by 43,560 (the number of square feet in an acre), and the result is 121.21 acres; rounded up, is 125 acres.[51] That just proves that Congress does not always use a dart board to draft legislation.

Forest Service officials believed that they alone should be involved in acquiring inholdings. To get the states involved, as the legislation required, would muddle the entire matter, and great confusion would result. John Kirby, assistant regional forester for Region 8 (headquartered in Atlanta), was concerned that landowners, knowing that there were potentially two bidders, would play off the states against the Forest Service and get a higher price. It was hard for Kirby to believe that the states would come up with the money in any case.[52] In this, he was very realistic — in fact, that was what happened (or rather, what didn't happen.)

Trail Miles to be acquired by the U.S. Forest Service by State

State	Forest	Miles	Miles to acquire	Percent
Georgia	Chattahoochee	83.0	1.0	1.0
North Carolina	Nantahala	68.0	12.0	5.0
	Pisgah	68.6	32.0	46.7
Tennessee	Cherokee	176.0	30.0	17.0
Virginia	Jefferson	210.0	17.0	8.0
	Georgia Washington	58.0	4.0	7.0
Vermont	Green Mountain	56.6	15.7	28.0
New Hampshire	White Mountain	110.0	5.8	5.0
Total		**844.0**	**111.7**	**13**

The Forest Service had a relatively manageable problem. In total, only thirteen percent of the trail through national forests needed pro-

50. See below, page 404, for the Pennsylvania State University study that recommended a new corridor width.
51. Sherman e-mail, unknown date.
52. ATC archives, Dunning papers, Kirby to Stan Murray, June 6, 1972.

tection, and, unlike the Park Service, the Forest Service had a plan. Moreover, they already had control of the territory within the proclamation boundaries. Rangers culturally were inclined to solve problems in a very direct way.

The raw statistics were deceptive. It appeared that Pisgah National Forest had done virtually nothing and would inherit a huge problem. To a lesser extent, this seemed to be true of the Green Mountain National Forest. But, it all depended on local issues. How all that played out in practice depended on the nature of the tracts they needed to buy and who was on the other end. The Forest Service preferred to buy whole tracts, rather than small slices of large tracts, and legislation in 1983 gave them the specific authority to do so. A huge Kimberly-Clark Tract in the Cherokee National Forest, 10,000 acres, was a good example of this policy, and it represented a major acquisition cost.[53]

In 1973, a new issue emerged for the Forest Service. A bill was introduced in Congress to begin designating wilderness areas in the eastern forests. Included in the proposal was the James River Face in Jefferson National Forest, along with study areas such as The Priest, Peters Mountain, Mountain Lake, and certain other areas not directly impacting the Appalachian Trail. Fearing that they would lose control of those areas, the Forest Service initially opposed this push. Their official rationale was that no forested areas in the East had not experienced the "hand of man" at some point in history. But, with strong backing from such congressional titans as Henry "Scoop" Jackson, chairman of the Senate Interior Committee, the bill became law the next year. ATC supported the bill and was at odds with its Forest Service allies.

The Forest Service over all had a good record on corridor acquisition in the 1970s — far better than the laggard Park Service. By 1976, the Forest Service had acquired about half of the inholdings needed to protect the trail.[54] Had it been entirely up to the Forest Service, no additional legislation would have been needed. But, of course, more than 600 miles of trail

---

53. *Ibid*, Murray to Thomas Frazier, Assistance Forest Supervisor, Cherokee National Forest, July 6, 1973.

54. *Oversight Hearings before the Subcommittee on Parks and Recreation on Oversight on the National Trails System Act of 1968 and Various Proposals to Study Proposed Additions to the National Scenic Trails System: March 11 and 12, 1976*, Serial No. 94-50.

corridor did not run through national forests, and that was a Park Service task.

One interesting historical issue in terms of long-term agency perspectives surrounded the White Mountain National Forest. That national forest contained 110 miles of the A.T. within its boundaries, through some of the most spectacular scenery on the trail. Back in the 1920s, Harlan Kelsey, a prominent member of the national park commission appointed in 1924 and a former president of the Appalachian Mountain Club (AMC), advocated for creating a national park. Considering the scenery, it should have been an easy sell, but the Forest Service was in the process of purchasing additional lands and advised that, if the Park Service became a "competitor," it would drive up the price.

That was one reason, but probably not the main one. Kelsey was opposed strongly by other prominent AMC members, particularly Allen Chamberlain and Philip Ayres. They contended that the Forest Service was doing a splendid job of protecting the land, the wildlife, and the timber[55]. Moreover, and this argument was not heard as often, the Park Service would bring a stronger federal presence and more regulation. New Englanders wanted to keep control of their resources.

The ANSTAC Revolt

The 1968 legislation had created the Appalachian National Scenic Trail Advisory Council (ANSTAC). Since an advisory committee could not itself act, it was supposed that it would monitor progress and weigh in when "advice" was needed. Assuming that the states would acquire the corridor, a central body to meet and discuss was perhaps a good idea, but the idea was visited by the same conceptual confusion that greeted the state-federal relationship.

ANSTAC met first in November 1969 in Washington. It was a huge and unwieldy body, more than thirty members, dominated by representatives from the Park Service and Forest Service. (ATC was awarded a number of seats, so it was not all government.) The com-

---

55. Loren Wood, *Beautiful Land of the Sky* (Bloomington, Indiana: iUniverse, 2013), p. 353.

An ANSTAC meeting.

mittee was officially chaired by the assistant director of the Park Service, Robert Moore, but he quickly turned the proceedings over to Richard Stanton, the Park Service's designated project officer for the A.T. Stanton was a known opponent of federal action on the trail.

According to a book by a later committee chairman, Charles H. W. "Hank" Foster, committee members from volunteer clubs were confused about the role of the committee and frustrated by attending meetings when no action was taken.[56] The committee seemed to have no substantive role, and no one was assigning it any actions. Volunteers were used to taking action. Was this what it was like in the federal bureaucracy? they wondered.

As the years and the meetings rolled along, the committee learned that most states had passed legislation establishing a trail in their states, but little funding had been authorized. Led by the irrepressible Ben Bolen, Virginia had become the first state to sign a cooperative agreement with the Park Service (1970), and it was hoped that

56. Charles H.W. Foster, *The Appalachian National Scenic Trail: A Time to Be Bold* (Needham, Mass.: Charles H.W. Foster, 1987). Most information directly related to ANSTAC in this book comes from Foster.

perhaps this would lead to other states doing the same thing. (It did not.) A meeting in 1972 had the first mention of LWCF funding in the context of state use to protect the trail. But, by the time the committee met at the Mather Training Center in Harpers Ferry in 1973, the volunteers had heard it all before and were discouraged both with the progress of the trail and in the influence, or lack thereof, of ANSTAC.

That session in Harpers Ferry was the last meeting for three years. In that year, Congress passed the Federal Advisory Committee Act, which terminated all such committees and required that they be recreated by statute and renewed at two-year intervals. Essentially, it was a sunset law, and the sun had set on ANSTAC. According to Foster, the Park Service, which intended to take no action on the A.T. in any case, viewed this as an excuse to ignore creating a new committee, claiming that it had no recourse under the act. He blamed Chairman Edward Gray, departing for another NPS position, stating that Gray had "drafted an inaccurate and rather self-serving report stating that the Trail protection job, in essence, had been completed." Trail club leaders were outraged. They began a steady drumbeat of protest, intended first for the National Park Service and later for members of Congress.

In the background, Conway, Oliphant, and Garvey, the three PATC leaders, went directly to Roy Taylor in 1974. "The three signers of this letter are writing to you because of our very deep concern over the failure of the Department of the Interior to implement the provisions of the National Trails System Act."[57] Furious at the evident thwarting of the 1968 legislation, they knew that they had a friend in Congress.[58]

ANSTAC was recreated in 1975 and held its first meeting at the ATC meeting in Boone, North Carolina. That particular conference proved to be a hotbed of revolutionary fervor, and it infected ANSTAC, beginning the "ANSTAC revolt." (See below.) With Ed Garvey on the floor, the committee decided that the National Park Service should play a much more prominent role in corridor acquisition.

---

57. PATC archives, Box 16, letter to Taylor, April 22, 1974.
58. PATC archives, Box 13 (Oliphant), Bob Wolf to Conway, Garvey, and Oliphant, April 7, 1975; *Potomac Appalachian*, April 1975.

It was time to take the job away from the states, which had failed to act. With Hank Foster, a former Massachusetts secretary of environmental affairs, in the chair, the committee contended that the Department of the Interior now owned the task.

Virginia's Ben Bolen was a strong advocate for federal action when states did not act. He proposed that the Land and Water Conservation Fund be used to accelerate surveys, title work, and appraisals necessary for acquisition at the federal level, reducing the state LWCF allocation in proportion to the amount of money the National Park Service needed to do the job. The position of the new ANSTAC reversed the earlier position that it was a state job.[59]

In assessing the impact of ANSTAC, Dave Startzell felt that it had no impact at the federal level. It was a useful forum, however, for making connections at the state level.[60] It was important — looking at its longer-range impact — to have those allies at the state level when Startzell began looking for money for corridor acquisition after 1978.

Dave Sherman, who was appointed as a representative to ANSTAC from Georgia, felt that ANSTAC did not provide a high-enough level of representation. In his view, it was a way for states to cling to their share of LWCF money.[61]

Crisis in Northern Virginia (Again)

The flash point was the very same area that led Stan Murray to begin working on a project to protect the Appalachian Trail through federal legislation in 1963. The forty-five-mile section from Harpers Ferry to the northern boundary of Shenandoah National Park was threatened by development. Parallel roads were paved, and new homes were springing up,

Concerned about pot parties and accumulating trash, landowners began closing shelters in northern Virginia, beginning with the Ashby Gap Shelter in 1950. Gradually, one shelter after another was closed: Manassas Gap, Wilson Gap, Yellow Rose. The landowner who

59. Foster, *op. cit.,* pp. 34-35.
60. Startzell interview, February 21, 2014.
61. Sherman interview, December 9, 2013.

closed Yellow Rose complained about cars driving to the shelter, littering, and large groups overloading the facility. (One group, he stated, showed up with more than 200 Boy Scouts.)

Eventually, the trail wound up on newly paved Va. 601 for an entire fourteen miles. By 1972, a north-bound hiker arriving at Linden, Virginia, was confronted with twenty-six consecutive miles of road-walking.[62] One landowner who had recently purchased a tract that had a portion of the trail on it said, "He does not like the looks of some of the people using the trail."[63] It was becoming a common refrain.

PATC began quietly purchasing critical properties. In 1972, the club purchased a ten-acre tract west of Mount Weather to protect the corridor, and the next year they bought a tract just north of Shenandoah National Park, using the cabin reserve fund.[64] In 1974, Ed Garvey, noting the painfully slow acquisition process so far, issued a challenge to the club to raise money to protect the trail. Ruth Blackburn, John Oliphant, Ray Fadner, and others had researched land records, and the club knew where they needed to buy land. By 1976, PATC had authorized $120,000 for land purchases and had purchased seventeen tracts from its land-acquisition fund.[65] All this was done prior to NPS funding and represented volunteers directly paying for land to protect "their" trail. Most of the purchases were in Virginia, where the state legislature had granted a tax exemption that gave the club considerable latitude in land purchases.

The distressed condition of the A.T. was hardly unique to PATC. Road walks in New York east of the Hudson surely rivaled that in northern Virginia, and, in many areas of New England, corridor acquisition was going nowhere and long road walks were the result. The difference was that this was happening to PATC — not the largest club, but still the most influential. Myron Avery was long dead, but it hardly mattered. Garvey, Grant Conway, Oliphant, Fred and Ruth Blackburn, Phil Stone, and others still dominated the policy agenda in Harpers

---

62. *ATN*, May 1972, pp. 58-59.
63. ATC archives, Murray Boxes, 1952-1974, Holmes to Murray, July 26, 1972.
64. *Potomac Appalachian*, August 1972, September 1973.
65. PATC archives, Box 17, p. 100; *Potomac Appalachian*, January 1976.

Ferry, and the PATC voice was the loudest. And, PATC headquarters was in the nation's capital, where the political decisions were made.

When one reviewed the situation in 1975, it was apparent that the idea that the states would act to purchase the corridor and protect the Appalachian Trail had not worked. The deadline passed in October 1973, and the corridor was not protected, with a few obvious exceptions, such as parts of New Jersey. Garvey was becoming agitated, and an agitated Garvey was not someone easy to deal with. He was not happy sitting on the sidelines, collecting Washington Senators box scores.

Boone

When the ATC assembled in Boone in June 1975 for its now-biennial meeting, revolution was in the air. People who had never been to an ATC conference before caught the whiff of discontent. Side conversations were overheard, and longtime volunteers had come to the meeting to challenge the status quo. Something was about to break.

The instigators — Garvey, Conway, and Oliphant — had sent a letter to the new chair of ANSTAC, Hank Foster, a month before the conference, requesting that ANSTAC recommend that the federal government get serious about land acquisition and trail rights-of-way.[66] It was a shot across the bow, a precursor to what was to come.

Even so, a surface calm prevailed through the opening phases of the conference. Boone was Stan Murray's last conference — he was to turn the gavel over to George Zoebelein. In his address, he talked about the new ATC headquarters in Harpers Ferry, the first ATC employee (Lester Holmes), the huge increase in the popularity of backpacking (leading to the hiring of Peter Dunning), the importance of the greenway concept. He reminisced about the meeting at Long Pond in Maine in 1963 that ultimately resulted in the National Trails System Act of 1968, and the momentous changes that had come to pass since then. He marveled at the progress and commissioned the

---

66. PATC archives, Box 16, draft from Garvey, Conway, and Oliphant to ANSTAC, May 13, 1975.

Conference to continue. It was essentially a speech looking backward and came across as exactly that. Giving Stan (the most significant ATC leader since Myron Avery) his due, it was not what the Conference in Boone was going to be about.

Gary Everhardt, who headed NPS, was on tap as the keynote speaker. Everhardt's keynote address offered little but platitudes. His long and rambling introduction provided no substance — just excuses: Too bad, it was, indeed, that NPS had not moved more quickly to acquire the trail corridor. Ah, but there were many barriers to quick movement. The resources just weren't there. NPS had a three-billion-dollar backlog of unmet needs, and the A.T. had to compete with other high-priority programs.

In place of NPS inaction, he referred back to the by-now-tired program of involving volunteers more directly in the land-acquisition program. He announced a $10,000 grant to write a contract to conduct leadership training in the clubs. The idea, it seemed, was to turn corridor acquisition over to the clubs. He concluded with some platitudes on visiting the national parks and encouraging more visitors.[67] This was not what the conferees came to hear; the applause must have been light.

Back stage, even as Everhardt spoke, a ferocious argument raged between the conference leaders and Ed Garvey. Garvey had prepared a resolution demanding that the leadership of the A.T. be stripped from the National Park Service and handed over to the Forest Service. It was cataclysmic — the feds had never been challenged by volunteers in such a direct way. But, to Garvey, it was perfectly logical. The Forest Service was the good guy — it had been buying inholdings and protecting many miles of the A.T., while NPS had stood by and done nothing. It wasn't just retribution, although there was an element of that — it was the logical thing to do. Ultimately, they managed to restrain Garvey and convinced him to soften the resolution.

His address to the conference heaped praise on the Forest Service, but his criticism of NPS was, in typical Garvey fashion, acerbic and unrelenting:

---

67. ATC archives, Conference Meetings, 20th meeting (1975).

It has been almost seven years since the National Trails System Act was passed and now, in June 1975, there are still almost 800 miles of the Trail in private ownership — 800 miles where the property owner could have the trail removed from his property at any time he chose to do so.... In these same seven years, the National Park Service, the agency charged with primary responsibility for administration of the Trail, has acquired not one acre of land or obtained a single easement for protection of the Trail.

NPS, he pointed out, had not even asked for money for the trail. He then launched into a tirade against Bob Jacobsen of Shenandoah National Park for closing all seventeen shelters. Finally, he offered a resolution taking NPS to task: "The members and delegates assembled at Boone, N.C., for the 20th general meeting...have voiced their dissatisfaction with the lack of progress in acquiring the Appalachian Trail right-of-way since passage of the National Trails System Act of 1968." His resolution directed the conference chairman (that would be Zoebelein) to send a letter to each member of the interior and insular affairs committees of the House and Senate and to both appropriations committees, making them aware of the situation and demanding corrective action.[68]

Zoebelein was on board with the Garvey resolution. His conference report later that summer was dominated by the controversy, and the need to somehow get NPS on board. He was very optimistic about the involvement of Dave Richie, who had recently taken on the A.T. job and had attended the conference in Boone. Richie must have been impressed by the fervor of the attendees.

At first, it seemed that nothing had changed. Everhardt could talk only about renewing the push for state involvement in acquisition.[69] But, the volunteers were already running in the opposite direction. The PATC lobbying group (consisting of the three usual suspects)

---

68. *Ibid.*
69. ATC archives, Zoebelein papers, Box 1-2-5, Everhardt to Zoebelein, September 3, 1975.

had already contacted Roy Taylor in the House of Representatives, and Taylor had scheduled hearings on the situation.[70]

Taylor brought Department of the Interior officials to the Capitol to demand to know why NPS had taken no action on his 1968 legislation. The answers hardly mollified Taylor. Nathaniel Reed, the assistant secretary for fish and wildlife (NPS was under Reed), wanted to give the states more time. He simply was not interested in national scenic trails — he favored national recreation trails because Interior had more control. Taylor then pressed Reed directly: "I know that you are concerned that ever since 1968 not one foot of the Appalachian Trail has been federally acquired and protected outside of existing Federal areas. [Was he using Garvey's words?] Do you see now a good chance that we could improve quickly on that record?" Reed claimed that he could do so but complained that, owing to the interruption of ANSTAC, NPS had had "two bad years." Representative Lloyd Meeds of Washington State countered that it looked like eight bad years to him.

Later that day, NPS Director Everhardt reiterated Reed's contention that they were trying to get the states to move on the project, ignoring the fact that the clock had run out on the states six years earlier. When they discussed the matter of the five million dollars that had been authorized for NPS to support the A.T., did Everhardt contemplate using any of that money for land purchases? Everhardt did not.[71]

A long list of volunteers, headed by Garvey and Ruth Blackburn, testified about the Park Service's unwillingness to acquire the corridor. Garvey, who was clearly annoyed that neither Reed nor Everhardt attended his testimony, attacked the Park Service for torpedoing the original legislation. He knew, and said all the volunteers knew, that NPS had decided at the outset not to acquire any land — a "conspiracy," he implied. And, while NPS had been completely inactive, PATC, on its own and using its own financial resources, had protected 5.6 miles of trail. It wasn't very much, but it was a great deal more than the Park Service had done. And, as he left the room, with

---

70. Foster, *op. cit.*, p. 37.
71. *Oversight Hearings, op. cit.*

a great flourish he laid on the table the same resolution that he had introduced at Boone, as if daring anyone to contradict him.[72]

In his testimony, Stan Murray wanted the committee to understand the need to protect a wider corridor. He also cited off-road-vehicle invasions, the use of motor bikes, bombing ranges across the trail, timber cuts on national forest land, and other incursions that diminished the hiking experience.[73] But, it did not have the emotional impact of the club volunteers' complaint. The assault on NPS was led, not by ATC, but by PATC.

The hearings were devastating for the Park Service, but, as long as the Ford administration continued, it appeared that no action would be forthcoming. In November 1976, however, Jimmy Carter won the presidency. It was known that he was concerned about the environment, and Paul Pritchard, the ATC executive director, had been Carter's chief of natural resources planning. The new administration seemed to offer a window of opportunity.[74]

Earlier that year, a Pennsylvania State study of optimum corridor width was unveiled. Done in the School of Landscape Architecture, it defined what protection was needed to buffer the Appalachian Trail from the sight and sound of modern intrusions. Overturning an earlier Forest Service study that proposed a width of just 200 feet (100 feet on either side of the trail), the Penn State study justified an optimal 1,000-foot corridor and, in some cases, a 2,000-foot buffer.

Following Carter's inauguration, in early 1977, during a luncheon at the Boston Union Club, Tom Deans (who headed AMC), Hank Foster, Paul Pritchard, Hank Lautz, and Dave Richie conferred about the next step. They had consensus to federalize the trail — that is, take the action away from the states, which had failed to protect the trail, and place protection in NPS.[75]

---

72. *Ibid; Potomac Appalachian,* May 1976.
73. *Potomac Appalachian, ibid.*
74. Foster, *op. cit.,* p. 55.
75. *Ibid.*

Herbst

In May 1977, ATC convened its first conference since the unsettled Boone meeting. The scheduled keynote speaker was to be Nathaniel Reed, the assistant secretary for fish and wildlife in the previous administration. Given Reed's track record, no one really expected a change in the position of the federal government. But, on January 20, a new administration had come into office and with it, a new assistant secretary (for fish, wildlife, and *parks*), Robert L. Herbst.

Herbst, who almost certainly owed his new job to Vice President Walter Mondale, came from Minnesota, where he had been the commissioner of natural resources. Minnesota had a very fine trail system, more than 7,500 miles long, consisting of many different trail types and user groups. Herbst was proud of his accomplishments in the job and brought that experience with him to his new position. PATC, the host club, crossed out Reed and penciled Herbst's name into the program instead.

When he took the microphone at the opening of the conference in Shepherdstown, West Virginia, no one expected anything in particular, but, since Herbst had come in with the Carter administration, perhaps the attendees could get a glimpse of how the new administration viewed the trail. Herbst's speech began ordinarily enough, with reminiscences about his experiences with trails in Minnesota. It also included sops to the federal-state relationship, pledging to work cooperatively with the states, even with those that had taken little or no action on protecting the Appalachian Trail.

But, as it went on, listeners heard more about the *federal* obligation to protect the A.T. Herbst stated outright that 200 feet per mile for the corridor was insufficient, and he was adopting the Pennsylvania State University study that recommended a 1,000-foot corridor. Here then was new policy — people sat up and started listening closer. A sense of anticipation gripped the room.

They hadn't long to wait. Herbst then pledged to recommend thirty-five million dollars to protect the trail. (One might remember that the sum authorized for the A.T. in the 1968 legislation was five million, and most of that had not been used for corridor protection.) And then he got to the clincher: "It is my objective that we will be able to protect at least 300 miles of the Trail's 600 unprotected miles…by our next meeting in 1979."

The audience, at first stunned, suddenly rose and cheered. *Washington Post* reporter Hank Burchard was in the room when the pandemonium broke out and described the scene. The speech, he wrote, was delivered in stentorian tones, and, when Herbst came to the climax, he raised his arms in Billy-Graham style. It was an electric moment.[76]

Where had this come from? Hank Foster credits Paul Pritchard, who now worked for Herbst, with pushing the idea. Chuck Rinaldi (see chapter 9) credited Dave Richie. Dave Sherman,

Herbst at the 1977 conference

who was coordinating the A.T. program in Herbst's office, probably had a larger role than others. So, the new assistant secretary was hearing from several advocates that something had to be done about the A.T.

Even before the conference, Herbst had laid out his program to Cecil Andrus, the new secretary of the interior. Reliance on the states had failed, he wrote. Protecting the trail was a federal obligation, and he proposed to accept it. "Failure to preserve it for future generations would be viewed by many as an unconscionable failure of government responsibility." Federal acquisition did not mean an active federal presence. Volunteers would continue to manage the trail, and he would have agreements with ATC and the trail clubs themselves.[77]

Sherman asked Herbst later how he came up with the number 300. Herbst replied that, if his state could protect thirty miles of trail

76. ATC archives, Conference Meetings (1977), *Washington Post* article, June 9, 1977.
77. ATC archives, Zoebelein papers, draft letter from Herbst to Andrus, April 18, 1977, written by Dave Richie.

in two years, he figured that the federal government could easily do ten times more than a state could do.[78]

Herbst, certain that OMB would object to the budgetary and policy implications in the speech, told Sherman that he did not go through the normal clearance process. According to Sherman, "Bob, being new, felt he could get away with pleading ignorance as to the formal review required for speeches involving policy and funding issues."[79]

The Herbst speech was the touchstone for all that followed. Foster, the new chairman of ANSTAC, promptly contacted William J. Whalen III, then the Park Service director, pointing to the steadfast refusal of his agency to acquire any land to protect the trail. "May I urge you to reconsider the present position of the National Park Service?"[80]

It did not take NPS long to begin backpedaling. Whalen had already agreed to take action even before receiving Foster's demand. He wrote, "Working together, and with your support and that of Secretary Andrus, we are prepared to meet the Federal responsibility for the Appalachian Trail."[81] In a long memo to Herbst the same date, he outlined the steps needed. Much crow was eaten in the early days after the Herbst speech.

The next step was to prepare the legislation. Working on the bill was Representative Phil Burton's staff. Burton, a Democrat from California, had taken the subcommittee leadership from Roy Taylor after he (Taylor) was defeated for reelection. Also working with Burton was Keith Sebelius, a Republican from Kansas. The members, Burton and Sebelius, and the key staffers — Cleve Pinnix and Clay Peters — worked harmoniously together, and the legislative process was much less messy than had been the work-up to the 1968 act.[82]

Burton's committee crafted a bill that was independent of other environmental legislation, such as the coastal redwoods legislation. Working closely with the committee staff was the ever-present Ed Garvey. The bill, introduced by Goodloe Byron, a liberal Democrat

78. Sherman e-mail, May 13, 2014.
79. Sherman e-mail, January 23, 2017.
80. ATC archives, Zoebelein papers, Foster to Whalen, August 17, 1977.
81. Hunter Library, Sherman Collection, Whalen to Director, Bureau of Outdoor Recreation, July 28, 1977.
82. Ronald J. Tipton interview, November 8, 2013..

from Maryland, passed easily in the House. Gaylord Nelson, who was still very much involved with the trail, helped move the bill through the Senate, where it likewise passed easily.

The bill that went through Congress to fund trail protection had new numbers. The authorization was raised to $90 million. The draft legislation adopted the standard proposed in the Pennsylvania State study and raised the total condemnation authority per mile from twenty-five to 125 acres. The corridor width was thus raised to 1,000 feet. The 1978 legislation gave ANSTAC statutory authority, to avoid the embarrassing two-year hiatus in the mid-1970s. Six months before the final bill was adopted, its proposed provisions were called "a turning point, a double blaze" in A.T. history by the then-editor of the *Appalachian Trailway News*.[83]

Could 300 miles of trail corridor be acquired in three years? The impossibility of doing such a job in three years dawned only gradually on those closest to the task. They came to understand that a whole mechanism had to be created, an entirely new office had to be staffed, experts in land acquisition had to be recruited, and a massive data-collection job would be necessary. But, in the flush of success, those finer points were obscured and became visible only gradually.

Bob Herbst stayed involved with the Appalachian Trail. He got ANSTAC reauthorized and agreed to be the chair of the council. In 1979, as he was leaving ANSTAC, he wrote Ruth Blackburn, "Today, the Appalachian Trail project ranks among the most important conservation programs of the Department, with achievements that should ensure its priority with the new administration.... The Appalachian Trail will remain an abiding concern with me, as I am sure it will with you."[84]

The 1978 act set the table for what was to follow. It proved to be the most complex land-acquisition program in the history of the National Park Service.

And, that was Dave Richie's problem.

---

83. *ATN*, September 1977, p. 1, article by Lyn Anderson.
84. ATC archives, Ruth Blackburn correspondence, 1981-1983, undated letter (1979 penciled in).

The Appalachian Greenway

Stan Murray brought new energy to the idea of broadening the trail corridor. To him, the Appalachian Trail was not simply a narrow ribbon of dirt. It was a whole environment that needed to be preserved. It was simply the extension of Benton MacKaye's concept of the trail. Myron Avery had hoped to implement MacKaye's vision, once the trail itself could be secured. Now that the trail had supposedly been secured through legislation, it gave Murray and ATC an opportunity to look beyond the narrow dirt path.

In 1966, the trail was not yet secured, but, as Murray worked with Congress to get federal protection, he began to talk about this wider corridor. He wrote to Walter Boardman and Ed Garvey:

The ideal that I hold in my mind is something like this: When I look at a map of the eastern United States, I visualize a strip of green, winding but continuous, from Maine to Georgia. This I see as a prime, high-quality outdoor recreation area for the eastern population; a museum piece of wilderness…; a forested, mountainous land where the sense of remoteness can be real….[1]

He hoped to get his greenway concept into the language of the bill and wrote to Daniel Ogden of the Bureau of Outdoor Recreation, proposing that the draft be changed to include this broader concept. He proposed that the section discussing twenty-five acres per mile include "scenic easements of some depth are highly desirable to provide the environmental protection a wilderness foot trail needs." He also discussed the idea with Representative Taylor.[2] No such language was inserted, and broadening the trail concept might have caused the legislation to stall. Roy Taylor needed simplicity.

So, Murray began thinking about organizing the effort outside of the legislation and discussed it with Boardman. He used the example of the Roan Highlands' balds as a model for a broader

1. ATC archives, Murray files, materials *re* National Trails System Act, 1966-69, Murray to Boardman and Garvey, July 27, 1966.
2. *Ibid*, Murray to Ogden, August 2, 1966; Murray to Taylor, August 7, 1967.

greenway.[3] In November 1966, he formed a committee of ATC, beginning with a meeting in Johnson City.

His concept always was intertwined with his desire to preserve the Roan Highlands, and, in 1972, he formed a separate committee, the Roan Mountain Preservation Committee, to work on preserving the Highlands. In order to raise money to protect Roan lands that the Forest Service was not yet authorized to buy, the committee in 1974 incorporated as a not-for-profit, the Southern Appalachians Highlands Conservancy.[4]

Murray proposed the committee to the board of managers in November 1972, and the committee engaged Ann Satterthwaite, a Washington-area consultant, to do a study. She published her report in 1974, urging that a greenway be established and outlining what it would involve and how it would unfold.

She first pointed out that nothing could be accomplished before the trail corridor had been acquired. Her research did not demonstrate a great deal of optimism concerning the role of the states, because so few had responded to the mandate of the National Trails System Act, so Phase I was in jeopardy at the outset. Phase II would involve acquiring small beads of property that had special historical or environmental important. Phase III would expand these nodes into larger protected zones, similar to what the state of California had done to protect its coastline. Phase IV would be a regional plan, with all the states involved

*Ann Satterthwaite and
George Zoebelein*

3. *Ibid*, Murray to Boardman, December 29, 1966.
4. Interview with Jay Leutze and Judy Murray, September 25, 2014.

in trail protection beyond the narrow legal corridor, and Phase V would involve a massive protection program, principally through easements and outright purchases. Funding would come from both governmental and private money.[5]

The "wilderness zone" that involved the trail corridor would be in public ownership, but the "countryside zone" would remain in private hands and controlled by a regional corporation, chartered by Congress, the Appalachian Greenway Corporation. It would operate similar to COMSAT, a quasigovernmental corporation that had been set up to build and launch communications satellites. That corporation would acquire and hold lands up to ten miles from the Appalachian Trail corridor, thus controlling use out to a considerable distance. Only those tracts with significant historic, environmental, cultural or scenic values would actually be owned — others would simply be regulated, probably by easement.

A problem at the outset was how to get all fourteen states on board. The California program was easier because it involved only one state. A similar program for the Appalachian Trail would require an unprecedented level of interstate cooperation. Cooperation on the trail project was rare enough *within* an individual state — cooperation *among* them was difficult to imagine.

A meeting to discuss the report was held in Amagansett, New York, October 5 and 6, 1974. Already, the Appalachian Trail was in trouble, with little or no action by the states, and no action at all at the federal level. So point one, corridor acquisition, was not occurring, and optimism had seriously eroded.

The group discussed how to organize the effort going forward. A separate Appalachian Highlands Association should be organized and was, in fact, created, with $1,000 in the bank. Satterthwaite recommended that membership on the board should be considerably broadened from its current fairly narrow base, with influential political figures and economically powerful people. This would be necessary because serious amounts of money would have to be raised to fund the corporation. Satter-

---

5. Ann Satterthwaite, "An Appalachian Greenway: Purposes, Prospects and Programs," November 1974.

Hump Mountain along the Roan Massif, with the A.T. crossing the center of the bald.

thwaite estimated that $500,000 would be needed to get started, and seed money was needed immediately.

The project began to fall apart immediately. Phil Hanes, from the family that manufactured Hanes underwear, was an experienced fund-raiser with access to money and noted to George Zoebelein, "I saw that the Appalachian Trail Conference to the best of my knowledge did not have the strength to do this job itself." Hanes had offered to help Murray raise money for the Roan Mountain project and had given Stan some names to contact, people who could provide large amounts. Murray made the contacts but had gotten turned down by every one, so Hanes had taken it on and had raised $200,000 within four months. This had convinced him that the committee could not actually do what Satterthwaite had laid out for it.[6]

ATC tried to bring the maintaining clubs into the project but got no response. By 1975, the concept of land-use planning was

6. ATC archives, Murray papers, Hanes to Zoebelein, October 15, 1974.

beginning to diminish, and the greenway project as an organized entity was put on hold.[7] An attempt was made to revive it in 1976, with a big meeting at the Key Bridge Marriott in Rosslyn, Virginia, across the Potomac from Washington. A number of key people were assembled, including Pat Noonan of The Nature Conservancy, Elvis Stahr of the National Audubon Society, Rep. Gilbert Gude, and others. Several more attempts were made to resuscitate the effort, and, in 1979, Ann herself was elected president of the organization. But, nothing worked. Hank Foster, chairman of the Appalachian National Scenic Trail Advisory Committee (ANSTAC), believed that the time was just not right for the greenway, and that it would have to wait for another day.[8] The AHA was dissolved after Hanes and George Zoebelein stepped down as trustees, with its $1,000 in assets transferred to ATC.

Murray's other effort, the protection of the Roan Highlands, took off and has been highly successful. In 1966, he had formed the Roan Mountain Preservation Committee and, in 1974, the Southern Appalachian Highlands Conservancy (SAHC). The Roan was always his first love, and he worked with the Forest Service to acquire the highlands. The last of the highlands to be acquired and the most northerly was Hump Mountain. The top of the mountain was, fortunately, in single ownership, and the owner, Oscar Julian, was not averse to selling, but the Forest Service placed the obligation of acquiring the mountain on the volunteers.

SAHC set about raising money, and, after fourteen years, the tract was finally deeded over in 1981.[9] So, Phil Hanes was not entirely correct in his appraisal of Murray's fund-raising abilities. When it came to the Roan Highlands, the needed funds were raised. Perhaps the difference was that Hump Mountain was a specific tract, and donors could come and look at it, hike over it, and estimate its value. The greenway project had no specific objective — it was all concept.

7. *Ibid*, Murray speech recalling the greenway effort, September 20, 1989.
8. ATC archives, Murray papers, workshop summary, April 1976; Foster, *ibid*, p. 45.
9. *ATN*, May/June 1982, pp. 6-7; November/December 1998, pp. 13-16; Jay Leutze, "Grace Under Pressure." *A.T. Journeys*, November/December 2012, pp. 18-24.

ATC Moves Upriver

The Appalachian Trail Conference still rented space from PATC in downtown Washington. This had begun (without rent) in 1927 in the Union Trust Build-ing. As PATC's locations migrated, so did ATC's quarters. But, the tenant always got the less desirable quarters. If there were a basement, ATC was there. If there were a top floor with a long climb up, that was where ATC was put. In 1966, PATC purchased its own building at 1718 N Street. The new building had four floors, and, of course, ATC got the top floor.

1718 N Street NW

ATC was unhappy with its situation. Its spaces were small, and PATC had just raised the rent. The crunch point occurred over ATC guidebooks. They were heavy, and, as the organization sold more of them, the process of moving the new books up to the ATC spaces became unendurable. ATC considered an elevator, but it would cost $8,000. Even a dumbwaiter, at $4,500, was unaffordable.

So, in 1971, Stan went to Paula Strain, the PATC president, complaining that they needed more space. Paula's response did not help matters much. She informed Stan that PATC itself needed more space and was about to take over ATC's room. A housing crisis was upon ATC.[1]

Murray cast desperately for something ATC could afford. At that critical point, the National Park Service came to the rescue, offering a vacant building in historic Harpers Ferry.

The Brackett House had come available for a rent at the same price ATC was paying PATC. In June, Les Holmes, the first execu-

1. Interview with Paula Strain, March 14, 1999; ATC archives, Murray papers: Laud Pitt to Strain, July 27, 1971; Strain to Murray, July 25; Strain to Lester Holmes, April 14, 1971.

tive secretary/director who lived in frederick, Maryland, began moving files and furniture from the N Street location and found that the Brackett House also provided a one-third increase in space from the PATC location.[2]

Brackett House during ATC's tenure.

The building dated back to 1857 and 1858 on land acquired for the antebellum federal armory. The clerk of the armory had lived there, but the armory was destroyed during the Civil War and was never rebuilt. Some of the buildings remaining from the military presence were assigned to General Oliver O. Howard's Freedmen's Bureau, and the Reverend Nathan Brackett, the superintendent of the Freedmen's Bureau school, made it his residence. That is how it acquired the name. It later became the nucleus for Storer College, established by John Storer of Stanford, Maine, who donated half the money for a "Negro school" in Harpers Ferry. The college, a "normal school" (*i.e.,* teacher's college) was established in 1867 in four federal buildings, one of which was the Brackett House, which then became a dormitory.

When the college was closed in 1955, the board of trustees voted to sell the buildings back to the federal government, and they were incorporated into Harpers Ferry National Historical Park.

Completing the Tuscarora-Big Blue

The Tuscarora Trail scouting to the west was stalled in the mid-1960s. The entire Pennsylvania route was laid out, but since PATC had stopped scouting north of Forest Service land in northern Virginia, the Pennsylvania clubs waited. Stan Murray grew impatient and told Lloyd Felton in March 1966 not to wait for

2. *ATN*, September 1972, p. 51; Luxenberg, *op. cit,* p. 27.

PATC: Build the scouted route south to Hancock, and, if no trail connection developed south of the river, a hiker could at least walk the towpath back to Harpers Ferry.[3] (This would not, however, have solved the trail blockages south of Harpers Ferry.)

PATC leaders were unsettled about the abandonment of their obligation. In early 1967, Fred Blackburn agreed to renew the project south of the Potomac and wrote to Felton that PATC would restart the effort.[4]

But, progress was stalled by an area of lowland and rolling hills with houses and farms that would be difficult to route a trail through. This was what had stopped Jim Denton several years earlier, but Blackburn was undeterred. He worked both road-walking and handshake agreements[5] with landowners to get the new trail to the Potomac River at Hancock.

The Potomac section of the new trail needed a name. One day, when Blackburn was scouting for a route with park rangers, they came up with the name. According to Blackburn, "When we were trying to find a route, we got to talking about it, a big blue-blazed trail, and [someone said] 'Call it Big Blue.'" North of the river people were calling it Tuscarora, the name of the farthest-south mountain.[6] So, the trail had two names: Tuscarora and Big Blue. The Tuscarora was blazed orange, because Pennsylvania rangers pointed out that blue was used as a lumbering blaze.[7]

Once work resumed south of the Potomac, the Pennsylvania clubs got to work building the trail that they had already scouted. KTA organized the effort. It was agreed that the Batona Club would work on the northern two-thirds of the trail south to U.S. 30, where it crossed Tuscarora Mountain, and Mountain Club of Maryland (MCM) would build the southern third. For MCM, the president, Thurston Griggs, who was to play a major role in the Appalachian Trail in Pennsylvania and Maryland, led the effort.[8]

---

3. ATC archives, Murray correspondence, Murray to Felton, March 1, 1966.
4. PATC archives, Box 11, Big Blue Trail, Blackburn to Felton, March 21, 1967.
5. True to tradition, Blackburn preferred verbal agreements to formal documentation.
6. Quoted from Floyd, *op.cit.*
7. PATC archives, Box 11, Big Blue, Felton to Blackburn, April 16, 1968.
8. *Potomac Appalachian*, March 1982.

The last blaze to the combined Big Blue–Tuscarora was painted by Fred Blackburn on October 10, 1981, at the foot of Great North Mountain, about nine miles north of the northern boundary of the national forest.[9] By that time, all the legislation needed to protect the Appalachian Trail was on the books, and the National Park Service was in the process of acquiring the corridor. So, in the end, the new trail never played a role as a new section of the Appalachian Trail. Continued work on it was justified solely as a new 250-mile hiking trail through terrain west of the A.T.

Trail Preservation Amid a Hiking Boom

In the ten years between the passage of the National Trails System Act and the 1978 amendments that finally brought the beginnings of Park Service land acquisitions, the situation on the Appalachian Trail grew worse, not better. This was the period of the counterculture movement. People began reading about this strange group of long-haired people in the San Francisco Bay area that allegedly smoked marijuana and never shaved. American youth, caught up partly in the culture, and partly in the antiwar movement resulting from the Vietnam war, painted old school buses psychedelic colors and took off on long, cross-country jaunts.

Along with all this was a strong back-to-nature movement. Crowds of people who had never hiked before took off for the forests, camping for long periods. Much of their behavior did not comport well with the existing hiking culture. The invasion of the forests often involved Appalachian Trail shelters and campsites, with loud music, pot, and piles of litter, because no one had thought about the need to move it to a dump. The invasion affected all areas of the trail and was a big reason why landowners in northern Virginia were insistent that the A.T. be removed from their part of the mountains.

The backpacking boom hit in the 1960s and 1970s, and membership in hiking clubs surged. Between 1969 and 1976, AMC hut use increased by ninety-seven percent. Kelty introduced the ex-

---

9. Floyd, *op. cit.*

ternal frame pack, and the company became almost synonymous with the backpack.[10]

The Appalachian Trail, created for a primitive and pristine forest experience, was overwhelmed by the surge in hikers. The volunteer clubs that maintained the Trail were confronted with conditions of which they never dreamed. The good thing was that the Appalachian Trail had become a magnet for hikers. The bad thing was that it had become a magnet for too many hikers without experience in the woods. Ann Satterthwaite commented, "Tramping in a single file, bumper to bumper along noisy litter strewn trails is not the hiking experience the Appalachian Trail Conference is committed to promote."[11]

Something had to be done. In New York, Elizabeth Levers of the New York chapter of AMC launched one of the earliest and most effective antilitter campaigns; it was copied up and down the mountain chain. The by-now-well-known slogan, "Take nothing but pictures, leave nothing but footprints," originated from the Forest Service in this period.

At Katahdin, rangers reacted with a severe law-enforcement campaign, while, in other places, clubs and rangers relied more on education. Some

A one-woman army, Elizabeth Levers was singular phenomenon. Born in 1905, she was president of the New York–New Jersey Trail Conference in the early 1970s, about the same time that she launched the antilitter campaign. But, her long-term role and title was corridor monitor for New York, and her area of concentration was the perpetually difficult section east of the Hudson. One NY–NJ TC volunteer wrote after her death in 1998, "She inspired us because she was there all the time, urging us on, keeping us motivated. And working herself." All volunteers marveled at her energy level, and few could keep up. She is shown here with a bag of litter on her back.

10. Watermans, *op. cit.* p. 563.
11. Ann Satterthwaite, *op. cit.*

clubs in New England hired people to take care of overnight shelters, paying a nominal salary for employment in the summer months.[12] GMC hired two young hikers, Preston Bristow and Lee Allen, to stay the summer at Stratton Pond, one of the most popular destinations, and, over the summer, they took out tons of trash. In some places, AMC tore down shelters and replaced them with tent pads ATC established an education committee in 1972, and Jeannette Fitzwilliams of PATC developed "Guidelines for Individual Behavior." GMC's Shirley Strong began a leave-no-trace program.

In 1973, PATC instituted a new program, initially called the Patrol, later the Trail Patrol. The first patrolman, Keith Conover, was instructed to hike back and forth along the trail, educating hikers and campers on what became Leave No Trace™ principles. He had no law-enforcement authority — only moral suasion. Conover was paid a nominal salary of $300 for the summer hiking season. ATC applauded the new program and urged other clubs to do the same.[13] Trail Patrol was a success and was expanded the next year from northern Virginia into Maryland and Pennsylvania.[14]

ATC, seeing the success of PATC's program, noted a similar program in the Adirondacks, and Peter Dunning of ATC laid plans for expansion of Trail Patrol up and down the trail. Hank Lautz, later ATC's executive director, headed the project and invited every club north of Damascus, Virginia, to join.[15]

The greatest impact on the A.T. from the hiking surge was on shelters. Shelters had become such a standard appurtenance on hiking trails that the necessity was unquestioned. Avery had wanted shelters on the trail every eight to twelve miles. Although it was found impossible to rigidly adhere to the Avery standard, shelters had been proliferating. But, huge parties, drinking bouts, overturned privies, and a long list of destructive behavior brought a change in attitude about shelters. Land managers, trail clubs, and even the members themselves began looking at shelters as more of a nuisance than a benefit. Thurston Griggs commented

12. *Ibid*, p. 581; also, interview with Preston Bristow and Lee Allen, July 9, 2014.
13. ATC archives, Peter Dunning papers, letter to Ruth Blackburn, June 13, 1973.
14. Interview with Keith Conover, April 1, 2012.
15. ATC archives, Peter Dunning papers, Dunning to Murray, April 4, 1974.

that MCM had lost so many shelters to vandalism that they had decided not to build more because they could not keep up.[16] Other clubs experienced the same, and momentum began building to either tear them down or, at the least, build no more.

The hiking surge led to a flurry of shelters being closed on federal lands. Some governmental entities proposed rationing, issuing permits, and even obscuring Appalachian Trail signs so that the trail would be harder to find. Following Superintendent Bob Jacobsen's decision to close shelters in Shenandoah National Park, similar actions were taken in Great Smoky Mountains National Park, and pretty soon it seemed that every land manager would "solve" the problem by making it go away. ATC wanted to step back and assess the attitude of their hikers. Was this the right solution?

In 1974, as the Great Shelter Closure movement was just getting under way, ATC's Peter Dunning sent a survey to all then-sixty-seven maintaining clubs, asking for their opinions. The survey could be filled out by clubs (and most were) or by individuals (a few chimed in, mostly club leaders). The choices were:

- Build more shelters
- Build no more, but hold at the present level.
- Permanently remove all shelters.
- Relocate "problem" shelters.

A consensus was clear: Build no more, but keep those that were already there. (Some advocated for also removing problem shelters to new locations.)[17] Stan Murray himself was in the "no new shelters" camp and was emblematic of how volunteer clubs thought about shelters at the time.

The strongest advocacy for removing shelters entirely came from the Smoky Mountains Hiking Club, and the membership cheered the decision by the Park Service to remove all shelters from Smoky Mountains trails. This was hardly surprising —

16. *ATN*, November 1973, p. 53.
17. ATC archives, Peter Dunning papers, various letters.

SMHC had played a large role in the creation of The Wilderness Society, and Benton MacKaye had been one of its members in earlier years before helping found TWS.

The only club that stood firmly on the side of keeping all shelters was PATC. Ed Garvey was the driver and was the strongest shelter defender in ATC. Garvey's answer to Jacobsen was caustic. He argued that SNP shelter policy discriminated against backpackers by evicting them from the only facilities that had ever been built for their benefit. He contrasted that with the huge campgrounds in Shenandoah National Park, built and maintained for the benefit of the car-driving public, at taxpayers' expense, and no one had ever proposed that they be closed, regardless of misuse. "I ask you, fellow members of the backpacking fraternity, what have we done to deserve such discrimination?"[18]

A side issue was shelters in designated wilderness areas. Part of the argument turned on an interpretation of the language in the Wilderness Act. How primitive did they have to be? There was a consensus that hiking trails should be permitted — how else would one ever experience wilderness in the East? Most Forest Service superintendents, however, declared that they would tear down shelters in wilderness areas. In 1977, that policy was flipped by Rupert Cutler, assistant secretary of agriculture for conservation, research, and education, who declared that Forest Service policies on wilderness had long been misunderstood. Quoting none other than Bob Marshall — that "trails and temporary shelters are entirely permissible"[19] — he legalized them at a stroke of his pen. Congress formalized this in the 1980s.

Many landowners reacted in near panic over the great hiking surge, quickly closing their property to hikers, and the A.T. began to fragment.

Dave Sherman commented to Dave Richie, the originator of the Park Service's A.T. Project Office, "I was shocked to see the great number of people who have signed the register on Springer stating their intentions of going to Katahdin.... If the use of the

18. *Potomac Appalachian*, February 1976.
19. ATC archives, Zoebelein papers, Cutler to a wide distribution, April 17, 1977.

Trail continues to increase over the next three years at the same astronomical rate it has over the last three years, then I don't know what its future will be. Its overuse is becoming apparent."[20]

Sherman had identified a new problem that was to confront ATC — the physical deterioration of the trail tread. Too many hikers would cause erosion, and the trail would be physically damaged. This spawned thinking about how to minimize the impact of so many boots on the ground and eventually resulted in research into how to build sustainable trails.

Proper drainage was a key to the improvement of the trail tread, as were new benching techniques and surface hardening. Much information came from the Forest Service, and the Appalachian Trail, to be sustainable, needed to follow USFS standards.

Garvey had an "ideal" shelter plan. Location was critical. Keep it away from the main trail, in a clearing where light could get through. Paint the inside white, not black. Provide tables and shelf space, otherwise "every piece of camping equipment must be put on the ground. Try to imagine a home or apartment like this." In the shelter, wooden floors were best. And, no wire bunks! The wire always became frayed, sharp, and cut holes in sleeping bags. Provide brooms on pegs to keep the shelter clean. And, for heavens sake, mark the side trail to the shelter in a way that a hiker knew that an actual shelter would greet him at the end of his quest. (*ATN*, September 1970, p. 41)

20. Hunter Library, Sherman Collection, Sherman to Richie, April 19, 1976.

Inside the Appalachian Trail Conference (Late 1970s)

The Conference needed stability, and George Zoebelein, an accountant from New York, provided stable leadership from 1975 to 1979. Zoebelein took a business approach to the Conference and worked on expanding the fund-raising programs. He followed a $40,000 deficit the previous year with a $40,000 surplus the next. When discussing the new relationship with the federal government, he emphasized the need to give volunteers new trail-

George Zoebelein

building skills — they were now building a federal trail, not an informal footpath with no national impact. Zoebelein provided steady leadership at a formative time when the trail and ATC itself were moving toward a new relationship with the federal government.

After three years in the National Park Service Brackett House, the lease cost jumped to $13,000. Again, it was time to pack and move. The board formed a committee to survey the prospects. They found an old building on the main street, owned by two Harpers Ferry school teachers. The building was structurally sound but needed internal changes from a four-apartment design. ATC moved in 1976, and the building became ATC's permanent home.[1]

ATC had hired its second executive director in 1975. Paul Pritchard grew up in Kansas, and, after college, he joined the Army and served in the Mekong River Delta during the Vietnam War. (The Phoenix program[2] was one of his tasks.) After Vietnam, he took a degree in economics and natural resources at the University of Tennessee. Out of college, he moved to Georgia,

1. Interview with Paul Pritchard, May 12, 2014.
2. The delta was south of Saigon, a flat rice-growing area. Phoenix was a CIA program to find and eliminate Viet Cong guerilla leaders. It gained a reputation for extrajudicial killings.

met Jimmy Carter when Carter was just a state senator, and became chief of natural resources for the state government. Later he worked in Washington State on coastal zone management with the Smithsonian Institution, and, while there, he got a call from ATC. The organization was in the process of hiring an executive director to succeed Les Holmes, and Pritchard was invited to apply.[3]

Paul Pritchard

Pritchard came to the job when the states were still being held to the task of acquiring the corridor, and NPS was refusing to buy its first tract of land. He pushed the relationship with the states, but it was by then (1975) obvious to anyone involved with the problem that that was not going to work. Nevertheless, Pritchard was very upbeat and pushed trail clubs to complete a trail corridor inventory, as if the volunteers were going to do the job themselves.

He also concentrated on improving trail guides. He felt that the quality was inconsistent. The control of trail guides had been fraught with local opposition since the days of Myron Avery, and this was true with Paul Pritchard as well.

Pritchard didn't intend to be at ATC very long. "I want to be a meteor, not a star," he once said.[4] He left in 1977, amid emerging chaos at the top. He went to the Department of the Interior, in order, he said, to ensure that the trail was adequately funded.

Succeeding Pritchard was Hank Lautz. Dave Startzell, the preeminent federal fund-raiser in ATC history, gave Lautz considerable credit for establishing an initial relationship with Congress. But, Lautz was not a good manager, Startzell contended, nor did he bring in the money that ATC needed to operate in those more

3. Pritchard interview.
4. *Ibid.*

professional times. Instead, he hired a private secretary with a staff of seven, and the organization began sinking into debt.

Finally, his top staff members — Startzell, Doug Blaze, and Rita Malone — went to Charlie Pugh, who had succeeded Zoebelein as chairman in 1979, and threatened to resign if Lautz was not replaced. The board essentially fired Lautz but gave him a grace period of several months to clear out. Startzell became acting executive director until Larry Van Meter arrived to stabilize the situation in 1981.[5]

Pugh was a stockbroker who had had unspecified problems with the Securities and Exchange Commission and resigned from his ATC position.[6] After a certain amount of turmoil, Ruth Blackburn

Hank Lautz and Charles Pugh

was chosen as the ATC chair, and her firm but polite, no-nonsense approach to management soon brought things under control.[7]

After four decades, the details are blurred, and even the basic facts were difficult to confirm, but the timing of that turmoil was extraordinarily bad. The organization had moved three-and-half years before to a new building it was buying, hired new staff, and begun trying to raise serious money. It was not a good way to begin a new era. Fortunately, Blackburn and Larry Van Meter were there at the critical moment and saved the organization.

5. Interviews with Startzell, Van Meter, and Sherman.
6. Startzell interview; Sherman e-mail, June 17, 2014.
7. Interview with Charles Sloan, May 19, 2014.

APPALACHIAN TRAILWAY NEWS

SEPTEMBER 1976
$1.25

ATC's new home in 1976

Chapter 9

RICHIE, RINALDI, AND SHERMAN

Think decentralization and grassroots. Shun bureaucratic and professional egotism. Share responsibility and credit generously. Respect the intelligence and ability of volunteers. Listen well. Don't waste money.
— Dave Richie to Steve Golden, February 26, 1975

In 1974, Dave Richie, a veteran Park Service officer, became deputy director of the Northeast Regional Office in Boston. As part of his job description, he assumed oversight of this new Appalachian Trail that had been authorized by federal legislation in 1968. The Park Service had not become directly involved in the trail — he had no staff for it and no central management program. He was expected to devote only ten percent of his time to this part of his job.

Richie looked at the job and came to believe that it would require more direct oversight than the Park Service was giving it. In 1975, he argued for twenty-five percent of his time and got it. In 1976, he argued for a separate park office for the Appalachian Trail and got that, too. For eleven years more, he could devote all his time to the trail.

He began a relationship with the Appalachian National Scenic Trail Advisory Council (ANSTAC) and began talking to trail volunteers. Ed Garvey was one of those with whom he talked, and he attended his first ATC conference, the incendiary meeting in Boone in 1975 (see chapter 8). He realized the conflicts that were ahead be-

David A. Richie

tween volunteers and NPS, and this probably served to move him toward a full-time position for NPS.

In the beginning, his was a voice in the wilderness. His direct bosses were opposed to NPS' getting involved with the Appalachian Trail. Gary Everhardt, who headed NPS at the time, was completely dismissive of the effort, as was Richard Stanton, the Park Service's designated project officer for the A.T. in Washington. Why would they want to devote any effort to this trail? Steve Golden, who became Richie's deputy, years later described the situation:

> *At the time, I'll give them a little bit of credit. This was a pretty crazy notion. This was a pretty wild notion that the Park Service could get involved in something like this. It's this long thin thing that had a noisy constituency, but we had a lot of noisy constituencies; we have a hard time managing things that we own, and now you want us to manage something we don't own? And it's long and thin, and it has the Forest Service, and the states, roads — you know, it was something that was blowing their minds."[1]

---

1. Interview with Steve Golden and Dave Sherman, April 2, 2014.

Dave Richie, the man who would come to represent the federal face of the Appalachian Trail, seemed a contradiction. Growing up a Quaker in Moorestown, New Jersey, he attended local Friends schools, then went to a Friends boarding school. He showed unusual academic, leadership, and athletic abilities all through school. He was student body president in high school and went on to Haverford College.

Quakers are known for pacifism and opposition to war. When Dave joined the Marines to become a jet pilot, he raised some eyebrows in his family. His motive was to fly — not to fight — and he was fortunate to be in the Marines between wars. However, that jet pilot and Marine side of Dave would inform his leadership style as much as his Quaker upbringing. Dave later came to oppose the Vietnam War and finished his military service flying transports, but his stint in the combat arms marked the first, but hardly the last, contradiction in his personality.

After returning to Haverford to finish his degree in 1958, he joined the federal government with the Bureau of Land Management and later transferred to the National Park Service. (He served a year as a congressional fellow for Senator Charles McC. Mathias of Maryland before returning to NPS.) His first field assignment was to Mount Rainier National Park from 1966 to 1967, and he was then transferred across the state to become superintendent of Lake Roosevelt National Recreational Area/Grand Coulee Dam from 1967 to 1969. He left the Park Service for two years to teach history at Westtown Friends School in Pennsylvania before returning. By 1971, he was superintendent of George Washington Memorial Parkway in northern Virginia. The Park Service clearly recognized Richie's ability and made him a park superintendent very early in his career.

When he transferred to Boston as deputy director of the Northeast Region in 1974, he knew little about hiking trails. He had, however, a strong attraction to outdoor recreation and was a longtime hiker, backpacker, and birder. A lifetime runner, he ran the Boston Marathon while he was assigned to the Boston office. His love of physical fitness might have been a factor in his insistence in taking on the Appalachian Trail full-time.

Richie attracted many friends but could also frustrate his colleagues in the Park Service. He was highly idealistic and liked to try to apply cosmic principles to the work place. His insistence on "first principles" caused him to change his mind so many times that people had trouble keeping up with him. Larry Van Meter, who became ATC's executive director in 1981, once commented that it was hard to keep Richie focused. He oscillated among the various approaches to land acquisition, and this lack of consistency could drive his colleagues crazy. He might one day focus strictly on easements, to the frustration of those who thought that fee acquisition was the only viable approach. The next time, he might prefer the fee approach. At other times, he thought that working with private land trusts was the best way and at times even thought that his office was superfluous, and he should hand the job to ATC's Trust for Appalachian Trail Lands.[2]

Yet Dave Richie was an engaging personality. He was warm and friendly, informal to a fault, very sincere, without a trace of the authoritarian. He was easy to talk to, and his door was always open. Even when dealing with his contradictions, no one could possibly dislike him.

The National Trails System Act that in 1968 created the first two "national" trails (the Appalachian Trail and the Pacific Crest Trail) required some sort of National Park Service management. The NPS was dragging its feet, reluctant to become directly involved in managing a new entity that had no bureaucratic underpinnings. The Park Service simply refused to act — it was a minefield.

When Richie stepped into the competing constituencies surrounding the Appalachian Trail in 1975, he was the ideal person for the job. The project needed Richie because it required compromise, and long, frustrating delays were inherent as the various players were slowly brought to the table. Everyone involved believed that the

---

2. E-mail from Larry Van Meter, February 4, 2016; Sherman e-mail, February 17, 2016. After Richie retired, he in fact headed the trust for a period before moving to North Carolina.

trail had no chance without Dave Richie at the helm.

When he took over the job and created the Appalachian Trail Project Office (ATPO), he began arguing that the job should not be in Boston. It needed to be near ATC in Harpers Ferry.

Richie told Steve Golden, his deputy, to pack up the Boston office and move to Harpers Ferry. Just where in Harpers Ferry was still uncertain. The General Services Administration (GSA) officer who was supposed to get space for ATPO was no longer working there. Steve put the Boston files in his car and drove to Harpers Ferry, put the files in the GSA building, and set up the new ATPO office temporarily on the porch.[3] Until GSA got them their own space, Richie and Golden worked out of the ATC offices up the street.

When he first assumed his new position in 1974, Richie adopted the National Park Service line. It was a state responsibility, and NPS would not get involved with land acquisition. In talking with Ann Satterthwaite about his new responsibilities, he emphasized that his role, he felt, was to ensure that the states moved forward in a coordinated fashion.[4]

At the ATC board of managers meeting in 1975, he announced that new contracts would be awarded to ATC for on-

Steve Golden *became Dave Richie's longtime assistant and alter ego. A New Yorker by birth, with multiple degrees in forestry and resource management, he was a sports enthusiast and outdoorsman who thru-hiked the Appalachian Trail in 1972 and then got a job with New York Department of Environmental Conservation, running a trail crew in the Catskills. He went to Boone in 1975 and had a chance meeting with Richie on the lawn outside the venue. They ran into each other on a field trip the next day, hit it off, and Richie hired him on the spot. Although officially named the "safety officer," Richie told him to forget about that — he would be working on the trail project.*

---

3. Golden and Sherman interview.
4. ATC archives, Box 5-3-5, Murray undated interview.

the-ground trail education and for beginning the process of bringing volunteers into determining land status in preparation for some form of protection.[5] At this point, Richie still assumed that the states would protect the trail, assisted by volunteers who actually knew where the trail was.

His conversion to the idea that this was a national-park responsibility came gradually and began at the ATC conference in Boone. Hearing Garvey speak came as a revelation to Dave Richie. "That came as a personal blow to me," he said later.[6] By April 1977, only a month before Robert Herbst's speech, Richie was among the converted. The states had not protected the trail, and only federal action could change the playing field. He would exempt only New Jersey and Maryland, two states whose acquisition programs had already been launched.[7] (Maryland did not follow through; New Jersey did.)

Richie was good at building bridges and began working closely with ANSTAC. He soon recognized the critical role that volunteers played, agreeing with Benton MacKaye (in a 1975 interview often cited afterward) that they were the "soul" of the trail. (MacKaye actually said the *clubs* were.) This was not going to be just another National Park Service management program. It was, if Richie had his say, to remain a volunteer project.

Richie did not want a large staff that was typical of other Park Service entities, and he grew the staff slowly. It came to include Karen Wade, Chris Brown, Pam Underhill, and Larry Henson, and it became a tight-knit group. Richie, Dave Startzell from ATC, Karen Wade, and Larry Henson, all key figures in the history of the trail, also all lived in Reston, a Washington suburb. They carpooled together from Reston to Harpers Ferry. Dave Sherman believed that the carpool gave the other three face time with Richie, and they would all bounce ideas around and try to keep Richie focused on approaches that would work in the cold reality of the trail environment.[8] His staff and acquaintances still thought of him as something of a dreamer.

5. *ATN*, August 1975.
6. ATC interview with Dave Richie, January 7, 1985, with Tom Floyd.
7. ATC archives, Murray papers, Richie to Bill Rennebohm, April 18, 1977.
8. Sherman e-mail, July 8, 2016.

When the 1978 amendment was passed, the Appalachian Trail had changed little since 1968. The threats to the land remained. In the ensuing decade after 1968, the amount of private land crossed by the A.T. was still about the same, but private property was actually a more serious threat than earlier, as second-home development continued to move to the eastern ridges of the Appalachians. The kindly farmer who was happy to acquiesce to hikers coming across a corner of his land was being replaced by the city dweller, who just wanted to get away from other people.

Hiking was still going through its adolescent phase, and park rangers continued to complain about pot parties, trash on the trail, and other forms of abuse. Many shelters were closed simply because rangers did not trust the public to use them properly.

Several clubs, among them the Potomac A.T. Club (PATC) and the Green Mountain Club (GMC), were paying club members to monitor the trail and shelters to curb the worst abuses. And now, a huge land-buying program was about to launch. The leader was Chuck Rinaldi, a blunt-talking, no-nonsense administrator. He and his office worked for Dave Richie, the thoughtful, mild-mannered Quaker from New Jersey. The relationship was going to be interesting.

The Approach

Stepping into the changed environment mandated by the 1978 legislation, Dave Richie set forth some overarching principles that would characterize the trail. That was his strength — setting broad principles — and they became, henceforth, the governing principles for the Appalachian Trail.

The first principle was volunteerism. The National Park Service managers wondered if this new responsibility would require them to hire a large staff, with rangers walking the trail, checkpoints at access locations, building parking lots and shelters and side trails, essentially replacing the volunteers.[9] Richie's answer was no: This trail

9. NPS Director William J. Whalen III, in a July 28, 1977, memo to Bob Herbst, wondered if he would have to replace the volunteers and emphasized the large increase in operating costs that would result.

was created by volunteers, and it would be managed by volunteers. The Park Service would be only the top layer and would do only those things that volunteers could not legally perform. This accorded with Richie's personality — inclusive, compromising.

When acquiring land, Richie strongly favored easements in lieu of purchase. He wanted to retain the loyalty of the landowner who had given permission for volunteers to walk on his land, and easements were, he believed, much more to a landowner's liking. Further, the easement should pertain only to the part of the property on which the trail was, in order to be the least intrusive document possible.[10]

Going back to the 1968 legislation, he emphasized the need to keep the original character of the trail — its scenic, historic, natural, and cultural features. He attempted to harmonize the need to maximize the quality of the user experience with simplicity of design and ease of maintenance. Those were difficult characteristics to combine, and Richie, at that point inexperienced with the trail itself, did not actually understand how hard all that would be.

Finally, he wanted to emphasize the experience of the individual hiker. Large groups, commercial tours, or competitive events were not what Benton MacKaye and Myron Avery had been thinking.[11] It was the wilderness experience that counted, and Richie understood that at the outset.

An additional principle, articulated by Richie as early as 1976, was what one might call "connectivitis." That is, the trail had to be considered as a single, 2,000-mile trail, not as individual segments. That was what Myron Avery was advocating all along. Benton MacKaye did not consider it important and stated on more than one occasion that it was more important for the segments to be in wilderness — connecting the segments was not that important. Thus, in the end, the National Park Service adopted Avery's principle.[12]

Much discussion ensued about how much latitude volunteers would have. Richie felt that they should continue to maintain the

---

10. PATC archives, Box 21, ATPO Land Protection Plan 1983.
11. ATC archives, Zoebelein papers, Richie draft action plan, August 22, 1978.
12. "Policy Analysis: The Appalachian Trail in New York, East of the Hudson River," A.T. Project Office (ATPO), Boston, June 22, 1976.

In the mid-1980s (left to right): Dave Startzell, U.S. Rep. Beverly Byron (Md.), Dave Richie, Chuck Rinaldi, and Larry Van Meter.

existing trail and should be involved with any rerouting proposals. Landowner relations also should be the domain of volunteers, at least until proposals were made for land acquisition. Even then, the volunteer contacts with landowners would be the first step in the process. And, once a corridor was established, volunteers should monitor the corridor. Dave Sherman advocated for a philosophy of buying the corridor and then turning management of the trail back to the volunteers who had built it in the first place.[13]

Opinions about new trail-construction standards were divided four decades after Avery laid them down for the A.T. Richie initially favored uniform standards imposed by the federal government, the standards

13. Hunter Library, Sherman Collection, letter to Lautz and Richie, January 27, 1979.

adopted by the Forest Service. That would have imposed stringent grade-elevation standards and would have required switchbacks.

Others argued for a lack of uniformity. As a National Park Service official, Dave Sherman wrote, "Uniform trail construction standards for the footpath, bridges, latrines, signs, shelters, *etc.*, should be absolutely avoided…. Diversity…now exists because of the often extreme independence of the clubs as well as their individual members. Every effort should be made to assure that the large number of clubs continues to exist."[14]

How wide should the corridor be? In that was widespread agreement. The standard of an average 1,000-foot corridor recommended in the Pennsylvania State University study was accepted by all parties. The problem would be in the implementation of that standard on a 2,000-mile-long trail that had, up to that point, no standard at all except that which was in the federal legislation. That is, the Park Service could condemn up to an average of 125 acres per mile. Somehow that number got linked with the width of the corridor, so that the corridor would be at least 500 feet either side of the trail. Nowhere in the legislation was such a number mentioned, and Congress had not imposed any corridor width at all, except to say, "Where practicable, such rights-of-way shall include lands protected for it under agreements in effect as of the date of enactment of this Act, to which Federal agencies and States were parties." The 125-acre-per-mile restriction had nothing at all to do with corridor width, only with the authority to condemn. The Pennsylvania State standard of a 1,000-foot corridor was the first one to be published and accepted.

Imposing a post-Avery construction standard on a trail that was owned and managed by many different jurisdictions would be an impossible task. That was why one government (the federal government) had to be the sole manager.

Dave Field in Maine argued against what came years later to be called the "green tunnel." Diversity of experience was to be retained. Hiking through forest should be broken up occasionally by passage through valleys and farm lands. Volunteer groups should continue to

14. *Ibid.*

work with local communities to manage a diverse experience. It was a view widely held in 1979, partly because that was where the trail was routed in many places, and hikers enjoyed the experience. Richie did not disagree.

With Richie in the lead, the principle of volunteer control won out. The Appalachian Trail was an unique beast. It would be the world's first national park created and managed by volunteers. That was what made it special. It was a marvelous coincidence that it was to fall under a National Park Service manager whose character and temperament were so uniquely suited to that task.

Rinaldi

Charles (Chuck) Rinaldi was viewed by some as Dave Richie's polar opposite. Rinaldi was hired by NPS to buy the land that was required for this 1,000-foot corridor. After a long career in NPS, he had become head of all land acquisition, and any position of lesser importance would be a step down. But, through an interesting set of circumstances, that was what happened, in a manner of speaking.

Working at Cape Cod National Seashore,[15] he was transferred to Washington in 1966. There, in 1972, he had a heart attack, and his doctor advised him to retire. But, he was stubborn and continued on, steadily increasing his level of responsibility until, in 1978, the doctor again advised him to retire for health reasons. This time, he took the advice seriously and went to his boss, Phil Stewart, to discuss retirement.

Stewart knew that an A.T. land-acquisition office was being set up in Martinsburg, West Virginia, and that Rinaldi was originally from West Virginia. To Stewart and Rinaldi, taking on that office, at a lower level than he occupied at the time, would be an easier job with less responsibility, a good transition into full retirement. That is how Chuck Rinaldi, the no-nonsense, hard-driving federal officer, wound up heading what became the most complex land-buying program in Park Service history. Some retirement job!

---

15. According to Chris Brown, Rinaldi acquired the Cape Cod National Seashore, the first national park unit to be acquired through direct purchase rather than by state donation. Brown interview, March 24, 2014.

Originally, A.T. land acquisition was handled by three offices — in Martinsburg; Allentown, Pennsylvania; and in New Hampshire. Herbst was disenchanted with the performance of the other two and urged Rinaldi to assume responsibility for all three offices. That is just what Rinaldi did. He began to build a staff, given a good deal of latitude by Herbst to name the number of positions, and the specific individuals that he wanted for the jobs. Unlike other office chiefs, he did not have to accept just any bureaucrat who came his way. With Herbst's backing, Rinaldi picked his staff of around twenty-five and got to work.[16]

Cleo Layton, one of Herbst's assistants, visited with Rinaldi and probably had a lot to do with the decision to establish an oversight office. He also appears to have had a major impact on Rinaldi's authority to organize his office and recruit his staff members.[17]

Rinaldi was not a hiker. He did do some hiking in Maine after he took the job, even climbing a portion of the very strenuous Saddleback. But, he brought a wealth of previous experience to the task of acquiring property, and he had already developed his favorite method. That was what people called "three strikes and you're out," otherwise known as "take out the two-by-four."

That method was used after sufficient landowner contacts had been made to purchase a parcel of land, but the acquisition was stalled. He favored purchase over easements or other forms of acquisition and was not shy about condemning land if the landowners showed signs of reluctance to sell. He would approach a landowner up to three times, but, if he could not get agreement, he would condemn. Just the threat of condemnation usually brought a reluctant landowner around.[18]

Rinaldi had little experience, and no patience at all, with easements, and he had good reason:

The National Park Service has had extremely poor experience with easements. When the Blue Ridge Parkway and the Colonial National Park were authorized, there were a lot of easements required. Easements need to be managed. The person that you acquire

---

16. Interview by Ronald Brown with Charles Rinaldi, May 17, 2007.
17. Sherman e-mail, December 12, 2015, and interview, December 13, 2013.
18. Rinaldi interview (by author), November 7, 2014.

the easement from knows what the restrictions are. When they sell that land to someone else, they seem to forget about it. The next thing you know, you've got a house built on your easement area. And it is too late, you can't get it removed.[19]

The "take out the two-by-four" method clashed with Richie's softer approach and, to some extent, with the legislative history. In 1977, even before the passage of the 1978 legislation and any purchases, Richie advocated a hybrid approach to land acquisition, combining easements with purchases. By 1979, he was promoting easements over purchase. Easements come in many

Richie and Rinaldi on the Trail corridor.

different forms, but he felt that, whatever types were used, any easement was better than a purchase.

As hard-nosed as he was, Chuck Rinaldi, the consummate professional, could be emotionally engaged in the job. In 1985, he reported to Richie at the end of the year that his office had acquired more than 85 miles of corridor that year: "Think of it — 85.2 miles to walk upon."[20] It could have been Dave Richie speaking.

When Rinaldi began work, several states were still involved with corridor acquisition, but leaving even part of the acquisition program to the states held inherent contradictions. Each state corridor had to match up with those in the adjoining states, so this required a certain element of coordination, a requirement that was not in the statute. Management of those long, thin corridors could become a nightmare. As Dave Sherman once noted to Richie and Hank Lautz of ATC, "Frankly, I can't imagine why the states would want to keep

19. Rinaldi interview by Brown.
20. Hunter Library, Sherman Collection, Rinaldi report to Richie, October 15, 1985.

these narrow linear tracts once they have been acquired. It would appear that they would consider them a management liability."[21]

One could not assume that the trail through state land was adequately protected. No central standard for protection could be applied in all fourteen states. For instance, what if a municipal government should choose to sell land that it had conserved for a watershed? Eminent domain was not available. This happened in both Virginia and Maryland, where the A.T. ran through watershed lands that the local municipality later decided that it did not need. This, too, argued strongly for fee-simple ownership since eminent domain could not be used against municipalities.

How wide a corridor would the states acquire? Even Richie, very early indeed, became nervous about the corridor width. Although the accepted federal standard was an average of 1,000-foot corridor, each state could interpret the requirement differently. When Richie began thinking about an expanded federal involvement by 1977, he reasoned that perhaps a corridor protected by the federal government was not such a bad idea after all.[22] That was all part of Dave Richie's education.

The task ahead was indeed daunting. The Appalachian Trail was not some nice, round, fenced-in park with a clearly defined boundary. The task consisted of acquiring more than 2,500 parcels of land scattered across fourteen states, owned by literally hundreds of landowners with greatly varying degrees of sympathy for the federal government. The Park Service alone had to acquire a poorly defined corridor of varying widths along more than 600 miles of rugged mountain lands, sparsely settled, the ownership of which was often questionable. Land records and tax maps had to be acquired, and ownership had to be identified, sometimes the most difficult part of the process. Then the tracts had to be plotted on NPS "segment maps" that served as the basis for beginning negotiations.

Who believed that it could all be acquired in three years? Perhaps some of Richie's staff did, and evidently Bob Herbst did, too. Chuck

---

21. *Ibid*, Sherman to Lautz and Richie, January 27, 1979.
22. ATC archives, Zoebelein papers, Richie letter to "meeting participants," April 1, 1977.

Rinaldi was more realistic. He was in the business already and knew how difficult it would be. It is safe to say that no one, not even Rinaldi, realized that the last major tract of land, through the Celanese plant near Pearisburg, Virginia, would finally be acquired in 2015, thirty-seven years after the passage of the 1978 act and long after Rinaldi had taken a position in the Everglades.

Acquisition was a team sport — surveyors, cartographers, realty specialists, appraisers, lawyers, and, of course, volunteers. The process began with an identification of the location of the trail on private property. That involved a visit to the county courthouse to pull the land records. Sometimes this was done by volunteers — for instance, Ruth Blackburn did almost all the work in Maryland. More often, it was done by a member of Rinaldi's staff or by a contractor working for the A.T. Land Acquisition Office (ATLAO), often assisted by volunteers, who knew best exactly where the trail was and whose property it crossed.[23] The process was not foolproof, however, and sometimes both volunteers and ATLAO staff were surprised to find later that the trail was not in the place the volunteer thought it was.

Next, the tract had to be appraised, and that was done by a local land appraiser under an ATLAO contract. Once the appraisal was approved, it went to an ATLAO realty specialist, who would make the offer to the landowner. The hardest part was the negotiation with the landowner, who often would not accept the appraisal. Although the entire process could be completed in about eight weeks, the negotiations could drag on for years. ATLAO usually acquired only part of a tract, and the landowner would remain the closest neighbor. Having a hostile landowner close to the corridor boundary made no sense, and Rinaldi, the former "take out the two-by-four" advocate, was reluctant to condemn unless it was absolutely necessary.

The initial meeting with the landowner was intended to be as pleasant as possible. The threat of condemnation was almost never brought up. It became well-known that the Park Service had that au-

---

23. Interview with Donald T. King, Chuck Rinaldi's successor as chief of land acquisition, June 12, 2015.

thority, but that club was kept hidden. It was enough that the landowner was aware of the potential.[24]

A fee-simple purchase was used in more than eighty percent of the
cases, with some other form, usually an easement, used in other cases.
Condemnation was used over about ten percent of the acreage.[25] Not
paying more than the appraised value was the rule, and it placed some
restrictions on the negotiating process. When the landowner disagreed
with the appraised price, NPS went to condemnation so that both sides
could present their arguments in court and the judge could decide what
the fair price would be. Condemnation also allowed NPS to negotiate
without the fair-market-value rule it had to follow otherwise.

Condemnations were sometimes used simply to clear a title. The
ownership of many mountain properties was unclear, some dating to
the Civil War, and that would always technically involve condemnation and paying any heirs who were found. The opposite of this, the
most extreme form, was a declaration of taking. When no agreement
could be reached, the ATLAO might just go to the court with the money for the appraised value and file it, and the property would instantly
go to the government. Property owners sometimes opted for that form
of acquisition so that they could get their money immediately and not
have to wait months or years for the condemnation action to play out.

Having volunteers involved in a land-purchase program was not
the culture that Rinaldi was used to, and he resisted at first. But, Ruth
Blackburn was doing fine work in Maryland, and, with volunteers
like that, how could Rinaldi continue to hold them at arm's length?
Dave Startzell gave Ruth much credit for breaking down Rinaldi's
resistance to dealing with volunteers.[26]

Once a new corridor segment had come under federal government control, often a new trail section had to be selected to get the
trail off roads. That was a job for volunteers, and Elizabeth Levers,
the enthusiastic volunteer for the New York–New Jersey Trail Conference, described the process of selecting and laying out a new trail

24. Sherman e-mail, June 25, 2016; Brown interview with Rinaldi.
25. E-mail exchange with Donald T. King, December 3, 2020.
26. Startzell interview, February 21, 2014.

in order to get it off road shoulders. In the case of the A.T. east of the Hudson, the Park Service flew some volunteers in a helicopter over the segment, so that they could get some sense of the terrain. Then, the volunteers went out on the ground with flagging tape, walking back and forth over the ground. They would tentatively select a route and then would move the flagging tape as they slowly improved the trail route. [27] Said Jane Daniels, a key volunteer in the process, "You really have to go over that estimated route five or six or eight times, back and forth in both directions to be sure you've got everything in it that should be in it.... Oh, but it was wonderful fun!"[28]

Dave Richie carefully prioritized tracts to be acquired. An "A" tract was a right-of-way tract that the A.T. would cross, and it was critical and must be acquired no matter what, even by condemnation. A "B" tract would be part of the corridor but would not be crossed by the footpath. It was important, but condemnation was not to be used. A "C" tract was a nice-to-have, often to protect the viewshed. Those were usually referred to the Trust for Appalachian Trail Lands for acquisition.[29]

After clashing many times with Rinaldi over the approach to acquisition, Richie eventually came around to fee-simple purchase as the best way to acquire the corridor. As he retired from ATPO in 1987, he said, "I have come to recognize that acquiring easements to provide permanent protection for the Trail is undesirable. Adequate easements are almost as expensive as buying the 'fee,' which is land-acquisition jargon for full ownership.... My education on the process of protecting land could have been accelerated considerably if I had listened sooner and more carefully to Chuck Rinaldi, whose vision has been clearer than my own from the beginning."[30]

The process of acquiring the corridor yielded some unexpected judicial rulings. In one case, a volunteer convinced Rinaldi that a tract of land completely outside the corridor should be purchased to protect the environment. The family that owned the tract took the matter to court, contending that only Congress had the authority for

27. Glenn Scherer interview with Elizabeth Levers, 1993, in N.Y.–N.J. TC archives.
28. Jane Daniels e-mail to author, July 25, 2015.
29. ATC archives, Raymond F. Hunt papers, Richie letter to Van Meter, May 9, 1985.
30. Excerpts of a farewell speech by Richie at the ATC meeting, in *ATN*, July/August 1987, p. 14.

such an extensive reroute. The judge ruled that, as long as a tract fell within the published right of way of the mapping panels produced in 1971, it was not a "substantial" reroute within the meaning of the statute, even though it might amount to a lateral displacement of a mile or more.

David Sherman and the Optimal Location Review

In 1978, Ron Tipton, a future CEO of ATC (2013–2017), thru-hiked the trail at NPS request and on its dime and, by prior agreement, submitted his comments about the adequacy of the trail and its facilities to the NPS land-acquisition office. Although he was generally satisfied with the experience, it was not a glowing endorsement of the trail conditions.

In his report, he stated, "The lack of a stable route is a serious problem managers of the A.T. must deal with. Recent trail relocations and relocations of relocations are common along most of the Trail." Commenting on a relocation in the Sinking Creek area southwest of Roanoke, he complained that the relocation had been done because of landowner problems. "The new route...is rough, rocky, narrow, overgrown and was almost obliterated by spring blowdown of trees. It is easily the worst section of the entire Trail to hike."

Dave Sherman in 1980

He was aghast at the timbering activity in the section from Sherburne Pass in Vermont to Glencliff in New Hampshire, where one hiked through slash and across haul roads. Discussing the route on the north slope of Cube Mountain, he wrote that the property was owned by Meldrim Thomson, Jr., the governor of New Hampshire at the time. "When approached last fall about selling his property to the federal government in order to protect the Trail, the Governor not only refused, but ordered his property along the Trail to be clearcut!"

There were not enough blazes in Massachusetts, but, in other areas, volunteers had blazed just about every tree. There were long gaps in the shelter system, and the shelters in Shenandoah National Park were closed to overnight use at the time.

Despite the criticism of certain trail sections in his report, he was generally positive about the experience. Still, Sherman was conflicted about the upcoming acquisition program. It would be necessary to condemn some properties, because those landowners would never come to terms. He wondered how the government would do this without alienating the many friendly landowners who had permitted hikers across their land for decades.[31]

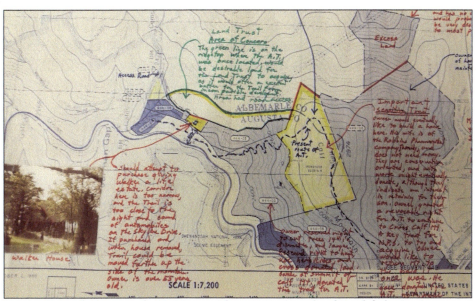

One of Sherman's 1984 corridor maps (north of Rockfish Gap).

31. Ron Tipton, "The Appalachian Trail: Ideas and Priorities for Land Acquisition," prepared for the Land Acquisition Division, NPS, October 13, 1978.

Now that the Park Service, in 1978, had the requirement to acquire the parts of the corridor that were on private land, it began thinking about what it was that they had to acquire. The only comprehensive survey of the trail location had been the aerial survey in 1971. That was where the trail had been at the time, but it was not necessarily where it *should* be. As the federal government (both Park Service and Forest Service) proceeded to purchase tracts, were they the *right* tracts? No one had ever done a comprehensive end-to-end survey of the corridor lands the Park Service was to acquire to answer that question.

That bothered Chuck Rinaldi a great deal, and, in late 1983, he asked the Park Service if it would be willing to loan Dave Sherman for six months to study the problem. Sherman, who was at the time working in the Washington, D.C., Park Service office, was the best choice for the job.

Born in 1943 in Columbus, Georgia, Sherman's education and experiences were in this home state. After college, he worked in banks but felt that he didn't want to spend the rest of his life indoors. In 1973, after having done extensive hiking, he began work with the Georgia Department of Natural Resources as the state coordinator for the Georgia Heritage Trust Program, the land-acquisition arm of the Department of Natural Resources under Governor Jimmy Carter. In 1975, he became the state historic preservation officer and finally the director of the office of planning and research.

In 1978, he moved to the federal level, becoming the special assistant for fish and wildlife and parks, working directly for Assistant Secretary Bob Herbst. From 1973 to 1983, he section-hiked the entire A.T., so he knew the trail from personal experience. Back in 1977, he had proposed the Benton MacKaye Trail, which branches off the Appalachian Trail near its southern terminus at Springer Mountain and continues on for 288 miles to Davenport Gap at the northeastern end of the Great Smokies.

For six months in 1984, Sherman studied the entire Appalachian Trail corridor from Katahdin to Damascus, a distance of approximately 1,688 trail miles. His office was in Martinsburg, West Virginia, with Rinaldi, but he spent most of those months in his car and on the trail. He visited all the tracts where he believed that additional acreage should be acquired. He met with local volunteers, usually in small groups, but, in the case of PATC, he met with the entire council. He discussed his findings with them, took photographs on site, and compiled the most detailed data on corridor conditions ever done.[32]

His maps, with photos and detailed analysis of the conditions, like the one shown on the next page, had never been matched before and only in the past decade have geographical information systems (GIS) technology and detailed on-the-ground analysis by clubs and ATC staff allowed a modern version.

Sherman had high standards. A partial list of things that concerned him included:

- Was there a high potential for development immediately adjacent to the existing trail? If houses were built, could they be seen from the trail?
- Was there a large enough land base for shelters at appropriate sites?
- If it was an easement, what were its terms, and did they need to be modified to protect the trail values?
- Was there the potential for ski slopes within site of the trail?
- If there was a vista, was the corridor wide enough to permit a side trail to it?
- Was more land needed to control off-road-vehicle use?
- Were the sources of springs protected?
- Was the trail too close to the corridor boundary?[33]

Opposition sometimes came from unexpected quarters. For instance, volunteers who had built the original trail, or who had been maintaining their trail section for years, often resisted rerouting the trail even to get it off steep, rocky sections. Sometimes a title search had not been done, and a trail section thought to be on corridor land was not, in fact, where it was thought to be. Sometimes a decision was required to change the trail route solely to conform with the rather vague

---

32. Sherman e-mail to the author, April 20, 2016.
33. Sherman, "Appalachian Trail Scenic Trail Corridor Review Project, unknown date {probably 1984}.

requirements of the 1968 act to "provide for maximum outdoor recreation potential and for the conservation and enjoyment of the *nationally significant scenic, historic, natural, or cultural qualities.*"[34] (Emphasis added.)

Sherman viewed landowners with a certain reserve. He wrote on the margins of one document, "The NPS should buy this land in fee so there will be no misunderstanding with the adjacent condominium owners who ultimately will want a view of the lake and will illegally cut trees on this easement to get it."[35] Later, Sherman wrote, based on his prior experiences with easement violations, "I have found that the human animal is never more creative than when it is to their economic advantage to figure out a way around the terms of an easement."[36] Like Rinaldi, Sherman favored acquisition in fee as the only truly safe way to protect the trail and the corridor.

Coming up with the money

Although Robert Herbst could proclaim the requirement to fund the corridor, only Congress could appropriate the money. That left a huge hole in the acquisition plan that depended on an uncertain political process. The Carter administration was friendly to the trail, and it had an initial Democratic majority in both the House and Senate. But, Carter lost the election in 1980, and, in January 1981, a new president, Ronald Reagan, took office, with decidedly different views on federal land acquisition.

The Herbst program started out in the hole. Although $90 million was authorized to fund the entire acquisition process (which was supposed to take only three years), Herbst got only about $7-$10 million appropriated the first two years, and that out of a supposedly friendly Democratic Congress and a Democratic administration. Yet, the news was not all bad. The fact was that it took Chuck Rinaldi almost three years to get a program organized, so that the National

34. Straight from the wording in the 1968 act, those were the scenic trail values as Congress defined them, and they have been used ever since to justify land acquisition.
35. Marginal note on a Sherman corridor map, 1984.
36. Hunter Library, Sherman Collection, Sherman to King, February 7, 1994.

Park Service could not possibly have spent the $90 million in three years anyway.

In early 1981, the Interior Department reported to Senator James A. McClure of Idaho, who had just become chairman of the Committee on Energy and Natural Resources, that NPS had so far protected 103.7 miles of trail. With just more than 400 NPS miles yet to acquire, the program was hardly off the ground. [37]

Aside from regular congressional appropriations, other potential ways to fund corridor acquisition were available at the beginning. The secretary of the interior had a contingency reserve fund, and five percent of the federal side of the Land and Water Conservation Fund (LWCF) could be used at the secretary's discretion. According to Steve Golden, the first corridor purchase was funded through that source.[38]

Other friendly sources were The Nature Conservancy (TNC), the Conservation Fund, the Trust for Public Land, and other nonprofit organizations. Beginning in the mid-1980s, they sometimes purchased corridor lands and held them in trust awaiting federal funding. TNC selected the Appalachian Trail as a high priority and stepped in many times to save corridor land, the acquisition of which had not yet been funded by Congress.[39]

Dave Sherman was concerned about escalating land values and noted to Herbst that the initial assumption that an acre would cost $800, on average, would soon be obsolete.[40] In the 1970s, the price of forest land in the mountains had run between $250 and $550 per acre. By the early 1980s, the average cost had crept up to more than $1,000 per acre. Second-home development was one of the main factors pushing up price.

The road ahead was daunting, and the political winds were blowing against the program. With Ronald Reagan came a Republican Congress, much less inclined to support federal land purchases. As if this news were not bad enough, Reagan's first secretary of the interior was James G. Watt.

---

37. Hunter Library, Sherman Collection, Herbst to McClure, January 26, 1981.
38. Interview with Golden and Sherman, May 20, 2014.
39. *Op. cit.*, "Policy Analysis: The Appalachian Trail in New York, East of the Hudson River."
40. Hunter Library, Sherman Collection, Sherman to Herbst, February 7, 1979.

Watt, who came from Wyoming and had been deputy assistant secretary of water and power development and director of the Bureau of Outdoor Recreation during the Nixon administration (see chapter 8), was one of the most polarizing figures in the history of the Department of the Interior. A known antienvironmentalist as founder of the Mountain State Legal Foundation, he favored not protection, but exploitation, of federal lands by mining and timber interests. One of his first official acts was to impose a moratorium on federal land purchases nationwide.

Secretary James Watt, no land-acquisition fan, came around and presented the prestigious Conservation Service Award to ATC Chair Ruth Blackburn in 1983. Startzell received it many years later, as had Benton MacKaye decades earlier.

David N. Startzell, who seemed to be the most politically attuned ATC staffer, alerted Ruth Blackburn, the chair of ATC, that Watt was very conservative and would probably not favor the purchase of A.T. lands.[41]

Yet Appalachian Trail funding did *not* disappear. All through the 1980s, it continued at a sustainable level, generally between $6 million and $10 million per year. In some years, A.T. corridor land purchases were the only federal land purchases in the entire country! The genius behind this remarkable development was Startzell (see chapter 11).

---

41. ATC archives, box 11-4-1, Hunt papers, Startzell to Blackburn, January 8, 1981.

The Contestants

Startzell knew that the trail ran through fourteen states. Each state had two senators, so, if he could get both senators in each of the fourteen states on board, he would have twenty-eight favorable votes out of a total of one hundred senators, more than one out of four. It was that group that he targeted and enlisted volunteers from the trail clubs to assist him in his effort to secure the votes.

ATC developed an information packet that volunteers could use to brief their own Congress members' staffs. In dealing with the House, it would include some potential purchases in the district, with some iconic photos to capture attention. After testimony in committees, ATC would send representatives and senators copies of the testimony and suggest they sign on to a bipartisan "Dear Colleague" letter supporting funding.[42]

Behind the scenes, a process for coming up with a required amount was developed. All the players would get together prior to the development of the federal budget for the coming year and decide on a total dollar amount to support. Each club would lobby for its own interests but would also support the total dollar amount to staffers on the Hill, so that there was no daylight among the clubs. When the White House would cut the agency-proposed budget to be submitted to Congress, ATC and the clubs would make sure that committee staffers had the internal numbers that were being requested for the Appalachian Trail.[43]

Every year, like clockwork, the Reagan administration would request very minimal appropriations from LWCF, and, every year, like clockwork, Congress would vote to approve the funds requested by ATC to purchase the corridor lands. In 1983, NPS Director William Penn Mott told ANSTAC, "The A.T. has the largest institutionalized lobby in the Senate — the Administration isn't going to fight

42. Startzell interview.
43. Sherman e-mail, April 28, 2016.

From left, Bob Jacobsen, Dave Richie, Dalton Du-Lac of the USFS, and ATC Regional Representative Mike Dawson on a site visit in September 1982.

a program that has the support of 28 senators."[44]

The lobbying effort had to be co-ordinated with Rinaldi's acquisition program. In some cases, ATC was given the opportunity to lobby for specific tracts, but, because of the complex land-acquisition process that Rinaldi's staff was going through, it was not always possible to pin down when specific tracts would be ready for purchase. That made lobbying more difficult, because Startzell could not always go to a specific lawmaker and promise that a certain tract was on the list. Rinaldi had to have the flexibility to acquire lands according to how the acquisition process was playing out.[45] So, throughout the acquisition process, there was always a certain amount of ambiguity, and flexibility was a requirement.

In 1985, Mott was able to report that just more than half of the 643 miles of the trail that the Park Service was committed to protect had been acquired. So far, 55,000 acres had been acquired, on 1,288 tracts of

44. Memorandum for the record by Bill Hutchinson, PATC president, April 24, 1983. The number was actually 26 — Jesse Helms of North Carolina and Harry Byrd, Jr., of Virginia never supported the acquisition program.
45. Interview with Startzell, Underhill, Sherman, and Wade, January 23, 2015.

land.[46] The land-acquisition program was working, and long stretches of the trail were being protected.

In the "race" to buy the corridor, the Forest Service got off to a much faster start than the Park Service. Viewing the 1968 legislation as a much-needed justification for buying inholdings, the Forest Service launched an aggressive land-acquisition program. The leadership at the time favored buying whole tracts rather than narrow strips. As a result, by 1988, they had protected 99 percent of the trail through forest lands.[47]

Some Park Service entities understood the new relationship with the volunteers, but some did not. Great Smoky Mountains National Park superintendents, for instance, persisted in managing without regard to volunteers, and closure of shelters was haphazard.

In Shenandoah National Park (SNP), Superintendent Bob Jacobsen simply did not believe that volunteers could maintain the trail or the facilities along the trail. First, he closed all shelters, and, when they were finally reopened, it was only with a new hut-keeper system. Users were being asked to pay $1 per visit per hut to help fund the hut-keeper system. Ed Garvey was so fed up with the relationship that he wrote to Jacobsen's supervisor, "I am now convinced that further discussion, at our level, with Bob Jacobsen is useless."[48]

When the A.T. Project Office (ATPO) purchased the trail corridor from the southern end of the park to Rockfish Gap, a distance of 8.5 trail miles, Jacobsen tried to take possession of it for his park staff, using the theory that giving it to PATC meant failure to maintain the trail section. Karen Wade in ATPO (later to become superintendent of a number of much larger national parks) informed Jacobsen that the territory in question belonged to her agency, not SNP.[49] In truth, that was an internal NPS territorial squabble — the land belonged to the United States.

---

46. ATC archives, Chuck Sloan files, address by Mott, August 3, 1985, at the ATC meeting in Vermont.
47. *ATN*, May/June 1989, p. 11, article by Dave Startzell.
48. PATC archives, Box 3, Garvey to Dick Stanton, April 9, 1979.
49. Sherman e-mail, January 31, 2016.

The Land Trust Movement

When the Reagan administration zeroed out land-acquisition funding in 1981, ATC needed a contingency plan, in case the administration's edict stuck. The organization commissioned Les Brewer and Chris Brown to study private funding. That led to a report to ATC in April 1982 recommending that the organization create a "land trust." The concept was so new that most people did not know what it was.

The Trust for A.T. Lands was created to act in a manner similar to The Nature Conservancy. It would look for lands that should be added to the corridor either for trail or environmental protection. The trust raised private funds, and, like TNC before it, often sold the lands it acquired back to the government.

Many were skeptical — private funding could never replace federal acquisition. In that, they were right, but the new "organization" — really a program of ATC, not a separate entity — became a significant player in the game, supplementing federal funding and buying and holding tracts that the government did not yet have the appropriated funds to acquire, selling later.

Ruth Blackburn chaired the new trust, and John Farrell became the first trust administrator. The advisory committee included Charles (Chuck) Sloan, who later assumed leadership for almost twenty years. It became a significant player, acquiring in total more than 39,000 acres through 1997. A Wintergreen resorts property along the trail in central Virginia was its first participation in a major acquisition (see page 485).[50]

Trust Land Acquisitions	
Year	Acres
1982	137
1983	3,426
1984	2,284
1985	125
1986	736
1987	693
1988	614
1989	2,062
1990	670
1991	644
1992	895
1993	988
1994	1,856
1995	85
1996	1,056
1997	21,192

50. Startzell, "The Long Journey of Dave Richie, 1932-2002," in *ATN*, March/April 2003; Sherman interview, December 9, 2013; *ATN*, July/August 1982, p. 20; interview with Chuck

The Volunteers

Chuck Sloan, as a board member and volunteer counsel for ATC, wrote in 1986 of the 1984 delegation of responsibility for the Appalachian Trail to volunteers (see below), "This delegation is widely believed to constitute the largest transfer of governmental authority to a private organization in recent history." It was indeed, probably in the entire scope of American history. It made it unnecessary for the Park Service to staff up a large office and, in the first year alone, was estimated to have saved the Park Service well more than a million dollars.

ATC at first got an annual subsidy of $300,000, but that was less than two-thirds of what ATC spent annually, and it raised the rest on its own. Dave Richie believed this to be one of the great bargains for the federal government.[51] The system worked, largely because of Richie's personality. Chuck Rinaldi, not one to necessarily get on the volunteer bandwagon, commented, "If you would have had your typical Smoky the Bear park superintendent in there, you had an entirely different outcome."[52]

Not everyone was happy at first. The influential Maryland/Pennsylvania volunteer Thurston Griggs, for instance, viewed Park Service intervention with considerable suspicion. To him, these professionals would foul up a system that was already working without them. On the other side were the park superintendents. And, they had a point. To a park superintendent or forest ranger, it seemed unimaginable that an unpaid volunteer could take over aspects of their job and do as well. What the volunteer had going for him or her, though, was passion. They had been there at the creation, and to them it was not just a job.

It was messy, especially at first. Not all the maintaining clubs were as large and well-trained as the Appalachian Mountain Club, Green Mountain Club, PATC, or New York–New Jersey Trail Conference. Karen Wade, for instance, complained that clubs in southwest Virginia were doing a poor job of maintenance and seemed to lack

---

Sloan, May 19, 2014; *ATN*, May/June 1983, p. 5; *Potomac Appalachian*, September 1982, p. 8.
51. ATC archives, Sloan article, July 1986, "Park Management by Volunteers: A History of Private Initiative on the Appalachian Trail."
52. Rinaldi interview with the author.

the capacity to fulfill their responsibilities. Her response was to recommend that ATC pour money and people into a training program.
Training, indeed, became the long-term solution to those problems,
and ATC became at least partly a volunteer-training organization.
Training occupied an ever-increasing portion of ATC staff time.

Occasional complaints came from many sides on the early performance of volunteers in the land-acquisition process. One unusually stark
complaint came from a landowner on Hosner Mountain in eastern New
York. Volunteers tore down a shed that was on her property (but close
to the trail), and the resulting pile of boards was not removed until she
hired a lawyer.[53] Such mistakes were probably inevitable, given the number of volunteers involved, and it was a good thing that a mediator like
Richie was running the show. And, as Rinaldi said, what choice did you
have? The volunteers knew the trail and the landowners.

The maintaining clubs sometimes got into disputes with each other,
and ATC was often called on to mediate. PATC, for instance, engaged
in jurisdictional disputes with the Mountain Club of Maryland and
the Old Dominion Appalachian Trail Club about which club would
be maintaining which trail sections. PATC, perhaps because Myron
Avery had pioneered its entire section (and much else beyond it), was
quite territorial and resisted attempts by anyone to interfere with what
they regarded as its territory (Pine Grove Furnace to Rockfish Gap).[54]

The Delegation Agreement

Once it was clear that the federal government was going to hand
over management of a national park property to volunteers, it was
obvious that there had to be a rule book. The eventual rule book was
to be called the "delegation agreement."

The first step was a comprehensive plan, which was required by
the 1978 legislation. Dave Richie wrote a broad plan that laid out general principles, something that Richie was exceptionally good at. The
task of writing a detailed comprehensive plan fell to Chris Brown

---

53. ATC archives, Hunt papers, correspondence in 1983 between Eileen Silver and ATC.
54. *Ibid*, undated memo from Bob Proudman..

of ATPO. Brown's plan placed volunteers at the center. According to Dave Startzell, "The notion that private organizations, consisting mostly of volunteers, were capable of developing management plans that would guide not only their own actions, but also those of federal and state agency partners on public lands, was truly radical at the time."[55] It was this 1981 document, signed by the secretaries of the interior and agriculture, that first officially enshrined the principle of volunteer leadership in the enterprise.[56]

A controversial aspect of the "comp plan" was that the 1978 legislation had not specifically named ATC, let alone any of the maintaining clubs. It had mentioned "private organizations," without any specific references.

The delegation agreement, publicly signed in 1984, described what could, specifically, be delegated to volunteers and what authorities had to reserve to the federal government. The rule book was written in March 1983 by Pete Raynor in his role as the assistant solicitor for parks and recreation in the Interior Department. Raynor named five things that the Park Service could not legally delegate:[57]

- Law enforcement.
- Title to lands. The Park Service would always own the land that was acquired for the trail.
- The authority to relocate the trail right-of-way. (NPS could delegate to ATC the authority to change the route within the existing right-of-way, which was generally within the corridor maps prepared in 1971.)
- Land acquisition (as distinct from land title).
- "Use of proceeds." All proceeds (*i.e.*, profits) resulting from management of the trail must be returned to the U.S. Treasury.

With those five exceptions — as well as compliance with the National Environmental Policy Act and similar statutes — the delegation

---

55. Startzell, *op. cit.*, "The Long Journey of Dave Richie, 1932-2002."
56. Interview with Chris Brown, March 24, 2014.
57. Memorandum from Raynor to ATPO, March 17, 1983.

After the public signing of the delegation agreement: left to right, ATC Executive Director Larry Van Meter, ATC Chair Raymond Hunt, Interior Secretary William Clark, and ANSTAC Chairman Arthur Brownell of International Paper.

agreement, which during a later renewal became a cooperative agreement under Office of Management and Budget regulations, basically handed over the responsibility to manage a national park to a nonprofit organization consisting of a paid staff of ten and more than thirty maintaining clubs consisting of thousands of volunteers. Nothing like it had ever been done — had even been contemplated — before 1978.

ATC lawyer Chuck Sloan drafted the initial agreement, working closely with Raynor. The final agreement was signed on January 26, 1984, by Raymond F. Hunt, chairman of the ATC, and Russell Dickenson, the National Park Service director, with Secretary of the Interior William P. Clark as a witness, on the mezzanine of the American Institute of Architects, publisher of Benton MacKaye's 1921 proposal for an Appalachian Trail.

The agreement, so significant to subsequent history, actually covered only 250 miles of the Appalachian Trail, the portion that was owned by NPS outside the boundaries of existing parks. Thus, it did not cover Shenandoah National Park, Great Smoky Mountains National Park, and other smaller park units. Nor did it cover Forest Service lands and those lands through state and local jurisdictions. To say that it was the *principle* that counted would be an understatement.

The Forest Service was not a problem. The relationship between ATC and the Forest Service was worked out in a series of memoranda applying the principles of the delegation agreement to USFS lands.[58]

The Blue Ridge Parkway was more problematic and moved very slowly. Getting an agreement with the parkway involved years of entangled negotiations. A draft agreement was exchanged between Larry Van Meter, ATC executive director, and previous NPS Director Gary Everhardt, who had become the parkway superintendent, in 1984. Yet four years later, the draft was still in limbo, and, according to ATC staff member Bob Proudman, "The current ATPO draft agreement, when contrasted with BRP's draft, obviously indicates that A.T. direction and policy — to Gary and his staff — represent some kind of threat that overlooks what they consider their fundamental interest to control park activities and resources."[59] What seemed to be bugging Everhardt and his staff was that some of the maintaining clubs in the area did not have a very good relationship with the parkway staff, and Hunt advised to go slow and try to work through the problems. The document finally was signed in March 1989. Modeled after the NPS–ATC delegation agreement, it assigned most maintenance responsibility to ATC, with a provision to subdelegate to the clubs.

Subdelegation to the clubs occurred on October 22, 1984, when an ATC letter went out, simultaneously to every club, assigning each one responsibility for a specific trail section. That was followed by a meeting with club representatives in Harpers Ferry in April 1985. The clubs had created the trail — the federal government now owned the trail — and the government was giving it back to them to manage and main-

---

58. ATC archives, Hunt correspondence in 1983 and 1984.
59. ATC archives, Hunt papers, Proudman memo to Rinaldi, August 19, 1988.

tain, as if nothing had ever changed. But now, people were looking over their shoulders, just to make sure that it was being done right.[60]

Clubs needed guidance, and the matter was already being discussed as early as 1978, when ATC established a trail standards committee. Much discussion ensued about how the trail was to be built and maintained, and Bob Proudman and Ed Garvey were prominent in the deliberations. Subsequently, ATC issued a manual, *Trail Design, Construction and Maintenance*, by William Birchard and Proudman, in 1981. Not unlike a similarly titled AMC book, it was the first comprehensive and authoritative trail maintenance manual for the Appalachian Trail since Avery's death.

Buying Land

In the beginning, ATPO was committed to working cooperatively with the states, and every state was different.

Corridor width was a bone of contention. New England clubs, having created many of their trails before Benton MacKaye proposed the Appalachian Trail, felt that their corridor width, dating back decades, had served perfectly well, and they didn't need to expand it to 1,000 feet.

The various states had their own programs, with greatly divergent ideas about how much land to protect. So, when ATLAO began acquiring land, it was a different process in all fourteen states. Four states — Maine, Massachusetts, New Jersey, and Maryland — decided to do their own protection program and claimed that they didn't need federal help.

In Maine, all but twenty-one miles of the trail had achieved "protected" status, mostly through zoning by the Land Use Regulation Commission (LURC). New Jersey was working through its Green Acres program, but the Green Acres program, owing principally to development pressures in northern New Jersey, acquired a corridor that was much too narrow for Sherman and NPS (and even drifted into New York). In many cases, Rinaldi had to go back to purchase tracts to widen the corridor.

---

60. *Ibid*, Proudman memo to Hunt and Van Meter, October 16, 1984, and Van Meter letter to clubs, March 19, 1985. Another set of MOUs was sent out during David Field's chairmanship of ATC and a new round was being prepared as this book went to publication.

Bob Proudman

In 1984, the master trail-builder on the East Coast was Bob Proudman. Bob was from Connecticut and had begun his hiking there, around Bear Mountain (the Connecticut version, not to be confused with Bear Mountain in New York). In 1964, he hiked half of the Long Trail in Vermont, and, after that, he met Tom Deans, the AMC executive director, in the AMC library on Joy Street in Boston. Deans encouraged Proudman to join an AMC trail crew. Bob joined the trail crew, which at the time was centered at Pinkham Notch in New Hampshire. He immediately got hooked on trail construction.[1] Fortunately for ATC, Proudman eventually joined the staff at Harpers Ferry after a stint at ATPO under Dave Richie and brought his trail-building skills south. He set the standard for trail construction for ATC and was a coauthor of *Appalachian Trail Design, Construction, and Maintenance*, first published in 1981, with a second edition in 2000, a follow-up to an AMC book with a similar title. It became the bible for volunteers who worked on the trail.

1. Interview with Bob Proudman, June 20, 2014.

Maryland already had committed to acquire the entire forty miles in that state, but the process had never gotten off the ground. In New Hampshire and Vermont, much of the A.T. was in state forests, and the process of acquiring inholdings was well along. In Massachusetts, acquisition was divided between NPS and the Department of Environmental Protection.

Virginia was the most complex situation — the state was acquiring part of the corridor and relying on NPS to acquire the rest, but the sheer length of the trail in that state (more than five hundred miles) meant a complex and drawn-out process involving both state and federal acquisitions. South of Virginia, most of the trail was on Forest Service land, which simplified the process.

In the valleys, the trail was often through agricultural lands, and ATPO wanted to keep it in its historic locations. How this would match up with Chuck Rinaldi's program of acquisition in fee was the question.

When the federal government purchased an entire tract, they wrote a special-use permit that allowed the farmer to continue farming even while the government now owned the land. In other cases, easements were written that permitted the trail to cross private property.

In some of the important valleys, ATPO hoped to preserve the view of rolling countryside from the hills. In Massachusetts, the valley views around Great Barrington and Tyringham were preserved as hikers descended from Jug End and The Cobble, and farmers continued to farm the fields as hikers walked along the edges. In Connecticut, ATPO preserved the fields around Rand's View. A concentration of agricultural leases in New Jersey between High Point and the Wallkill River followed suit.[61]

According to Dave Barr, an ATC board member from Pennsylvania at the time, the initial meeting with farmers tended to have government officials and volunteer trail maintainers on one side of the room and a coterie of grumpy farmers on the other. But, even in the Cumberland Valley (see page 475), the two sides eventually were able to work toward an accommodation. The feds brought scientific farming with them and insisted that farmers rotate crops and use the latest fertilizers and pest-control methods, so farmers got better yields. The long-term result of that new relationship between farmers and the government was a grudging acceptance and a working relationship that still characterizes many areas of the trail.[62] For hikers, it kept the trail in its original location and offered an often welcome change from the "green tunnel."

Local governments owned parts of the trail corridor, and Rinaldi distrusted the relationship. He felt that they often would not understand or appreciate the trail values that his office was trying to protect. He especially feared that they would sell watershed lands. A 1984 amendment to the federal legislation gave the ATLAO the authority to purchase lands from local governments. Long-running negotiations with Roanoke, Virginia; Hagerstown, Maryland; Hanover, New Hampshire; and Loudoun County, Virginia, eventually resulted in acquisition in fee in order to guarantee permanent protection.[63]

61. Sherman e-mail, February 25 2015. In 1990, the 5,100-acre Wallkill River National Wildlife Refuge was established, and two miles of the A.T. cross through it now.
62. Deborah Smith interview with Dave Barr, June 6, 2006.
63. For Roanoke, see ATC archives, Avery correspondence. Also, Sherman interview, De-

In 1979, Assistant Secretary Bob Herbst directed Dave Richie to "please begin immediate negotiations for a footbridge across Maryland's Potomac River utilizing the existing B&O trestle." This project required a great deal of muscle, because railroad companies always opposed pedestrian traffic near their rights-of-way, citing potential liability concerns. The bridge opened in December 1985 (see page 145), from Harpers Ferry National Historical Park on the West Virginia side to the Chesapeake and Ohio National Historical Park on the Maryland side. Congress at the time of the dedication legislatively named the walkway after U.S. Representative Goodloe Byron of Maryland, a longtime A.T. supporter and primary sponsor of the 1978 A.T. amendments to the National Trails System Act, who had died of a heart attack at the age of 49 in October 1978 while jogging on the C&O Canal towpath. The walkway itself was significantly damaged and closed just before Christmas 2019 by a freight-train derailment and not reopened until the following July Fourth.

Rep. Byron and his family on Weverton Cliffs. His wife, Beverly, would succeed him in office; his son, "Geb," would later serve on the ATC board.

463

Throughout the process, uncertain land titles bedeviled the AT-LAO staff. They would spend hours at county courthouses, trying to sort out land titles that sometimes went back to the Revolutionary War. West of the Mississippi River, following the Louisiana Purchase, the federal government had laid out the land in 640-acre sections, but east of the river, the system used was called metes and bounds, which could be any shape. Sometimes the land would be described as "walk 120 paces from the large oak tree at the corner of the lot, then turn left and walk 60 paces to the beech tree." (Would the oak or beech tree still be alive 200 years later?) Land titles described in that way had to be resurveyed, which introduced additional time and expense into the process. Some mountain tracts had no owner listed who could be found alive. In those cases, condemnation was the only way to proceed, and many of the condemnations were to resolve land titles so that the land could be purchased. Maryland turned out to be an especially difficult case, because so many land titles were unresolved. Ruth Blackburn played a large role in researching those titles so that ATLAO didn't have to.[64]

Some acquisitions could be quixotic. Tom Speaks, the supervisor for the Cherokee National Forest and later the George Washington/Jefferson National Forest, tells the story of approaching landowners on a ridgeline south of Pearisburg, Virginia. The Forest Service needed to purchase the trail corridor along a three-mile ridge, and the land was owned by about twenty-three or twenty-four landowners whose properties began along a road in the valley west of the ridge and went up to the top. All he needed was the very top, and he began approaching landowners to get their agreement. Every one of them turned him down, but some of them mentioned one particular owner who was well-respected, and it appeared that some of the owners might follow his example.

So, Tom drove to the man's house and found him baling hay in a field. Tom had grown up on a farm and knew how to bale, so he pitched in. After a while, the owner asked Tom why he was there. That led eventually to a meeting in the living room, and the man

cember 13, 2013; Hunter Library, Sherman Collection, Box 11-3-2, Partnership Committee meeting, August 15, 1984. Hanover was one of the most difficult negotiations, and the process required eight years to complete.
64. Interview with Donald King, June 12, 2015.

agreed to sell the top of his property to the Forest Service. After that, all but one owner agreed to sell. (Speaks had to condemn one tract.)[65]

When all was said and done in 1978, a "first purchase" by NPS still was needed. ATPO wanted publicity, and Steve Golden figured that a purchase near New York City would attract reporters from *The New York Times*. So, for that purchase, they arranged a public event, with speakers and reporters, on the Harry Beinert tract on Hosner Mountain, east of the Hudson River. The great day was set for January 29, 1979. But, the day before, Steve got a call from Chuck Rinaldi. The understanding of the actual trail location was so flawed that it turned out that the trail was not actually on the land that had been purchased. Steve called the New York–New Jersey Trail Conference,

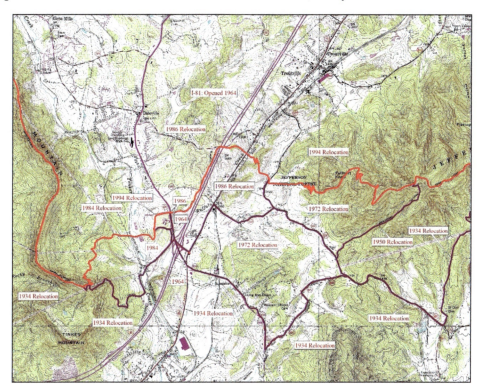

A myriad of relocations around the busy interchange for I-81 at Daleville, Virginia, over the decades.

65. Interview with Tom Speaks, March 4, 2014.

and, early the next morning, volunteers were out rerouting the trail onto the Beinert land. When the speeches began just after noon, a new trail section was in place.[66]

Despite the linearity of the A.T., in some areas it was anything but linear, and reroutes tended to be placed on top of reroutes, as the situation on the ground changed. A good example of the complexity was the A.T. crossing of Interstate 81 at Daleville, Virginia. The map on the next page resembles nothing so much as a pile of spaghetti.

In acquiring almost 2,000 individual tracts over a period of years, the National Park Service got involved in some controversial negotiations, but, in the vast majority of cases, the process was amicable, if somewhat puzzling for the landowner. (What was all this fuss about a hiking trail, and why did the federal government insist on routing it through their property?) That so few of the negotiations resulted in unfriendly condemnation was a credit to both the federal negotiators and the landowners who gave up a portion of their land for a recreational trail that few of them really cared about.

The story had many heroes.

Leading them were the soft-spoken Dave Richie, a cerebral Quaker more inclined toward compromise to get things done, and the determined Chuck Rinaldi, the National Park Service's top land buyer. That two people with so different personalities could end up working cooperatively together was a credit to both men.

Their supporting cast included Karen Wade, Pam Underhill, and many others who sometimes risked their personal safety in the process of acquiring the tracts needed to fill out the corridor. Also in the pack was Dave Startzell, the resident genius at getting the money from Congress. And last, but not least, was Dave Sherman, who bounced between Forest Service and Park Service positions but was always in the picture, working to ensure that the trail was in the best location possible.

---

66. Interview with Golden and Sherman, April 2, 2014. See also *ATN*, Mach/April 1979, p. 17.

Inside the Appalachian Trail Conference (Early 1980s)

In the late 1970s, a crucial time in the history of the Appalachian Trail, firm leadership was needed in Harpers Ferry, but ATC was ineffectively led. The chaotic period lasted for only a relatively short time, and, since the trailwork was really done by the maintaining clubs, it had no permanent effect. Still, ATC had to settle itself internally before it could become an effective participant.

Fortunately, ATC found safe harbor in both chair and executive-director positions. For the chair, Charlie Pugh was succeeded by Ruth Blackburn, and Hank Lautz was succeeded by Larry Van Meter. They both calmed the waters and charted ATC toward its present-day structure and influence.

Arguably, no ATC chair since Avery was more popular than Ruth Blackburn. Originally, she came into the trail enterprise through her husband, Fred. She became known first as the researcher who found all the tract maps for the Appalachian Trail from northern Virginia through Maryland. Her almost three-year term, November 1980–June 1983, was during the tumultuous early days of the corridor-acquisition project, and her testimony to Congress to

ATC's Harpers Ferry Headquarters

Fred and Ruth Blackburn on a work trip.

obtain funding was so effective that James Watt, who annually refused to voluntarily purchase property for the federal government, acknowledged her effectiveness in defeating him every year. In 1983, Watt gave her a Conservation Service Award, the department's highest civilian recognition (see page 450). The citation read, in part, "She has been the single most influential volunteer in shaping the successful National Park Service trail protection program."

She was trusted implicitly by the Park Service. That trust played a role in convincing the leadership to turn over trail management to volunteers.[1] It was said by many that it was impossible not to like Ruth Blackburn.

Larry Van Meter came to ATC through the Green Mountain Club. Like Dave Richie, he came from a Quaker background and attended Moorestown Friends School in New Jersey. He was an enthusiastic hiker and, in the early 1970s, became a lodge keeper in the Green Mountain Club program. In 1975, he was hired as the first executive director for GMC. And, in late 1981, the ATC board hired Van Meter — a board member at the time — as its fourth executive director after the departure of Hank Lautz.

His mission was to professionalize the staff, increase salaries, and stabilize an organization that had been in turmoil. As with Ruth Blackburn, it was hard not to like Larry Van Meter, and his pleasing personality helped to reduce friction within the board of managers.

---

1. *ATN*, July/August 2000, Judy Jenner article, p. 35.

On the day he arrived in Harpers Ferry as a staff member in 1981, he announced that he would be leaving in five years, and he departed, right on schedule, in 1986.[2]

When Ruth's term as chair ended in 1983, Raymond F. Hunt succeeded her. He was a native of Pennsylvania and had graduated from Yale in chemical engineering. He had taken a job with Tennessee Eastman in Kingsport, Tennessee, as had Stan Murray. Hunt continued Ruth Blackburn's push as a peacemaker and consensus-builder. He, too, appeared often before Congress to advocate for trail funding.[3]

In 1978, ATC began opening its first field offices. That was a big departure for an organization that had been geographically moored to Harpers Ferry, and it was also a stretch financially. But, it made sense, because the trail was more than 2,000 miles long, and ATC needed to connect with local clubs, front-line agency officials, and local communities. Initially, three offices were established — north, central, and south.

The first field person hired was Rima Farmer. A forty-six-year-old with a master's degree in planning, she had known Dave Startzell when they were both studying at the University of Tennessee in Knoxville. Recently divorced, she had nothing else on her plate and grabbed the job in July 1978.

The next two regional representatives were Doug Blaze, who took the office in Allentown, Pennsylvania, and Roger Sternberg, in New England. Rima's territory (Springer Mountain to Damascus) was far too large, and, in 1980, Mike Dawson was hired to take an office in southwest Virginia.

The objective was to colocate regional offices with partner organizations, and ATC eventually achieved this in all cases but the mid-Atlantic, although that has changed in this decade. In the very early days, regional offices were wherever there was space. Rima Farmer's first office was her own kitchen in Norris, Tennessee. Sternberg opened his first humble office above a movie theater

2. Foster, *op. cit.*, pp. 87-88. However, most of this information on Van Meter came from interviews: Van Meter himself (June 13, 2014), Ron Tipton (November 8, 2013), and Mike Dawson (February 4, 2016).
3. *ATN*, July/August 2000, Judy Jenner article.

in downtown Hanover, New Hampshire. In those early days, ATC regional representatives grabbed whatever cheap loft was available, and the constant shifting of locations took on the aspect of a floating crap game.

ATC had always been viewed as some far-off entity in Harpers Ferry, a place few volunteers had ever visited and knew nothing about. But, when regional offices opened, all of a sudden ATC was in their backyard. It was sure to be viewed as an infringement on the independence of the maintaining clubs, and those offices were viewed with great suspicion by many of the volunteers. "We're just here to help" did not sell at first. Rima, as the only woman, had a particularly difficult job convincing hardened male volunteers that she had anything at all to contribute.

Basically, the same story unfolded in all the regions. The regional representatives began showing up at club meetings. Then, they began calling their own meetings, which often became training sessions. They began holding trail-construction workshops, and the volunteers found that these ATC staff members knew how to build trails. They introduced new, and more effective, construction techniques that produced more sustainable trails and fewer steep inclines and handled many of the training and education demands. Bob Proudman from the Appalachian Mountain Club (and then the ATC board and then ATPO before joining the staff) became the principal teacher of trail building after 1981 and spread the New England construction techniques up and down the Atlantic Seaboard. In a few years, the regional representatives held a respected place and were relied on to assist.[4]

Regional representatives also began establishing trail crews that would help the clubs. The first to be established, Konnarock, in 1983, in Sugar Grove, Virginia, proved to be the most active. In addition to training and education, the regional representatives spent a lot of their time on land-acquisition scouting and courting. In that, they relied partly on volunteers who knew the private landowners who hosted sections of the trail.

4. Interviews with Rima Farmer (October 3, 2016), Mike Dawson (February 4, 2016), and Roger Sternberg (by telephone, June 20, 2016). Rima also provided a copy of her first letter to the southern clubs, January 2, 1979.

Chapter 10

SPECIAL CASES

The process of acquiring the Appalachian Trail corridor took forty-seven years after the 1968 National Trails System Act, far longer than anyone had envisioned. Most acquisitions were pain-free, but some involved resistant landowners, fierce arguments, court proceedings, and condemnations. A few are emblematic of the bumpy road forward.

Tyringham

The trail in the area of Tyringham, Massachusetts, and Upper Goose Pond was a good example of how trail values were preserved. When Dave Sherman hiked through Massachusetts in 1984, he commented on the area around Tyringham:

> *Proper location of the footpath through Tyringham is one of the important corridor designs yet to be decided on.... Massachusetts and the Berkshires have beauty, but it is largely unseen by the hiker.... Tyringham has it all and is a high point of hiking in this state. It is one of only a few places on the A.T. where a visitor's ideal vision of a New England farming community is met. The view one gets from the Cobble of the pastoral landscape and church steeple of the small community is a signal to the hiker that one has definitely reached New England.*[1]

---

1. Sherman A.T. corridor maps, 1984, map 246.

The trail in 1984 passed Upper Goose Pond, just south of Tyringham, but barely touched one end, and the hiker could easily pass by without seeing this iconic lake.

As the acquisition process moved forward, three landowners in the Tyringham area opposed the trail and took the Park Service to court. The town itself opposed the acquisition, arguing that it would take property off its tax rolls.[2] Two years later, ATPO secured a favorable court judgment, an event that, according to Rinaldi, "will have a positive impact on Trail protection issues up and down the Appalachian Trail."[3] The courts took very literally the provision of the National Trails System Act of 1968 that the "significant  scenic, historic, natural or cultural qualities" were to be preserved and permitted the National Park Service great latitude in deciding if the trail sections in question were important to retain those values.

The Tyringham matter was not put to rest finally until 1990. Upper Goose Pond already had been acquired, in cooperation with the state of Massachusetts in 1980,[4] and the trail was rerouted to follow the lake bank for almost half a mile, one of the most delightful stretches of trail on the East Coast.

Working with Massachusetts was an uneven process. The state was jealous of its prerogatives, and, as ATPO became more insistent on directly acquiring the corridor, the state officials became more touchy, according to then-ATC Regional Representative Roger Sternberg.[5]

2. ATC archives, Hunt papers, article in the *Berkshire Eagle*, April 27, 1984.
3. Hunter Library, Sherman Collection, Rinaldi report to Richie, October 8, 1987. ???? Richie retired in June 1987.
4. *Ibid*, Rinaldi report, October 10, 1980.
5. Sternberg interview, June 20, 2016.

Nuclear Lake

Few properties on the East Coast seem more pristine than Nuclear Lake, but a more poorly chosen name could hardly have been devised.

Originally called Pawling Lake because of its proximity to Pawling, New York, the lake was actually an artificial body of water that became a lake when a swamp was dammed up. When Chuck Rinaldi took over the ATLAO office, Bob Herbst named three sites that he especially wanted Rinaldi to acquire, one of which was this lake. He expected that the trail would be placed in close proximity.

The property had acquired its daunting name because it had been used once to test nuclear-reactor fuel rods but had been long since abandoned and was up for sale. So Rinaldi purchased the lake site from the owner, United Nuclear Corporation, a subsidiary of Gulf General Atomic, without an environmental assessment.

With such a history, volunteers approached this property with some trepidation. The New York–New Jersey Trail Conference formed a Nuclear Lake management committee to make recommendations regarding its use as a trail route. A site-clearance subcommittee began meeting. In 1983, New York state notified the National Park Service that the property was on its list of suspected hazardous-waste sites, and Nuclear Energy Services Company began radiological testing. The company inspected and surveyed the abandoned structures on the site, including a building where the plutonium testing had been conducted. A Nuclear Regulatory Commission contractor, Oak Ridge Associated Universities, surveyed a "hot spot" at the waste storage building and removed the contaminants. After that, the Trail Conference recommended that the property be opened to hikers but with warning signs to prevent entry to the remainder of the property (the plant and lake area) until final tests had been performed. In 1986, NPS agreed to open the trail through the site.

But then the matter hit *The New York Times* and generated a firestorm of controversy. An article in *Outside* magazine (which did not have a reputation for the most careful journalism) reproduced local rumors of an explosion at the facility in 1977 where the company was testing nuclear-reactor fuel rods. Another rumor began circulating that the company had loaded its contaminated materials into fifty-five-gallon drums, loaded them onto a barge, floated them to the middle of the lake, and sank them by firing at them with rifles. This rumor appeared to have some validity when ground-penetrating radar located something that might have been a drum or drums.

So the Park Service organized a thorough assessment of the buildings. They did find low-level radiation in a few places and set to work fixing the problem. NPS brought in machines that ground up concrete floors in the waste-disposal building, put the material in two freezer-chest-sized radioactive-material containers, and shipped them to South Carolina for disposal. Finally, they drained the lake to see if they could find those drums. All they found was a Jeep that had fallen through the ice years earlier and had never been recovered. No drums of radioactive material were found. However, the

dam was rated as nearly collapsing, so it was replaced, and the lake again filled with water.

The Trail Conference had waited until all testing was done before certifying the trail along the lake as safe to walk, and, for those who might have been nervous about walking that route, a blue-blazed trail skirted the edge of the property, well away from the lake. In 1994, the lake and environs were pronounced clean.[6]

Nuclear Lake was a matter of some embarrassment to the Park Service, but only on the public-relations front. When all the testing was finished, and everyone involved had had their say, banging the nuclear drum simply made a hollow sound.

Cumberland Valley

The route of the Appalachian Trail through Cumberland Valley in Pennsylvania has been judged by many to have been the single most controversial acquisition of the entire process. In the 1970s, the existing route was still a road walk of more than twelve miles, ten of which were on a paved road, blazed by Avery and Schairer in 1930. At the time, few houses were in the valley, and it was just one of many long roadwalks down the shoulders of rural roads with little traffic.

By 1976, the road route had become suburbanized, a long walk along heavily traveled roads chock-a-block with houses, stores, and farms, and the trail clubs involved began discussing where the trail should be moved. Three potential routes were identified, including the existing road route, a railroad route (along an abandoned rail line), and the so-called ridge route. The latter followed Ironstone Ridge, a geologic volcanic dike through which lava had welled up. That last option would involve purchasing many tracts of land from valley farmers. Farmers could do nothing with lava, so it provided a narrow strip of unfarmed land and, to NPS and ATC, was the best

6. "Nuclear Lake Property Chronology," a document supplied by Ron Rosen of N.Y.–N.J. TC; interview with Ron Rosen and James Haggett, June 4, 2014; Rinaldi interview; Sherman and Golden interview; ATC archives, Hunt papers; *Outside* article, October 1986, p. 14; *ATN*, March/April 1994, p. 5; Sherman interview, December 9, 2014.

route of the three. The trail followed the ridge from Blue Mountain south to a place just north of Pa. 641, where it branched off to the east. (See map.)

Volunteer Thurston Griggs explored a fourth route that was never actually considered. It was the historical trail route along Blue Mountain to Colonel Denning State Park, then across the valley through Newville, and on south to Pine Grove Furnace. Referred to as the Newville route, it was judged unacceptable because it actually crossed more private property than any of the other three. It was virtually identical to the proposed A.T. route mapped out by Eugene Bingham in 1927. (See chapter 3.)

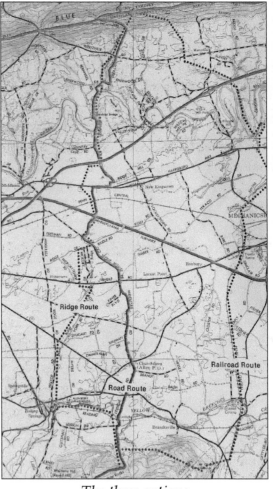

The three options

A first meeting involved NPS, Griggs' Mountain Club of Maryland (the club that was responsible for trail maintenance through the valley), PATC, the Susquehanna Appalachian Trail Club, state forests and game lands officials, and other interested groups. The group recommended the ridge route, which was already being used in part. Dave Richie commissioned Thurston to contact landowners and begin the process of acquiring a route along Ironstone Ridge.

The meetings did not go well. The first landowners that Thurston sat down with were on Deer Lane, a gravel road just south of Blue

Mountain in the northern part of the valley. To his surprise, he found a very upset group of landowners — they wanted to know what authority Griggs had to take their land and promised to take him to court.

The reception in the southern part of the valley was even worse. Landowners had all heard rumors that the Park Service was going to condemn their land and were up in arms. Some threatened to shoot him on sight. One fellow told Thurston that he would go home in a box.

The opponents organized, the first being the small group that lived on Deer Lane. Their first public statement referred to the "trickery and lies plus harassment from a representative of the U.S. Park Service for such a ridiculous cause." Hikers were stereotyped as a small minority who would litter and represented a security threat. (According to Thurston, most of them were giving up farming and hoped to sell their land to developers.[7]) Thurston hotly defended his approach, but, back in Harpers Ferry, his initiative came to be regarded as a mistake. The approach had alarmed landowners and farmers unnecessarily and could have been handled more tactfully. Larry Van Meter commented, "Bless his heart, Thurston created a total mess."[8] Looking back on it, though, the initial approach sounded logical on the surface, and it was hard for Richie and Griggs to anticipate the firestorm that resulted. Hindsight was far better than foresight.

Other groups sprang up like mushrooms. An immediate problem was a group called CANT (Citizens Against the New Trail) that went to township supervisors and convinced them to oppose a route — any route — across the valley. They were joined in 1979 by Charles Cushman, a gadfly heading the American Land Rights Association who would bedevil A.T. acquisition for more than two decades. (President Reagan appointed him to the National Parks Advisory Committee in 1983.) Despite claiming to be neutral, his group opposed almost anything the Park Service wanted to do, and Cushman joined forces with

---

7. Thurston Griggs, "Cumberland Valley: Location for a National Foot-Trail." (Maurice Forrester files.)
8. Interview with Larry Van Meter, June 13, 2014. Van Meter's daily logs reflect an ongoing preoccupation with the Cumberland Valley.

CANT.[9] The opponents organized first and, supported by the township, held the high ground.

Richie urged the volunteers to get organized, and a protrail group consisting of the various trail groups in the area coalesced around Carol Witzman, president of the Susquehanna A.T. Club, with Craig Dunn as the most active participant and real leader. It also included Dave Barr, Warren Hoffman from Pennsylvania Audubon, and Karen Lutz. Gradually, the protrail group became a significant player and acted as a check on the obstructionist tactics of the antitrail groups. Local meetings became better balanced, and discussion slowly became more rational.[10]

In the early 1980s, however, hostility was palpable, and meetings sometimes turned into shouting matches. A committee was organized to find a solution, and, although it brought the two sides together, it achieved nothing and eventually disbanded. The matter seemed to be at a standstill.[11]

In 1984, the Park Service tried again, discussing the three options with local authorities and landowners, and did an environmental assessment of the proposed routes. Then, quite unexpectedly, in 1985, a decision was rendered.

President Reagan's new director of the National Park Service was William Penn Mott. A California Quaker by birth, he was already in his early 80s when he took the job. One of the most controversial matters on his plate was Cumberland Valley. Without telling anyone, he drove to Pennsylvania, inspected the various routes, walked them himself, and drove back to Washington. On November 26, 1985, Mott announced that the National Park Service had selected the ridge route.[12]

And, just like that, the matter was resolved. Some of the hardliners in the valley never came over to an accommodation, but, with the decision finally rendered, the controversy seemed to die. Trail clubs built those sections of the ridge route that were not yet constructed.

9. CANT and Cushman's role in the controversy can be found in many sources. See, for instance, the Carlisle *Evening Sentinel*, March 2, 1979; ATC archives, Zoebelein papers, Blaze and Wade letter, July 27, 1979; and Foster, *op. cit.*, pp. 71-72.
10. Interview with Craig Dunn by Deborah Smith, unknown date.
11. *Ibid.*
12. ATC archives, NPS letter in Cumberland Valley file; *ATN*, March/April 1986, p. 6.

Craig Dunn emerged as the leader for the trail in the Cumberland Valley, where he was a respected banker. Born in the Panama Canal Zone, his dad was a golf pro, so the family moved around quite a bit. They eventually settled in Pennsylvania, and Craig went to high school in Philadelphia and then graduated from Dickinson College with a major in history and economics. After college, he got a job in a bank and stayed in banking for his professional career. He joined the Susquehanna A.T. Club  in 1976, became a trail maintainer, and began helping Griggs with his early research on the valley route. Dunn had a calming influence on everyone, and, when people began yelling at each other during meetings, he was the one who always kept his head. Later, as a member of the ATC board, he served for years as chair of the Trust for A.T. Lands Advisory Committee.

The Park Service arranged pacts with willing farmers who wanted to continue to farm, often on lease-back arrangements. And, in still-later years, Cumberland County became a big supporter of the Appalachian Trail, viewing it as the most significant recreational resource in the county. It was a classic example of a trail turning trail haters into trail lovers — or at least not hostile.

Farther north in Pennsylvania, the Reverend and Mrs. Charles Evans owned property on Blue Mountain and proposed to build a house where the trail had a fine viewpoint. Reverend Evans took it upon himself to reroute the trail away from his building site, and, when negotiations hit a dead end, he called in CANT for support. Evans brought in politicians, including Senators Ted Stevens of Alaska and Richard Schweiker of Pennsylvania and local U.S. representatives. Rinaldi, unafraid of political pressure and convinced that the Evanses were negotiating in bad faith, invoked condemnation, the first such instance since the 1978 legislation.[13]

Northern Virginia

Northern Virginia had been the flash point in 1968. An impetus for the trails act had been to a considerable degree the situation along the fifty-seven miles of the A.T. from Harpers Ferry to Shenandoah National Park. It was hardly a surprise, then, that the National Park Service put considerable emphasis on that part of the corridor after 1978.

PATC members knew the territory and became some of the first volunteers on the ground to contact landowners. In addition, the club was fairly wealthy by ATC standards, and, through concentrated fund-raising, it had secured enough money to begin buying tracts of land that it knew would fall in the corridor. In 1980, PATC purchased a large tract along the corridor that had a substantial house on it, and the club named it after Fred and Ruth Blackburn. This became the Blackburn Trail Center, open to the public and a destination for hikers in northern Virginia.

Tom Floyd, then supervisor of trails, used his own resources to buy tracts that he knew were directly in the planned corridor. John Oliphant and his brothers similarly began acquiring tracts that were on corridor maps. PATC, Floyd, and Oliphant held their tracts in trust for later NPS acquisition. In the matter of corridor protection, PATC was the most active club on the trail.

Most negotiations were successful, if somewhat tense on occasion. A few holdouts were encountered. The most recalcitrant was one Reed Thomas, who held property just south of U.S. 50 (Ashby Gap) and refused to sell. NPS acquired property to route the trail around to the west of the Thomas tract but held out hope that the A.T. eventually could be moved to the east because of the magnificent views to be had from the pastureland on the Thomas property.[14]

---

13. *Ibid,* ATC archives, Cumberland Valley files: Golden memo, May 31, 1978, and Richie memo, September 10, 1978; interview with Sherman, December 2013; Rinaldi interview, December 7, 2014; ATC archives, Zoebelein papers, Richie letter to Evans, July 2, 1979.

14. It was not finally acquired by NPS until 2003. Records for the acquisition of property in northern Virginia by PATC are held in Vienna, Va.

Bears Den

The acquisitions in Northern Virginia were not concluded, however, without a major controversy inside PATC. The issue was a tract south of Va. 7 that was to become a flashpoint — Bears Den.

The 620-acre property that was astride the trail had been owned by an ophthalmologist and his wife, Huron and Francesca Lawson, who had built a faux Tudor mansion reminiscent of estates that they had seen in their travels through Europe. The Lawsons died in the 1960s, and the tract of land was purchased by a family-owned development company, the Assateague Island Realty Corporation. The Rodenbergs (who owned the development company) planned to develop the land with many houses on small lots, with a central community center and swimming pool. That would prevent the A.T. from entering the planned forest route at its northern end. The developer barred hikers from the tract.

Things didn't work out for the Rodenbergs. Clarke County turned down their proposal for the development because of septic issues and disapproved of the proposed swimming pool. Realizing that the development was not going to be profitable without the permits, they put the entire tract on the market for $1 million.

The tract was needed badly for trail protection, and every indication was that it would slip away to become the site of vacation homes. The National Park Service and Appalachian Trail Conference went to the Potomac Appalachian Trail Club, and, in 1981, Bill Hutchinson, the PATC president, appointed a special committee headed by Agriculture Department lawyer Jim Snow to deal with the problem.

The Rodenbergs owned all 620 acres, stretching from Va. 601 down the west side of the ridge, almost to the Shenandoah River. An adjacent landowner purchased 360 acres near the river, but that still left 260 acres near the ridgetop. NPS was only interested in a narrow corridor to protect the A.T., and the lodge built by the Lawsons was not part of the deal. That left about 66 acres at risk.

The ensuing debates within the council tore PATC apart. One faction, favored by President Jack Reeder, did not want PATC to get

involved with the property
— the club had no capability
to manage such a tract, they
claimed, and not enough
money to do so. A second
group, led by Chuck Sloan
and Ruth Blackburn, argued
that this tract was inherently
a PATC responsibility. After
much argument, the final
council vote was to purchase
the property with the house
on it and offer it to ATC at

the same price. If ATC refused, PATC would sell it to another (unspecified) owner. With that gun to its head, ATC, which was also reluctant to get involved in property management, agreed to purchase
and manage it. PATC sold the property in June 1984, and ATC in turn
had the NPS encumber it with enough easements and buy it in parts,
enough to cover the cost. The new, completed route of the Appalachian Trail from Harpers Ferry to the northern boundary of Shenandoah National Park was dedicated in July 1985.

The controversy did not completely subside within PATC. Jack
Reeder lost the next election, and the club lost much of its reputation in Harpers Ferry.[15] The issue with ATC was not just the palpable
dissension within the club. The problem was that it forced ATC into
a land-management role, something that the organization opposed
and was unprepared to assume. ATC's mission was to manage the
trail, not manage property along the trail.

Other Virginia Flare-ups

The trail crossing of Interstate 81 at Daleville, Virginia, just north
of Roanoke, produced another precedent-setting decision. The area was

---

15. PATC archives contain thick files on the controversy. The dispute was noted in Larry
Van Meter's daily logs.

becoming heavily developed (see page 465), and the county contended that, since it was making local plans for development, it should decide just where the trail route should be. Karen Wade of NPS asserted that the National Park Service had precedence over local jurisdictions in the matter of trail routing. Wade recruited local volunteers to show the county planner, Martha Williams, where the trail was and to discuss alternative routes.

Eight years later, the county once again protested NPS acquisitions because the purchases were taking tracts off the tax rolls. Botetourt County officials called their member of Congress and the Chamber of Commerce, to no avail. The National Trails System Act gave NPS the decision-making power, and local judges chose to interpret the legislation in favor of the federal government.[16]

Other acquisitions underlined the authority of the National Park Service to decide the trail route, regardless of local opposition. Several Virginia towns protested the trail as being within their watersheds, to no avail. (In fact, NPS preferred to buy those properties owned by local governments, fearing that they would eventually sell them for development. Dave Sherman's distrust of elected politicians influenced those decisions.) A local development company in Warren County opposed acquisition of its land but was overridden. South of Shenandoah National Park, before NPS acquisition began and states were still in a lead role, the Royal Orchard Land Corporation wanted to negotiate an easement between Rockfish and McCormick gaps back in the mid-1970s, but Stan Murray wrote to Virginia's Ben Bolen, "The relocation for the Appalachian Trail proposed by the Royal Orchards Land Corporation…is inferior to the existing route. To accept this relocation would be contrary to the general relocation policy of the Conference, that the relocation not be inferior to the existing route."[17]

Tempers could get hot. In one incident, Pam Underhill from ATPO was visiting a family outside Ceres, in southern Virginia, that ada-

16. Appalachian Trail Land Acquisition Office files, Martinsburg, W.Va.: Wade memo to Rima Farmer, Larry Henson, and Chuck Rinaldi, May 14, 1979; Don King letter to John B. Williamson of Botetourt County, April 15, 1987.
17. ATC archives, Dunning papers, various letters. See especially Murray to Bolen, April 12, 1974.

mantly opposed the trail, and, when she returned to her car, someone had loosened the lug nuts. (Fortunately, she discovered it before the car crashed.)[18] Incidents like this were not unknown in the lives of ATPO officials and led to a certain sense of caution in approaching rural families.

Yet opposition could turn into support on a dime. When hiking through that same area a few years later, Dave Sherman and Ron Tipton encountered one of the greatest outpourings of support they had ever seen. Sherman wrote later, "Word had gotten around that hikers were there, and we had groups taking us to the store for supplies 5 miles away, installing electric lights in the shelter for our use, bringing us firewood, the largest bowl of popcorn I have ever seen, sharing with us their wedding pictures, offering to carry gallon jugs of water by truck 18 miles north and leaving them for us along a dirt road the next day."[19]

McAfee Knob

West of Roanoke was Catawba Mountain, with the iconic McAfee Knob (arguably the most photographed spot on the Appalachian Trail) and Tinker Cliffs, another famous viewpoint. The mountain was in private ownership, and the trail was pushed over to North Mountain

in 1978 because not all the landowners would agree to the trail. So, when ATPO became involved, the A.T. was on North Mountain, avoiding Catawba and bypassing McAfee and Tinker.

In the early 1980s, ATPO began contacting the landowners to

18. Underhill interview.
19. Hunter Library, Sherman Collection, letter to Laura Waterman, June 28, 1985.

discuss fee acquisition of a trail corridor. Donald T. King, longtime leader of the A.T. Land Acquisition Office who did much of the negotiating for this twenty-two-mile stretch, reported that most landowners were friendly, and the Reverend and Mrs. Clyde Carter enthusiastically donated their land to protect the trail on Tinker Ridge. But, atop Catawba itself, from which the knob protrudes off the footpath itself, ATPO found just confusing land titles, a situation that dated back to the time of postcolonial Governor Patrick Henry, when warrants were provided to two different owners. Negotiations for this land began in 1979 and were not successfully concluded until 1987, when owner Harry Johnson agreed to an out-of-court settlement.[20]

Wintergreen

Wintergreen was a planned vacation and ski development about ten miles south of Rockfish Gap in Virginia. It lay astride the route of the A.T. and, at 2,733 acres, was one of the largest private developments that ATPO had to contend with. Eight miles of the A.T. ran through the property. It included Humpback Rocks, another iconic viewpoint on the A.T.

The developer, future U.S. Representative Lewis F. Payne, began to develop the property above the Blue Ridge Parkway in 1976. He was not unfriendly to the trail and permitted the route to continue through his development, but part of it was actually on streets with houses on both sides, not the environment envisioned in the National Trails System Act. It was clear that an accommodation had to be negotiated with Payne, so, in 1981, negotiators sat down with him to see what could be worked out. For reasons of his own, Payne was anxious to move forward with an agreement and agreed to sell a tract of land for the trail for $2 million, a bargain sale about $400,000 below the appraised value.

The National Park Service was required to offer the appraised price, so ATC agreed to step in and become an intermediate pur-

---

20. Edward B. Garvey, *The New Appalachian Trail* (Birmingham, Ala., Menasha Ridge Press, 1997), p. 278; interview with Don King, June 12, 2015; Carter donation discussed in *ATN*, July/August 1982, p. 20; Hunter Library, Sherman Collection, Rinaldi to Richie, January 14, 1987. The Carters had purchased their tract without knowing that the trail was on it, but, when they found out, they fully supported federal protection over their land.

chaser, employing the fledgling Trust for Appalachian Trail Lands as the buyer. But, NPS funds were not sufficient for a purchase at the time, so three Virginia congressmen — Senator John Warner and Representatives Dan Daniel and Kenneth Robinson — got a $10-million appropriation for the trail in 1983, including a specific earmark for the Wintergreen purchase.[21]

Wintergreen was an example of a relatively friendly acquisition, although the local maintaining club, the Old Dominion A.T. Club, was no fan of Wintergreen in the early years of the development. Payne did not object to the trail and intended all along to negotiate a sale below market. The deal was negotiated with Larry Van Meter of ATC and Pat Noonan, former president of The Nature Conservancy.

As rerouted, the new trail was a five-mile section that completely bypassed Wintergreen on the west. The new route was no longer on subdivision streets and had one nice view on Cedar Cliffs Overlook. (But, when hikers swung north along the A.T., the ski trails on Wintergreen were clearly visible, an unfortunate blot along the scenic trail.)

New York

In 1976, the longest series of road walks on the Appalachian Trail was in New York, east of the Hudson River. Of the sixty-two miles, thirty-nine were on road shoulders. The situation was getting worse, as the New York suburbs were quickly expanding north along the east side of the Hudson. Development was rampant, and landowners were putting up no-trespassing signs.

Two counties comprised the land from the Hudson to the Connecticut border. On the west, Putnam was one of the fastest-growing counties in the country. Opposition to any trail at all sprang up in 1979. Residents formed the Hudson Highlands Taxpayers Association and began lobbying local government entities to deny trail access to their properties. Public meetings were held, where residents voiced opposition to the trail. To the east, Dutchess County was slower to or-

---

21. *ATN*, July/August 1983.

ganize, and community meetings were more civil. Still, the potential for organized opposition was significant.[22]

Once an eastbound hiker left Anthony's Nose, no public land for the trail was available until Clarence Fahnestock State Park. The original land, a donation of about 2,400 acres, was donated in 1929 by Dr. Ernest Fahnestock as a memorial to his brother Clarence.[23] But, houses blocked the southwest entrance to the park, and the trail remained on roads for several miles before getting access to park land. New York state had made plans to allocate money for the trail corridor, but, as of 1976, no money had appeared.[24]

East of Fahnestock and south of the Taconic State Parkway was Hosner Mountain. Homes clustered on the top of the ridgeline, and it was there that the trail met its most determined opposition. The trail was forced onto roads in the valley paralleling the ridge.

In Dutchess County, then-ATC Regional Representative Bob Leone began organizing community meetings to discuss the trail route. He also set up advisory committees, where various options could be examined. If they did not like what NPS was proposing, what route did they favor? Actually talking about the options for the trail seemed to calm things — people began thinking about alternatives, and, in many cases, they didn't sound all that bad. Leone's decision to hold meetings began to turn the tide in Dutchess County and proved to be the antidote to organized community opposition.[25] By 1982, Leone was able to report that the remaining problems in Putnam County also had been resolved, and only three properties remained to be acquired to complete a ten-mile relocation to get the A.T. off roads.[26]

Another factor in success east of the Hudson was the inimitable Elizabeth Levers, who had been the first woman to lead the New York–New Jersey Trail Conference (see page 418). This diminutive woman met with an estimated 150 landowners and sometimes jawboned

---

22. Hunter Library, Sherman Collection, summary of the situation, July 22, 1979.
23. Source: Wikipedia.
24. "Policy Analysis: The Appalachian Trail in New York, East of the Hudson River," *op. cit.*; *ATN*, March/April 1990, pp. 10-13.
25. Glenn Scherer interview of Elizabeth Levers, 1993, in N.Y.–N.J. TC archives.
26. ATC archives, Ruth Blackburn papers, Leone memo to the board of managers, August 16, 1982.

many into doing what their instincts told them not to do. Bob Proudman once described Elizabeth: "She was just very pushy. She would get right in your face and treat you like a 14-year-old truant. She was very effective; she loved the trail."[27] Elizabeth began her trail-building effort in 1980, and it continued into the 1990s. Calling herself the "Coordinator of the Appalachian Trail in New York State," she seemed to be everywhere at once: Canopus Hill, Depot Hill, Stormville Mountain, Hosner Mountain.[28]

In January 1981, Levers wrote a summary of a landowner visit:

> *Ted[29] and I visited the family in the evening. Mrs. Worgull is 90, very deaf and with cataracts in both eyes, but has nothing wrong with her mind — very sharp and with a good sense of humor. Francis Oakley was out jogging — we waited an hour beyond our 8-8:30 appointment time. He was very argumentative, and evidently was mixed up in his thinking, in insisting on a new deed for the property she will keep — not necessary or required. About 9:30 his wife arrived....and after a few minutes of very pertinent questions she took him outside. In a few minutes she came back in and told her mother, Mrs. Worgull, to sign the right of entry form for both surveying and assessment.[30]*

One imagines many such encounters on the way to a secured corridor.

One landowner controversy in New York became a high-profile relocation. Near the Connecticut border, Dr. Joyce Brothers, a noted television personality at the time, owned a home in the path of the trail. At the time, the trail was on a road in front of her house. When she got the letter from NPS suggesting a reroute off the road, she started calling the director of NPS almost daily, and, when officials visited her in her Manhattan apartment, she became very emotional and started crying. She threatened to discuss her "ill treatment" on her nationally syndi-

---

27. Interview with Bob Proudman, June 20, 2014.
28. Notebook of New York work trips, donated by Ron Rosen.
29. "Ted" is unidentified.
30. ATC archives, Levers papers.

cated television show. NPS officials were afraid that she would start crying on the show, something that she had done on a previous show, and they backed down. NPS moved the trail farther from her house, to what proved to be a better and more remote location.[31]

Connecticut

The New York–Connecticut border region, a favored area for the wealthy away from the city, seemed to breed notable opponents. S. Dillon Ripley, the retired secretary of the Smithsonian Institution, insisted that the trail not go near his house, and it was moved accordingly in order to not agitate a prominent opponent. A local landowner group was organized under one Jim Gollin to oppose the Park Service acquisition process, if not the acquisitions themselves. A wealthy absentee landowner, William Ray (he owned a luxury resort south of San Francisco), held out to the bitter end, claiming that the Park Service trespassed on his land. (Ken Lutters, the New York park official working the problem, acknowledged that volunteers had marked a proposed route on his land but stated that this was permitted by the statute in order to assess potential trail routes.) Ray's lawyer was informed that the roadwalk was incompatible with the legislation authorizing the trail.[32]

Connecticut was home to the largest and most expensive single land acquisition up to 1985. The Stanley Works tool company had owned a long stretch of the east bank of the Housatonic River since 1910. The company had planned to build a hydroelectric plant to power its New Britain plant, but it was never needed, and the land remained undeveloped for decades. Convinced that it would never need it, Stanley was willing to sell the land but argued about the price, contending that what NPS was offering was below market. Such claims were often made at the outset, but sometimes proved to be just an initial bargaining position. After negotiations failed in

---

31. Brown interview; Sherman e-mail, 2015; interview with Ron Rosen and James Daggett, June 4, 2014.
32. Hunter Library, Sherman Collection, Rinaldi report, October 14, 1982; Sherman e-mail, July 7, 2016; ATC archives, Levers papers, Gollin and Ray, and the *Lakeville Journal*, January 11, 1979. See also Garvey, *op. cit.*, p. 279.

1979, the company suggested that the Park Service buy the entire tract and eventually agreed to a price of $3.1 million for 1,276 acres of prime land along the river in eastern Connecticut. The purchase provided five miles of flat walking along a scenic river, one of the most agreeable stretches of trail in any state.[33]

Connecticut was a state that provided little direct assistance to the Park Service in securing the corridor, but, on the plus side, it did provide the Park Service with free rein to negotiate a trail corridor of adequate width.

Vermont

Vermont, being the state that already had its own version of a "long trail," kept its distance from the A.T. Vermont Yankees viewed themselves as part of a separate country and were determined to keep to themselves when it came to hiking, as in just about everything else.

When the Appalachian Trail was being created, the Green Mountain Club was already well-organized. In the early 1970s, GMC began a program of hiring caretakers for its huts in order to combat a rising problem of trash on the trails from the back-to-nature movement. By 1975, it had hired twenty-five caretakers for the summer months. That same year, the club hired its first executive director, Larry Van Meter. Larry had been the caretaker at Montclair Glen and later served as a part-time ranger-naturalist on Camel's Hump for the Vermont Forest and Parks Department.[34]

In the beginning, Vermont had little interest in being part of the Appalachian Trail. GMC opposed designation of any part of the Long Trail, and, in 1975, Governor Thomas P. Salmon wrote to Secretary of the Interior Rogers Morton requesting that the Long Trail and the Appalachian Trail not be coaligned.[35] No record of an answer from

---

33. *ATN*, July/August 1985; Hunter Library, Sherman Collection, Rinaldi report for March 1985; Van Meter daily logs, October 2, 1984, and July 26, 1983.
34. Vermont State archives, Box 241/8, *Long Trail News*, August 1971, May 1975, and November 1975.
35. *Ibid, Long Trail News*, August 1975.

the secretary could be found, and the National Park Service paid no attention to the request.

When Van Meter took over, he immediately hired Preston Bristow for GMC, a recent college graduate. Two years later, Preston chanced to meet Steve Golden of ATPO while attending congressional hearings. Golden needed someone to identify property owners in Vermont, part of the NPS program to protect the A.T. There were questions as to exactly where the A.T. was and whose land it was on, which involved time-consuming visits to county offices to pull tax maps. In Vermont, all those records were maintained at the township level, were difficult to access, and hard to copy. (Some town employees viewed Preston's effort with suspicion and refused to give him any help.) He concentrated on the thirty-mile section from Sherburne Pass to the New Hampshire border, in order to connect GMC territory with the Dartmouth Outing Club section (at the time, from Vt. 12 to Hanover and on to Mount Moosilauke).[36]

The process of acquiring the corridor was agonizing at first. Each acquisition had to be taken to a town hall meeting and approved under a state consent agreement. Long predating the A.T., the Long Trail did not have a 1,000-yard standard for corridor width, 300 feet being much closer to the standard for that state, and there was some resistance at first to changing the width. Vermonters held less concern for the section from Sherburne Pass to the New Hampshire border — that was not part of the Long Trail and was viewed by some with a certain amount of disdain.

Although Vermont was slow to start, it ultimately became one of the most supportive states. The congressional delegation, headed by Senator Patrick Leahy, secured funding for the acquisition of corridor lands, and Governor Howard Dean pushed for state funds to purchase lands for the Sherburne–New Hampshire section.[37] The quirky Vermonters could be your best friend or your worst enemy, depending on their mood.

36. Interview with Preston Bristow and Lee Allen, July 14, 2014.
37. Sherman e-mail, July 14, 2016.

Two acquisitions in Vermont merit special mention. Stratton Mountain, where both James Taylor and Benton MacKaye claimed to have had their respective visions of a long trail, was owned by International Paper Company, and, when the National Park Service began acquiring the corridor, the trail was not actually on the mountain. But, in May 1985, after a long struggle that began in the mid-1970s, the company agreed to sell the western part of the mountain. Returning the trail to the top of the mountain became a major theme of the ATC biennial conference in Vermont in 1985. Special funding was needed, and Roger Sternberg, who was ATC's New England representative, began gathering signatures for a letter to Vermont's congressional delegation. Dave Startzell, too, was working with the delegation, and, with strong support from Leahy, Senator Robert Stafford, and Representative Jim Jeffords, Congress appropriated $6.7 million for the Green Mountain National Forest to acquire the land from International Paper. The Vermont delegation got Congress to fund the purchase, but it then was stalled by the Gramm–Rudman–Hollings budget-control act.[38] The Nature Conservancy stepped in and bought the land and held it until the Forest Service got the money and purchased it from TNC.[39] International Paper soon would become ATC's first corporate member.

And then there was the Killington–Pico showdown. As the Appalachian Trail moves from New Hampshire into Vermont, it crosses U.S. 4 and hits the Long Trail just north of a place called Sherburne Pass, which is the only known "pass" in the East, the first home of the Green Mountain Club (see page 237). (The term of art in New England is "notch," while south of New England they are called "gaps." Pass is a western term — Berthoud Pass, Donner Pass, *etc.*) There, it turns south and coaligns with the Long Trail all the way to the Massachusetts border.

Southbound, it struggles first up Pico Peak and then across the shoulder of Killington, with the slopes in between. Killington, at more

---

38. The Gramm–Rudman–Hollings Balanced Budget and Emergency Deficit Control Act of 1985 and the Balanced Budget and Emergency Deficit Control Reaffirmation Act of 1987 (both often known as Gramm–Rudman) were the first binding spending constraints on the federal budget. It permitted sequestration in case an appropriation would add to the deficit.

39. *ATN*, September/October 1989, pp. 10-11.

than 4,000 feet, is the highest point on the Appalachian Trail in Vermont. It was, in 1980, the largest ski resort in the state. That is why the trouble began.

The owners of Killington had big plans. They wanted to connect Killington with Pico, which also had a ski resort, but a smaller one, into one large resort. The corporate owners of Killington were aggressive developers; they were well-connected politically but were also confronted with the Vermont antidevelopment mentality that had, in earlier years, frustrated other developers and saved the environment of the trail.

Negotiations with the developers began as early as 1980. In 1983, a tentative agreement was reached between Sherburne Corporation (then the Killington owners) and the National Park Service to move the trail over the ridge to the west and would have allowed a ski lift and nine ski trails to cross the trail. That led to public outrage in Vermont and a cancellation of the agreement. A 1985 plan was also cancelled, because it would have violated a statewide ordinance that prohibited mechanized ski development above 2,500 feet. Preston Bristow, then working for the National Park Service, described the viewpoint of Preston Smith, owner of Sherburne Corporation, to Joe Cook, president of the Green Mountain Club: "As a businessman, Preston Smith feels that a deal is a deal and when you sign a contract and real estate changes hands you learn to live with what you got. The concept that significant public criticism, expressed through the NEPA process, can cause a deal not to be a deal and can authorize a federal agency to renegotiate is quite foreign."[40]

The National Park Service and the Killington folks decided that anything that went public would get the obstreperous Vermonters involved and whatever deal was negotiated would wind up not being a deal. So further negotiations were conducted in private — that is, they were held behind closed doors and not disclosed to the public.

In 1989, a new agreement became public, one that had been negotiated in secret, largely by William P. Barr, then a lobbyist in private practice and eventually (twice) U.S. attorney general. Signed on January 19, 1989, without public comment or an environmental impact

---

40. ATC archives, Hunt papers, Bristow to Cook, August 30, 1986.

statement, it moved the Appalachian Trail off to the western side of Killington and Pico. As purely a matter of trail location, it provided a rather scenic route. It also permitted unlimited tree removal, ski trails in the corridor lands, and two ski trails actually crossing the trail. Further, it permitted future development using mechanized equipment. Dave Startzell complained to Secretary of the Interior Manuel Lujan, the only secretary to visit ATC offices, calling the new agreement a "violation of trust."

There turned out to be a story behind the story. The new deal was negotiated by the Park Service under fierce pressure from Assistant Secretary of the Interior for Fish, Wildlife and Parks Becky Norton Dunlop, with Barr the intermediary. Described as "a Reagan ideologue," Dunlop had been appointed by President George H.W. Bush during a Senate recess and had never received confirmation. According to an article in the *Journal of National Parks*, NPS professionals had been overruled by a "handful of Interior officers intent on carrying out the Reagan-era agenda of encouraging commercial use of public resources."[41] The NPS director, William Penn Mott (who had saved the Appalachian Trail in Cumberland Valley), succumbed to the pressure and left NPS for a preretirement post in California, before the deal was announced.

The Killington agreement resulted in ATC's suing its partner, the National Park Service, for the first time. Meantime, the resourceful Startzell began mobilizing public opinion, secured a day-long hearing by a U.S. House committee, and prompted congressional votes to void the deal. He also attempted to smoke out the documents relating to the deal by initiating a Freedom of Information Act request.

J. Bennett Johnston, chair of the Senate Committee on Energy and Natural Resources, refused to consider further Interior appointments until Dunlop was replaced. In 1990, Senator Patrick Leahy of Vermont introduced language in the appropriations bill for the Department of the Interior that blocked the agreement and likewise moved on the assistant secretary. Under this pressure, Ms. Dunlop was unhorsed the following May.

41. *ATN*, article by John Kenney, September/October 1989.

After those tense hearings in Congress and legislative riders, an agreement was finally announced by Vermont Governor Howard Dean in 1996. A land exchange was involved that satisfied the American Skiing Company, which had purchased Killington in June of that year.[42] The new route was not nearly as scenic as the original trail layout, but it was out of view of the ski trails.

Maine

Ten generations down from Darby Field, who first climbed Mount Washington in 1642, was one David B. Field. Dave's father was in the timber business, and Dave grew up in Phillips, a remote village in the shadow of Saddleback Mountain. In 1955, at the age of 14, Dave, an older brother, and three friends began a section hike in the Bigelow Range, where they encountered hundreds of blowdowns from a recent hurricane. They decided to help clear the trail, went home to get equipment, and returned to the trail, taking out 240 blowdowns in a single day.

They had never heard of ATC or the Maine Appalachian Trail Club (MATC) but found a register at Horns Pond Lean-to and signed in. Dave soon got a letter from Louis Chorzempa inviting them to join MATC, and that began his long-running involvement with the Appalachian Trail.

Field studied forestry at the University of Maine, and, after graduation, went to work for the Forest Service in the White Mountains. He went back to school for a master's degree in forest economics and still later a doctorate at Purdue University. After his doctorate, he taught at the Yale School of Forestry, and, in 1976, he moved back to Maine, eventually becoming chairman of the department of forestry management at the University of Maine. He served as western Maine trail overseer from 1967 to 1977 and president of MATC from 1977 to 1987, succeeding Steve Clark, another key Maine volunteer, and

---

42. The complex history of Killington–Pico can be followed in: *ATN*, July/August 1989, p. 5; March/April 1991, p. 5; July/August 1994, p. 8; July/August 1996, p. 6; ATC archives, the Hunt papers with numerous pieces of correspondence and a large box of Startzell's and regional office files on the matter. Also consulted were Underhill (interview, March 7, 2014) and Dave Sherman (by e-mail, February 12, 2015).

also served on the ATC board for twenty-six years, including as chair from 1995 to 2001.

Field maintained seven-and-a-half miles of the A.T. on Saddleback, but his influence went far beyond a single section. He realized that the trail, laid out in the 1930s, had never been in an optimal location and asked himself, "Where would Avery have put this trail if he had had the time and resources?" Considering the entire trail, he worked with the rest of the MATC executive committee to design a reroute of the A.T. in Maine, beginning in the late 1960s.[43] His effort in Maine was similar to Dave Sherman's "optimal corridor review" study.

Most of the Appalachian Trail in Maine was on land owned by large forest-products companies — Boise Cascade, Saint Regis, International Paper, Georgia Pacific, and Great Northern Paper, as well as family estates. The companies were not hostile to the trail, because it rarely impacted their logging operations, but the situation was far from optimal. It was their land, and, when they needed a haul road to cross the trail, they didn't need to get anyone's permission. (In many locations, Avery had selected haul roads to route the trail.) If they decided to cut timber on a tract where the trail was located, it was their choice.

When dealing with those companies, Field enjoyed a unique position. He was a forester himself and dealt with the companies in the normal course of business. So, when he needed to talk to someone about the trail, he was talking to friends and colleagues.

When the National Trails System Act was passed in 1968, MATC began working with private landowners to obtain cooperative agreements and was able to begin rerouting the trail off roads. The list of major reroutes was long: Pleasant Pond, Elephant Mountain, Old Blue, Moody Mountain, Sawyer Notch, and on and on. Ultimately, about 170 miles were rerouted onto more optimal locations.[44] (Ski resorts were the biggest obstacle, and a ski resort forced the trail off Sugarloaf and onto a reroute.)

So when, in 1978, the National Park Service became involved in the trail corridor, Maine was already working on the route. As of

---

43. Interview with Dave Field, June 2014.
44. Ibid.

Dave Field with his chainsaw in 1984 on Big Wilson Ledges.

1980, 208 miles of the trail was located on private lands, and sixty-seven on public lands (including six miles of road-walking).[45]

Because the acquisition process in Maine was relatively mature when Chuck Rinaldi began buying land, MATC was, at first, stand-offish, and Steve Clark of MATC did not believe that Maine needed any help — MATC was developing a trail route of its own. Suspicious of federal intentions, Clark wrote to Richie in 1978, "The proposed depth of data collection strongly suggests that policy decisions and management on individual trail sections will be made from a central focal point."[46] MATC managed to stave off direct federal involvement in the process for six years.

Working independently, Maine began its own corridor-acquisition program in 1979 with a major donation of 1,200 acres from International Paper covering 7.2 miles of trail, but the program lasted only

45. David B. Field, *Along Maine's Appalachian Trail* (Charleston, S.C.: Arcadia Publishing, 2011), p. 121.
46. ATC archives, Zoebelein papers, Clark to Richie, May 21, 1978.

until 1983. Although MATC was doing an admirable job, NPS policy was, in all cases, to oversee the process to ensure that permanent protection was achieved, and, in that year, at a "summit meeting" in Greenville, Maine, NPS assumed leadership.

MATC, and Field particularly, remained engaged. For years, Dave felt that, with his and the club's longstanding and close personal working relationships with the timber companies, that they would either donate the lands needed or protective easements over them, which would be adequate to protect them. Over the years, it became obvious that this was not going to occur to the degree that was hoped. While they talked about doing the right thing, companies' proposed easement documents, once studied, reserved all types of exceptions and exclusions that still gave them a lot of control over the land, control that the Park Service felt would not be acceptable to protect the A.T. The massive amount of acceptable donations of land and interests in lands from the timber companies just never materialized in a manner that would have met minimum protection standards and be the same as lands being acquired up and down the trail. Moreover, awareness of federal funds for land acquisition reduced landowner interest in negotiating for donations. The 1984 agreement transferring trail-management authority from the NPS to the ATC and the clubs reduced MATC resistance to federal involvement.

No one knew the terrain as well as Field did, and, in January 1984, he sat at his dining-room table and drew the corridor as he saw it. He widened the corridor from six hundred to one thousand feet, the federal standard width, and tried to make the corridor match the existing trail, location of which was uncertain in many places. Then, after getting concurrence from MATC's executive committee, he met with Maine state officials in Augusta and rolled out the new corridor maps.[47]

Following intervention by ATPO, the protected trail miles began to be added more quickly. The first Park Service acquisition in Maine was in October 1984. The first *major* purchase, in October 1985, protected the rugged Barren–Chairback Range, the trail section scouted by Walter Greene in 1933. In April 1985, lands acquired from International Paper

---

47. Field interview.

protected 14.5 miles of trail; in September, Boise Cascade sold property protecting more than twenty trail miles, the largest single land purchase to that time by the ATLAO.[48]

Land trusts and the Appalachian Mountain Club also played a later role in Maine, protecting large tracts in the A.T. viewshed. The Nature Conservancy acquired several large tracts. Roxanne Quimby, a philanthropist with a conservation bent, helped preserve land in the Monson area early in this century.[49] Maine itself had a land-preservation program and

Dave Startzell, NPS Realty Agent Boyd Sponaugle, MATC's Lester Kenway, Pam Underhill of ATPO, and ATC Regional Representative Roger Sternberg on a scouting trip below Saddleback Mountain.

established a 22,000-acre preserve around Namahkanta Lake,[50] with NPS acquiring lakeshore lands for the A.T.

Not all went well. In 1978, a Boston developer named Donald Breen acquired 12,000 acres of land outside Rangeley, land that held a down-at-the-heels ski resort originally opened in 1959. Despite its being a longtime losing proposition, Breen proposed to expand the resort, hoping that doubling the size would bring it to profitability. Breen planned to add many miles of ski trails and three new ski

48. Hunter Library, Sherman Collection: Rinaldi to Richie, August 8, 1980, April 12, 1985, and October 15, 1985.
49. Quimby, a donor to ATC, made her money through cocreating the Burt's Bees products and sold the business for $190 million in 2007. Her acquisitions are not part of the corridor, but her thru-hiker daughter briefly served on the ATC board, and she served on one of the board committees about the time she was divesting herself of Burt's Bees and beginning to buy tens of thousands of acres of Maine forest.
50. Clark interview.

lifts, two of which would take skiers to the very top of the mountain into the alpine zone of rare species. The new development would be mostly in what was known as the "bowl," a part of the mountain clearly visible from the Appalachian Trail as it crossed the summits of Saddleback Mountain. Along with the rest of the MATC leadership, Field, who had maintained the Saddleback section of the Appalachian Trail for decades, was adamantly opposed.[51] Thus began a dispute between Breen and the National Park Service that was to continue for twenty-two years (see chapter 11).

Down South

On the North Carolina–Tennessee border, several NPS acquisitions filled in gaps in national forest lands. The most significant was Max Patch, one of the most iconic balds on the trail. Originally, the A.T. followed a road around the mountain, but, in 1968, the Carolina Mountain Club proposed a relocation onto the bald. That would involve landowners agreeing to sell, because the entire bald was privately held. The Forest Service tried to purchase a corridor over the mountain but could not find landowners willing to sell, so the Atlanta regional office called a halt in 1975. ATC badly wanted the reroute and continued lobbying ANSTAC and the Forest Service, hoping to revive negotiations.

In 1982, a group of investors proposed to build a high-end development atop the mountain. Arch Nichols (see chapter 4), an ATC board member and Forest Service official, found out about a meeting at which the proposal was to be put to the Madison County Planning Board and notified Carolina Mountain Club and others who he knew would oppose it. When the meeting was called to order, the planning board was surprised to find a full room, with fifty people, local residents and CMC members, opposed to the proposal. The board turned down the request to rezone the property, and the next day the Forest Service reopened its stalled negotiations with landowners.

---

51. *ATN*, September/October 1986, pp. 5-6.

The deal was sealed in September, and Max Patch was saved for the hiking public.[52]

The Roan Mountain story continued, and the Forest Service acquired Hump Mountain, near the northern end of the Roan area, in 1983 from a friendly landowner, Oscar Julian. The final settlement was a complex deal involving three separate tracts totaling about 1,500 acres. One parcel, containing the trail and summit, was purchased by the Forest Service; a second was purchased by the Southern Appalachians Highlands Conservancy (SAHC); a third, smaller tract was placed in a charitable remainder trust that would provide an annuity for Julian and his wife until their death, at which time it would go to SAHC. That was how the Appalachian Trail acquired Hump Mountain, one of the largest balds in the South, for a permanent trail route.[53]

Northeast of Sams Gap was Big Bald, another grassy eminence. The trail corridor was acquired from the Big Bald Development Corporation when the Forest Service acquired the Little Bald ridge line in 1977. Wolf Laurel ski resort occupied the eastern and southern flanks, and the trail was along the edge of this large development.[54]

Down south, tempers sometimes ran high when the federal government got involved. The most infamous family to oppose the trail route were the Oaks, a family of lawless brothers and their mother whose house was very near the trail, just a few miles north of Hump Mountain. The family became notorious for stringing fishing lines with fish hooks at eye level across the trail, along with violent crimes against hikers, harassment along roads, and much else. Sometimes, physical confrontations with the Oaks brothers could have ended in federal employees and volunteers getting beaten up. In the end, no one got hospitalized during those tense acquisition meetings, although four teen-aged hikers were gang-raped on Buck Mountain

---

52. *ATN*, November/December 1982, pp 5-8, article by Judy Jenner.
53. Hunter Library, Sherman Collection, Roan Highlands folder, note from Stan Murray, October 26, 1981; *ATN*, July/August 1983. Land acquisition along the A.T. in the Roan Highlands has continued to this day, and many thousands of acres have been protected by SAHC and the Forest Service.
54. Marci Spencer, *Pisgah National Forest: A History* (Charleston, S.C: History Press, 2014), p. 143; Van Meter logs, September 7, 1982.

in the late 1970s. The Oaks brothers eventually violated so many laws that the worst of them were brought to justice and locked up for years. That and relocations ended the threats of harassment and violence that hikers had had to endure once they crossed U.S. 19E.[55]

---

55. Sherman e-mail, March 2016. For years, A.T. guides cautioned hikers about that section of the trail.

COMPLETING THE TRAIL: STARTZELL AND UNDERHILL

These Americans are the most peculiar people in the world. You'll not believe it when I tell you how they behave. In a local community in their country, a citizen may conceive of some need which is not being met. What does he do? He goes across the street and discusses it with his neighbor. Then what happens? A Committee comes into being...and begins to function in behalf of the need. You won't believe this, but it's true: All of this is done without reference to the bureaucracy. All of this is done by private citizens on their own initiative. The health of a democratic society may be measured by the quality of functions performed by its private citizens.
— Alexis DeToqueville

If the land-acquisition process for the Appalachian Trail were ever to be completed after Dave Richie retired, a new partnership was needed. The team that eventually developed, Dave Startzell and Pamela Underhill, was a veteran duo. In the A.T. program, they developed long experience in trail management, and each had worked closely with Richie and Rinaldi for almost a decade.

Dave Startzell was born in Washington and lived first in the District of Columbia suburbs. His father, James Startzell, was an agent for the FBI, and they moved around the country as he took different positions in FBI offices. When the family lived in Cleveland, Dave entered college at Miami University of Ohio. He decided to major in sociology and came away with a bachelor's degree. By that time, his family had moved to Memphis, Tennessee, and he entered the University of Tennessee, at first intending to get a doctorate in sociology. He realized at one point that it would be hard to get a job in sociology, so he switched to urban planning.

At the time, Paul Pritchard came to Knoxville looking for urban planners for the ATC staff and was impressed with Dave but didn't have money to hire him. He kept Startzell in the back of his mind, though.

The offer didn't come right away, so Startzell took a job in urban planning in Oxnard, California, in 1977. He was there less than a year when he got a call from Hank Lautz, the new ATC executive director. Lautz had a position open as "director of education," and Pritchard had recommended Startzell. Dave accepted immediately and drove back east to take the job in Harpers Ferry. He began there in January 1978. The 1978 amendments to the 1968 National Trails System Act were passed just weeks later, and his job was to educate people about its implications.

In the hinterlands, he found lots of opposition. People were upset about this new federal program that could ultimately take their land or parts of it, and strong support did not even exist in some trail organizations. The Green Mountain Club, for instance, still viewed its Long Trail as separate and apart from the rest of the Appalachian Trail.[1]

Startzell immediately became the real leader of Lautz's small staff and was the catalyst in 1980 when the staff revolted and the board of managers decided to keep the rest of the staff and fire Lautz. It was Startzell who came up with the advocacy formula that provided congressional funds for corridor acquisition. His policy and advocacy skills were the best in the history of the ATC; he was indeed a policy wonk. Larry Van Meter departed in August 1986, and Startzell was first named acting executive director, a title he had held between

---

1. Interview with Startzell, February 21, 2014.

Lautz and Van Meter. He became permanent executive director in November of that year until March 2012.

Startzell's impact on the Appalachian Trail was absolutely seminal and began long before he became executive director. It is very possible that the corridor acquisition would never have been completed without him. Chuck Rinaldi, who headed the NPS acquisition program, stated, "We did receive acquisition funds pretty steadily, and it's mainly because of Dave Startzell and his ef-forts. I just can't emphasize enough the role that he has played."[2]

Dave Startzell in 1986

The second person to provide the leadership the new trail needed had been working for Chuck Rinaldi when she was named to head ATPO. Born in Boston in 1949, Pamela Underhill (who normally goes simply by "Pam") soon moved to a farm outside Princeton, New Jersey, where her father, Heaton Underhill, became the first director of fish and game for the state, so her heritage was securely in land con-servation. In 1962, Heaton Underhill took a job with the Department of the Interior as assistant director of the Bureau of Outdoor Recreation (see chapter 7), and the family moved to Arlington, Virginia.

Pam began college at Wellesley in 1967 but completed her undergraduate work the University of California at Berkeley, from which she was graduated in 1971 with a de-gree in urban studies. She then moved back to the Washington area, where she married a leathersmith and moved to Harpers Ferry. That was her initial connection to the Ap-palachian Trail.

Startzell and Pam Underhill atop Springer Mountain in 2006.

2. Ronald Brown interview with Rinaldi, May 17, 2007.

Out of college and looking for work, she applied to the National Park Service and took a temporary secretarial position. After a brief stop-over working elsewhere at the Department of the Interior, also as a secretary, she took a job working as a secretary for Dave Richie in the Appalachian Trail Project Office but moved quickly to Chuck Rinaldi's office in Martinsburg, West Virginia (see chapter 9) as a realty specialist, contacting landowners whose property was in the path of the planned corridor. In 1981, she moved back to Dave Richie's office in Harpers Ferry as a "trail project coordinator." She worked with Karen Wade on the corridor design for the southern half of the trail, and, when Chris Brown departed Richie's staff as the National Environmental Policy Act specialist, she took that on, too. With that long background in Appalachian Trail land acquisition, she was named project manager of the A.T. Project Office in 1995, with her title later changed to park manager as the Project Office became the A.T. Park Office.

Dave Startzell comes across as quiet and deliberative. It is as if he is deciding every word in his next sentence. Pam Underhill, however, does not. She strikes one as at once more forceful and more direct. She has decided opinions about the A.T. and doesn't worry if the people across the table don't agree with her. The Appalachian Trail was her trail — she had been hired to protect it from all threats, and that was her job. She was at once the trail's first line of defense and its last.

Both Dave and Pam are now retired, each having served the longest tenures for their respective positions, but their influence lives on in a completed trail and a public corridor. The Appalachian Trail has benefitted greatly from their presence.

Organizing for the Future

Although the two events were unrelated, Dave Startzell's new job as ATC executive director closely coincided with the retirement of Dave Richie. Searching for a replacement, the Park Service asked two veteran officers, Chuck Rinaldi and then Dave Sherman, to serve as acting A.T. project managers until NPS named a permanent replacement. Chuck held that position until he retired, and then Sherman took over for five months in 1989 until the Park Service eventually settled on John Byrne to become the manager.

When he arrived from the superintendency of the George Washington Parkway (as Richie had), Byrne was a more traditional Park Service officer than Richie, but he grew and changed in the job. He became very concerned about a rock-slide problem at the troublesome Lehigh Gap in Pennsylvania, and, when NPS refused to allocate money to fix the problem, he resigned. He was succeeded by Don King, who became the acting head of ATPO.[3] Finally, Pam Underhill was promoted in 1995, and the job stabilized under her leadership. (Don King had taken over Rinaldi's land-acquisition office.)

Dave Startzell continued to be the key to finding money from Congress, approaching members of Congress he came to know who would be the strongest supporters. Surprisingly, he found that the split was about fifty-fifty between Democrats and Republicans. Another surprise was that the supporters were not all from trail states. Sidney Yates, a Democrat from Chicago, was a strong supporter, as was Ralph Regula, a Republican from Ohio; the two led the key House interior appropriations subcommittee for years. Others, however, had more direct interests: Senators William Cohen from Maine, Patrick Leahy from Vermont, and Warren Rudman from New Hampshire, Representative Silvio Conte and Senator Edward Kennedy from Massachusetts, and Representative Beverly Byron from Maryland, widow of Goodloe Byron (see page 435).[4] Finding the money every year was an art form, and only Startzell seemed to know which levers to pull.

The funding source was a complex issue, and the money didn't always come from the same pocket. For both the Park Service and the Forest Service, the Land and Water Conservation Fund (LWCF), created in 1965, was the established funding source. Land acquisition was supposed to be the sole purpose of the fund, and, until the Reagan administration, that was what it was used for. But, beginning in

---

3. Interview with Pamela Underhill, March 7, 2014.
4. Startzell interview, *op. cit.*

1981, each administration found it a convenient source of money for various general-fund purposes beside land acquisition.

Most corridor-acquisition money did come from the LWCF, averaging for the first twelve years (up to 1995) around $8 million per year, with the Park Service getting $6-7 million and the Forest Service getting the rest. Despite varying degrees of support from federal administrations, and raids on the funding sources for other purposes, the funding for A.T. land acquisition was the longest running, most consistently funded federal conservation program in the country.

By spring 2014, the Park Service had acquired 2,569 parcels of land, adding up to 118,470 acres, protecting 621.5 map miles of the trail, on top of the 215 miles in the two large national parks. For its part, the Forest Service by then had acquired 468 more tracts and 56,710 more acres, adding 149 more miles to the 699 miles it had protected before February 1978. Between October 1968 and April 2014, states had protected 407 miles covering about 20,000 acres. One can only marvel at this consistent record of success over a period of years. It was a testament to careful work at Harpers Ferry and Martinsburg.

The Forest Service first used Weeks Act money to buy inholdings, and later LWCF money replaced Weeks Act funds. Forest Service acquisitions were at once more simple and more complicated than they were for the Park Service. It was simpler in that the tracts that it needed were already within the proclamation boundary. What was needed was to come to an agreement with the landowner, and the Forest Service could acquire the entire tract. But, the trail ran through eight national forests, each handling the matter in its own way. Despite some central coordination, not everyone was moving in lock step. Each national forest supervisor enjoyed considerable independence.

One year, the Forest Service did not spend its entire appropriation for the fiscal year, so ATC went to the Forest Service and explained that, if they wanted continued appropriations, they would have to spend all the money. What they needed was a master acquisition plan, Startzell explained. Working with ATC, the Forest Service did come

Vice President Al Gore and President Bill Clinton working on the trail in April 1998. In the photograph above, current ATC President Sandra Marra is at left, and the author is at top right, speaking with NPS Regional Director (and future ATC board member) Bob Stanton.

up with a plan, and Congress was so impressed that they passed a supplemental appropriation for the Forest Service for that year.[5]

As president, Bill Clinton's interests were not focused on national trails and environmental protection, but Vice President Al Gore had an abiding interest in both. On Earth Day, April 23, 1998, both Clinton and Gore appeared in Harpers Ferry to "help" with building the trail, in a highly publicized media event instigated by Gore staffers on the White House Council on Environmental Quality. The president and vice president were accompanied by a virtual army of Secret Service and military security agents, some hiding in trees along and across the river, out of camera range.

It demonstrated the administration's commitment to both the environment and to recreational trails and was staged partly to urge

5. Startzell interview, *op. cit.*

Congress to pass a $15-million appropriation to "finish" land acquisition for the A.T. by the end of the century. It had the desired effect, and the amount, $15 million, was more than double the normal annual appropriation. Representative Regula called Startzell from the lobby off the House floor to give him the news.[6]

In the end, it was insufficient, and the process continued into the next century. The last major acquisition to purchase A.T. treadway was not completed until an agreement was worked out with the Celanese plant on the New River above Pearisburg, Virginia, in 2015.

Internally, Startzell oversaw the myriad changes in July 2005 resulting from the shift in the organization's name from Conference to Conservancy — designed to emphasize its roles since the 1980s in land conservation and management, rather in holding meetings as a confederation of clubs, its superficial image driven by the name.

Getting the Land

By 1996, the corridor-acquisition program was closing in on a completed trail. The Park Service had purchased just less than 600 miles of trail, involving the acquisition of 2,338 individual tracts scattered over the fourteen states of the Appalachian Trail. Over the same time, the Forest Service had acquired 45,573 acres, and eleven of the fourteen states had added 20,239 acres. Challenges remained, and land needed to be acquired.

Dave Startzell named the most difficult areas: Cumberland Valley (where individual tracts had not yet been acquired); Phillipstown, New York; Salisbury, Connecticut; Sheffield and Tyringham in Massachusetts; and Saddleback in Maine (see chapter 10).[7]

The process was helped by favorable judicial rulings. Perhaps the most significant came early, in 1990, when Judge Charles Haight ruled in favor of the National Park Service in a lawsuit in Putnam County, New York. In a case pitting Park Service authority against a private landowner, Haight backed the broadest interpretation of the

6. *Ibid* and *ATN*, July/August 1999.
7. Startzell, *op cit.*

National Trails System Act of 1968. He ruled that the land acquired by condemnation did not need to be specifically for the trail itself. Rather, it could be acquired to protect trail values and the environment around the trail route. Moreover, rerouting of the trail, as long as it fell within the published right-of-way panels of 1971, was not a substantial rerouting and did not require congressional authorization. The ruling gave the Park Service enormous leverage in acquiring corridor lands and backed the clear intent of Congress in 1968 to preserve "the scenic, historic, and cultural values" of the Appalachian Trail and the hiking experience.[8] Benton MacKaye himself could not have written a better justification.

Maine was characterized by large land acquisitions. Timber companies placed huge tracts under easement. For instance, Great Northern Paper Company donated to the state 4,476 acres south of Millinocket (the most northerly town close to the trail). The easement placed significant restrictions on development and added buffer zones and tightened restrictions on road crossings of the trail.[9] A Scott Paper Company sale of 4,887 acres was the largest single transaction in the history of the National Park Service trail-protection program, and that single purchase protected 31.6 trail miles. The tract included the area east of Saddleback, including Spaulding Mountain, the Spaulding–Sugarloaf area, and the Crocker Mountain range.[10]

In Connecticut and New York, the Park Service acquired property that permitted a 3.5-mile relocation of the Appalachian Trail off roads and onto the ridges of Schagticoke Mountain on the states' border. The purchase ended decades of a contentious relationship with William Ray, an absentee landlord who clung to the property (see page 489). It involved members of Congress from both states, two Park Service directors, and three project managers. The purchase was not closed until after Ray died in 1991.[11]

---

8. U.S. District Court, Southern District of New York, *in re* United States of America *v.* Christina Mattin, tax collector, town of Putnam Valley; unknown heirs of Philip Philipse; and unknown others.
9. *ATN*, May/June 1990, p. 5.
10. *ATN*, March/April 1988, p. 3.
11. *ATN*, July/August 1994, p. 7.

In Pennsylvania, the relocation of the trail through the Cumberland Valley (see chapter 10) onto the ridge route brought it squarely into Boiling Springs. This picturesque little town had a privately owned lake in the center. The Bucher family owned the lake and a cottage on the shoreline, but they put it on the market in the mid-1970s to avoid a split among the heirs after the patriarch died. Local citizens formed a Citizens United for Preservation (CUP) in 1983 to preserve the lake for the community. At that point, Craig Dunn, then chairman of the ATC's Trust for Appalachian Trail Lands (TATL) advisory committee, got TATL involved, along with Anthony DeLuca, a Boiling Springs lawyer representing the town residents anxious to prevent development on the lake, and a local industrialist/philanthropist. In 1987, the family sold the lake, a small parking lot on the western shore, and about three acres of lakeside land to the trust, which resold the lake to the Pennsylvania Fish Commission. The cottage and the land along the lake bank was sold to the National Park Service, and the A.T. was routed along the lake bank.[12]

In Virginia, no more intriguing story exists than the acquisition of Spy Rock. South of The Priest, where the A.T. had been rerouted back in the 1940s to avoid the Blue Ridge Parkway, was a large rock with a spectacular view. It was in private hands, owned by a family of two aging brothers and a sister. They were born there, had a small farm, lived in a cabin without electricity or running water, and still farmed with a mule. They had no heirs and were not averse to selling to the Park Service but wanted to live their lives out on that land. Since they refused to sell at the time, condemnation was considered, but the Park Service rethought the problem and agreed that the family could continue to live on the land until the last one died, at which point the property would become public.[13]

In the South, Tom Speaks, who had been so effective in dealing with landowners, eventually concentrated solely on the Appalachian Trail. His job was to supervise land acquisition for the Forest Service in the South. Around 1991, the Forest Service began focusing more

---

12. *ATN*, November/December 1987, pp. 24-25; March/April 1988, p. 7.
13. Sherman interview, December 9, 2013. The last heir died in 2015.

and more on A.T. acquisitions, and Speaks moved to Unicoi, Tennessee, to pursue purchases. He worked closely with Dave Startzell, and once said, "Your job is to go to Congress and ask for the money. My job is to figure out how to buy those pieces of property."[14]

As the corridor was acquired, ATC leaders had less and less concern for actual footpath protection and more concern for protecting the hiking experience and the broader environment in which it developed. Slowly, the focus turned from Avery back to MacKaye. How could the environment surrounding the trail be preserved?

TATL became a major player in land acquisition in the South. Near U.S. 19E, an area made infamous by the Oaks brothers (see chapter 9), was a roadwalk along Campbell Hollow Road near Elk Park, North Carolina. The Forest Service had taken an option on the Augusta Campbell tract, but the price was above the appraised value, so TATL covered the cost above the appraised price, and the acquisition moved the trail off a road walk inhabited by vicious dogs.[15]

Rocky Fork near Unicoi proved to be one of the most complex acquisitions in the South. Rocky Fork was a 10,000-acre tract that hosted about eight miles of the trail. The Forest Service contacted the landowners, who seemed to change regularly, but never got a response. In 1980, it was sold to a developer, which was a red flag. Four years later, Speaks got in touch with The Conservation Fund (TCF), which agreed to purchase the tract and hold it in trust for the Forest Service. TCF led a coalition that included ATC, the Southern Appalachian Highlands Conservancy, and about thirty other local, regional, and national organizations. It was a huge risk, because TCF had no assurance that federal money would be there.[16] But eventually, in 2008, thanks largely to Senator Lamar Alexander and U.S. Representatives David Price and Phil Roe, the Forest Service got the initial funding for this major, $40-million acquisition, completed seven years later.[17]

In New Hampshire, the Lyme Timber Company, a private group specializing in conservation investments, approached ATC and other

---

14. Interview with Speaks, *op. cit.*
15. *Trail Lands*, an ATC newsletter, 1999.
16. The state of Tennessee also contributed money to secure Rocky Fork.
17. Speaks interview; Sherman interview.

groups to explore the acquisition of a large block of timberland along the borders of Lyme and Dorchester. Initially owned by International Paper, Lyme Timber bought it in 1992 and assembled several parcels on either side of the trail. The state of New Hampshire, through its Land Conservation Investments Program, purchased a conservation easement on 2,200 acres within the viewshed of the trail and extinguished all development rights in order to protect the trail environment.[18]

In 1974, Thomas P. Clephane, a forest products analyst with Morgan Stanley & Company, published a paper that revealed that the total value of timber for the forest products companies in New England far exceeded the value of the stock of the timber companies. In 1988, a British financier named James Goldsmith, following Clephane's report, purchased large tracts of timberland and promptly put it on the market. Goldsmith undoubtedly made a killing, but, when developers purchased some 200,000 acres, it led to concerns for the future of the northern forests. Congress then tasked USFS to do a Northern Forest Lands Study, and Maine, New Hampshire, New York, and Vermont created a sixteen-member task force to assist.

In 1990, Congress authorized and funded the Northern Forest Lands Council, a seventeen-member advisory body to make recommendations for policy and legislative changes. In 1990, twenty-four conservation, recreation, environmental, and forestry groups, including ATC, formed a Northern Forest Alliance to monitor activities of the council. The council released a "Citizen's Agenda for the Northern Forest," a compilation of public comments recorded during the council's spring listening sessions.[19] The report, "Finding Common Ground," was sent to Congress in September 1994. It called for improved stewardship of private land, along with thirty-seven specific recommendations.

In 1999, ATC's TATL became involved in the preservation of the viewshed for the A.T. on Mount Abraham, one of the last 4,000-footers in Maine not in public ownership. (Abraham was on Arthur Comey's proposed Appalachian Trail route in the 1920s but never came into public ownership, and the trail was never routed over the mountain.)

---

18. *Trail Lands*, 1994.
19. *ATN*, March/April 1996, p. 11; Field interview.

At $924,000, preserving the viewshed on the slopes of Abraham was one of TATL's largest projects ever.[20]

TATL joined a public-private coalition in an effort to protect the idyllic Pierce Pond in Maine. A sporting camp called the Carrying Place once was nearby, and the pond itself was within the viewshed of the trail. The corridor was protected by NPS, but the shoreline was still in private hands. One owner was discussing marketing his shoreline property. A new land trust — the Maine Wilderness Watershed Trust — was formed specifically to protect the pond.[21]

In northern Virginia, ATC, through its land trust, joined with the Niles/Rolling Ridge Foundation to protect a 1,600-acre tract west of the trail in 1993, conserving the timber and viewshed resources while developing a recreation plan with trails and a campsite. A short distance south of the Niles/Rolling Ridge property, the Adam Foster family donated a conservation easement on viewshed property, the Raven Rocks overlook.

And, in Pennsylvania, the trust and the Wildlands Conservancy pooled resources with the Pennsylvania Game Commission to protect 2,000 acres on Blue Mountain known as the Boyer estate. Those lands stretched nearly three miles along the A.T. from near Swatara Gap to the Lebanon–Schuylkill county line.

Likewise, TATL served as a catalyst to acquire two important land parcels in Connecticut, joining forces with The Nature Conservancy, local organizations, and the state Department of Environmental Protection.[22]

The list of projects involved TATL with such conservation organizations as The Nature Conservancy and The Conservation Fund that had much larger resources, along with citizens' organizations and state agencies. None of the other groups had the knowledge on the ground about what needed to be protected and why. It took trail maintainers and hikers to provide that critical input and to organize other groups. And, it was in the context of ATC's gradual swing toward broader conservation protection along the trail, officially adopted as ATC policy in 1989.[23]

---

20. *Trail Lands*, 1999.
21. *ATN*, July/August 1989, p. 9.
22. *ATN*, May/June 1990, p. 7; March/April, p. 6; March/April 1989, p. 3; September/October 1991, p. 9.
23. *ATN*, March/April 1989, p. 3.

Threats

Acquiring the corridor was one thing. Keeping it protected was quite another. Sometimes it seemed to ATC and the Park Service that defending their territory was a full-time job. Even though the trail was authorized by Congress, threats still came from all directions.

The Telecommunications Act of 1996, intended to promote cellular-telephone use, provided untold benefits to the American population. It was not, however, an unmitigated benefit to trails. Within a year, some 25,000 cell towers dotted the American landscape. Tall, metal spears intruded on what Benton MacKaye imagined pristine wilderness. The transformation of cell technology from analog to digital, and the move up the frequency spectrum, provided better telephone service but also meant that cell towers would be spaced closer together. By the act, local authorities could regulate the industry but could not prohibit

Startzell in the 1990s.

towers.[24] The Telecommunications Act bumped up against the words of the National Trails System Act. The best resolution would always be thoughtful negotiation to mitigate the effects of cell towers. Soon after the act passed, Startzell negotiated with the cellular-phone companies trade association a detailed system of prior notices and location negotiations that was effective for about a decade before changes in officials saw it fade from use.

Powerline crossings provided more cause for concern. Much of the electric power for the East Coast came from electric generation plants in the West, and that electricity had to get to the power-hungry East somehow. New proposals for wide powerline crossings of

---

24. *ATN,* November/December 1997, p. 6, article by Dave Startzell.

the Appalachian Trail were constant. Each new proposal had to be negotiated to mitigate, as much as possible, the values decreed in the National Trails System Act — to protect the natural, scenic, historic, and cultural values of the trail. As with cell towers, no over-arching solution to the problem of powerline crossings could be found. It was just a long-running series of negotiations, although it did lead to a specific ATC policy — drafted as a win-win solution — that defined the organization's values when it came to pipeline proposals and whether to oppose them or seek alternative routes and mitigations.

Environmental devastation was yet another threat. In many places on the trail, toxicity had become a problem. The most famous (or infamous) example was Lehigh Gap in Pennsylvania (see page 219), where decades of lead residue blown from the zinc smelters in Palmerton had poisoned the mountain and left a moonscape. Only a few miles away, near Port Clinton, Pennsylvania, the Sun Pipeline Company cleared a right-of-way across NPS-owned land during which they moved and possibly overturned barrels of unknown substances, potentially containing hazardous materials. Volunteers went to the site in 1987 and tried to clean up the 4.2 acres, finding additional hazardous material.[25]

Then a messy radon lawsuit in New Jersey complicated many relationships. In 1982, the New Jersey Green Acres fund was used to purchase a 16.5-acre site near Wawayanda State Park. The A.T., which was on roads in the area, was supposed to be moved to the property, but the site was contaminated by radon from a World War II defense contractor that made luminous watch dials. In 1986, Vernon Township sued the New Jersey Department of Environmental Quality (DEP), and the New York–New Jersey Trail Conference joined the lawsuit.

Dave Richie was concerned that the lawsuit could damage relationships with DEP, an essential partner in New Jersey, and did not support the lawsuit. That produced internal turmoil at ATC. Ray Hunt tried to get JoAnn Dolan, executive director of the New York–New Jersey Trail Conference, to withdraw the lawsuit. Dolan took the position that defending the trail environment was the right thing

---

25. ATC archives, Hunt papers, Sherman memo of September 11, 1989

to do, regardless of the potential for damaging relationships with DEP. Bob Proudman recommended that ATC and ATPO take Dolan's side, and eventually the ATC executive committee voted to support the Trail Conference, without joining the lawsuit.[26]

The National Park Service took the position that the federal legislation protecting the A.T. required intersecting roads be minimized, but it was a constant struggle. In North Carolina, the proposed North Shore Road along the southern boundary of Great Smoky Mountains National Park kept bobbing up (see page 328). In 2000, Congress appropriated $16 million to resume road construction. Morgan Sommerville, who headed the southern regional office of ATC, testified at public hearings, and the Park Service fought it and managed to fend it off.[27]

The Forest Service itself was occasionally the culprit. As tracts were logged, haul roads crossed the trail. That was especially prevalent in the South, where active logging was an on-going issue. In some ways, the Forest Service was its own worst enemy.

Elsewhere, errant property owners refused to cooperate. A classic example of this was Phil Physioc, a Maryland owner of tracts along the A.T. where he would cut and then sell the timber. Physioc claimed ownership of lands that were clearly in the acquired corridor and built haul roads across corridor land without informing the Park Service.[28]

ATPO staff members were sometimes greeted with firearms when approaching families to negotiate land purchases. The physical threats were not at all typical of the acquisition process, but violence was never far from the minds of the staff members. Corridor acquisition was not supposed to be a contact sport, but landownership can be an intensely personal matter.

Occasional homicides on the trail — eleven men and women were murdered in nine instances between 1974 and 2019 — garner a great deal of publicity. Occasionally, hikers simply died on the trail. Heart attacks claimed some hikers. Heat stroke was a frequent culprit and

26. Extensive correspondence in the Hunt papers.
27. *ATN*, July/August 2003, p. 17.
28. Sherman interview, December 9, 2013. PATC records from the Maryland Appalachian Trail Management Committee provide detailed information on the Physioc problem.

sometimes the opposite, hypothermia. Falls sometimes killed hikers, a reminder that mountains were steep and had dangerous drop-offs. The notorious Kennebec River crossing in Maine in 1985 claimed a victim, leading ATC to attempt, with considerable success, to reaffirm a ferry as the official route there and provide, with financial help from the Maine A.T. Club and corporations, a canoe and operator to save hikers the potentially dangerous prospect of wading across a swift river.[29] Falling trees occasionally claimed an unlucky hiker. And, once in a while, a hiker got lost and died of exposure. Significant previous hiking experience was no guarantee of safety.

Two firing ranges — Indiantown Gap and Anthony's Nose — were close enough to make both hikers and the U.S. Army nervous. Although the A.T. was moved away from Indiantown Gap, hikers reported hearing artillery shells whizzing past them in 1997 and spent shells were found on state game lands, so they were not always imagining things.[30]

Continued on page 532

---

29. The problem with the Kennebec crossing relates to the unpredictable release of water from an upstream dam. The potential threat cost ATC up to $35,000 a year to mitigate. Still, one A.T. hiker since 1985 has drowned in the Kennebec.
30. *ATN*, November/December 1997, p. 8.

April Hill

ATC's policy was to manage the trail and let others manage lands and resources along the trail. Occasionally, ATC was forced to violate this dictum in order to ensure trail protection. One such conservation project got ATC directly involved in land management. That was April Hill, the Kellogg property just down the road from South Egremont, Massachusetts.

The story of the Kellogg land began in the 1980s with then-New England ATC Representative Roger Sternberg, who became acquainted with Mary-Margaret Kellogg. Mrs. Kellogg owned the house and property adjacent to the Appalachian Trail. Sternberg wanted Mrs. Kellogg to add her property to the corridor. She had no children, just a niece and nephew who did not live locally and had no interest in moving to Massachusetts.

When not in Carlisle, Pennsylvania, she lived in a large New England salt-box home, built in 1744, with adjoining farmland that could be seen clearly from Jug End, a place where the A.T. began climbing out of the valley. The entire property, initially 150 acres when she and her husband bought it in 1978 with its colonial boundar-

ies intact, was on the National Register of Historic Places.

Sternberg began discussions with Mrs. Kellogg in 1985, and ATC made an exception to policy, receiving a conservation easement on thirty-three acres the following year. She sold sixty-three acres along one edge of the property to NPS for the trail corridor and transferred the development rights on fifty acres to Massachusetts' agricultural-preservation program. In time, ATC's trust provided management oversight for the forty farmed acres and the woodlands.

In 1991, Mrs. Kellogg donated to ATC a historic preservation easement on the house and a conservation easement on the four acres encompassing the house and three outbuildings dating to between 1750 and 1850. Two adjacent property owners, influenced by Mrs. Kellogg's commitments, agreed to conservation easements totaling sixteen acres.

Given all the encumbrances and ATC's long-standing reluctance to get involved with property management (except for the trail and the corridor), Dave Startzell was reluctant to commit resources directly. When Mrs. Kellogg died in 2004, the 1991 assets were inherited by ATC.

Searching for a use, ATC made the back of the house an office for the New England regional staff, rented office space to the Appalachian Mountain Club, and used the large barn mainly for trail-crew training and storage. Mrs. Kellogg's bequest included a trust fund from which ATC received a certain amount per year that went into the expense of managing the property but did not cover the entire cost. ATC had to allocate funds.[1]

ATC sold the property in 2019 to a local nonprofit.

Belview Mountain

One of the classic viewshed stories concerns Belview Mountain, in North Carolina, in clear view below the Appalachian Trail as the footpath crosses Hump Mountain.

In 1982, Avery County, North Carolina, issued a permit for the Putnam Mine, a 151-acre tract on Belview Mountain. Paul Brown, the owner of the tract, started a rock-crushing operation that began to eat into Belview and created an enormous scar that became ever wider as the crusher chewed up more and more mountain. Local resident Jay Leutze could hear the back-up beeps from the rock crushers, to say nothing of the noise from the actual crushers as they slowly ground up Belview Mountain into small bits. Leutz, a lawyer, launched a lawsuit to stop the operation from his house, only a mile and a half below the path of the trail.

Brown was just a small businessman, hoping to make a living, but Leutze and other residents in the area were alarmed, and they fastened onto trail protection. The provisions of the

---

1. Interview with Adam Brown of ATC, October 3, 2016; Sternberg e-mail, July 2, 2016; *ATN*, November/December 1991, pp. 4-5; Startzell e-mail, October 8, 2016.

National Trails System Act did not seem to permit incompatible activities of this nature so close to the Appalachian Trail.

The residents tried to enlist ATC, but it was, at first, a hard sell. The original permit was for the old Cranberry Mine, which ran under Hump, and ATC reasoned that it could not be seen from the Trail. So, Leutze enlisted Dan "Wingfoot" Bruce of Hot Springs, North Carolina, a well-known thru-hiker and sometime hostel owner. Bruce began a letter-writing campaign that turned ATC around. Regional officials went out to see the site and were immediately convinced that ATC should join the lawsuit.

Eventually, the National Park Service got involved, and Pam Underhill voiced her opposition to the Putnam mine at a critical public hearing. Her testimony in behalf of NPS was key and the state permit for the Putnam mine was revoked, a signal victory for viewshed protection.[2]

Pochuck Boardwalk

Many structures on the Appalachian Trail are built to keep hikers' feet dry. Bog bridges characterize the trail in Vermont (otherwise referred to by hikers as Vermud). Pilings and boardwalks appear in many places. But, when one speaks about boardwalks over swamps, the Pochuck Boardwalk is in a class by itself.

An easy commute from New York City, northern New Jersey was one of those places on the trail afflicted by rampant development. A portion of the route was on the narrow shoulder of Sussex County 517. The only alternative was the vast Pochuck swamp. Assistant Director Anne Lutkenhouse of the

---

2. Jay Leutze, *Stand Up That Mountain* (New York: Scribner, 2012); interview with Leutze and Judy Murray, September 25, 2014.

New York–New Jersey Trail Conference (NY–NJ TC) took on the project, working with Karen Lutz of the mid-Atlantic ATC regional office in Boiling Springs. The first step, beginning in 1993, was a 110-foot suspension bridge, and a civil engineer, Tibor Latincsics, volunteered to head that part of the project. After a lengthy permitting process, construction began in 1995. Volunteers and trail crews pitched in, and, within a year, the bridge was complete — thirty-four feet in the air, five feet above flood stage. Called the "bridge to nowhere," it stood isolated near the edge of the swamp.

Next came the boardwalk itself. Volunteers began building it in 1999, and, when it was finally complete, it was a mile and a half. Working up to their hips in water, volunteers sank countless metal screw pilings and, on top, built a seemingly endless plank bridge, with turnouts and resting benches. It was one of the greatest volunteer projects in Appalachian Trail history.[3]

The Appalachian Trail Foot Bridge

Seventy-seven miles south of Rockfish Gap, the Appalachian Trail crosses the James River. The original route crossed the river on a narrow automobile bridge, and hikers had to dodge lumbering log trucks and speeding cars. On the south side of the river, the trail passed a hydroelectric plant. It was hardly the environment that Benton MacKaye envisioned for his trail but was the best that could be done at the time, unless hikers wanted to swim.

This began to change with Bill and Laurie Foot. Laurie was from Chicago, and Bill came from Akron, Ohio. They met and married at Purdue University, and Bill became a purchasing agent for Babcock and Wilcox, while Laurie became a school psychologist. Both were avid hikers.

In 1987, after returning from an A.T. thru-hike, they became involved with the A.T. and the Natural Bridge A.T. Club (NBATC). Bill was constantly scouting for a more optimal route for the trail and fastened on the James River crossing. He became intrigued with five stone piers sitting in the river. He dis-

---

3. *ATN:* March/April 1996, p. 13, by Glenn Scherer; March/April 2000, p. 14.

covered that they were owned by one Henry Smiley, owner of a mining company in the area. Smiley had purchased the piers from the railroad company for $125. Since the railroad no longer used the crossing, and the bridge itself had been removed, they didn't need them. Now 80, he, too, no longer required the piers. Sitting at his home and talking to Bill and Laurie, he offered to sell them for $1.

Bill and Laurie now had bridge piers. They got a friend to evaluate the soundness and had to add height to elevate them above the flood line. (The James River coursed through a narrow gorge at that point, and flooding was always a concern.) Monetary grants would be necessary, but first they had to own the land on both ends of the planned bridge. On the north side, Virginia Power donated 35 acres. On the south side, a hunt club owned the land and held out for a price above the appraisal. The Park Service prepared to condemn the tract, but TATL stepped in first to get the agreement and pay above the appraised price. Now, the club owned the piers, and the land on both sides of the river was in public hands. All they needed was a bridge.

NBATC applied for a series of highway-fund grants to cover the cost of construction. They needed a twenty percent match, but the piers were considered part of the match, and the appraised value of $262,000 covered the match. The club submitted a total of four grant requests, finally getting enough money to cover the cost of construction. They were required to bid out to small companies, and the bridge was built in prefabricated sections and floated down the James River to be hoisted on top of the piers.

Legal issues dominated much of the project. The bridge was given to the Forest Service, but the Forest Service had to own the land under the piers to make it legal. That required an act of the Virginia legislature to donate ownership of the land under the river. Once the trail reached the south bank, it had to cross CSX rail-

road land. The railroad had a huge staff of lawyers and always refused permission for an at-grade crossing. The company, however, eventually agreed to a trail under the tracks, a departure from its norm. Aside from the huge mound of paperwork necessary to complete the bridge, the role for volunteers was to construct the trail approaches to the bridge.

The bridge, dedicated on October 14, 2000, is the longest span on the Appalachian Trail. Tragically, Bill Foot had died of cancer the preceding April. The club named the Foot Bridge after Bill.[4]

Saddleback

West of the Bigelow Range stands Saddleback Mountain (see also chapter 9). One of only four peaks above 4,000 feet on the Maine Appalachian Trail (the others are Crocker, Avery, and Katahdin), the battle to protect it has attained notoriety as one of the most controversial acquisitions in the history of the project (see chapter 10). Pam Underhill reminisces, "I think that's where my ashes should be scattered. Lord knows I spilled enough blood up there."[5]

The original trail over the peak was built by the CCC in 1935. It traversed an environmentally sensitive subalpine zone over the bald summit, and the trail route stayed there, unmarred by development. In 1960, a small ski area was established in Sandy River Plantation on the north slope. The resort installed ski lifts with two T-bars and later added a chair lift. The facilities terminated at the 3,000-foot elevation and did not approach the 4,120-foot summit. Owing to some poor snow years, the resort went bankrupt, and property ownership changed hands several times.[6]

---

4. "James River Foot Bridge Story," July 2, 2005, by Laurie Foot, as presented at the ATC biennial conference in 2005; interview with Laurie; *ATN*, March/April 2000, p. 12.
5. Underhill interview, *op. cit.* The mountain is notorious for blood-sucking blackflies.
6. Much of the detailed quarter-century history of the trail over Saddleback was found in a ^IDave Field memo written in February 10, 1985, in the Hunt papers in the ATC archives, which also contain a three-foot box of Startzell's files, numerous NPS documents, and a plethora of regional-office photographs and notes. See also Field's memo to Gloria LeVasseur, LURC Project Analyst on November 16, 1983, in the same Hunt papers.

Ski-resort developers continued to show interest in Saddleback and launched various proposals. In 1973, Maine Appalachian Trail Club (MATC) President Steve Clark petitioned for a trail-protection zone that included all the land above the point where tree height averaged six feet, and ATC endorsed the MATC position. All subsequent development proposals by the ski resort were opposed by MATC, and, for several years, nothing much changed on top of Saddleback.

In 1978, a Boston developer named Donald J. Breen acquired 12,000 acres of land outside Rangeley, land that held the down-at-the-heel ski resort. Despite being a longtime losing proposition, Breen proposed to expand the resort, hoping that doubling the size would bring it to profitability. Breen planned to add many miles of ski trails and three new ski lifts, two of which would take skiers to the very top of the mountain into the alpine zone of rare species. The new development would be mostly in what was known as the "bowl," a part of the mountain clearly visible from the Appalachian Trail as it crossed the three peaks of Saddleback Mountain. Breen planned to file his phase-one development plans with the Maine Land Use Regulation Commission (or LURC, replaced in 2012 by the Land Use Planning Commission).

Dave Field, who maintained the Saddleback section of the Appalachian Trail, was adamantly opposed.[7] Thus began a dispute between Breen and the National Park Service that was to continue for twenty-two years.

In 1983, Saddleback Mountain Ski Resort applied to LURC for permission to construct a chair lift above 4,000 feet, ending within 200 feet of the existing trail. Again, MATC strongly opposed the proposal. Over several subsequent years, developers continued to send in proposals, but LURC kept the ski resort development at bay — the development did not come closer than 450 feet from the trail, and none of the resulting development was visible from the A.T. The ATC board of managers continued to support MATC and passed a resolution that "the National Park Service, the Appalachian Trail Conference, and the Maine Appa-

7. *ATN,* September/October 1986, pp. 5-6.

lachian Trail Club should take all feasible measures to assure the protection of the Appalachian Trail and the environment of the Appalachian Trail across the Saddleback Mountain Range."[8]

Dave Sherman, in his 1984 optimal location review, characterized Saddleback as "the single most important unprotected area remaining on the Appalachian Trail."[9]

In 1987, Breen proposed a four-season resort, focusing chiefly on the winter months, when he expected the resort to be in the black. It was all about skiing.

In order to make a profit, he planned more ski trails, more chair lifts higher on the mountain, with some trails actually crossing the Appalachian Trail in the alpine zone. Some experts felt that the resort could never make money because of competition from existing resorts at Sugarloaf and Sunday River. Sno Engineering, a firm engaged by ATC to evaluate the economic potential for Breen's ideas about expanding the resort, characterized Breen's proposals as "not viable because the area has poor development potential for skiing."[10] An environmental assessment in 1987 recommended protection of the trail area because it passed through a "krummholz zone" of rare native plants and stunted and deformed trees typical of alpine areas.

Breen was undeterred by negative evaluations, but he met firm opposition from ATC. Startzell wrote letters to both Maine state and National Park Service officials, citing the environmental assessment and the National Trails System Act, the provisions of which protecting the "nationally significant scenic, historic, natural, or cultural qualities" of the trail would clearly be violated by Breen's plans. Startzell even felt that the Saddleback section had been there so long that it might qualify to be listed with the National Register of Historic Places and compared the top of the mountain with other famous balds — Roan, Katahdin, and the Presidentials.[11]

---

8. ATC archives, Hunt papers, ATC board resolution, November 1984.
9. Sherman corridor-review maps, marginal note.
10. ATC archives, Hunt papers, undated ATC position paper (probably 1987).
11. *Ibid*, Startzell letter to Robert LaBonta (commissioner of the Maine Department of Conservation), March 9, 1987, and to Rinaldi, March 30, 1987.

Early in the process, antigovernment land-acquisition gadfly Chuck Cushman of the American Land Rights Association, who had gotten Cumberland Valley residents stirred up (see chapter 10), entered the fray — predictably on the side of the ski resort. Cushman got local residents in Maine riled up, and one public meeting in Rangeley degenerated into an emotional tirade by local residents, who strongly favored development.[12]

Although the ATC position received consistent concurrence from LURC, the organization was not supported by the politicians in Maine in that process.

Negotiations stalled in the late 1980s but restarted in 1996. When they heard that NPS was thinking about condemnation, freshman Senators Olympia Snowe and Susan Collins — while always respectful of ATC and the Maine club — jumped into the controversy and subjected Pam Underhill to what she described as "abusive tirades" at the Capitol. "I felt I had Senators Snow and Collins dancing on my head for two solid years."[13]

After long and difficult discussions, the Park Service finally acquired 1,435 acres from Breen, with another 320 acres under scenic easement without significant visual protections. The cost to the Park Service was $4 million, a sum reached under intense political pressure from Maine's congressional delegation. That pressure resulted in the White House, in the waning days of the Clinton administration, cutting NPS out and bringing in former Maine Senator George Mitchell, who had gained more fame as a diplomat, to wrap up the details behind closed doors. Along with Snowe and Collins, Mitchell was on the side of the developer and crafted a "compromise" that favored Breen.[14]

If all is well that ends well — with the footpath protected but the longterm viewshed less so — then the Saddleback mess turned out well, but ATC and the Park Service were very unhappy to have had to buy off Breen with an amount they considered excessive. And, the performance of Maine's congressional delegation *vis-a-vis the agency* can be compared very unfavorably with that of Vermont. That state had a long-standing tradition of

---

12. *Ibid.*
13. Underhill interview.
14. *ATN*, November/December 1996, p. 7; November/December 2000, p. 8.

protecting the Green Mountains, and their senators and representatives acted completely opposite to those of Maine, who caved to an out-of-state developer who sold his holdings three years later.

Breen's buyer also announced significant expansion plans, never fully realized, and the resort has been idle since 2015, with a new, 2020 buyer planning to reopen and expand it in 2021.

Sterling Forest

West and south of the state-owned Palisades Interstate Park Commission (PIPC) land in New York state stood a vast forest. The name, Sterling, was contorted from Revolutionary War General William Alexander, heir to a Scottish title, earl of *Stirling*. It became a home for iron smelting and produced most of the cannons, rifles, anchors, and the like that were used by colonials during the Revolution. Two iron operations, Ringwood and Sterling, produced a chain that was placed across the Hudson River during the war and played a role in stopping British ships and troops trying to secure the river. The Ringwood mines eventually came under the control of Peter Cooper and Abram Hewitt. It was Cooper who built the first American locomotive and funded Cooper Union in New York City. (Cooper Union hosted a February 1860 speech by unannounced presidential aspirant Abraham Lincoln that proved pivotal for his nomination and election a few months later.) Working at Cold Spring, Peter Parrott devised the Parrott gun, the largest artillery piece used during the Civil War.

Sterling Forest eventually was purchased by railroad magnate Edward H. Harriman as an extension of his land holdings farther north and east. Harriman eventually assembled a land empire of 70,000 acres, owning all the way from the Hudson River to Greenwood Lake on the New York–New Jersey border. But, the land in Sterling Forest had been largely logged off, and the iron mines were depleted. (Just as well, since they had been replaced in the larger economy by the Wasabi Range in Minnesota, which produced more iron at a cheaper price.) So, in 1953, the Harriman family sold the land to an investment company, City Investing.

The investment company sold some of the land to IBM, International Paper, International Nickel, and Union Carbide. On the land that they kept, the investors envisioned a large town development, but their initial proposal was defeated by local zoning. By the early 1980s, the idea of a large town was dormant. City Investing still had plans to develop the land and proposed what would have become the largest residential and commercial real-estate development in the nation. They planned 14,500 residential units and 7.4 million square feet of commercial and light industrial space, scattered through the forest in various clusters.

In the middle of the forest was the small town of Tuxedo. City planners were enthused by this development plan in which Tuxedo would be the center of the action. The benefit to the town would be in tax revenue, and dollar signs sold the proposal. It was simply irresistible.

Paul and JoAnn Dolan, New York City residents, had a vacation cottage on Greenwood Lake very close to the A.T. JoAnn became executive director of New York–New Jersey Trail Conference in 1981 (and an ATC board member in 1985), and Paul worked as an editorial manager for ABC-TV's "20/20" news program. The Appalachian Trail ran along the north edge of Sterling Forest, past Fitzgerald Falls and Little Dam Lake. The proposed development in the forest was within the viewshed of the trail.

The Dolans became concerned about what was happening south of their cabin in the forest. In 1985, they held a meeting at the cabin to discuss the matter. The company had just thrown Sterling Forest on the market, and the objective of the Dolans was to get people interested in preserving part of this huge tract as a viewshed. It was attended by Paula Leicht of ATC (the land trust's administrator at the time), Nash Castro of Palisades Interstate Park Commission (who was instrumental in securing the 1968 statute as a NPS official assigned to the East Wing of the White House), representatives of The Nature Conservancy, and others. After the meeting, they took the attendees on an informational hike on the A.T., past Little Dam Lake and Fitzgerald Falls, to build support for protecting the viewshed. The Dolans had a son, Jamie, who was disabled, and they used his condition as a background theme, focusing on preserving the land for their children and their children's children.

Part of Sterling Forest was in New Jersey, and that state already had its Green Acres land-protection program. Governor Thomas Kean took the first step, approving a $2 million grant from the fund to purchase the 2,074 acres in New Jersey.

The developer pushed ahead with the master plan to develop the land around Tuxedo, but it had problems. All the data that it had submitted to the town was false. The problem was water. The wetlands were not mapped properly, the soil composition was wrong, and the hydrological data was invented to get the required approvals.

The biggest problem that the developer had was the New York State Thruway Authority. Sterling Forest needed a new exit off the highway to make the development profitable. The problem was that the exit would have to use land purchased by federal money, and that placed the National Park Service in control. The Park Service position was that they would grant the exit only if the Palisades Interstate Park Commission (PIPC) requested it. PIPC refused, and the exit became a nonstarter. This placed the entire development in Tuxedo in jeopardy.

In 1997, Governor George Pataki, a dedicated conservationist, announced the purchase of the first 1,400 acres of the 17,000-acre Sterling Forest tract in New York. The remaining 15,280 acres were purchased for $55 million with federal money, and the land became public property.

Sterling Forest became the largest single purchase of *viewshed* lands to protect the Appalachian Trail corridor. ATC worked on it quietly in Congress and within its membership. This accorded with its policy at the time of engaging in specific footpath and corridor lands, while relying on local interests to provide resources for view-shed protection. Senators Bill Bradley and Frank Lautenberg of New Jersey were key supporters of the $55-million federal grant.

In Tuxedo, the Sterling Forest Corporation was capped at 3,000 residential units and 2.1 million square feet of commercial space, a fraction of what it had originally planned. No developed lands would abut the Appalachian Trail corridor. The result was a huge win for the Dolans and their efforts to bring together a coalition of like-minded conservationists.[15] In 2014, N.Y.–N.J. TC and ATC supported a local group to convince New York to disallow a massive casino in Tuxedo below the A.T.

15. Sources for this section were from: Robert O. Binnewies, *Palisades: 100,000 Acres in 100 Years* (New York: Fordham University Press and Palisades Interstate Park Commission, 2001); *The Trail Walker*, February/March 1988; *ATN*, September/October 1995, p 8; *ATN*, July/August 1996, p. 5; and extensive interviews with Paul and JoAnn Dolan, May 31, 2014.

An Uncertain Finality

The story of the Appalachian Trail has a well-defined beginning with Benton MacKaye's 1921 article proposing a trail along the spine of the Appalachians, but the project has no end. Federal acquisition of the trail corridor may be complete, but land purchases continue as the protection zone expands to improve the user experience.

Just as a hiker might stand on Tinker Cliffs in central Virginia and look across the vast forest stretching in every direction, so, too, the view of the future for the Appalachian Trail appears endless.

EPILOGUE

We are guideless walkers who have lost our way, we are poor little
Hikers who have gone astray, gentlemen trampers off on a spree,
Doomed to wander for eternity, God have mercy on such as we.
　　　　　　　　— Report of the ATC Publications Fund,
　　　　　　　　　　　　date and author unknown

The Hiking Culture

The Appalachian Trail spawned a new phenomenon in America — the long-distance hiker. It inspired thousands of people to throw on a backpack and flee to the woods, many of whom would never have thought of it otherwise. The trail became a magnet that drew people to it. It changed lives and, in the process, changed generations of Americans. There were other trails in the country, but the Appalachian Trail was regarded as the premier trail. It exercised a pull and became a significant recreational force in the country.

After Earl Shaffer's thru-hike in 1948, the idea that one could hike the entire trail at one time captured the imagination of succeeding generations of hikers. Eventually, backpackers competed to see who could do the fastest thru-hike. Benton MacKaye dismissed that as an aberration of his idea and suggested that an award be given to the person who did the slowest thru-hike, so that they could enjoy the experience as it was originally intended. His idea didn't catch on, and the mystique of thru-hiking exercised a greater pull each year. Ed Garvey's 1971 book, *Appalachian Hiker: Adventure of a Lifetime*, had a significant influence on thru-hiking (as well as Appalachian Trail hiking in general) and led to a geometric increase in long-distance A.T. hiking.

The magic of hiking was not confined to the obviously fit and athletic. In 1955, after a failed attempt in 1954. Emma Gatewood, a sixty-seven-year-old grandmother from Ohio, thru-hiked the A.T., carrying her belongings in a cloth sack thrown over her shoulder (see page 284). In 1990, Bill Irwin, a blind hiker, succeeded in thru-hiking the A.T. and recorded his experiences in a book. (Both became national celebrities of a sort.) Bob Barker, a victim of multiple sclerosis, thru-hiked the trail three times on crutches.

Hikers competed to do "different" thru-hikes. Seeing a backpacker with a large guitar slung over the pack was not unique, and one hiker walked from Georgia to Maine carrying a tuba, which he played occasionally at shelters for the entertainment of incredulous hikers. The surge was accompanied by a blizzard of autobiographical accounts, a publishing niche that only served to encourage more hiking. There was more than one novel about the culture of thru-hiking, children's books, several videos, and a handful of stage plays.[1]

Overnight accommodations on the trail expanded as it became more popular, and many of them became quite famous in the hiking culture. In Monson, Maine, Shaw's Boarding House was a destination for north- and southbound hikers. In Virginia, Woods Hole, run for many years by Tillie Wood, was an almost mandatory stopover in southwest Virginia. Just a few miles north, in Pearisburg, was the Holy Family Hostel. The Partnership Shelter in southwest Virginia became famous because a local pizza restaurant would deliver directly to the shelter. In New York, Graymoor Monastery began taking in hikers in 1974 almost by accident and became a place that hikers looked forward to visiting.

As the popularity of thru-hiking burgeoned, thru-hiker extraordinaire Warren Doyle organized in Pipestem, West Virginia, in October 1982 a get-together of hikers who had done all 2,000 miles. The meeting met with such enthusiasm that the group decided to create a permanent organization that would allow them to stay in touch. They met in Harpers Ferry in March of the next year to officially create the Appalachian Long Distance Hikers Association (ALDHA).

---

1. For one: Richard Judy, *Thru: An Appalachian Trail Love Story* (Gardeners, Pa.: Appalachian Trail Museum Society, 2014).

In 1987, Dan "Wingfoot" Bruce proposed that hikers get together on a day in May in Damascus, Virginia. It was the fiftieth anniversary of the completion of the trail, and it was time to celebrate. Thus was born "Trail Days," the most enduring event on the trail. It became a boisterous gathering marked by a big parade down the main street of Damascus.

The Appalachian Trail Conservancy has kept track of thru-hikers and thru-hiker wannabes as they surge through its Harpers Ferry headquarters, as well as those who register at various places on the trail, especially at Springer and Katahdin. But, Harpers Ferry was the most "official" place, and ATC took and kept photographs. A chart on the next page, current as of 2018, shows the numbers of north- and southbound thru-hikers, flip-floppers, and those reporting completed section-hikes.

"Wingfoot" (left) at the first Trail Days with Gene Espy

The surges in numbers seem related to external publicity. The first big surge followed the publication of Ed Garvey's book in 1971. Bill Bryson's 1998 U.S. publication of *A Walk in the Woods* had a major impact on thru-hiking, section-hiking, and ordinary day-hiking. People who had never heard of the Appalachian Trail wanted to set foot on it after reading Bryson's book, and even people who never hiked at all were enthralled by his amusing account. The book, a continued favorite of book clubs, spawned a movie seventeen years later.

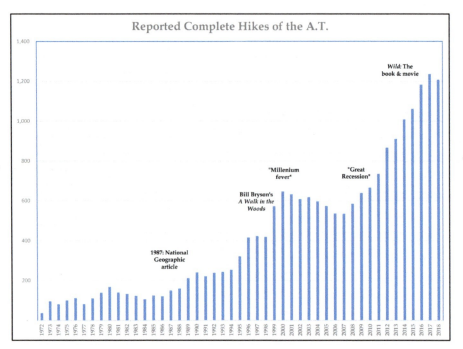

Reported thru-hikes and completed section-hikes, 1972-2018[1]

1. Source: Appalachian Trail Conservancy; thanks to Laurie Potteiger and Dave Tarasevich.

Today, an estimated three to four million people from the United States and around the world walk some portion of the Appalachian Trail in any given year.

Studies have shown that hikers tend to be intellectual and introverted, but one would never know it by reading the hiker logs that exist at shelters along the trail. What comes across is a boisterous and exuberant culture, strongly tinged with humor. The humor is often displayed in trail signs, such as:

"Walking on this bridge of rocks keeps the water from my socks. Burma Shave."

"Posted. No Poachin'. No Trespassin'. NO NUTHIN'. This applies to friends, relatives, enemies and YOU. Violators [crossed out] Survivors will be prosecuted."

And then there was this sign, right, outside the Smithsonian Conservation Biology Institute in northern Virginia. (The sign disappeared years ago, probably a prize decorating a wall in some teen-ager's bedroom.[2])

Building the trail became the greatest volunteer-centered project in America and possibly the world. People who might otherwise have avoided mowing the lawn bolted enthusiastically from suburb to forest, where they grabbed loppers, paint brushes, and Pulaskis and toiled uncounted hours under a hot sun on a project that consumed their imagination. The camaraderie was infectious, and trail-builders tended to identify with the group they were working with, be it digging waterbars or building shelters.

And, it was an egalitarian experience so typical of the American culture. The following quote was typical of what many volunteers experienced. In this case, it was written by then-GMC Executive Director Ben Rose:

> 'Well, I am the executive director...,' Rose recalled. 'Then I saw the president of the club, Andrew Nuquist, working nearby, the head of the Montpelier Section, Bill Clark, and a couple of other people who happened to be very skilled carpenters and builders...and I realized that I had no idea who was in charge!'[3]

Still, many volunteers toil alone. They are the section maintainers, who opted to work on a specific section, usually without assistance, keeping the trail fit for hikers. This particular culture was emblematic of the breed, and the PATC *Bulletin* in 1949 published a description of the overseer, in an article entitled "Take a Bow, Mr. Overseer:"

---

2. Both quotes appear in the *ATN* for July/August 1986. The photo was taken by the author before the sign disappeared in the 1990s.
3. Nuquist, *op. cit.*, p. 24.

It is his duty to clear and mark this trail, in accordance with the specifications recommended by the Appalachian Trail Conference, and to make periodic reports.... How and when he gets this work done is his own business.... He is responsible only for keeping the trail up to standard at all times. His is the pride — and the blisters — of owner-ship, and the very real thrill of being able to look at a long stretch of cleared trail and think, "This I did, for others, for free."[4]

Volunteers and the Government

The Appalachian Trail is a successful partnership among private citizens and governments. Many different entities participate, but all are led by the "cooperative management system" of ATC and the federal agencies laid out in the 1981 comprehensive management plan.

Federal bureaucracies are an unrevealed mystery to volunteers, and the volunteers are often surprised when they get different responses from different organizations. The problem goes back to very different missions. The Park Service mission is preservation and recreation. The over-all Forest Service mission is varied but begins with timber management and harvesting. Recreation, while important, often takes a back seat to commercial operations but special values zones for the A.T. have become embedded in the agency's DNA. Clear-cutting timber tracts has been a central way to manage timber resources and is opposed by hiking organizations, for example, but the A.T. is recognized as a special place.

A certain amount of infighting has occurred over the years between the two agencies. In the 1960s and 1970s, volunteer organizations leaned strongly toward the Forest Service for support. The Forest Service was actively acquiring inholdings on its lands to protect the trail; the Park Service was not acquiring any land to protect the trail. Although the National Trails System Act of 1968 named the parent departments of both the Park Service and Forest Service as managers of the federalized Appalachian Trail, the Park Service was accorded primacy, and, if the states did not acquire the corridor within two years, it was the Park Service that was supposed to step forward. It was not until after the passage of 1978

---

4. PATC *Bulletin*, January 1949, p. 8. Author unknown.

amendments that the Park Service took leadership of the enterprise with ATC and the Forest Service.

Completing the corridor acquisition did not resolve all the disagreements and latent animosity between the two agencies, but it did force a solution. The two agencies still have their different cultures, but arguments generally occur behind closed doors. They have agreed to cooperate on the Appalachian Trail project and to work cooperatively with volunteers.

Complete?

The last major official footpath tract acquired with federal funds was in Virginia, just north of the New River and the Celanese plant, in 2015. The federal government must take a bow for its decision to support the Appalachian Trail and other recreational trails across America. But, the Appalachian Trail is unique among those trails and stands as a monument to determined volunteers who have worked for ninety-nine years since Benton MacKaye first proposed it. The Park Service position is that it is now, officially, complete, although scattered snippets remain to be acquired. But, as Myron Avery said in 1937, it was a living thing and would never really be finished. Ask any volunteer who has just spent his or her weekend working on an official reroute.

SOURCES AND
ACKNOWLEDGMENTS

A book of this nature is not the sole product of one mind. So many people helped that there is a risk in writing an acknowledgments section that might fail to include all the names. Nonetheless, one must try.

Dave Sherman is almost a coauthor. His guidance took me through all the chapters of the book. He sent long and detailed e-mails and long and detailed critiques of each chapter. I asked him why he was not writing the book, and he claimed not to be a writer (a claim made hollow by his e-mails).

Nearly every chapter has a section on the trail in Maine. Dave Field has been the guiding hand behind the Appalachian Trail in Maine for many decades. He also provided me much of the information about the A.T. in Maine. He has copied the very voluminous Avery papers now residing in the Maine State Archives, once he "rescued" them from the ATC archives in the 1980s.

Interviews

Critical pieces of information have come from interviews. Those who I personally interviewed were Larry Anderson, Keith Argow, Hal Avery, Chris Bolgiano, Preston Bristow and Lee Allen, Chris Brown, George Case, Steve Clark, Keith Conover, Mike Dawson, JoAnn and Paul Dolan, Craig Dunn, Rima Farmer, Dave Field, Laurie Foot, Steve Golden, Don King, Jay Leutz and Judy Murray, Paul Pritchard, Bob Proudman, Chuck Rinaldi, Ron Rosen and Jim Daggett, Dave Sherman, Chuck Sloan, Jim Snow, Tom Speaks, Dave Startzell, Roger Sternberg, Paula Strain, Ron Tipton, Pam Underhill, and Larry Van Meter. Some other interviews that I had access to (of Gaylord Nelson is a good example) were done by others.

Archives

I visited archives up and down the East Coast. The largest and most important were those of ATC and PATC. Consulted were (north to south):

Rauner Library, Dartmouth College, Hanover, New Hampshire. Contains most of the papers of Benton MacKaye. Thanks to Maria Fernandez and Eric Asau.

Appalachian Mountain Club, Boston, Massachusetts, has an excellent reference library and various documentary collections of its activities, but I found few records directly related to the Appalachian Trail.

Green Mountain Club, Barre, Vermont. The Green Mountain Club has established a very valuable archive of records donated to the state archives.

The headquarters of the *New York-New Jersey Trail Conference in Ramapo, New Jersey,* has important historical correspondence relating to the establishment and history of that organization. At the time of my research, there was no archivist, and the collections have suffered as a result. Thanks to Tim Messerick.

In *Pennsylvania,* Barbara Wiemann has consulted and provided information from the various trail clubs in Pennsylvania. For that state, Barbara was my most important source of information. She was the Dave Sherman of Pennsylvania.

Earl V. Shaffer collection at the *Smithsonian Institution Museum of American History.*

ATC archives, located at the time of my work near Bardane, West Virginia. This is the mother lode for research on the history of the Appalachian Trail. Included are papers and scrapbooks of Myron Avery, Ruth Blackburn, Peter Dunning, Ed Garvey, Ray Hunt, Brian B. King, Elizabeth Levers, Benton MacKaye, Stan Murray, Florence Nichol, Arthur Perkins, Chuck Sloan, Dave Startzell, Jean Stephenson, Larry Van Meter, and George Zoebelein. At publication, ATC was in the process of donating its entire collection to a nearby university, with future access to this legacy to be determined.

Potomac Appalachian Trail Club, Vienna, Virginia. Includes five boxes of Myron Avery papers, along with more than seventy boxes of club records on almost every conceivable topic related to the club and hiking. The Bears Den collection is part of this archive, along with the records of the Red Triangle Club. PATC maintains collected correspondence of Jack Reeder and Chuck Sloan.

Shenandoah National Park, Luray, Virginia. Includes the Ferdinand Zerkel collection.

Natural Bridge Appalachian Trail Club, held by former president Laurie Foot.

Carolina Mountain Club archives, University of North Carolina–Asheville Special Collections. Includes Rep. Roy Taylor papers. Thanks to Gene Hyde and Colin Reeve.

McClung Collection, East Tennessee Historical Society, Knoxville, Tennessee. Contains the papers of the Smoky Mountains Hiking Club, Paul Fink, and Harvey Broome, among others.

Western Carolina University, Hunter Library, Sherman Collection, Cullo-whee, North Carolina. Thanks to George Frizzell and Jason Brady.

The *Georgia Appalachian Trail Club* has an archives in Atlanta, but it was not consulted because the club has extracted its most important records and published them in two volumes entitled, *Friendships of the Trail.* The two books, the first of which is listed below, are a must-have for any researcher on Georgia A.T. history.

Trail Club Histories

Only a few clubs have published histories, although some have local manuscript copies of unpublished histories. Most do not have archival collections. Papers, if they exist, are often stored in the garage or basement of the current president or secretary. Clubs that do have published histories relating to the Appalachian Trail are (north to south):

Judith Maddock Hudson, *Peaks and Paths: A Century of the Randolph Mountain Club* (Gorham, N.H.: Randolph Mountain Club, 2010).

Tom Slayton (editor), *A Century in the Mountains: Celebrating Vermont's Long Trail* (Waterbury, Vt.: The Green Mountain Club, 2009).

Glenn Scherer, "Vistas and Visions: A History of the New York–New Jersey Trail Conference" (New York: New York–New Jersey Trail Conference, 1995).

David Bates, *Breaking Trail in the Central Appalachians – a Narrative* (Washington: Potomac Appalachian Trail Club, 1987).

Georgia Appalachian Trail Club History Committee, *Friendships of the Trail: The History of the Georgia Appalachian Trail Club, 1930-1980* (Atlanta:

Georgia Appalachian Trail Club, 1981). This history reproduces early documents in the club's history and is a valuable source of information on GATC leaders.

Unbound Reports

Bureau of Outdoor Recreation, U.S. Department of the Interior, "Trunk Trail Report on The Appalachian Trail for the Steering Committee on A Nationwide Systems of Trails Study," October 1965. Written by Don Shedd.

Ann Satterthwaite, "An Appalachian Greenway: Purposes, Prospects and Programs." November 1974.

Virginia Division of Parks, "The Appalachian Trail: Pathway for the Future; a Planning Proposal," January 1974.

Sally K. Fairfax, "Federal-State Cooperation in Outdoor Recreation Policy Formation: the Case of the Appalachian Trail," doctoral dissertation submitted to Duke University, 1973.

Published sources

Unrivaled as published historical sources are the periodic newsletters of ATC, under various titles, beginning with *Appalachian Trailway News (ATN)* in 1939; the bound documents must be consulted.

Close in significance are the periodical publications of PATC, beginning in 1928. These can be found in bound and unbound issues at the PATC headquarters in Vienna.

Most other trail clubs circulate newsletters, but they are not donated to a central location, except insofar as they are part of a donated archival collection, such as GMC's.

Selected Bibliography

Leonard M. Adkins and ATC, *Images of America: Along the Appalachian Trail in Georgia, North Carolina, and Tennessee* (Charleston, S.C.: Arcadia Publishing, 2012).

— *Along Virginia's Appalachian Trail* (Charleston, S.C.: Arcadia Publishing, 2000)

Larry Anderson, *Peculiar Work: Writing About Benton MacKaye, Conservation, Community* (Little Compton, R.I.: Quicksand Chronicles, 2013).

— *Benton MacKaye: Conservationist, Planner, and Creator of the Appalachian Trail* (Baltimore: The Johns Hopkins University Press, 2002).

Jennifer A. Bauer, *Roan Mountain: History of an Appalachian Treasure* (Charleston, S.C: Natural History Press, 2011).

Robert O. Binnewies, *Palisades: 100,000 Acres in 100 Years* (New York: Fordham University Press and Palisades Interstate Park Commission, 2001).

Chris Bolgiano, *The Appalachian Forest: A Search for Roots and Renewal* (Mechanicsburg, Pa.: Stackpole Press, 1998)

Douglas Brinkley, *The Wilderness Warrior: Theodore Roosevelt and the Crusade for America* (Audible Studios, 2009).

Maurice Brooks, *The Appalachians* (Morgantown, W.Va.: Seneca Books, Inc., 1965).

V. Collins Chew, *Underfoot: A Geologic Guide to the Appalachian Trail* (Harpers Ferry: Appalachian Trail Conference, second edition, 1993).

Allen R. Coggins, *Place Names of The Smokies* (Gatlinburg, Tenn.: Great Smoky Mountains Natural History Association, 1999).

David Donaldson and Maurice J Forrester, *A Grip on the Mane of Life: An Authorized Biography of Earl V. Shaffer, 1918-2002* (Gardners, Pa.: Appalachian Trail Museum Society, 2014).

Gene Espy, *The Trail of My Life: The Gene Espy Story* (Macon, Ga.: Indigo Publishing Group, Inc., 2008).

David B. Field, *Along Maine's Appalachian Trail* (Mount Pleasant, S.C.: Arcadia Publishing, 2011).

Paul M. Fink, *Backpacking was the Only Way* (Jonesborough, Tenn.: Research Advisory Council, 1975).

Charles H.W. Foster, *The Appalachian National Scenic Trail: A Time to Be Bold* (Needham, Mass.: Charles H.W. Foster, 1987)

Edward B. Garvey, *Appalachian Hiker: Adventure of a Lifetime* (Oakton, Va.: Appalachian Books, 1971).

— *The New Appalachian Trail* (Birmingham, Ala.: Menasha Ridge Press, 1997).

Dave Gilbert, *A Walker's Guide to Harpers Ferry, West Virginia* (Harpers Ferry: Harpers Ferry Historical Association, 1992).

Bill Irwin with David McCasland, *Blind Courage: A 2,000 Mile Journey of Faith* (Waco, Texas: WRS Publishing, 1991).

Horace Kephart, *Our Southern Highlanders* (Knoxville: University of Tennessee Press, 1913).

Darwin Lambert, *The Undying Past of Shenandoah National Park* (Lanham, Md.: Roberts Rinehart, Inc., 1989).

David Lilliard, *Appalachian Trail Names: Origins of Place Names Along the A.T.* (Mechanicsburg, Pa.: Stackpole Books, 2002).

Larry Luxenberg, *Walking the Appalachian Trail* (Mechanicsburg, Pa.: Stackpole Books, 1994).

George Perkins Marsh, *Man and Nature; or, Physical Geography as Modified by Human Action* (London: S. Low, Son and Marston, 1864).

David Mazell (ed), *Pioneering Ascents: The Origins of Climbing in America, 1642-1873* (Vienna, Va.: Potomac Appalachian Trail Club, 1991).

John McPhee, *In Suspect Terrain* (New York: Farrar, Straus and Giroux, 1982).

George Freeman Pollock, *Skyland: the Heart of the Shenandoah National Park* (Richmond, Va.: Virginia Book Company, 1960).

Glenn Scherer, *Vistas and Visions: A History of the New York–New Jersey Trail Conference* (New York: New York–New Jersey Trail Conference, 1995, magazine format, available on-line only).

Earl V. Shaffer, *Walking with Spring* (Harpers Ferry: Appalachian Trail Conference, 1983).

Robert Sorrell, *Roan Mountain* (Charleston, S.C.: Arcadia Publishing, 2014).

Paula Strain, *The Blue Hills of Maryland: History Along the Appalachian Trail on South Mountain and the Catoctins* (Vienna, Va.: Potomac Appalachian Trail Club, 1993).

Doris Tomaselli, *Ned Anderson: Connecticut's Appalachian Trailblazer, Small Town Renaissance Man* (Sherman, Conn.: The Sherman Historical Society, 2009).

Raymond Torrey, Frank Place, Jr., and Robert L. Dickson, *The New York Walk Book* (New York: American Geographical Society, 1923).

Laura and Guy Waterman, *Forest and Crag: A History of Hiking, Trail Blazing, and Adventure in the Northeast Mountains* (Boston: Appalachian Mountain Club, 1989.

Sources of Illustrations

If not otherwise noted in the caption

Appalachian Trail Conservancy — viii

Appalachian Trail Conservancy Archives — cover map, 2, 4, 28–29, 33, 36, 38–39, 47, 53, 56–57, 69 (Welch family), 72, 76, 79, 83, 85–86, 88, 92, 99–100, 11, 120, 125, 127, 130 center, 145, 153, 156, 179, 182–183, 187, 189–193, 196, 199, 202, 205, 213, 228, 232, 237, 241, 245, 248, 252–253, 255 top, 257–258, 263, 270, 276, 284–285, 289, 291, 295 top (by Laurie Potteiger), 297–299, 301, 308, 312, 335, 356, 360–362, 364, 368, 373, 376, 396, 410, 415, 418 (by Bob Proudman), 423–426, 428, 435, 439, 450, 452, 463, 476, 499, 505, 509, 516, 520, 535

Jennifer Bauer (*Roan Mountain: History of an Appalachian Treasure*) — 7

DeLorme Maps (modified by author) — 180, 304, 307, 319, 465

Gene Espy — 283 top

David B. Field, partly from the Maine State Library and Myron H. Avery family albums — 95–97, 254, 267, 292, 295 bottom, 497

Friends of Peace Pilgrim — 283 bottom

Georgia Appalachian Trail Club — 201

Steve Golden — 431

Google Maps — 414

Green Mountain Club Archives — 238

Historicalpix.com — 41

Hunter Library/Sherman Collection — 185

Thomas Johnson (author) — 34, 142, 177, 208, 249, 329, 412, 467, 472, 474, 479, 482, 484, 486, 523–524, 532, 537

Maine Appalachian Trail Club — 255 bottom

Philbrick's A.T. Public Transportation Guide (Facebook) — 117

Pinnacles of Dan Hiking Web site — 172

Potomac Appalachian Trail Club Archives — 59, 106, 130 top and bottom, 133, 135, 146–147, 170, 266, 384, 406, 468, 570

Roanoke Appalachian Trail Club Archives — 173

David Sherman — 444–445

Tom Slayton (*A Century in the Mountains: Celebrating Vermont's Long Trail*) — 32

Smoky Mountains Hiking Club Archives — cover, 194

Larry Van Meter — 458

Wikipedia — 10, 74, 101, 165, 343, 352

INDEX

ABOUT THE AUTHOR

An avid hiker, Tom Johnson was born on October 10, 1940, and reared in Longview, a small town in Washington State. He began hiking in his early teens near Mount Saint Helens in the years before it erupted. His hiking was interrupted when he went away to college in Oregon and married his wife Sharon in 1959.

Out of college in 1964, he joined the Air Force and became a professional intelligence officer, retiring as a lieutenant colonel. He and his wife traveled the world, living in four different foreign countries. Returning permanently to the United States in 1991, he became active in the Potomac Appalachian Trail Club (PATC) and resumed his life of hiking. He was alternately president or vice president of PATC for twelve consecutive years, beginning in 1996. He was also a hike leader and took members of the club hiking in foreign countries for six consecutive years. At the time of this writing, he was the PATC archivist and historian and active with the Appalachian Trail Museum Society and other trail groups in several capacities.

Professionally, he remained an intelligence officer, having served for thirty-four years with the National Security Agency (NSA) and twenty-one years with the Central Intelligence Agency (CIA). He wrote the official history of NSA in four volumes, and his volumes twice won NSA's cryptologic literature award. His publications include *American Cryptology During the Cold War* (the history of NSA), the history of PATC, and numerous books and articles for NSA and CIA, most of them still classified. His NSA history has been partially declassified, and that portion is now an Amazon book with the same title.

While hiking in Shenandoah National Park on December 5, 2020, after giving a history talk to fellow club members (in tan cap at right side of shelter), Tom suffered a fatal heart attack.